FREE Study Skills DVD Offer

Dear Customer,

Thank you for your purchase from Mometrix! We consider it an honor and a privilege that you have purchased our product and we want to ensure your satisfaction.

As a way of showing our appreciation and to help us better serve you, we have developed a Study Skills DVD that we would like to give you for FREE. This DVD covers our *best practices* for getting ready for your exam, from how to use our study materials to how to best prepare for the day of the test.

All that we ask is that you email us with feedback that would describe your experience so far with our product. Good, bad, or indifferent, we want to know what you think!

To get your FREE Study Skills DVD, email freedvd@mometrix.com with *FREE STUDY SKILLS DVD* in the subject line and the following information in the body of the email:

- The name of the product you purchased.
- Your product rating on a scale of 1-5, with 5 being the highest rating.
- Your feedback. It can be long, short, or anything in between. We just want to know your impressions and experience so far with our product. (Good feedback might include how our study material met your needs and ways we might be able to make it even better. You could highlight features that you found helpful or features that you think we should add.)
- Your full name and shipping address where you would like us to send your free DVD.

If you have any questions or concerns, please don't hesitate to contact me directly.

Thanks again!

Sincerely,

Jay Willis
Vice President
jay.willis@mometrix.com
1-800-673-8175

FSOT

Study Guide

FSOT Prep Secrets for the Foreign Service Officer Test

Full-Length Practice Test

Step-by-Step Review
Video Tutorials

4th Edition

Written and edited by Mometrix Test Prep

Printed in the United States of America

This paper meets the requirements of ANSI/NISO Z39.48-1992 (Permanence of Paper).

Paperback
ISBN 13: 978-1-5167-1483-4
ISBN 10: 1-5167-1483-0

DEAR FUTURE EXAM SUCCESS STORY

First of all, **THANK YOU** for purchasing Mometrix study materials!

Second, congratulations! You are one of the few determined test-takers who are committed to doing whatever it takes to excel on your exam. **You have come to the right place.** We developed these study materials with one goal in mind: to deliver you the information you need in a format that's concise and easy to use.

In addition to optimizing your guide for the content of the test, we've outlined our recommended steps for breaking down the preparation process into small, attainable goals so you can make sure you stay on track.

We've also analyzed the entire test-taking process, identifying the most common pitfalls and showing how you can overcome them and be ready for any curveball the test throws you.

Standardized testing is one of the biggest obstacles on your road to success, which only increases the importance of doing well in the high-pressure, high-stakes environment of test day. Your results on this test could have a significant impact on your future, and this guide provides the information and practical advice to help you achieve your full potential on test day.

Your success is our success

We would love to hear from you! If you would like to share the story of your exam success or if you have any questions or comments in regard to our products, please contact us at **800-673-8175** or **support@mometrix.com**.

Thanks again for your business and we wish you continued success!

Sincerely,
The Mometrix Test Preparation Team

Need more help? Check out our flashcards at:
http://mometrixflashcards.com/FSOT

TABLE OF CONTENTS

Introduction

Thank you for purchasing this resource! You have made the choice to prepare yourself for a test that could have a huge impact on your future, and this guide is designed to help you be fully ready for test day. Obviously, it's important to have a solid understanding of the test material, but you also need to be prepared for the unique environment and stressors of the test, so that you can perform to the best of your abilities.

For this purpose, the first section that appears in this guide is the **Secret Keys**. We've devoted countless hours to meticulously researching what works and what doesn't, and we've boiled down our findings to the five most impactful steps you can take to improve your performance on the test. We start at the beginning with study planning and move through the preparation process, all the way to the testing strategies that will help you get the most out of what you know when you're finally sitting in front of the test.

We recommend that you start preparing for your test as far in advance as possible. However, if you've bought this guide as a last-minute study resource and only have a few days before your test, we recommend that you skip over the first two Secret Keys since they address a long-term study plan.

If you struggle with **test anxiety**, we strongly encourage you to check out our recommendations for how you can overcome it. Test anxiety is a formidable foe, but it can be beaten, and we want to make sure you have the tools you need to defeat it.

Secret Key #1 – Plan Big, Study Small

There's a lot riding on your performance. If you want to ace this test, you're going to need to keep your skills sharp and the material fresh in your mind. You need a plan that lets you review everything you need to know while still fitting in your schedule. We'll break this strategy down into three categories.

Information Organization

Start with the information you already have: the official test outline. From this, you can make a complete list of all the concepts you need to cover before the test. Organize these concepts into groups that can be studied together, and create a list of any related vocabulary you need to learn so you can brush up on any difficult terms. You'll want to keep this vocabulary list handy once you actually start studying since you may need to add to it along the way.

Time Management

Once you have your set of study concepts, decide how to spread them out over the time you have left before the test. Break your study plan into small, clear goals so you have a manageable task for each day and know exactly what you're doing. Then just focus on one small step at a time. When you manage your time this way, you don't need to spend hours at a time studying. Studying a small block of content for a short period each day helps you retain information better and avoid stressing over how much you have left to do. You can relax knowing that you have a plan to cover everything in time. In order for this strategy to be effective though, you have to start studying early and stick to your schedule. Avoid the exhaustion and futility that comes from last-minute cramming!

Study Environment

The environment you study in has a big impact on your learning. Studying in a coffee shop, while probably more enjoyable, is not likely to be as fruitful as studying in a quiet room. It's important to keep distractions to a minimum. You're only planning to study for a short block of time, so make the most of it. Don't pause to check your phone or get up to find a snack. It's also important to **avoid multitasking**. Research has consistently shown that multitasking will make your studying dramatically less effective. Your study area should also be comfortable and well-lit so you don't have the distraction of straining your eyes or sitting on an uncomfortable chair.

The time of day you study is also important. You want to be rested and alert. Don't wait until just before bedtime. Study when you'll be most likely to comprehend and remember. Even better, if you know what time of day your test will be, set that time aside for study. That way your brain will be used to working on that subject at that specific time and you'll have a better chance of recalling information.

Finally, it can be helpful to team up with others who are studying for the same test. Your actual studying should be done in as isolated an environment as possible, but the work of organizing the information and setting up the study plan can be divided up. In between study sessions, you can discuss with your teammates the concepts that you're all studying and quiz each other on the details. Just be sure that your teammates are as serious about the test as you are. If you find that your study time is being replaced with social time, you might need to find a new team.

Secret Key #2 – Make Your Studying Count

You're devoting a lot of time and effort to preparing for this test, so you want to be absolutely certain it will pay off. This means doing more than just reading the content and hoping you can remember it on test day. It's important to make every minute of study count. There are two main areas you can focus on to make your studying count:

Retention

It doesn't matter how much time you study if you can't remember the material. You need to make sure you are retaining the concepts. To check your retention of the information you're learning, try recalling it at later times with minimal prompting. Try carrying around flashcards and glance at one or two from time to time or ask a friend who's also studying for the test to quiz you.

To enhance your retention, look for ways to put the information into practice so that you can apply it rather than simply recalling it. If you're using the information in practical ways, it will be much easier to remember. Similarly, it helps to solidify a concept in your mind if you're not only reading it to yourself but also explaining it to someone else. Ask a friend to let you teach them about a concept you're a little shaky on (or speak aloud to an imaginary audience if necessary). As you try to summarize, define, give examples, and answer your friend's questions, you'll understand the concepts better and they will stay with you longer. Finally, step back for a big picture view and ask yourself how each piece of information fits with the whole subject. When you link the different concepts together and see them working together as a whole, it's easier to remember the individual components.

Finally, practice showing your work on any multi-step problems, even if you're just studying. Writing out each step you take to solve a problem will help solidify the process in your mind, and you'll be more likely to remember it during the test.

Modality

Modality simply refers to the means or method by which you study. Choosing a study modality that fits your own individual learning style is crucial. No two people learn best in exactly the same way, so it's important to know your strengths and use them to your advantage.

For example, if you learn best by visualization, focus on visualizing a concept in your mind and draw an image or a diagram. Try color-coding your notes, illustrating them, or creating symbols that will trigger your mind to recall a learned concept. If you learn best by hearing or discussing information, find a study partner who learns the same way or read aloud to yourself. Think about how to put the information in your own words. Imagine that you are giving a lecture on the topic and record yourself so you can listen to it later.

For any learning style, flashcards can be helpful. Organize the information so you can take advantage of spare moments to review. Underline key words or phrases. Use different colors for different categories. Mnemonic devices (such as creating a short list in which every item starts with the same letter) can also help with retention. Find what works best for you and use it to store the information in your mind most effectively and easily.

Secret Key #3 – Practice the Right Way

Your success on test day depends not only on how many hours you put into preparing, but also on whether you prepared the right way. It's good to check along the way to see if your studying is paying off. One of the most effective ways to do this is by taking practice tests to evaluate your progress. Practice tests are useful because they show exactly where you need to improve. Every time you take a practice test, pay special attention to these three groups of questions:

- The questions you got wrong
- The questions you had to guess on, even if you guessed right
- The questions you found difficult or slow to work through

This will show you exactly what your weak areas are, and where you need to devote more study time. Ask yourself why each of these questions gave you trouble. Was it because you didn't understand the material? Was it because you didn't remember the vocabulary? Do you need more repetitions on this type of question to build speed and confidence? Dig into those questions and figure out how you can strengthen your weak areas as you go back to review the material.

Additionally, many practice tests have a section explaining the answer choices. It can be tempting to read the explanation and think that you now have a good understanding of the concept. However, an explanation likely only covers part of the question's broader context. Even if the explanation makes sense, **go back and investigate** every concept related to the question until you're positive you have a thorough understanding.

As you go along, keep in mind that the practice test is just that: practice. Memorizing these questions and answers will not be very helpful on the actual test because it is unlikely to have any of the same exact questions. If you only know the right answers to the sample questions, you won't be prepared for the real thing. **Study the concepts** until you understand them fully, and then you'll be able to answer any question that shows up on the test.

It's important to wait on the practice tests until you're ready. If you take a test on your first day of study, you may be overwhelmed by the amount of material covered and how much you need to learn. Work up to it gradually.

On test day, you'll need to be prepared for answering questions, managing your time, and using the test-taking strategies you've learned. It's a lot to balance, like a mental marathon that will have a big impact on your future. Like training for a marathon, you'll need to start slowly and work your way up. When test day arrives, you'll be ready.

Start with the strategies you've read in the first two Secret Keys—plan your course and study in the way that works best for you. If you have time, consider using multiple study resources to get different approaches to the same concepts. It can be helpful to see difficult concepts from more than one angle. Then find a good source for practice tests. Many times, the test website will suggest potential study resources or provide sample tests.

Practice Test Strategy

If you're able to find at least three practice tests, we recommend this strategy:

Untimed and Open-Book Practice

Take the first test with no time constraints and with your notes and study guide handy. Take your time and focus on applying the strategies you've learned.

Timed and Open-Book Practice

Take the second practice test open-book as well, but set a timer and practice pacing yourself to finish in time.

Timed and Closed-Book Practice

Take any other practice tests as if it were test day. Set a timer and put away your study materials. Sit at a table or desk in a quiet room, imagine yourself at the testing center, and answer questions as quickly and accurately as possible.

Keep repeating timed and closed-book tests on a regular basis until you run out of practice tests or it's time for the actual test. Your mind will be ready for the schedule and stress of test day, and you'll be able to focus on recalling the material you've learned.

Secret Key #4 – Pace Yourself

Once you're fully prepared for the material on the test, your biggest challenge on test day will be managing your time. Just knowing that the clock is ticking can make you panic even if you have plenty of time left. Work on pacing yourself so you can build confidence against the time constraints of the exam. Pacing is a difficult skill to master, especially in a high-pressure environment, so **practice is vital**.

Set time expectations for your pace based on how much time is available. For example, if a section has 60 questions and the time limit is 30 minutes, you know you have to average 30 seconds or less per question in order to answer them all. Although 30 seconds is the hard limit, set 25 seconds per question as your goal, so you reserve extra time to spend on harder questions. When you budget extra time for the harder questions, you no longer have any reason to stress when those questions take longer to answer.

Don't let this time expectation distract you from working through the test at a calm, steady pace, but keep it in mind so you don't spend too much time on any one question. Recognize that taking extra time on one question you don't understand may keep you from answering two that you do understand later in the test. If your time limit for a question is up and you're still not sure of the answer, mark it and move on, and come back to it later if the time and the test format allow. If the testing format doesn't allow you to return to earlier questions, just make an educated guess; then put it out of your mind and move on.

On the easier questions, be careful not to rush. It may seem wise to hurry through them so you have more time for the challenging ones, but it's not worth missing one if you know the concept and just didn't take the time to read the question fully. Work efficiently but make sure you understand the question and have looked at all of the answer choices, since more than one may seem right at first.

Even if you're paying attention to the time, you may find yourself a little behind at some point. You should speed up to get back on track, but do so wisely. Don't panic; just take a few seconds less on each question until you're caught up. Don't guess without thinking, but do look through the answer choices and eliminate any you know are wrong. If you can get down to two choices, it is often worthwhile to guess from those. Once you've chosen an answer, move on and don't dwell on any that you skipped or had to hurry through. If a question was taking too long, chances are it was one of the harder ones, so you weren't as likely to get it right anyway.

On the other hand, if you find yourself getting ahead of schedule, it may be beneficial to slow down a little. The more quickly you work, the more likely you are to make a careless mistake that will affect your score. You've budgeted time for each question, so don't be afraid to spend that time. Practice an efficient but careful pace to get the most out of the time you have.

Secret Key #5 – Have a Plan for Guessing

When you're taking the test, you may find yourself stuck on a question. Some of the answer choices seem better than others, but you don't see the one answer choice that is obviously correct. What do you do?

The scenario described above is very common, yet most test takers have not effectively prepared for it. Developing and practicing a plan for guessing may be one of the single most effective uses of your time as you get ready for the exam.

In developing your plan for guessing, there are three questions to address:

- When should you start the guessing process?
- How should you narrow down the choices?
- Which answer should you choose?

When to Start the Guessing Process

Unless your plan for guessing is to select C every time (which, despite its merits, is not what we recommend), you need to leave yourself enough time to apply your answer elimination strategies. Since you have a limited amount of time for each question, that means that if you're going to give yourself the best shot at guessing correctly, you have to decide quickly whether or not you will guess.

Of course, the best-case scenario is that you don't have to guess at all, so first, see if you can answer the question based on your knowledge of the subject and basic reasoning skills. Focus on the key words in the question and try to jog your memory of related topics. Give yourself a chance to bring the knowledge to mind, but once you realize that you don't have (or you can't access) the knowledge you need to answer the question, it's time to start the guessing process.

It's almost always better to start the guessing process too early than too late. It only takes a few seconds to remember something and answer the question from knowledge. Carefully eliminating wrong answer choices takes longer. Plus, going through the process of eliminating answer choices can actually help jog your memory.

Summary: Start the guessing process as soon as you decide that you can't answer the question based on your knowledge.

How to Narrow Down the Choices

The next chapter in this book (**Test-Taking Strategies**) includes a wide range of strategies for how to approach questions and how to look for answer choices to eliminate. You will definitely want to read those carefully, practice them, and figure out which ones work best for you. Here though, we're going to address a mindset rather than a particular strategy.

Your chances of guessing an answer correctly depend on how many options you are choosing from.

How many choices you have	How likely you are to guess correctly
5	20%
4	25%
3	33%
2	50%
1	100%

You can see from this chart just how valuable it is to be able to eliminate incorrect answers and make an educated guess, but there are two things that many test takers do that cause them to miss out on the benefits of guessing:

- Accidentally eliminating the correct answer
- Selecting an answer based on an impression

We'll look at the first one here, and the second one in the next section.

To avoid accidentally eliminating the correct answer, we recommend a thought exercise called **the $5 challenge**. In this challenge, you only eliminate an answer choice from contention if you are willing to bet $5 on it being wrong. Why $5? Five dollars is a small but not insignificant amount of money. It's an amount you could afford to lose but wouldn't want to throw away. And while losing $5 once might not hurt too much, doing it twenty times will set you back $100. In the same way, each small decision you make—eliminating a choice here, guessing on a question there—won't by itself impact your score very much, but when you put them all together, they can make a big difference. By holding each answer choice elimination decision to a higher standard, you can reduce the risk of accidentally eliminating the correct answer.

The $5 challenge can also be applied in a positive sense: If you are willing to bet $5 that an answer choice *is* correct, go ahead and mark it as correct.

Summary: Only eliminate an answer choice if you are willing to bet $5 that it is wrong.

Which Answer to Choose

You're taking the test. You've run into a hard question and decided you'll have to guess. You've eliminated all the answer choices you're willing to bet $5 on. Now you have to pick an answer. Why do we even need to talk about this? Why can't you just pick whichever one you feel like when the time comes?

The answer to these questions is that if you don't come into the test with a plan, you'll rely on your impression to select an answer choice, and if you do that, you risk falling into a trap. The test writers know that everyone who takes their test will be guessing on some of the questions, so they intentionally write wrong answer choices to seem plausible. You still have to pick an answer though, and if the wrong answer choices are designed to look right, how can you ever be sure that you're not falling for their trap? The best solution we've found to this dilemma is to take the decision out of your hands entirely. Here is the process we recommend:

Once you've eliminated any choices that you are confident (willing to bet $5) are wrong, select the first remaining choice as your answer.

Whether you choose to select the first remaining choice, the second, or the last, the important thing is that you use some preselected standard. Using this approach guarantees that you will not be enticed into selecting an answer choice that looks right, because you are not basing your decision on how the answer choices look.

This is not meant to make you question your knowledge. Instead, it is to help you recognize the difference between your knowledge and your impressions. There's a huge difference between thinking an answer is right because of what you know, and thinking an answer is right because it looks or sounds like it should be right.

Summary: To ensure that your selection is appropriately random, make a predetermined selection from among all answer choices you have not eliminated.

Test-Taking Strategies

This section contains a list of test-taking strategies that you may find helpful as you work through the test. By taking what you know and applying logical thought, you can maximize your chances of answering any question correctly!

It is very important to realize that every question is different and every person is different: no single strategy will work on every question, and no single strategy will work for every person. That's why we've included all of them here, so you can try them out and determine which ones work best for different types of questions and which ones work best for you.

Question Strategies

Read Carefully

Read the question and answer choices carefully. Don't miss the question because you misread the terms. You have plenty of time to read each question thoroughly and make sure you understand what is being asked. Yet a happy medium must be attained, so don't waste too much time. You must read carefully, but efficiently.

Contextual Clues

Look for contextual clues. If the question includes a word you are not familiar with, look at the immediate context for some indication of what the word might mean. Contextual clues can often give you all the information you need to decipher the meaning of an unfamiliar word. Even if you can't determine the meaning, you may be able to narrow down the possibilities enough to make a solid guess at the answer to the question.

Prefixes

If you're having trouble with a word in the question or answer choices, try dissecting it. Take advantage of every clue that the word might include. Prefixes and suffixes can be a huge help. Usually they allow you to determine a basic meaning. Pre- means before, post- means after, pro - is positive, de- is negative. From prefixes and suffixes, you can get an idea of the general meaning of the word and try to put it into context.

Hedge Words

Watch out for critical hedge words, such as *likely, may, can, sometimes, often, almost, mostly, usually, generally, rarely,* and *sometimes.* Question writers insert these hedge phrases to cover every possibility. Often an answer choice will be wrong simply because it leaves no room for exception. Be on guard for answer choices that have definitive words such as *exactly* and *always.*

Switchback Words

Stay alert for *switchbacks.* These are the words and phrases frequently used to alert you to shifts in thought. The most common switchback words are *but, although,* and *however.* Others include *nevertheless, on the other hand, even though, while, in spite of, despite, regardless of.* Switchback words are important to catch because they can change the direction of the question or an answer choice.

Face Value

When in doubt, use common sense. Accept the situation in the problem at face value. Don't read too much into it. These problems will not require you to make wild assumptions. If you have to go beyond creativity and warp time or space in order to have an answer choice fit the question, then you should move on and consider the other answer choices. These are normal problems rooted in reality. The applicable relationship or explanation may not be readily apparent, but it is there for you to figure out. Use your common sense to interpret anything that isn't clear.

Answer Choice Strategies

Answer Selection

The most thorough way to pick an answer choice is to identify and eliminate wrong answers until only one is left, then confirm it is the correct answer. Sometimes an answer choice may immediately seem right, but be careful. The test writers will usually put more than one reasonable answer choice on each question, so take a second to read all of them and make sure that the other choices are not equally obvious. As long as you have time left, it is better to read every answer choice than to pick the first one that looks right without checking the others.

Answer Choice Families

An answer choice family consists of two (in rare cases, three) answer choices that are very similar in construction and cannot all be true at the same time. If you see two answer choices that are direct opposites or parallels, one of them is usually the correct answer. For instance, if one answer choice says that quantity *x* increases and another either says that quantity *x* decreases (opposite) or says that quantity *y* increases (parallel), then those answer choices would fall into the same family. An answer choice that doesn't match the construction of the answer choice family is more likely to be incorrect. Most questions will not have answer choice families, but when they do appear, you should be prepared to recognize them.

Eliminate Answers

Eliminate answer choices as soon as you realize they are wrong, but make sure you consider all possibilities. If you are eliminating answer choices and realize that the last one you are left with is also wrong, don't panic. Start over and consider each choice again. There may be something you missed the first time that you will realize on the second pass.

Avoid Fact Traps

Don't be distracted by an answer choice that is factually true but doesn't answer the question. You are looking for the choice that answers the question. Stay focused on what the question is asking for so you don't accidentally pick an answer that is true but incorrect. Always go back to the question and make sure the answer choice you've selected actually answers the question and is not merely a true statement.

Extreme Statements

In general, you should avoid answers that put forth extreme actions as standard practice or proclaim controversial ideas as established fact. An answer choice that states the "process should be used in certain situations, if..." is much more likely to be correct than one that states the "process should be discontinued completely." The first is a calm rational statement and doesn't even make a definitive, uncompromising stance, using a hedge word *if* to provide wiggle room, whereas the second choice is a radical idea and far more extreme.

BENCHMARK

As you read through the answer choices and you come across one that seems to answer the question well, mentally select that answer choice. This is not your final answer, but it's the one that will help you evaluate the other answer choices. The one that you selected is your benchmark or standard for judging each of the other answer choices. Every other answer choice must be compared to your benchmark. That choice is correct until proven otherwise by another answer choice beating it. If you find a better answer, then that one becomes your new benchmark. Once you've decided that no other choice answers the question as well as your benchmark, you have your final answer.

PREDICT THE ANSWER

Before you even start looking at the answer choices, it is often best to try to predict the answer. When you come up with the answer on your own, it is easier to avoid distractions and traps because you will know exactly what to look for. The right answer choice is unlikely to be word-for-word what you came up with, but it should be a close match. Even if you are confident that you have the right answer, you should still take the time to read each option before moving on.

General Strategies

TOUGH QUESTIONS

If you are stumped on a problem or it appears too hard or too difficult, don't waste time. Move on! Remember though, if you can quickly check for obviously incorrect answer choices, your chances of guessing correctly are greatly improved. Before you completely give up, at least try to knock out a couple of possible answers. Eliminate what you can and then guess at the remaining answer choices before moving on.

CHECK YOUR WORK

Since you will probably not know every term listed and the answer to every question, it is important that you get credit for the ones that you do know. Don't miss any questions through careless mistakes. If at all possible, try to take a second to look back over your answer selection and make sure you've selected the correct answer choice and haven't made a costly careless mistake (such as marking an answer choice that you didn't mean to mark). This quick double check should more than pay for itself in caught mistakes for the time it costs.

PACE YOURSELF

It's easy to be overwhelmed when you're looking at a page full of questions; your mind is confused and full of random thoughts, and the clock is ticking down faster than you would like. Calm down and maintain the pace that you have set for yourself. Especially as you get down to the last few minutes of the test, don't let the small numbers on the clock make you panic. As long as you are on track by monitoring your pace, you are guaranteed to have time for each question.

DON'T RUSH

It is very easy to make errors when you are in a hurry. Maintaining a fast pace in answering questions is pointless if it makes you miss questions that you would have gotten right otherwise. Test writers like to include distracting information and wrong answers that seem right. Taking a little extra time to avoid careless mistakes can make all the difference in your test score. Find a pace that allows you to be confident in the answers that you select.

KEEP MOVING

Panicking will not help you pass the test, so do your best to stay calm and keep moving. Taking deep breaths and going through the answer elimination steps you practiced can help to break through a stress barrier and keep your pace.

Final Notes

The combination of a solid foundation of content knowledge and the confidence that comes from practicing your plan for applying that knowledge is the key to maximizing your performance on test day. As your foundation of content knowledge is built up and strengthened, you'll find that the strategies included in this chapter become more and more effective in helping you quickly sift through the distractions and traps of the test to isolate the correct answer.

Now it's time to move on to the test content chapters of this book, but be sure to keep your goal in mind. As you read, think about how you will be able to apply this information on the test. If you've already seen sample questions for the test and you have an idea of the question format and style, try to come up with questions of your own that you can answer based on what you're reading. This will give you valuable practice applying your knowledge in the same ways you can expect to on test day.

Good luck and good studying!

Communication

Speaking and Listening

Public Speaking

Speech communication instructors often refer to public speaking as a "transaction," or a way of indicating the important active roles of both the speaker and audience. Too often, people consider speech-giving as a process in which one person actively provides information while another group of people passively receives information. Instead, the ideal public speaking relationship is one in which the speaker presents a message and the audience presents feedback. Even when the audience is not given an opportunity to speak, they provide feedback in the form of attention or inattention. By referring to public speaking as a transaction, instructors emphasize the roles and responsibilities of both speaker and audience. In general, speech communication instructors would define a transaction as any communication in which information passes from speaker to listener and vice versa.

For most people, the obvious goals of public speaking are political victories and support for social movements. Both are common motives of public speech, but they are not the only recognized intention of public communication. Public speech is often used to define an individual or a community. For instance, people may use speeches to describe particular attributes of themselves or of the group to which they belong. People also use speeches simply to disseminate information. Speeches can be used to inspire other people to action. Famous addresses like the "I Have a Dream" speech of Martin Luther King, Jr. exemplify this kind of speech. Finally, public speaking can be used to introduce arguments and to debate controversial questions in a community. The presidential debates before the general election are a good example of this.

There are a number of reasons for studying public speaking, but the most commonly cited are social, intellectual, and consumer motives. People need to learn to speak in public in order to function in society and to manage relationships, administrate social events, and minimize conflict. Intellectually, a study of public speaking gives insight into human thought, ethics, and persuasion. Public speeches can generate emotions and ideas in listeners as well as influence their existing thoughts and feelings. It is also important to study public speaking not only to improve one's own speaking skills, but to improve one's ability to analyze and interpret the speeches of others.

Pauses in Vocal Delivery

Human speech is not just a constant stream of syllables. The placement and use of pauses during speech also plays an important role in forming meaning. The study of pauses in human speech is a subcategory of paralinguistics. A short pause is often used to denote the end of a sentence or clause. In many ways, short pauses are used like commas. Long pauses, on the other hand, are more similar to periods or the ends of paragraphs. When a speaker takes a long pause, he or she may be allowing what has been said to sink into the minds of the audience. Individuals often pause as they search for the right word. Other times, individuals will insert a slight pause into a sentence to create a level of suspense before the thought is finished.

Nonverbal Communication

Nonverbal communication is the ability to enhance or elaborate on the words of the speaker. In particular, hand gestures and changes in vocal rhythm and volume have the ability to add expressiveness to what is being said. Many times, the gestures and vocal mechanisms of the speaker simply emphasize his or her message; at other times, however, the speaker may detract from or undermine his or her message with contradictory gestures. Hand gestures and gesticulations have the ability to dramatize a communication event.

By giving the audience things other than words to concentrate on, the speaker engages and entertains them. Although nonverbal communication is typically thought of as supplementary to the words being spoken during a communication event, it can also serve a vital purpose as feedback. The gestures, eye movements, facial expressions, and posture of the audience often indicates their level of engagement more accurately and honestly than verbal criticism. It is very difficult to hide extreme boredom or rapt attention. The nonverbal communication of the audience will indicate their level of interest and acceptance of the message of the speaker. The speaker can then adjust his or her message accordingly.

At times, the nonverbal communication produced by a speaker will give a slightly different message than that of the speaker's words. This is often the case when a speaker is attempting to introduce an element of irony into his or her message. For instance, if at the conclusion of a bad movie one friend says to another, "Well, that was a good use of my time," but smiles while saying the words, the other friend might assume that the message is being delivered with sarcasm. In other words, the speaker does not literally mean that the movie was a good use of time, but rather wishes to indicate that it was a waste of time. A message is being delivered, but the nonverbal communication accompanying the words creates a complex message different than the mere words being spoken.

Sometimes, a speaker's nonverbal communication is contradictory to the words he or she is speaking. This can often create confusion and conflict. For instance, imagine a person is in distress. In some cultures, it is not considered dignified to ask another person for help, even in emergency situations. So, a person in dire need of assistance might be saying he or she does not need help, even though observation of nonverbal signs says otherwise. Obviously, this will create conflict in the mind of the audience, who will want to obey the wishes of the person but will also want to lend assistance to a person in need. When an individual directly contradicts his or her words with his or her nonverbal communication, it becomes much more difficult for the communication message to be interpreted.

Listening

People often listen to one another as a demonstration of empathy. Empathy is the ability to understand and appreciate what another person is going through despite not having the same experience oneself. One of the ways a person can express understanding and compassion for others is simply by listening to them. Listening to someone indicates that his or her problems are worth your time. Most people find that not only is listening a good way to demonstrate empathy, but it is also a good way to develop empathy. It seems that when we listen to one another, we gradually develop a sense of each other's internal worlds, and we come to treat each other with more compassion.

Simply listening to another person can have profound psychological implications. Indeed, the entire field of psychoanalysis is largely based on the idea that having a sympathetic audience for one's problems is profoundly therapeutic. Many people pay a great deal of money simply to have a sympathetic listener who can offer some professional advice. Psychoanalysts are especially skilled at creative listening. That is, they are able to "unpack" the message of the speaker and discern new, possibly hidden meanings. Numerous studies have indicated that the process of verbally elaborating and describing personal issues eases the burden of stress on the mind, regardless of whether the interpretation of these issues is accurate or constructive.

Defensiveness can be extremely limiting to an individual's ability to listen properly. When a person is defensive, he or she is overly concerned with protecting his or her own interests. Defensiveness is especially prevalent in interpersonal communications in which the two parties do not trust one another. However, some paranoid individuals may be naturally more inclined to defensiveness than others. The problem with defensiveness is that it indicates that the attention of the listener is on his or her own concerns, rather than on the content of the message being delivered. To the degree that a listener is not focusing on the message being delivered, his or her ability to understand and respond to the message will be impaired.

Active Listening

Active listening is a technique of communication reception in which the listener tries to develop an empathic relationship with the speaker. Proponents of this form of listening declare that a great deal of listening contains an unhelpful evaluative aspect, to the extent that the speaker continually feels in danger of being criticized by the listener. In active listening, on the other hand, the listener makes an effort to fully experience the thought process of the speaker before even beginning to judge. Perhaps most importantly, active listening is a skill that is developed over time. To fully engage with what someone is saying, the listener must practice subverting his or her own ego and focus instead on the perceived interests of the speaker.

Defensiveness

Speech communication theorists identify a number of ways in which defensiveness can impair effective and accurate communication. These ways are basically defined by the attitude of the listener. For instance, some defensive listeners adopt an overly evaluative posture, in which they indicate that it is up to them to decide whether the speaker is competent or not. Other defensive listeners adopt a self-consciously apathetic attitude, as if to indicate that they are above being interested in the message of the speaker. Another common listening attitude for a defensive individual is certainty, or the assumption that he or she already knows the content of the message. This attitude draws the speaker up short and makes it difficult for him or her to continue communicating.

Types of Speeches

Introductory Speech

It is common for a speech of introduction to precede a keynote speech, a presentation, or a public performance of some kind. For instance, a symphony director will often give a brief speech of introduction before a concert. The best introductory speeches do not simply list the achievements or characteristics of the person or event that is to follow. Rather, they engage the interest of the audience and whet their appetite for what is to come. A good speech of introduction should not include any criticism of what is to follow. It is always a good rule of thumb for the introductory speaker to confer with those who are to follow so that his or her message can be as appropriate as possible.

Welcoming Speech

A welcoming speech is often given at the beginning of a convention, meeting, or special event of some kind. Typically, the welcome will be delivered by a representative of the group or organization putting on the event. For instance, the chairman of a professional organization administering a business convention might deliver a speech of welcome to convention attendees. Welcoming speeches are typically light on substance and primarily provide an overview of the events to follow. Also, a welcoming speech typically includes a message of thanks to the organizers and administrators of the event. The speaker often indicates his or her personal goals for the event and may tell the audience how to make their questions and comments known to the event administrators.

Presentation

Over the last few years, the presentation has emerged as the most common speech form in the United States. Members of the business community frequently give presentations, but this form is also common to academic lectures, community discussions, and religious gatherings. One of the defining characteristics of a presentation is that it contains other media besides simply a speaker. It is common for a speaker to include photographs, brochures and handouts, short videos, audio samples, in a presentation. In business, tables and charts are frequently used to illustrate the points of a presentation. Because presentations are often designed to be given over and over again to different audiences, they may be complex, detailed, and highly coordinated.

Another defining characteristic of a presentation is the use of presentation aids. Speakers often include supplementary audio or visual materials that elaborate or reinforce their presentation points. Currently, the most popular presentation aid is PowerPoint, a software program that allows speakers to assemble a collection of slides to accompany their speech.

Informative Speech

When one is delivering an informative speech, his or her primary goal is to instruct the audience on a particular subject. If the speech is effective, the audience members will leave with more knowledge and understanding. College lectures are a great example of an informative speech. Although informative speeches may be entertaining, the humor or "color" of the speech should not distract from the overall intention, which is to disseminate information. Informative speeches often contain specific statistical data and an organized set of arguments and supporting evidence. Many informative speeches contain mention of counter-arguments, including rebuttals.

Impromptu Speech

An impromptu speech is one delivered "off-the-cuff"; that is, one delivered with a minimum amount of preparation and in an informal style. Not everyone is capable of delivering an effective impromptu speech. Most people can give a successful impromptu speech only if the topic is one on which they have discoursed before or if they are extremely familiar with their topic. Of course, we all make impromptu speeches as a matter of course in our daily lives. Every time you are asked to give your opinion on a subject or to explain an idea, you are in effect making an impromptu speech. By studying speech communication, however, people can learn the elements of effective impromptu speeches and improve their ability to deliver them.

Extemporaneous Speech

An extemporaneous speech combines elements of preparation and improvisation. When one is delivering an extemporaneous speech, he or she is drawing on prepared research but not reading directly from a sheet of paper nor reciting the speech from memory. An extemporaneous speech is more conversational and informal than a written speech and is therefore more appropriate for casual gatherings. The colloquial and informal nature of an extemporaneous speech can be extremely helpful in cultivating a good rapport between speaker and audience. To deliver an effective extemporaneous speech, however, the speaker must be extremely familiar with his or her source material.

Persuasive Speech

Persuasive speeches are designed to change the minds of the audience or motivate the audience to action. The precise goals of a persuasive speech are dependent on the particular cause promoted by the speaker. Moreover, the methods employed in a persuasive speech will depend on the subject matter and the speaker's rhetorical style. Some speakers employ a dry, data-driven style when making a persuasive speech. They hope to overwhelm their audience with the strength and breadth of information. Other speakers seek to beguile their audience by amusing and entertaining them.

This kind of speech is appropriate for general audiences and non-technical subjects. When a persuasive speech is being delivered to an audience of experts, or is centered on a complex issue, it must include cogent reasoning and supportive data.

Problem-Solving Speech

In a problem-solving speech, the speaker outlines a particular problem, attempts to diagnose the cause, and then suggests a potential solution. Problem-solving speeches are at their heart persuasive speeches, since they attempt to convince the audience of the merits of adopting a particular strategy to solve a given problem. To be effective, however, a problem-solving speech needs to follow a logical pattern. These speeches typically begin with an introduction and a definition of the problem in question. The speaker will then summarize the possible causes of the problem and discuss some of the possible solutions. Following this, the speaker will make a case for one of the solutions and provide supporting evidence and argumentation. Finally, the speaker will attempt to rebut some of the possible counterarguments to the proposed solution.

Proof Speech

Speech communication instructors often refer to a "proof speech." This is a common type of speech, in which the speaker introduces his or her argument and then attempts to prove it. Proof speeches follow a consistent pattern. In brief, a proof speech has four components: introduction, argument, development, and conclusion. A speech that follows this pattern allows the audience to become acquainted with the thrust of the speaker's arguments before substantiation is offered. The lengths of the various components of a proof speech will vary, depending on the speaker's interests and the knowledge level of the audience. For instance, an audience already familiar with the subject matter may not require as much supporting material to be convinced.

Entertaining Speech

The only goal of some speeches is to entertain and amuse the audience. Standup comedy is a type of entertaining speech. Many speeches that also contain information or persuasive content are primarily entertaining. The keynote speakers at conferences and conventions often cloak their arguments in witty anecdotes and jokes. Obviously, serious subjects are not appropriate content for entertaining speeches. However, many speakers will introduce some elements of an entertaining speech to first capture the attention of the audience and then persuade them to engage seriously with the weightier elements of the speech.

Eulogy

A eulogy is a speech that praises a particular individual and highlights his or her best qualities. Eulogies are often given at funerals as the speaker remembers the deceased in a positive light. Eulogies are not the appropriate form for criticism or objective analysis of a person's life.

On the other hand, a eulogy may fail if the audience finds it so excessively laudatory that it is not believable. In some cases, a eulogy of sorts may be given in praise of a particular event, community, or culture. Typically, a eulogy is delivered to an audience that is already disposed to think favorably of the subject. The speaker is typically someone who has extensive personal experience with the subject of the eulogy.

Elements of Speechwriting

Basic Elements of Speechwriting

To master the speechmaking process, one should clearly understand a few basic elements. The central figure is the speaker; that is, the one delivering the speech. The speaker brings a self-conception as well as a conception, or impression, of the audience's general identity. In the study of speechmaking, the audience is sometimes referred to as the "receiver." Like the speaker, the audience members will have a self-image as well as an impression of the speaker. The setting in which the speech is delivered is known as the "situation." The speaker uses various channels of communication, including words and gestures, to communicate his or her message. The audience members will deliver their responses to the speech both verbally and through body language. This response to the speech is called feedback.

Preparing a Speech

To successfully prepare a speech it is best to follow a basic set of established steps. By following these steps, the speaker (or speechwriter) can more efficiently develop an organized and effective presentation. The first step in preparing a speech is to select a subject, if the topic has not been predetermined. Next, the speaker should articulate to himself or herself the key ideas and arguments to be included in the speech. As he or she begin to formulate these ideas and arguments, it is important to take into account the characteristics of the intended audience. At this point, the speaker should begin gathering materials for the speech, whether through research or brainstorming. The next step is to outline the speech, and finally, write a draft of the speech. It is always a good idea to practice delivering the speech and to make revisions or adjustments where necessary.

During the preparation phase of speech composition, a speaker will begin to organize his or her research material. Once the speaker has decided upon the basic angle and structure of the speech, he or she may need to acquire more research materials for elaboration and support. Of course, it may take the speaker a while to find the appropriate thrust of the speech. Speakers should not be discouraged by numerous blind alleys or false starts during the preparation phase. Even when it seems that progress is not being made, the speaker should remember that each false start eliminates a possible point of entry bringing the ultimate goal closer.

Selecting a Subject

Perhaps the most important component of an effective speech is an appropriate and interesting subject. When selecting a subject for a speech, one should look for a topic that is engaging to a general audience. While it is important for the speaker to have some familiarity with the subject, it is not necessarily a good idea to speak about a subject on which he or she is an expert. Too often, an expert delivering a speech to a general audience dwells too much in details and specificities, which has a tendency to bore the audience. It is a good idea for the speaker to have a passing familiarity with the subject, so that he or she will be able to find good research materials and judge what will be interesting to a general audience. However, the speaker should also make sure to emphasize the aspects of the subject that are relevant to the lives of the audience members.

Basic Message Units

In every speech, the content is divided into what are called basic message units. A basic message unit has two parts: the point the speaker is trying to make and the evidence or supporting material he or she has assembled. In order to be complete, a message unit needs to have both components. Otherwise, the speaker will be making points without offering any reasoning or evidence, or he will be giving factual information and argumentation without connecting the dots to make a larger point. The point stated by the speaker needs to be a complete and discrete thought. The supporting material must be pertinent to the point and sufficient to convince a reasonable person.

Composing a Speech Outline

Creating a detailed, comprehensive outline is the first step before actually writing the first draft of a speech. After assembling all the necessary material and information for the speech, the speaker can then begin organizing the main points of the speech and the arguments and evidence supporting his or her ideas and claims. It is important that all secondary ideas and claims also support the speech's main idea or claim. One should always introduce the most important claim, or thesis, at the beginning of the speech. The speaker can then spend the rest of the speech building a case for this thesis and elaborating other related points. When composing an outline, remember that the finished speech should ideally be much more colorful and engaging. An outline is not meant to entertain, but rather to clearly and succinctly indicate the organization of the speech.

Denotative Meaning

Denotative meaning is the way in which a word indicates something else. The word "table," for instance, denotes a flat surface with three or more legs. A speaker must always be conscious of the denotative meaning of the words he or she uses. The denotative meaning is not decided on an individual basis. Rather, it is the product of unconscious agreements on meaning made by the members of a community. In other words, to ensure that he or she communicates effectively with the audience, the speaker must have a familiarity with the denotative meanings that will be known to the members of that audience. Effective speakers continually refer to a dictionary during speech composition in order to solidify their understanding of denotative meanings.

Connotative Meaning

Connotative meaning is any implication or a suggestion connected to a word that extends beyond the denotative meaning of the word. The connotative meaning of the word, then, is not strictly the definition of the word. Connotative meanings are often quite emotional in character. For instance, the denotative meaning of the word "whale" is a large mammal that lives in the ocean. When the same word is used in a certain way, however, its connotative meaning may refer to someone who is overweight.

Speakers need to be aware of both the connotative and the denotative meanings of the words they use. Otherwise, they run the risk of confusing or even offending the audience members. A detailed dictionary will often have explanations of the various connotative meanings of common words.

Review Video: Denotation and Connotation
Visit mometrix.com/academy and enter code: 310092

Evidence for a Speech

Statistics

Speakers often use statistics to provide numerical evidence for their assertions. Basically, a loose definition of statistics is any information that contains numbers to be effective, statistics must be clear and accurate. Statistics can have a great deal of sway over an audience, since they carry with them the impression of objectivity and mathematical truth. That being said, audience members should keep in mind that statistics are often highly subjective. For instance, by manipulating sample size, information taken into consideration, and scope of a statistical survey, a speaker can present information to support his point no matter how incorrect it is. Audience members should always be wary of statistics and should press the speaker to provide more information on the origin and methodology behind any statistics he or she uses.

Numbers

There are a few different ways to use numbers in a speech. One way is to use numbers as markers of evaluation. When we say a person weighs 120 pounds, for instance, we are using numbers to evaluate their weight. In a similar way, numbers can be used as a basis for comparison. By comparing the prices of two dishwashers, for instance, we obtain an important piece of information we can use in making a consumer decision. Numbers can also be used to make illustrative points. For instance, speakers often cite various statistics in support of an argument. It is important to emphasize that, although numbers suggest impartiality, they are calculated by human beings, who are highly subjective and whose intentions should be rigorously questioned.

Testimony

Eyewitness Testimony

Many speakers incorporate eyewitness testimony into their speeches to great effect. Of course, this kind of supporting material is only appropriate for certain kinds of speeches. For instance, when delivering a speech about the Battle of the Bulge, it might be very useful to quote some soldiers who fought in the battle. On the other hand, eyewitness testimony seems less appropriate to a speech about climate change, which is so widespread that no one person could view its entire effect globally. When using eyewitness testimony, it is important to establish the credentials of the person being quoted. Also, a speaker should take care to indicate the particular vantage point of the eyewitness, so the audience can consider his or her testimony in light of that point of view.

Expert Testimony

Whenever possible, speakers attempt to incorporate expert testimony into their speeches. Any time a speaker can quote a well-known authority who agrees with his or her point of view, he or she will be eager to do so. Most members of an audience will probably feel relatively uninformed compared to the speaker and will be ready to listen to anyone who may be considered an expert. Of course, testimony is only expert and appropriate when it comes from an expert in that particular field. For example, most people would be less inclined to take seriously the political views of an expert in basketball than they would if those views came from a respected public servant. Nevertheless, an audience should remain skeptical about persuasive arguments, even when they are made by experts. The standards of logic required of experts apply to everyone else as well.

Purpose

Immediate Aim and Ultimate Aim

On occasion, a speaker will have a slightly different intention in making a speech than is apparent from the speech itself. In the field of speech communication, this is known as the distinction between immediate aim and ultimate aim. An example would be a particular speech intended to be a small part of achieving a long-term goal. A prominent businessman, for example, might make a speech about ethics in public policy. Whereas on its face the speech might seem to be a simple address about local community issues, it might be also be part of the businessman's plan to develop his reputation in advance of a political campaign. The immediate aim of the speech, then, is to inform, while the ultimate aim is to advance the political ambitions of the speaker.

Specific Purposes for a Speech

The first step in preparing a speech is knowing the specific purpose of that speech. This enables the speaker to focus on what is important and to research efficiently for relevant material. Knowing the specific purpose of the speech allows the speaker to emphasize the most important points within the speech. The specific purpose of a speech might be informing the audience on a particular point, changing a few minds on a particular subject, raising some money, or simply entertaining the audience. It is a good idea to make the specific purpose of the speech explicit in the speech. Although you do not want to beat your audience over the head with your intentions, there should be no question as to what the speech is meant to accomplish. In general, the specific purpose of a speech is defined in terms of the desired reaction from the audience.

Persuasion

Persuasion is the art of changing the attitudes, beliefs, or actions of other people. It can be used for any number of purposes: to sell a product, to make a friend, to advance a cause, or simply to win an argument. To a certain degree, even primarily informative speeches contain an element of persuasion. The speaker is encouraging his or her audience to understand a given subject in the same way he or she does. To be persuasive, the speaker must have a clear idea of what he or she is trying to accomplish. Also, it is important to understand the best persuasive strategy for achieving the desired effect. Persuasion can be styled as direct argument or as more indirect, even subversive, suggestion.

Students of rhetoric have long noticed the correlation between a charismatic personality and persuasion. Basically, if a speaker is able to establish strong personal relationships with his or her audience, he or she is much more likely to be an effective persuasive communicator. The most important thing a persuasive speaker can do is to establish trust from the outset. If a speaker can convince the audience that he or she has their best interests at heart and is a competent source of information, the work of persuasion is largely done. Establishing trust and respect with the audience is as much a matter of one's credentials as one's appearance and presentation. Speakers who can demonstrate expertise and empathy are likely to find success with the audience.

Competency

To be persuasive, an individual must be perceived as competent by the audience. Competence manifests itself in a number of characteristics, such as preparedness, poise, thoughtfulness, and clarity. A competent speaker should be able to answer questions from the audience on a specific subject, or should at least be able to explain where the answers could be found. A competent speaker must have supporting evidence for his or her arguments and must make this evidence clear to the audience. A competent speaker will also be able to organize his or her message effectively, giving the audience the best opportunity to educate themselves. Finally, a competent speaker will appear unhurried and calm.

Conviction

Audiences seem to have a sixth sense for insincerity. They can tell when a speaker does not really believe his or her message. For this reason, effective persuasion is greatly benefited by the speaker's deep conviction in what he or she is saying. It is often said that before a speaker can persuade anyone else, he or she needs to be persuaded.

When the strength of a speaker's convictions is evident in his or her delivery, the natural empathy of the audience will assist in persuasion. Historically, a survey of the great persuasive orators (Martin Luther King Jr., Abraham Lincoln, Pericles, etc.) confirms that strong belief is a boon to persuasive rhetoric.

Reputation

Another factor that can greatly influence a speaker's power of persuasion is reputation. When a speaker has a reputation for upright behavior and responsibility to the truth, an audience is much more likely to believe his or her message. The credibility of the speaker is imperative, regardless of the topic. If the content of the speech is highly specialized, the audience will want to know that the speaker has some advanced training in the subject. When an audience arrives for a speech already knowing the positive reputation of the speaker, the work of persuasion is almost complete. For many politicians and orators, building a reputation that encourages persuasion is the work of a lifetime.

Direct Experience

Having direct knowledge of sources can be extremely beneficial to a speaker's power of persuasion. For instance, imagine a motivational speaker on the subject of weight loss. If that speaker has had the experience of being overweight and then successfully losing weight and becoming healthier, the audience will be much more likely to take his or her words to heart. When a speaker can claim direct experience of the topic on which he or she speaks, the audience is unlikely to attribute the speaker's motives to personal gain or manipulation. The most effective speakers are able to present their personal experience as a model for the examination and consideration of the audience.

Imitation

Unconscious mimicry or imitation can be one of the most powerful forces for persuasion. Human beings have a natural tendency to imitate the behavior of those they perceive to be leaders or role models. People often adopt beliefs or act in ways uncharacteristic of whom they really are in order to mirror the behavior of a leader. This phenomenon is due in part to the tendency of human beings to minimize differences between one another as a means of preventing conflict. Of course, to inspire imitation on the part of the audience, a speaker must appear competent and have a good reputation. The members of an audience should be particularly skeptical of speakers who encourage them to adopt a point of view simply because others are doing so.

Authority

Human beings have a natural tendency to believe what designated authority figures tell them. In part, this is an inherited characteristic. Early humans, in order to survive in the wild, often had to rely on the advice and guidance of their peers. In many cases, people will follow directions from an authority figure without considering the ramifications of their actions. This phenomenon was evidenced during the Nuremberg trials after World War II, as numerous Nazi officials defended their actions as "just following orders." The educational system also encourages people to trust authority figures and follow directions. Audience members should be aware of this tendency and should guard against blindly accepting the recommendations of a speaker.

SUGGESTION

A persuasive speaker may sometimes use a suggestion rather than a direct command to achieve his or her goal. A suggestion is simply a less forceful recommendation; it implies that the audience has the ability to decide for themselves whether or not to accept the guidance of the speaker. Suggestion is a good strategy for dealing with naturally skeptical audience members, who will resist any overt attempts to change their minds.

Because it is an indirect form of persuasion, however, suggestion requires a bit more subtlety on the part of the speaker. But because it gives the listener the impression that he or she has arrived independently at a conclusion, suggestion can be more effective than direction.

MOTIVATION

When an audience is considering the elements of a persuasive speech, they will likely give some thought to the motivations of the speaker. For instance, when approached by a salesperson, a customer is likely to assume that the salesperson has a vested personal interest in making a sale and does not necessarily have the best interests of the consumer at heart. In other contexts, however, the motivation of the speaker may be harder to discern. In an academic speech, for instance, the audience will be aware that the speaker is attempting to promote a certain viewpoint, but they may not be able to determine exactly why the speaker supports that point of view. To the extent that the audience can discern the motivation of the speaker, they will be able to intellectually consider the merits of the speech, and not be swayed by emotion.

CALL TO ACTION

Audiences will naturally be resistant to persuasive arguments that attempt to take them out of their normal routine. People of all ages have a tendency to fall into habitual behaviors that can be difficult and even painful to interrupt. A persuasive speaker, however, is by nature one who attempts to convert an audience to a new way of living or thinking. He or she will therefore encounter the listeners' resistance, based on their entrenched habits. Habitual behavior can be attacked in a number of ways. One is to persuade the audience that these habits are detrimental. Another is to suggest the advantages that can be gained from a new way of living or thinking. In all cases, however, the speaker should remember that most behavioral change is incremental and not the result of sudden conversion.

One of the most common kinds of persuasive speech is one in which the speaker attempts to persuade the audience to change something. The speaker may be asking the listeners to change their behavior, their opinion on some subject, or the way in which some issue is handled in their community. These kinds of speeches usually follow a similar arc: first, the speaker describes the disastrous state of affairs at present. Second, the speaker introduces his or her proposal for remedying the situation. Third, the speaker indicates the rewards that the audience will obtain by accepting the proposal of the speaker. If the speech is effective, by its conclusion the audience should be practically intoxicated with the expansive vision of a positive future the speaker has outlined.

Another kind of persuasive speech is one in which the speaker attempts to persuade the audience to *not* change something. Like the speech in support of change, the speech against change has three classic components. First, the speaker argues that things are fine as they are. Second, the speaker argues against any proposals for change that have been made. Third, the speaker describes the negative consequences for the audience if changes are made. As with the speech in support of change, the speech against change begins by setting the general scene and only gradually works its way around to addressing the individual concerns of the audience members. In this way, the last impression the audience receives is that of the effects of change or stasis on their own lives.

Speech Development

Well-Organized Speech

All well-organized speeches have certain qualities in common. For instance, a well-organized speech is comprehensible, meaning it can be understood by all members of the audience. A well-organized speech also has a formal unity, which means all of its parts contribute to the main idea. A unified speech has no extraneous parts. A well-organized speech is also comprehensive—it covers all the issues an audience member would expect to be addressed by a speech on the given subject. Finally, a well-organized speech does not have any repetition. Every major point should be covered in its entirety, but no points need to be repeated once they have been clearly delivered.

Setting

When preparing a speech, a speaker should take into account any idiosyncrasies of the speech format or setting. For instance, in some situations a speaker will have specific guidelines and rules for his or her speech. When giving an address to the members of a particular religious or cultural group, for instance, one might need to abide by specific rules. Another thing to consider is the placement of the speech in the overall event. For instance, if other speeches are to follow, one might want to make sure there will be no overlap in speech content. Also, if the speech is to be given directly after a dinner, one should be aware that audience members will be less likely to pay close attention to the details of the speech. Finally, a good speaker will be aware in advance what the physical setting for the speech will be. That is, he or she will know beforehand such details as whether or not the speech is to be given standing or sitting and whether a podium will be available.

Location

When preparing a speech, one should always keep in mind the occasion for which the speech is intended as this will help determine what kind of speech is appropriate. Individuals who have gathered together for a summer picnic, for instance, will not be interested in hearing a long and complicated speech. A short, humorous address would be more appropriate for this setting. A convention of professors, on the other hand, will be receptive to a more substantive speech that might also include relevant technical information. On rare occasions, a speaker may decide it is necessary to deliver a speech not entirely appropriate for the setting; this should only be done, however, when it is absolutely necessary.

Time Limits

When preparing a speech, one must be aware of exactly how much time is available for presenting the material. The time limit will greatly influence the content of the speech. It is rarely possible, for instance, to effectively discuss a complicated subject in a short period of time. Nor will it be possible to hold an audience's interest over a long period of time without having a wealth of information and ideas. Giving an effective persuasive speech in particular requires sufficient time. This is especially true when one is trying to convert an audience's opinion on a subject with which they are unfamiliar or on which they already have firm opinions. Generally, it takes a strong argument, elaborated through a number of points, to alter an opinion already agreed upon by most members of the audience.

Many speakers handicap themselves from the start by selecting a subject that is either too expansive or too narrow for their needs. To be effective, a speech subject must be appropriate for the amount of time available for giving the speech. Obviously, a half-hour speech can go into much more detail and tackle a wider range of issues than can a five-minute speech. A very short speech should have only one main idea, whereas in a longer speech the speaker may have time to deliver several important points and give supporting information for each. Although the best way to determine the appropriate subject for the time limit is to gain experience as a public speaker, beginning speakers can nevertheless help themselves by considering the parameters of a speech as they begin to consider possible subjects.

Title

It is very important to settle on a clear and appropriate title for a speech early on in the preparation process. The title should make explicit the central idea or concept to be discussed in the speech. The title should also indicate the intention of the speech. For instance, if the intent of the speech is to inform the audience about a particular subject, the title should clearly state the name of the subject. If the intention of the speech is to persuade the audience, the title should indicate the main arguments to be made by the speech. To be effective, a title should be succinct, clear, and, if possible, engaging.

Main Idea

It is important when giving an informative speech to lay out the main idea in a manner comprehensible to the audience. The main idea of an informative speech should be presented near the beginning of the address and therefore should not require an audience to understand any concepts that will be explained later in the speech. The audience should be able to understand the gist of the main idea before the speaker goes on to elaborate. In the preparation of a speech, the speaker should define the main idea early on, so that he or she can procure evidence and supporting arguments appropriate to that main idea. Too often, speakers introduce evidence and arguments not directly supportive of the main idea of the speech. This causes confusion among the audience and waters down the effect of the speech.

When a speech is designed to present or advance a particular viewpoint, the speaker will need to pay special attention to the phrasing of the speech's main claim. The main claim should be phrased in such a way that it will be comprehensible to a general audience and will not offend casual listeners with a harsh or controversial tone. The degree of intensity appropriate to the claim will depend on the audience. A more strident tone can be used with an audience of like-minded individuals, whereas a diverse group of uncommitted listeners requires a more evenhanded tone. When constructing the main claim of a speech, the speaker should be sure to present only ideas that can be supported by available evidence and reasonable argument. If the main claim of a speech is far-fetched or unsupportable, even the more rational elements of the speech may be dismissed by a skeptical audience.

Idea and a Claim

The goal of a speech is to disseminate information or persuade the audience. In other words, a speaker will either deliver ideas or make claims. A speaker who is delivering ideas is expressing information and opinions for their own sake, and not necessarily trying to change the minds of the audience. Informative speeches are usually on subjects about which the audience is not expected to know very much. The purpose of such a speech is to increase the knowledge of the audience rather than to convert them to any particular viewpoint. When a speaker makes claims, on the other hand, he or she is introducing opinions that may or may not be held by the members of the audience. The intention of this type of speech will be to provide arguments and evidence to support the speaker's claims.

Logical Analysis of a Speech Topic

A speaker should always perform what is known as a logical analysis before presenting his or her speech. This is simply an analysis of the message units that make up the speech, as well as the connections between these message units. To be effective, the logic of any speech must progress in a systematic and discernible manner and should include ample evidence and supporting materials. Speakers often create a brief outline for their speech, in which they sketch the basic structure of the speech's logic, leaving out the supplementary material. In any case, it is essential to make sure the logical skeleton of a speech is sturdy before focusing on other aspects.

As the speaker reviews his prepared speech and performs a logical analysis, he needs to be constantly asking himself whether each point and piece of supporting material is essential. Everything included in the speech should be there for a clear and explicit reason or else it must be considered superfluous. The speaker must also determine whether all of the evidence clearly and directly supports the points it is intended to support. Finally, the speaker must make sure every point in the speech follows a proper order, progressing logically to the speech's climax and ultimate conclusion.

Logical Errors with Speeches

Faulty Attribution of Causation

One of the most common errors of logic one can make in a speech is the faulty attribution of causation. This occurs when the speaker erroneously assumes that just because one thing followed another, the second thing was caused by the first. For instance, I may grab my umbrella on the way out the door before it starts raining, but if I later use my umbrella, I cannot claim that bringing my umbrella caused the rain. When a speaker describes a major historical or social event and suggests such an event had only one cause, this is almost always a case of faulty attribution of causation. Major social and historical movements are simply too complex to be attributed to a single cause. At the very least, a speaker must provide detailed substantiation for any assertions of causation.

Circular Reasoning

A common logical error in speeches is circular reasoning. A chain of logic is described as circular when the assumptions made at the beginning of the argument depend on the conclusion of the argument being true. For instance, imagine a speaker declaring that the Tigers baseball team will certainly lose their playoff series. As evidence for this claim, the speaker declares that the Tigers always lose their playoff series. This reasoning clearly does not hold up: In order to believe the Tigers will lose their playoff series, we have to assume they always lose their playoff series, which we do not really know yet, and which depends on their performance in the upcoming playoffs series. In other words, the claims made by the speaker depend for their support on the speaker's assumptions.

Review Video: Circular Reasoning
Visit mometrix.com/academy and enter code: 398925

Contradictory Argument

Occasionally, a speaker will fall victim to the logical error known as the contradictory argument. A contradictory argument is one in which the speaker introduces information that directly contradicts his main argument. For the most part, this error should be easy to avoid. After all, a speaker will be careful not to include information that undermines his main point. Speakers do, however, sometimes include inconsistent arguments in a speech and this can be highly detrimental to their purpose. Contradictory argument is especially problematic in a persuasive speech, in which the speaker is attempting to persuade the audience from their pre-existing opinions and hoping to sell them on the merits of an alternative view.

EXPOSITORY SUPPORTING MATERIAL

Most speeches include expository supporting material. The word "expository" comes from the same root as "expose" and refers to information that sheds light on areas about which the audience may know little. Some of the common forms of expository information are examples, analogies, and narratives. Expository supporting material is distinguished from argumentative supporting material in that it strives to remain as objective as possible. When a speaker claims to be providing objective and impartial information, he or she will be held to that standard by the audience. For this reason, it is especially important for speakers who use expository supporting material to verify their sources.

EXAMPLES

A good speaker knows that examples can be effective because they provide concrete case studies through which the audience can assess the arguments of the speech. Examples are also good for humanizing an abstract speech. For instance, an audience may have a hard time listening to a speech about water conservation, but if the speaker introduces examples of how drought can affect individual people, they will be more likely to stay engaged. A good speaker includes examples that are appropriate and interesting, but which do not distract from his or her main points. Also, examples should not dominate a speech; they should simply add interest to the body of the speaker's message.

Successful speakers are likely to use both real and hypothetical examples in the course of a speech. Real examples are appropriate in speeches describing a particular historical or social topic that is grounded in reality. For instance, it would not be appropriate to use a hypothetical example in an argument about the Revolutionary War since there are plenty of real examples to illustrate points regarding that conflict. In more general speeches, however, it may be necessary to use a hypothetical situation as an example. When describing the possible results of some decision, for instance, a speaker might invoke the case of some hypothetical person as a means of dramatizing his or her argument. In general, real examples are treated with more respect by an audience and should be used whenever possible.

ANALOGIES

An effective speaker will often elaborate and clarify his or her ideas with analogies. An analogy is simply an extended comparison between two things. For instance, a speech on economics might describe a current downturn in the economy as it relates to the Great Depression. In other words, the speaker is drawing an analogy between a current problem and a known historical event. The important thing to remember about an analogy is that the two things being compared will probably not be identical in all respects. The speaker should take care to indicate this and should not make claims that suggest the analogy is perfect. On the other hand, an effective analogy can be a useful predictive tool and can give the audience a way of engaging with the subject.

NARRATIVES

Speakers often incorporate narratives into their speeches as a way of engaging interest and indirectly making a point. A narrative is simply a story. Narratives can be either fiction or nonfiction. As with examples, narratives tend to have more impact on an audience when they are true. However, an artfully told fictitious narrative can also captivate an audience.

Recent scientific research suggests that audience members are mentally programmed to pay attention to information when it is presented as a story. That is, the human mind is naturally receptive to a narrative. Good speakers take advantage of this tendency by delivering information in the context of a narrative.

Review Video: Narratives
Visit mometrix.com/academy and enter code: 280100

DEFINING THE PURPOSE OF THE SPEECH

In preparation for making a speech, it is important to strictly define the purpose of the speech. Without a firm idea of the intention of the speech, it will be too easy for the content to miss the mark. To begin with, the speaker should consider his or her own intentions as well as the intentions of the audience. As much as possible, the intentions of the speaker and those of the audience should be made to overlap. One should define the central argument or idea to be expressed in the speech and take care that this argument or idea is consistent with the intention of the speech. It is also important that the title of the speech indicates the intention as well as the central theme of the speech.

Delivery of a Speech

Important Attributes of a Speaker

To be an effective speaker, one must have a clear intention, a good attitude, and extensive knowledge of the subject of the speech, as well as a degree of credibility with the audience. The speaker should fully understand the intention of the speech, even if that intention is not directly expressed in the speech. Sometimes a speaker will have a hidden motive or a long-term goal that cannot be expressed in the speech. To establish credibility, the speaker should possess a solid working knowledge of the subject of the speech. When the speaker is fluent in the subject he or she is discussing, the speech will flow more naturally and the speaker will be able to tailor his or her message to the audience's level of understanding. Referring to a speaker's "attitude" simply means his or her self-conception; that is, the image the speaker has of himself or herself. If a speaker has a positive self-image, he or she is more likely to deliver an effective speech.

Memorizing and Reading a Speech

When delivering a speech, the speaker may need to decide whether to memorize or read the text. There are advantages to each approach. When a speech is memorized, the speaker can make eye contact with the audience and use his or her hands to make illustrative gestures. Memorized speeches run the risk of sounding overly rehearsed, however, and the speaker may falter if he or she loses track of the speech. Some speakers prefer to read their speeches, often because they prefer to have a copy of the speech for reference. If the speaker plans to read his or her speech, he or she should become extremely familiar with the speech so it is not necessary to read every word from the paper. Regardless of whether a speech is memorized or read, the speaker should practice delivery to increase fluency.

Practicing Speech Delivery

Excellent speech delivery does not just happen. It is the result of extensive practice. After the speaker has outlined and drafted the speech, he or she needs to practice delivering it. Practicing a speech serves a number of purposes. For one thing, the speaker might not detect weak points in the speech until he or she actually speaks the words aloud. In addition, it is helpful to record oneself practicing the speech and then play back the tape to identify weaknesses in the delivery. It is often a good idea to practice delivering a speech in front of friends or family and then have them critique the performance. Perhaps the most important point is that practice delivering the speech allows the speaker to further familiarize himself or herself with the material, thus increasing the level of comfort and fluency in delivery.

Avoiding Distractions

As much as possible, an effective speaker will minimize distractions during a speech. Distractions can include things done by the audience as well as by the speaker him- or herself. Of course, it is not possible for a speaker to control the behavior of an audience, but he or she can exercise self-control. Too many speakers challenge the patience of the audience by hemming and hawing over their words, making distracting gestures, or engaging in frequent vocal tics. For many speakers, making noises like "uh" and "er" while searching for the right word is natural and unconscious. It can be very distracting to an audience, however, so a speaker would do well to practice delivering his or her message without incorporating these filler sounds.

Formal Delivery

Ideally, with experience a speaker develops the ability to deliver his or her message in a manner appropriate to the topic, the audience, and the setting. For instance, when speaking to a group of five or six people, it is inappropriate to use a booming voice and wild, dramatic gestures. Likewise, it takes a very sophisticated speaker to deliver an intimate, informal lecture to a group of two or three hundred. One of the best ways to develop a sense of what is appropriate for a given setting is to study effective speakers in various settings. Notice how they vary their vocal quality and nonverbal communication repertoire in different environments. To gain the attention and respect of the audience, the speaker needs to deliver his or her message in a manner that will meet their expectations.

Channels of Public Communication

Normally, speech delivery is considered a simple transmission of words by one person to a group. However, this is only one of the channels through which information is delivered during a speech. In the technical language of speech communication, the speaker's words are said to pass through the verbal channel. At the same time, the speaker's tone of voice indicates his or her attitude through the aural channel. Some speakers use visual aids, which transmit information through the pictorial channel. Finally, a speaker transmits information about his or her attitude and self-image through gestures and facial expressions. This transmission is said to pass through the visual channel.

Importance of Nonverbal Communication

Many speakers underestimate the positive effects that nonverbal communication can have on their success in delivering a message. By making assertive and forceful gestures, a speaker can create an image of credibility and confidence. Similarly, by making easy gestures, a speaker can promote an image of relaxation and expansiveness. The trick is to know which gestures are appropriate in which situations. Furthermore, an effective speaker will be able to modulate the volume and pitch of his or her voice in accordance with the requirements of the speech.

A bombastic tone is not appropriate to an academic discourse, nor is a dry delivery appropriate for a political rally. A speaker needs to be aware of the expectations of the audience, and only challenge them when such a challenge is necessary.

Message

The message of a speech is communicated not only with the words being spoken but also through the speaker's self-presentation. In other words, the quality of the speaker's voice and his or her body language contribute to the message as well. The message of the speech is generally considered to have three basic components: structure, content, and presentation. The structure of the speech is the order in which information is delivered. To be effective, a speech must have a logical and coherent structure. The content of the speech is the information it contains; even an entertaining or persuasive speech must have good content. Finally, the presentation of a speech is the style in which it is delivered to the audience. Different kinds of speeches require different presentation styles. The most important thing is to match the presentation to the intention of the speech.

Procedure for Improving One's Own Public Speech

The process of improving public speech technique will vary depending on the individual's particular challenges. A few common remedies can be generally helpful however. For one thing, a person can record themselves and listen to the way they speak. Speakers are frequently unaware of their articulation problems while giving a speech, but these problems become clear upon review. With practice, speakers can train themselves to diagnose particular problems and can subsequently learn to self-correct them. Practice in producing the correct sound every day should result in almost immediate progress. After a while, the corrections will become habitual and will no longer need review or practice.

Posture

Many speakers fail to recognize the significance of proper posture in the delivery of a speech. As much as words or gestures, a speaker's posture transmits information about his or her attitude, credibility, and confidence. To present a message effectively, a speaker should stand up as straight and tall as possible. Slouching forward or bending over one's notes indicates a lack of interest and preparation. This kind of advice may seem trivial, but an audience will subconsciously pay closer attention to anyone whose posture indicates command and authority. Effective speakers pay close attention to their own posture and make sure that poor posture does not disrupt the transmission of their message.

Facial Expression

The facial expressions made by a speaker can have a significant impact on the effectiveness of message delivery. The facial expressions of the speaker can either reinforce or contradict his or her words. If the words being spoken are amusing or colorful, it is appropriate for the speaker to be smiling and have a relaxed facial expression. If the speaker is addressing a serious subject while grinning, however, the audience will most likely discount what he or she is saying. A speaker needs to match his or her facial expressions to the subject matter and to the expectations of the audience. A large audience can expect the facial expressions of the speaker to be slightly exaggerated, while a small audience may be put off by what seems like a leering or grimacing speaker.

Eye Contact

Speakers should never underestimate the importance of eye contact during message delivery. For one thing, it is very difficult for an audience member who is making eye contact with the speaker to lose interest. An effective speaker will often shift his or her gaze around the room, making eye contact with as many people as possible. Under no circumstances should a speaker look up in the air, stare at his or her notes, or fix his or her eyes on some point in the distance. At the same time, the speaker should not constantly move his or her eyes around the room, as this may be perceived as anxious behavior. Eye movements should be calm, regular, and smooth.

Gestures

A public speaker should make sure that his or her gestures are in harmony with the subject matter of the speech and the expectations of the audience. Many people are in the habit of either moving their hands frequently during speech or keeping their hands stationary. Both of these approaches are only appropriate in certain circumstances. When delivering a speech to a large audience, or delivering a speech with a high emotional content, a speaker may be advised to incorporate wide, energetic gestures. However, these kinds of motions are not appropriate for a more somber subject. And although gestures can amplify the meaning of the speaker's words, they should never become a distraction from the message of the speech.

Proper Use of Notes

Many speakers will require notes, but they should rely on these notes as little as possible during delivery of the speech. For one thing, notes tend to prevent a speaker from making effective eye contact and using his or her hands expressively while speaking. Also, speakers who become reliant on notes may not be able to orient themselves in a speech if something goes wrong with the notes. Notes should only be used as a reference point of last resort. They should be kept down in front of the speaker, preferably out of view of the audience. They should not be held and should be on as few pieces of paper as possible, to prevent excessive shuffling during a speech. Finally, a speaker who requires notes should carefully look them over before a speech to make sure they are understandable and arranged properly.

SPEECH ANXIETY

Speech anxiety is a common malady but not one that should cause a person to lose heart. Even the most successful speakers have a bit of anxiety when delivering a message. In a way, this anxiety is a positive thing, because it focuses the attention and encourages concentration. Speech anxiety is a natural response to confronting an uncertain and unfamiliar situation. Research suggests that those who suffer from severe speech anxiety are often the most effective public speakers. Also, most speakers report that the anxiety they feel before delivering a speech is much greater than the anxiety they feel when actually in the process of speaking.

The abundance of nervous energy felt before delivering a speech can be used to the speaker's advantage. For one thing, many people find that speech anxiety sharpens their senses and focuses their concentration on the task at hand. Human beings are naturally inclined to focus their attention when they perceive a threat. The good thing about speech anxiety is that the attention is sharpened even though the threat is not significant. Many accomplished speakers use speech anxiety to increase their level of excitement and dynamism while delivering a speech. Indeed, many speakers say that without speech anxiety, they would not be able to achieve the rhetorical effects that have made them successful speakers.

STATE APPREHENSION

To some extent, everyone grapples with speech anxiety. The fear of embarrassment or public disclosure can be overcome only with significant practice at public speaking. There are a couple of different kinds of speech anxiety. "State apprehension" is defined as speech anxiety that is only felt in specific situations. For instance, an individual who is comfortable talking in class but becomes anxious when required to speak informally with peers is experiencing state apprehension. Many people experience state apprehension in relation to delivering formal speeches in front of a group. State apprehension has both physical and mental symptoms, including vocal tics, sweaty palms, and a trembling voice.

TRAIT APPREHENSION

Some people experience speech anxiety to a greater degree than others. Those aspects of speech anxiety that are unique to an individual are known as trait apprehensions. For instance, someone might have an aversion to public speaking because of a past experience. People who have an unnaturally high level of trait apprehension tend to avoid situations in which they will be required to speak to a large group. The good news for these individuals is that trait apprehension can be overcome with experience. Unfortunately, however, this means practicing public speaking until it becomes natural.

CULTIVATING SELF-CONFIDENCE

Most people struggle with some degree of anxiety when they are required to speak in public. One of the best things a person can do to reduce speech anxiety is to present a confident image. Naturally, one should always practice delivering a speech several times beforehand. Through repetition, the speaker becomes familiar with the appropriate gestures and rhythms of the speech, which gives rise to increasing confidence in his or her ability to deliver. Another good way to build confidence is to make eye contact with the audience during speech delivery. A forthright, steady gaze from the speaker connotes a feeling of confidence. Finally, confidence can be communicated through posture and body language. Standing up straight and emphasizing key points with hand gestures is a great way to communicate self-confidence.

The Audience

Communication Rules

Sometimes a speech will be delivered in a particular environment or to a particular group that is governed by specific communication rules. For instance, a speech delivered in church is unlikely to be followed by a question-and-answer period. As another example, some debating societies have strict rules for the presentation and critique of a speech. In more informal situations, some groups will have different expectations for speaker behavior. For instance, a gathering of senior citizens is unlikely to respond well to coarse humor. In other words, communication rules may be explicit or implicit. While preparing a speech, the speaker needs to address the formal considerations that will influence his or her message.

Ethics

To be effective as a public speaker, one needs to maintain a high degree of ethical rectitude. This is true not only because of the inherent virtues of ethical behavior, but also because an audience will not trust a speaker whom they believe to be unethical. To promote good ethics as a public speaker, one should always be as honest as possible. One should also try to promote the interests of the audience whenever appropriate. It is important to give members of the audience responsibility for making up their own minds, rather than attempting to browbeat them into submission with one's argument.

Audience Analysis

In the study of speech communication, audience analysis is simply the practice of examining the characteristics and background of the audience in order to tailor a speech appropriately. For instance, one would want to know the general age, socioeconomic status, culture, and gender of an audience while preparing a speech. The type of speech appropriate to a group of elementary schoolgirls will be quite different from that appropriate to a group of older men, even if both speeches are on the same subject. The prejudices and pre-existing opinions of these two groups will be extremely different and thus, to be effective, a speaker must tailor and deliver his or her message to each group in very different ways.

When a seasoned public speaker conducts an audience analysis, he or she focuses on a few specific characteristics of the audience. For one thing, the speaker wants to know the audience's background as it relates to him or her and his or her subject matter. Although much of audience analysis consists of determining the approximate ages and socioeconomic backgrounds of the audience, this is primarily because such information enables the speaker to estimate the audience's opinions and degree of familiarity with the subject matter and speaker. A speaker who is well-liked by the audience can employ a different rhetorical strategy than one with whom most of the audience disagrees.

Characteristics of the Audience

The individual or group of individuals who listen to a speech bring their own characteristics to bear on the quality of the speech. For one thing, listeners will always have their own intentions. That is, they will always be seeking to obtain something from the speech, whether it is information or entertainment. Listeners will also have varying degrees of skill, meaning that some groups will be better at understanding a complex message. Listeners will also bring their pre-existing attitudes toward the speaker and the speaker's subject. To deliver an effective message, a speaker needs to perform an audience analysis to determine the characteristics of his or her listeners.

SOCIAL CONTEXT

When speakers consider the characteristics of the environment in which they will deliver their speech, they sometimes neglect to consider the social context. The social context is the set of relationships between the members of the audience and the speaker and between the members of the audience themselves. The speaker should know beforehand how he or she stands in relation to the audience. For instance, a speaker may be recognized as an expert, an entertainer, or an intriguing fraud. Also, the speaker should understand how the members of the audience st and in relation to one another; whether they are friends, colleagues, or strangers, for instance. The information gained by this consideration of social context should inform the construction and delivery of the speech.

PHYSICAL SETTING

The physical setting in which a speech is delivered exerts significant influence over the expectations of the audience and should therefore be taken into account by the speaker beforehand. For instance, an audience that is required to stand during a speech will have less patience for a long-winded and complex oration. On the other hand, if the audience is seated in soft, plush chairs, they may be too relaxed to pay attention to a serious lecture. When the subject of a speech requires a fair amount of technical detail, it is a good idea for the audience to be seated in upright chairs and for the room to have sufficient light. In any case, the speaker should consider how physical setting will influence the mood of the audience and should adjust his or her speech accordingly.

TAILORING THE SUBJECT OF A SPEECH FOR THE APPROPRIATE AUDIENCE

When deciding on the subject of the speech, the speaker must take into account the characteristics and ability level of the audience. The speaker should be aware of the audience's expectations. That is, whether they expect to be informed, entertained, or persuaded. Audience members may be annoyed if a speech has a drastically different tone from the one they were expecting. For instance, an audience expecting a serious speech will be impatient with a speaker who spends a great deal of time trying to make them laugh. In some cases, it may be necessary to thwart the expectations of the audience, as for instance when a serious moral point must be made instead of providing sheer entertainment.

When deciding upon the subject matter of a speech, the speaker should take into account the audience's general intelligence level and subject-related knowledge. A speech will be ineffective if it is either too elementary or too advanced for the audience. If the speaker is unfamiliar with the knowledge base of the proposed audience, he or she should take steps to determine this knowledge before preparing the speech. For an unschooled audience, it is a good idea to focus on the most basic and important principles of a given subject. For an audience of experts in a given field, however, it is important to provide information that will be stimulating and informative.

AUDIENCE ATTITUDE

It is important for a speaker to gauge the attitude of the audience before delivering his or her speech. Attitude, because it is more subtle than age, ethnicity, or belief system, can only be determined through direct observation. Thus, if a speaker is able to observe the audience before delivering the speech, he or she can benefit greatly. Observing the audience beforehand can provide clues to what kind of general mood the audience is in, whether good or bad. If the audience is in a hostile mood, the speaker may want to avoid trying to joke with them. An audience that seems jovial and engaged, on the other hand, should not be alienated with strident rhetoric or harsh words. The job of the speaker is to establish and maintain a good rapport with the audience.

Remembering the Audience's Capacity to Act

When developing a speech, one should always remember the characteristics and capabilities of the audience. This is especially important when producing a persuasive speech. It does not make sense to encourage the audience to take an action they are not capable of taking. For instance, a politician would be foolish to make an impassioned plea for votes to a bunch of elementary school students, all of whom are years away from voter eligibility. When developing a persuasive speech, then, it is essential to remember the capacity of the audience to act.

Beliefs

To accurately assess what an audience might be thinking, one must understand that audience's core beliefs. Strictly defined, beliefs are the facts, ideas, and opinions that the audience holds to be true. Objectively, some of these beliefs may actually be untrue. However, to deliver an effective message, a speaker must take into account the sum total of the audience's beliefs. If the purpose of the speech is to adjust the beliefs of the audience, the speaker must appeal to either the reasoning skills or the emotions of his or her listeners.

When describing the beliefs of an audience, speech communication instructors often distinguish between fixed and variable beliefs. The primary difference between the two is that fixed beliefs are harder to change. Typically, fixed beliefs have been held throughout an individual's life and most likely reinforced by his or her experience. Variable beliefs, on the other hand, may have been recently acquired and therefore may be less established in the individual's mind. A speaker is more likely to change variable beliefs and should therefore focus his or her attention on these. Variable beliefs are especially vulnerable to change when they are based on opinion rather than fact.

Facts and Opinions

When considering the convictions of an audience, it is good to distinguish between facts and opinions. Facts are those convictions that can be proven in an objective sense. Scientific assertions, for instance, are considered facts. Opinions, on the other hand, cannot necessarily be supported by hard data. People often hold opinions for rather arbitrary individual reasons, such as those based on personal experience. The fact that communities hold collective opinions must also be considered when making a speech. In general, it is easier for a speaker to adjust beliefs or convictions based on opinion than those based on fact.

Feedback

Feedback is the response of the audience to the message delivered by a speaker. Although feedback is typically thought of as verbal responses to the message, it also includes body language, attention or inattention, and participation in dialogue after the speech. To be effective, a speaker must be attuned to all these kinds of feedback. In other words, he or she must monitor the audience throughout the speech to identify signs of boredom or engagement. The feedback a speaker receives while delivering his speech is called immediate feedback. The feedback the speaker receives after delivering the speech is called delayed feedback. Delayed feedback usually takes the form of critical comments, praise, or questions. A practiced speaker will use feedback to improve subsequent speeches.

Correct Grammar, Organization, and Sentence Structure Required for Writing Reports

Foundations of Grammar

The Eight Parts of Speech

Nouns

When you talk about a person, place, thing, or idea, you are talking about a **noun**. The two main types of nouns are **common** and **proper** nouns. Also, nouns can be abstract (i.e., general) or concrete (i.e., specific).

Common nouns are the class or group of people, places, and things (Note: Do not capitalize common nouns). Examples of common nouns:

> *People*: boy, girl, worker, manager
>
> *Places*: school, bank, library, home
>
> *Things*: dog, cat, truck, car

Proper nouns are the names of a specific person, place, or thing (Note: Capitalize all proper nouns). Examples of proper nouns:

> *People*: Abraham Lincoln; George Washington; Martin Luther King, Jr.
>
> *Places*: Los Angeles, California; New York; Asia
>
> *Things*: Statue of Liberty, Earth*, Lincoln Memorial
>
> *Note: When you talk about the planet that we live on, you capitalize *Earth*. When you mean the dirt, rocks, or land, you lowercase *earth*.

General nouns are the names of conditions or ideas. **Specific nouns** name people, places, and things that are understood by using your senses.

General nouns:

> *Condition*: beauty, strength
>
> *Idea*: truth, peace

Specific nouns:

> *People*: baby, friend, father
>
> *Places*: town, park, city hall
>
> *Things*: rainbow, cough, apple, silk, gasoline

Collective nouns are the names for a person, place, or thing that may act as a whole. The following are examples of collective nouns: *class, company, dozen, group, herd, team,* and *public.*

Pronouns

Pronouns are words that are used to stand in for a noun. A pronoun may be classified as personal, intensive, relative, interrogative, demonstrative, indefinite, and reciprocal.

Personal: *Nominative* is the case for nouns and pronouns that are the subject of a sentence. *Objective* is the case for nouns and pronouns that are an object in a sentence. *Possessive* is the case for nouns and pronouns that show possession or ownership.

Singular

	Nominative	Objective	Possessive
First Person	I	me	my, mine
Second Person	you	you	your, yours
Third Person	he, she, it	him, her, it	his, her, hers, its

Plural

	Nominative	Objective	Possessive
First Person	we	us	our, ours
Second Person	you	you	your, yours
Third Person	they	them	their, theirs

Intensive: I myself, you yourself, he himself, she herself, the (thing) itself, we ourselves, you yourselves, they themselves

Relative: which, who, whom, whose

Interrogative: what, which, who, whom, whose

Demonstrative: this, that, these, those

Indefinite: all, any, each, everyone, either/neither, one, some, several

Reciprocal: each other, one another

Review Video: Nouns and Pronouns
Visit mometrix.com/academy and enter code: 312073

Verbs

If you want to write a sentence, then you need a verb. Without a verb, you have no sentence. The verb of a sentence explains action or being. In other words, the verb shows the subject's movement or the movement that has been done to the subject.

Transitive and Intransitive Verbs

A transitive verb is a verb whose action (e.g., drive, run, jump) points to a receiver (e.g., car, dog, kangaroo). Intransitive verbs do not point to a receiver of an action. In other words, the action of the verb does not point to a subject or object.

Transitive: He plays the piano. | The piano was played by him.

Intransitive: He plays. | John writes well.

A dictionary will let you know whether a verb is transitive or intransitive. Some verbs can be transitive and intransitive.

Action Verbs and Linking Verbs

Action verbs show what the subject is doing in a sentence. In other words, an action verb shows action. Unlike most types of words, a single action verb, in the right context, can be an entire sentence. **Linking verbs** link the subject of a sentence to a noun or pronoun, or they link a subject with an adjective. You always need a verb if you want a complete sentence. However, linking verbs on their own cannot be a complete sentence.

Common linking verbs include *appear, be, become, feel, grow, look, seem, smell, sound,* and *taste*. However, any verb that shows a condition and has a noun, pronoun, or adjective that describes the subject of a sentence is a linking verb.

Action: He sings. | Run! | Go! | I talk with him every day. | She reads.

Linking:

Incorrect: I am.

Correct: I am John. | I smell roses. | I feel tired.

Note: Some verbs are followed by words that look like prepositions, but they are a part of the verb and a part of the verb's meaning. These are known as phrasal verbs and examples include *call off, look up*, and *drop off.*

Review Video: Action Verbs and Linking Verbs
Visit mometrix.com/academy and enter code: 743142

Voice

Transitive verbs come in active or passive voice. If the subject does an action or receives the action of the verb, then you will know whether a verb is active or passive. When the subject of the sentence is doing the action, the verb is in **active voice**. When the subject receives the action, the verb is in **passive voice**.

Active: Jon drew the picture. (The subject *Jon* is doing the action of *drawing a picture.*)

Passive: The picture is drawn by Jon. (The subject *picture* is receiving the action from Jon.)

Verb Tenses

A verb tense shows the different form of a verb to point to the time of an action. The present and past tense are shown by changing the verb's form. An action in the present, *I talk,* can change form for the past: *I talked*. However, for the other tenses, an auxiliary (i.e., helping) verb is needed to show the change in form. These helping verbs include *am, are, is* | *have, has, had* | *was, were, will* (or *shall*).

Present: I talk	Present perfect: I have talked
Past: I talked	Past perfect: I had talked
Future: I will talk	Future perfect: I will have talked

Present: The action happens at the current time.

Example: He *walks* to the store every morning.

To show that something is happening right now, use the progressive present tense: I *am walking*.

Past: The action happened in the past.

Example: He *walked* to the store an hour ago.

Future: The action is going to happen later.

Example: I *will walk* to the store tomorrow.

Present perfect: The action started in the past and continues into the present.

Example: I *have walked* to the store three times today.

Past perfect: The second action happened in the past. The first action came before the second.

Example: Before I walked to the store (Action 2), I *had walked* to the library (Action 1).

Future perfect: An action that uses the past and the future. In other words, the action is complete before a future moment.

Example: When she comes for the supplies (future moment), I *will have walked* to the store (action completed before the future moment).

Review Video: Present Perfect, Past Perfect, and Future Perfect Verb Tenses
Visit mometrix.com/academy and enter code: 269472

Conjugating Verbs

When you need to change the form of a verb, you are **conjugating** a verb. The key forms of a verb are singular, present tense (dream); singular, past tense (dreamed); and the past participle (have dreamed). Note: the past participle needs a helping verb to make a verb tense. For example, I *have dreamed* of this day. The following tables demonstrate some of the different ways to conjugate a verb:

Singular

Tense	First Person	Second Person	Third Person
Present	I dream	You dream	He, she, it dreams
Past	I dreamed	You dreamed	He, she, it dreamed
Past Participle	I have dreamed	You have dreamed	He, she, it has dreamed

Plural

Tense	First Person	Second Person	Third Person
Present	We dream	You dream	They dream
Past	We dreamed	You dreamed	They dreamed
Past Participle	We have dreamed	You have dreamed	They have dreamed

Mood

There are three moods in English: the indicative, the imperative, and the subjunctive.

The **indicative mood** is used for facts, opinions, and questions.

Fact: You can do this.

Opinion: I think that you can do this.

Question: Do you know that you can do this?

The **imperative** is used for orders or requests.

Order: You are going to do this!

Request: Will you do this for me?

The **subjunctive mood** is for wishes and statements that go against fact.

Wish: I wish that I were going to do this.

Statement against fact: If I were you, I would do this. (This goes against fact because I am not you. You have the chance to do this, and I do not have the chance.)

The mood that causes trouble for most people is the subjunctive mood. If you have trouble with any of the moods, then be sure to practice.

Adjectives

An adjective is a word that is used to modify a noun or pronoun. An adjective answers a question: *Which one? What kind?* or *How many?* Usually, adjectives come before the words that they modify, but they may also come after a linking verb.

Which one? The *third* suit is my favorite.

What kind? This suit is *navy blue*.

How many? I am going to buy *four* pairs of socks to match the suit?

Articles

Articles are adjectives that are used to mark nouns. There are only three: the **definite** (i.e., limited or fixed amount) article *the* and the **indefinite** (i.e., no limit or fixed amount) articles *a* and *an*.

Note: *An* comes before words that start with a vowel sound. For example, "Are you going to get an **u**mbrella?"

Definite: I lost *the* bottle that belongs to me.

Indefinite: Does anyone have *a* bottle to share?

Comparison with Adjectives

Some adjectives are relative and other adjectives are absolute. Adjectives that are **relative** can show the comparison between things. Adjectives that are **absolute** can show comparison. However, they show comparison in a different way. Let's say that you are reading two books. You think that one book is perfect, and the other book is not exactly perfect. It is not possible for one book to be more perfect than the other. Either you think that the book is perfect, or you think that the book is not perfect.

The adjectives that are relative will show the different **degrees** of something or someone to something else or someone else. The three degrees of adjectives include positive, comparative, and superlative.

The **positive** degree is the normal form of an adjective.

Example: This work is *difficult.* | She is *smart.*

The **comparative** degree compares one person or thing to another person or thing.

Example: This work is *more difficult* than your work. | She is *smarter* than me.

The **superlative** degree compares more than two people or things.

Example: This is the *most difficult* work of my life. | She is the *smartest* lady in school.

Review Video: What is an Adjective?
Visit mometrix.com/academy and enter code: 470154

Adverbs

An adverb is a word that is used to **modify** a verb, adjective, or another adverb. Usually, adverbs answer one of these questions: *When?*, *Where?*, *How?*, and *Why?*. The negatives *not* and *never* are known as adverbs. Adverbs that modify adjectives or other adverbs **strengthen** or **weaken** the words that they modify.

Examples:

He walks *quickly* through the crowd.

The water flows *smoothly* on the rocks.

Note: Some words that end in *-ly* are adjectives, not adverbs. Examples include: *early, friendly, holy, lonely, silly*, and *ugly*. To know if a word that ends in *-ly* is an adjective or adverb, you need to check your dictionary. Also, while many adverbs end in *-ly*, you need to remember that not all adverbs end in *-ly*.

Examples:

He is *never* angry.

You talk *too* loudly.

Comparison with Adverbs

The rules for comparing adverbs are the same as the rules for adjectives.

The **positive** degree is the standard form of an adverb.

Example: He arrives *soon*. | She speaks *softly* to her friends.

The **comparative** degree compares one person or thing to another person or thing.

Example: He arrives *sooner* than Sarah. | She speaks *more softly* than him.

The **superlative** degree compares more than two people or things.

Example: He arrives *soonest* of the group. | She speaks the *most softly* of any of her friends.

Review Video: Adverbs
Visit mometrix.com/academy and enter code: 713951

Prepositions

A preposition is a word placed before a noun or pronoun that shows the relationship between an object and another word in the sentence.

Common prepositions:

about	before	during	on	under
after	beneath	for	over	until
against	between	from	past	up
among	beyond	in	through	with
around	by	of	to	within
at	down	off	toward	without

Examples:

The napkin is *in* the drawer.

The Earth rotates *around* the Sun.

The needle is *beneath* the haystack.

Can you find me *among* the words?

Review Video: What is a Preposition?
Visit mometrix.com/academy and enter code: 946763

Conjunctions

Conjunctions join words, phrases, or clauses and they show the connection between the joined pieces. **Coordinating** conjunctions connect equal parts of sentences. **Correlative** conjunctions show the connection between pairs. **Subordinating** conjunctions join subordinate (i.e., dependent) clauses with independent clauses.

Coordinating Conjunctions

The coordinating conjunctions include: *and, but, yet, or, nor, for,* and *so*

Examples:

The rock was small, but it was heavy.

She drove in the night, and he drove in the day.

Correlative Conjunctions

The correlative conjunctions are: *either...or* | *neither...nor* | *not only...but also*

Examples:

Either you are coming *or* you are staying.

He *not only* ran three miles *but also* swam 200 yards.

Review Video: Coordinating and Correlative Conjunctions
Visit mometrix.com/academy and enter code: 390329

Subordinating Conjunctions

Common subordinating conjunctions include:

after	since	whenever
although	so that	where
because	unless	wherever
before	until	whether
in order that	when	while

Examples:

I am hungry *because* I did not eat breakfast.

He went home *when* everyone left.

Review Video: Subordinating Conjunctions
Visit mometrix.com/academy and enter code: 958913

Interjections

Interjections are words of exclamation (i.e., great amount of feeling) that are used alone or as a part of a sentence. Often, they are used at the beginning of a sentence for an introduction. Sometimes, they can be used in the middle of a sentence to show a change in thought or attitude.

Common Interjections: Hey! | Oh, | Ouch! | Please! | Wow!

Agreement and Sentence Structure

Subjects and Predicates

Subjects

The **subject** of a sentence names who or what the sentence is all about. The subject may be directly stated in a sentence, or the subject may be the implied *you*. The **complete subject** includes the simple subject and all of its modifiers. To find the complete subject, ask *Who* or *What* and insert the verb to complete the question. The answer is the complete subject. To find the **simple subject**, remove all of the modifiers (adjectives, prepositional phrases, etc.) in the complete subject. Being able to locate the subject of a sentence helps with many problems, such as those involving sentence fragments and subject-verb agreement.

Examples:

The small red car is the one that he wants for Christmas.

(The simple subject is *the car*, and the complete subject is *the small red car.*)

The young artist is coming over for dinner.

(The simple subject is *the artist*, and the complete subject is *the young artist.*)

Review Video: Subjects
Visit mometrix.com/academy and enter code: 444771

In **imperative** sentences, the verb's subject is understood (e.g., [You] Run to the store) but not actually present in the sentence. Normally, the subject comes before the verb. However, the subject comes after the verb in sentences that begin with *There are* or *There was.*

Direct:

John knows the way to the park.

(Who knows the way to the park? Answer: *John*)

The cookies need ten more minutes.

(What needs ten minutes? Answer: *The cookies*)

By five o'clock, Bill will need to leave.

(Who needs to leave? Answer: *Bill*)

Remember: The subject can come after the verb.

There are five letters on the table for him.

(What is on the table? Answer: *Five letters*)

There were coffee and doughnuts in the house.

(What was in the house? Answer: *Coffee and doughnuts*)

Implied:

Go to the post office for me.

(Who is going to the post office? Answer: *You are.*)

Come and sit with me, please?

(Who needs to come and sit? Answer: *You do.*)

Predicates

In a sentence, you always have a predicate and a subject. The subject tells what the sentence is about, and the **predicate** explains or describes the subject.

Think about the sentence: *He sings*. In this sentence, we have a subject (He) and a predicate (sings). This is all that is needed for a sentence to be complete. Would we like more information? Of course, we would like to know more. However, if this is all the information that you are given, you have a complete sentence.

Now, let's look at another sentence:

John and Jane sing on Tuesday nights at the dance hall.

What is the subject of this sentence?

Answer: John and Jane.

What is the predicate of this sentence?

Answer: Everything else in the sentence (sing on Tuesday nights at the dance hall).

Subject-Verb Agreement

Verbs **agree** with their subjects in number. In other words, *singular* subjects need *singular* verbs. *Plural* subjects need *plural* verbs. Singular is for one person, place, or thing. Plural is for more than one person, place, or thing. Subjects and verbs must also agree in person: first, second, or third. The present tense ending *-s* is used on a verb if its subject is third person singular; otherwise, the verb takes no ending.

Review Video: Subject Verb Agreement
Visit mometrix.com/academy and enter code: 479190

Number Agreement Examples:

Single Subject and Verb: *Dan calls home.*

(Dan is one person. So, the singular verb *calls* is needed.)

Plural Subject and Verb: *Dan and Bob call home.*

(More than one person needs the plural verb *call*.)

Person Agreement Examples:

First Person: I *am* walking.

Second Person: You *are* walking.

Third Person: He *is* walking.

Complications with Subject-Verb Agreement

Words Between Subject and Verb

Words that come between the simple subject and the verb may serve as an effective distraction, but they have no bearing on subject-verb agreement.

Examples:

The joy of my life returns home tonight.

(**Singular Subject**: joy **Singular Verb**: returns)

The phrase *of my life* does not influence the verb *returns*.

The question that still remains unanswered is "Who are you?"

(**Singular Subject**: question **Singular Verb**: is)

Don't let the phrase *"that still remains..."* trouble you. The subject *question* goes with *is.*

Compound Subjects

A compound subject is formed when two or more nouns joined by *and*, *or*, or *nor* jointly act as the subject of the sentence.

Joined by And

When a compound subject is joined by *and*, it is treated as a plural subject and requires a plural verb.

Examples:

You and Jon are invited to come to my house.

(**Plural Subject**: You and Jon. **Plural Verb**: are)

The pencil and paper belong to me.

(**Plural Subject**: pencil and paper. **Plural Verb**: belong)

Joined by Or/Nor

For a compound subject joined by *or* or *nor*, the verb must agree in number with the part of the subject that is closest to the verb (italicized in the examples below).

Examples:

Today or *tomorrow is* the day.

(**Subject**: Today / tomorrow **Verb**: is)

Stan or *Phil wants* to read the book.

(**Subject**: Stan / Phil **Verb**: wants)

Neither the books nor the *pen is* on the desk.

(**Subject**: books / pen **Verb**: is)

Either the blanket or *pillows arrive* this afternoon.

(**Subject**: blanket / pillows **Verb**: arrive)

Indefinite Pronouns as Subject

An indefinite pronoun is a pronoun that does not refer to a specific noun. Indefinite pronouns may be only singular, be only plural, or change depending on how they are used.

Always Singular

Pronouns such as *each*, *either*, *everybody*, *anybody*, *somebody*, and *nobody* are always singular.

Examples:

Each of the runners *has* a different bib number.

(**Singular Subject**: Each **Singular Verb**: has)

Is either of you ready for the game?

(**Singular Subject**: either **Singular Verb**: Is)

Note: The words *each* and *either* can also be used as adjectives (e.g., *each* person is unique). When one of these adjectives modifies the subject of a sentence, it is always a singular subject.

Everybody grows a day older every day.

(**Singular Subject**: Everybody **Singular Verb**: grows)

Anybody is welcome to bring a tent.

(**Singular Subject**: Anybody **Singular Verb**: is)

Always Plural

Pronouns such as *both*, *several*, and *many* are always plural.

Examples:

Both of the siblings *were* too tired to argue.

(**Plural Subject**: Both **Plural Verb**: were)

Many have tried, but none have succeeded.

(**Plural Subject**: Many **Plural Verb**: have tried)

DEPEND ON CONTEXT

Pronouns such as *some*, *any*, *all*, *none*, *more*, and *most* can be either singular or plural depending on what they are representing in the context of the sentence.

Examples:

All of my dog's food *was* still there in his bowl

(**Singular Subject**: All **Singular Verb**: was)

By the end of the night, *all* of my guests *were* already excited about coming to my next party.

(**Plural Subject**: all **Plural Verb**: were)

OTHER CASES INVOLVING PLURAL OR IRREGULAR FORM

Some nouns are **singular in meaning but plural in form**: news, mathematics, physics, and economics.

The *news is* coming on now.

Mathematics is my favorite class.

Some nouns are plural in form and meaning, and have **no singular equivalent**: scissors and pants.

Do these *pants come* with a shirt?

The *scissors are* for my project.

Mathematical operations are **irregular** in their construction, but are normally considered to be **singular in meaning**.

One plus one is two.

Three times three is nine.

Note: Look to your **dictionary** for help when you aren't sure whether a noun with a plural form has a singular or plural meaning.

COMPLEMENTS

A complement is a noun, pronoun, or adjective that is used to give more information about the subject or verb in the sentence.

DIRECT OBJECTS

A direct object is a noun or pronoun that takes or receives the **action** of a verb. (Remember: a complete sentence does not need a direct object, so not all sentences will have them. A sentence needs only a subject and a verb.) When you are looking for a direct object, find the verb and ask *who* or *what.*

Examples:

I took the blanket. (Who or what did I take? *The blanket*)

Jane read books. (Who or what does Jane read? *Books*)

Indirect Objects

An indirect object is a word or group of words that show how an action had an **influence** on someone or something. If there is an indirect object in a sentence, then you always have a direct object in the sentence. When you are looking for the indirect object, find the verb and ask *to/for whom or what.*

Examples:

We taught the old dog a new trick.

(To/For Whom or What was taught? *The old dog*)

I gave them a math lesson.

(To/For Whom or What was given? *Them*)

Review Video: Direct and Indirect Objects
Visit mometrix.com/academy and enter code: 817385

Predicate Nominatives and Predicate Adjectives

As we looked at previously, verbs may be classified as either action verbs or linking verbs. A linking verb is so named because it links the subject to words in the predicate that describe or define the subject. These words are called predicate nominatives (if nouns or pronouns) or predicate adjectives (if adjectives).

Examples:

My father is a *lawyer.*

(Father is the **subject**. Lawyer is the **predicate nominative.**)

Your mother is *patient.*

(Mother is the **subject**. Patient is the **predicate adjective.**)

Pronoun Usage

The **antecedent** is the noun that has been replaced by a pronoun. A pronoun and its antecedent **agree** when they have the same number (singular or plural) and gender (male, female, or neuter).

Examples:

Singular agreement: *John* came into town, and *he* played for us.

(The word *he* replaces *John.*)

Plural agreement: *John and Rick* came into town, and *they* played for us.

(The word *they* replaces *John and Rick.*)

To determine which is the correct pronoun to use in a compound subject or object, try each pronoun **alone** in place of the compound in the sentence. Your knowledge of pronouns will tell you which one is correct.

Example:

> Bob and (I, me) will be going.
>
> Test: (1) *I will be going* or (2) *Me will be going*. The second choice cannot be correct because *me* cannot be used as the subject of a sentence. Instead, *me* is used as an object.
>
> **Answer**: Bob and I will be going.

When a pronoun is used with a noun immediately following (as in "we boys"), try the sentence **without the added noun**.

Example:

> (We/Us) boys played football last year.
>
> Test: (1) *We played football last ye*ar or (2) *Us played football last year*. Again, the second choice cannot be correct because *us* cannot be used as a subject of a sentence. Instead, *us* is used as an object.
>
> **Answer**: We boys played football last year.

Review Video: Pronoun Usage
Visit mometrix.com/academy and enter code: 666500

A pronoun should point clearly to the **antecedent**. Here is how a pronoun reference can be unhelpful if it is not directly stated or puzzling.

> **Unhelpful**: Ron and Jim went to the store, and *he* bought soda.
>
> (Who bought soda? Ron or Jim?)
>
> **Helpful**: Jim went to the store, and *he* bought soda.
>
> (The sentence is clear. Jim bought the soda.)

Some pronouns change their form by their placement in a sentence. A pronoun that is a subject in a sentence comes in the **subjective case**. Pronouns that serve as objects appear in the **objective case**. Finally, the pronouns that are used as possessives appear in the **possessive case**.

Examples:

> **Subjective case**: *He* is coming to the show.
>
> (The pronoun *He* is the subject of the sentence.)
>
> **Objective case**: Josh drove *him* to the airport.
>
> (The pronoun *him* is the object of the sentence.)

Possessive case: The flowers are *mine*.

(The pronoun *mine* shows ownership of the flowers.)

The word *who* is a subjective-case pronoun that can be used as a **subject**. The word *whom* is an objective-case pronoun that can be used as an **object**. The words *who* and *whom* are common in subordinate clauses or in questions.

Examples:

Subject: He knows who wants to come.

(*Who* is the subject of the verb *wants*.)

Object: He knows the man whom we want at the party.

(*Whom* is the object of *we want*.)

Clauses

A clause is a group of words that contains both a subject and a predicate (verb). There are two types of clauses: independent and dependent. An **independent clause** contains a complete thought, while a **dependent (or subordinate) clause** does not. A dependent clause includes a subject and a verb, and may also contain objects or complements, but it cannot stand as a complete thought without being joined to an independent clause. Dependent clauses function within sentences as adjectives, adverbs, or nouns.

Example:

Independent Clause: I am running

Dependent Clause: because I want to stay in shape

The clause *I am running* is an independent clause: it has a subject and a verb, and it gives a complete thought. The clause *because I want to stay in shape* is a dependent clause: it has a subject and a verb, but it does not express a complete thought. It adds detail to the independent clause to which it is attached.

Combined: I am running because I want to stay in shape.

Review Video: Independent and Dependent Clauses
Visit mometrix.com/academy and enter code: 556903

Types of Dependent Clauses

Adjective Clauses

An **adjective clause** is a dependent clause that modifies a noun or a pronoun. Adjective clauses begin with a relative pronoun (*who, whose, whom, which,* and *that*) or a relative adverb (*where, when,* and *why*).

Also, adjective clauses come after the noun that the clause needs to explain or rename. This is done to have a clear connection to the independent clause.

Examples:

I learned the reason *why I won the award.*

This is the place *where I started my first job.*

An adjective clause can be an essential or nonessential clause. An essential clause is very important to the sentence. **Essential clauses** explain or define a person or thing. **Nonessential clauses** give more information about a person or thing but are not necessary to define them. Nonessential clauses are set off with commas while essential clauses are not.

Examples:

Essential: A person *who works hard at first* can often rest later in life.

Nonessential: Neil Armstrong, *who walked on the moon*, is my hero.

Review Video: Adjective Clauses and Phrases
Visit mometrix.com/academy and enter code: 520888

Adverb Clauses

An **adverb clause** is a dependent clause that modifies a verb, adjective, or adverb. In sentences with multiple dependent clauses, adverb clauses are usually placed immediately before or after the independent clause. An adverb clause is introduced with words such as *after, although, as, before, because, if, since, so, unless, when, where,* and *while.*

Examples:

When you walked outside, I called the manager.

I will go with you *unless you want to stay.*

Noun Clauses

A **noun clause** is a dependent clause that can be used as a subject, object, or complement. Noun clauses begin with words such as *how, that, what, whether, which, who,* and *why*. These words can also come with an adjective clause. Unless the noun clause is being used as the subject of the sentence, it should come after the verb of the independent clause.

Examples:

The real mystery is *how you avoided serious injury.*

What you learn from each other depends on your honesty with others.

Subordination

When two related ideas are not of equal importance, the ideal way to combine them is to make the more important idea an independent clause and the less important idea a dependent or subordinate clause. This is called **subordination**.

Example:

Separate ideas: The team had a perfect regular season. The team lost the championship.

Subordinated: Despite having a perfect regular season, *the team lost the championship.*

Phrases

A phrase is a group of words that functions as a single part of speech, usually a noun, adjective, or adverb. A phrase is not a complete thought, but it adds **detail** or **explanation** to a sentence, or **renames** something within the sentence.

Prepositional Phrases

One of the most common types of phrases is the prepositional phrase. A **prepositional phrase** begins with a preposition and ends with a noun or pronoun that is the object of the preposition. Normally, the prepositional phrase functions as an **adjective** or an **adverb** within the sentence.

Examples:

The picnic is *on the blanket.*

I am sick *with a fever* today.

Among the many flowers, John found a four-leaf clover.

Verbal Phrases

A verbal is a word or phrase that is formed from a verb but does not function as a verb. Depending on its particular form, it may be used as a noun, adjective, or adverb. A verbal does **not** replace a verb in a sentence.

Examples:

Correct: *Walk* a mile daily.

(*Walk* is the verb of this sentence. The subject is the implied *you.*)

Incorrect: *To walk* a mile.

(*To walk* is a type of verbal. This is not a sentence since there is no functional verb)

There are three types of verbals: **participles**, **gerunds**, and **infinitives**. Each type of verbal has a corresponding **phrase** that consists of the verbal itself along with any complements or modifiers.

Participles

A **participle** is a type of verbal that always functions as an adjective. The present participle always ends with *-ing*. Past participles end with *-d, -ed, -n,* or *-t.*

Examples: Verb: *dance* | Present Participle: *dancing* | Past Participle: *danced*

Participial phrases most often come right before or right after the noun or pronoun that they modify.

Examples:

Shipwrecked on an island, the boys started to fish for food.

Having been seated for five hours, we got out of the car to stretch our legs.

Praised for their work, the group accepted the first-place trophy.

GERUNDS

A **gerund** is a type of verbal that always functions as a noun. Like present participles, gerunds always end with *-ing*, but they can be easily distinguished from one another by the part of speech they represent (participles always function as adjectives). Since a gerund or gerund phrase always functions as a noun, it can be used as the subject of a sentence, the predicate nominative, or the object of a verb or preposition.

Examples:

We want to be known for *teaching the poor.* (Object of preposition)

Coaching this team is the best job of my life. (Subject)

We like *practicing our songs* in the basement. (Object of verb)

INFINITIVES

An **infinitive** is a type of verbal that can function as a noun, an adjective, or an adverb. An infinitive is made of the word *to* + the basic form of the verb. As with all other types of verbal phrases, an infinitive phrase includes the verbal itself and all of its complements or modifiers.

Examples:

To join the team is my goal in life. (Noun)

The animals have enough food *to eat for the night.* (Adjective)

People lift weights *to exercise their muscles.* (Adverb)

Review Video: Gerund, Infinitive, and Participle
Visit mometrix.com/academy and enter code: 634263

APPOSITIVE PHRASES

An **appositive** is a word or phrase that is used to explain or rename nouns or pronouns. Noun phrases, gerund phrases, and infinitive phrases can all be used as appositives.

Examples:

Terriers, *hunters at heart,* have been dressed up to look like lap dogs.

(The noun phrase *hunters at heart* renames the noun *terriers.*)

His plan, *to save and invest his money,* was proven as a safe approach.

(The infinitive phrase explains what the plan is.)

Appositive phrases can be **essential** or **nonessential**. An appositive phrase is essential if the person, place, or thing being described or renamed is too general for its meaning to be understood without the appositive.

Examples:

> **Essential**: Two of America's Founding Fathers, George Washington and Thomas Jefferson, served as presidents.
>
> **Nonessential**: George Washington and Thomas Jefferson, two Founding Fathers, served as presidents.

Absolute Phrases

An absolute phrase is a phrase that consists of **a noun followed by a participle**. An absolute phrase provides **context** to what is being described in the sentence, but it does not modify or explain any particular word; it is essentially independent.

Examples:

> *The alarm ringing*, he pushed the snooze button.
>
> *The music paused*, she continued to dance through the crowd.

Note: Absolute phrases can be confusing, so don't be discouraged if you have a difficult time with them.

Parallelism

When multiple items or ideas are presented in a sentence in series, such as in a list, the items or ideas must be stated in grammatically equivalent ways. In other words, if one idea is stated in gerund form, the second cannot be stated in infinitive form. For example, to write, *I enjoy reading and to study* would be incorrect. An infinitive and a gerund are not equivalent. Instead, you should write *I enjoy reading and studying*. In lists of more than two, it can be harder to keep everything straight, but all items in a list must be parallel.

Example:

> **Incorrect**: He stopped at the office, grocery store, and the pharmacy before heading home.
>
> The first and third items in the list of places include the article *the*, so the second item needs it as well.
>
> **Correct**: He stopped at the office, *the* grocery store, and the pharmacy before heading home.

Example:

> **Incorrect**: While vacationing in Europe, she went biking, skiing, and climbed mountains.
>
> The first and second items in the list are gerunds, so the third item must be as well.
>
> **Correct**: While vacationing in Europe, she went biking, skiing, and *mountain climbing*.

Sentence Purpose

There are four types of sentences: declarative, imperative, interrogative, and exclamatory.

A **declarative** sentence states a fact and ends with a period.

Example: *The football game starts at seven o'clock.*

An **imperative** sentence tells someone to do something and generally ends with a period. (An urgent command might end with an exclamation point instead.)

Example: *Don't forget to buy your ticket.*

An **interrogative** sentence asks a question and ends with a question mark.

Example: *Are you going to the game on Friday?*

An **exclamatory** sentence shows strong emotion and ends with an exclamation point.

Example: *I can't believe we won the game!*

Review Video: Function of a Sentence
Visit mometrix.com/academy and enter code: 475974

Sentence Structure

Sentences are classified by structure based on the type and number of clauses present. The four classifications of sentence structure are the following:

Simple: A simple sentence has one independent clause with no dependent clauses. A simple sentence may have **compound elements** (i.e., compound subject or verb).

Examples:

Judy *watered* the lawn. (single subject, single *verb*)

Judy and Alan *watered* the lawn. (compound subject, single *verb*)

Judy *watered* the lawn and *pulled* weeds. (single subject, compound *verb*)

Judy and Alan *watered* the lawn and *pulled* weeds. (compound subject, compound *verb*)

Compound: A compound sentence has two or more independent clauses with no dependent clauses. Usually, the independent clauses are joined with a comma and a coordinating conjunction or with a semicolon.

Examples:

The time has come, and we are ready.

I woke up at dawn; the sun was just coming up.

Complex: A complex sentence has one independent clause and at least one *dependent clause.*

Examples:

Although he had the flu, Harry went to work.

Marcia got married *after she finished college.*

Compound-Complex: A compound-complex sentence has at least two independent clauses and at least one *dependent clause.*

Examples:

John is my friend *who went to India*, and he brought back souvenirs.

You may not realize this, but we heard the music *that you played last night.*

Review Video: Sentence Structure
Visit mometrix.com/academy and enter code: 700478

SENTENCE FRAGMENTS

Usually when the term *sentence fragment* comes up, it is because you have to decide whether or not a group of words is a complete sentence, and if it's not a complete sentence, you're about to have to fix it. Recall that a group of words must contain at least one **independent clause** in order to be considered a sentence. If it doesn't contain even one independent clause, it would be called a **sentence fragment**. (If it contains two or more independent clauses that are not joined correctly, it would be called a run-on sentence.)

The process to use for **repairing** a sentence fragment depends on what type of fragment it is. If the fragment is a dependent clause, it can sometimes be as simple as removing a subordinating word (e.g., when, because, if) from the beginning of the fragment. Alternatively, a dependent clause can be incorporated into a closely related neighboring sentence. If the fragment is missing some required part, like a subject or a verb, the fix might be as simple as adding it in.

Examples:

Fragment: Because he wanted to sail the Mediterranean.

Removed subordinating word: He wanted to sail the Mediterranean.

Combined with another sentence: Because he wanted to sail the Mediterranean, he booked a Greek island cruise.

RUN-ON SENTENCES

Run-on sentences consist of multiple independent clauses that have not been joined together properly. Run-on sentences can be corrected in several different ways:

Join clauses properly: This can be done with a comma and coordinating conjunction, with a semicolon, or with a colon or dash if the second clause is explaining something in the first.

Example:

Incorrect: I went on the trip, we visited lots of castles.

Corrected: I went on the trip, and we visited lots of castles.

Split into separate sentences: This correction is most effective when the independent clauses are very long or when they are not closely related.

Example:

> **Incorrect**: The drive to New York takes ten hours, my uncle lives in Boston.
>
> **Corrected**: The drive to New York takes ten hours. My uncle lives in Boston.

Make one clause dependent: This is the easiest way to make the sentence correct and more interesting at the same time. It's often as simple as adding a subordinating word between the two clauses

Example:

> **Incorrect**: I finally made it to the store and I bought some eggs.
>
> **Corrected**: When I finally made it to the store, I bought some eggs.

Reduce to one clause with a compound verb: If both clauses have the same subject, remove the subject from the second clause, and you now have just one clause with a compound verb.

Example:

> **Incorrect**: The drive to New York takes ten hours, it makes me very tired.
>
> **Corrected**: The drive to New York takes ten hours and makes me very tired.

Note: While these are the simplest ways to correct a run-on sentence, often the best way is to completely reorganize the thoughts in the sentence and rewrite it.

Review Video: Fragments and Run-on Sentences
Visit mometrix.com/academy and enter code: 541989

Dangling and Misplaced Modifiers

Dangling Modifiers

A dangling modifier is a dependent clause or verbal phrase that does not have a **clear logical connection** to a word in the sentence.

Example:

> **Dangling**: *Reading each magazine article*, the stories caught my attention.
>
> The word *stories* cannot be modified by *Reading each magazine article*. People can read, but stories cannot read. Therefore, the subject of the sentence must be a person.
>
> **Corrected**: Reading each magazine article, *I* was entertained by the stories.

Example:

Dangling: Ever since childhood, my grandparents have visited me for Christmas.

The speaker in this sentence can't have been visited by her grandparents when *they* were children, since she wouldn't have been born yet. Either the modifier should be **clarified** or the sentence should be **rearranged** to specify whose childhood is being referenced.

Clarified: Ever since I was a child, my grandparents have visited for Christmas.

Rearranged: I have enjoyed my grandparents visiting for Christmas, ever since childhood.

Misplaced Modifiers

Because modifiers are grammatically versatile, they can be put in many different places within the structure of a sentence. The danger of this versatility is that a modifier can accidentally be placed where it is modifying the wrong word or where it is not clear which word it is modifying.

Example:

Misplaced: She read the book to a crowd *that was filled with beautiful pictures*.

The book was filled with beautiful pictures, not the crowd.

Corrected: She read the book *that was filled with beautiful pictures* to a crowd.

Example:

Ambiguous: Derek saw a bus nearly hit a man *on his way to work*.

Was Derek on his way to work? Or was the other man?

Derek: *On his way to work*, Derek saw a bus nearly hit a man.

The other man: Derek saw a bus nearly hit a man *who was on his way to work*.

Split Infinitives

A split infinitive occurs when a modifying word comes between the word *to* and the verb that pairs with *to*.

Example: To *clearly* explain vs. *To explain* clearly | To *softly* sing vs. *To sing* softly

Though considered improper by some, split infinitives may provide better clarity and simplicity in some cases than the alternatives. As such, avoiding them should not be considered a universal rule.

Double Negatives

Standard English allows **two negatives** only when a **positive** meaning is intended. For example, *The team was not displeased with their performance*. Double negatives to emphasize negation are not used in standard English.

Negative modifiers (e.g., never, no, and not) should not be paired with other negative modifiers or negative words (e.g., none, nobody, nothing, or neither). The modifiers *hardly, barely*, and *scarcely* are considered negatives in standard English, so they should not be used with other negatives.

Punctuation

End Punctuation

Periods

Use a period to end all sentences except direct questions and exclamations. Periods are also used for abbreviations.

Examples: 3 p.m. | 2 a.m. | Mr. Jones | Mrs. Stevens | Dr. Smith | Bill, Jr. | Pennsylvania Ave.

Note: an abbreviation is a shortened form of a word or phrase.

Question Marks

Question marks should be used following a direct question. A polite request can be followed by a period instead of a question mark.

Direct Question: What is for lunch today? | How are you? | Why is that the answer?

Polite Requests: Can you please send me the item tomorrow. | Will you please walk with me on the track.

Review Video: Question Marks
Visit mometrix.com/academy and enter code: 118471

Exclamation Marks

Exclamation marks are used after a word group or sentence that shows much feeling or has special importance. Exclamation marks should not be overused. They are saved for proper **exclamatory interjections**.

Example: We're going to the finals! | You have a beautiful car! | "That's crazy!" she yelled.

Review Video: Exclamation Point
Visit mometrix.com/academy and enter code: 199367

Commas

The comma is a punctuation mark that can help you understand connections in a sentence. Not every sentence needs a comma. However, if a sentence needs a comma, you need to put it in the right place. A comma in the wrong place (or an absent comma) will make a sentence's meaning unclear. These are some of the rules for commas:

1. Use a comma **before a coordinating conjunction** joining independent clauses
   Example: Bob caught three fish, and I caught two fish.

2. Use a comma after an introductory phrase or an adverbial clause
   Examples:
   After the final out, we went to a restaurant to celebrate.
   Studying the stars, I was surprised at the beauty of the sky.

3. Use a comma between items in a series.
   Example: I will bring the turkey, the pie, and the coffee.

4. Use a comma **between coordinate adjectives** not joined with *and*

   Incorrect: The kind, brown dog followed me home.
   Correct: The *kind, loyal* dog followed me home.
   Not all adjectives are **coordinate** (i.e., equal or parallel). There are two simple ways to know if your adjectives are coordinate. One, you can join the adjectives with *and*: *The kind and loyal dog*. Two, you can change the order of the adjectives: *The loyal, kind dog*.

5. Use commas for **interjections** and **after *yes* and *no*** responses

   Examples:

   Interjection: Oh, I had no idea. | Wow, you know how to play this game.
   Yes and No: *Yes,* I heard you. | *No,* I cannot come tomorrow.

6. Use commas to separate nonessential modifiers and nonessential appositives

   Examples:

   Nonessential Modifier: John Frank, who is coaching the team, was promoted today.
   Nonessential Appositive: Thomas Edison, an American inventor, was born in Ohio.

7. Use commas to set off nouns of direct address, interrogative tags, and contrast

   Examples:

   Direct Address: You, *John,* are my only hope in this moment.
   Interrogative Tag: This is the last time, *correct*?
   Contrast: You are my friend, *not my enemy.*

8. Use commas with dates, addresses, geographical names, and titles

   Examples:

   Date: *July 4, 1776,* is an important date to remember.
   Address: He is meeting me at *456 Delaware Avenue, Washington, D.C.,* tomorrow morning.
   Geographical Name: *Paris, France,* is my favorite city.
   Title: John Smith, *PhD,* will be visiting your class today.

9. Use commas to **separate expressions like *he said* and *she said*** if they come between a sentence of a quote

   Examples:

   "I want you to know," he began, "that I always wanted the best for you."
   "You can start," Jane said, "with an apology."

Review Video: Commas
Visit mometrix.com/academy and enter code: 786797

Semicolons

The semicolon is used to connect major sentence pieces of equal value. Some rules for semicolons include:

1. Use a semicolon **between closely connected independent clauses** that are not connected with a coordinating conjunction.

   Examples:

   She is outside; we are inside.
   You are right; we should go with your plan.

2. Use a semicolon **between independent clauses linked with a transitional word.**

   Examples:

   I think that we can agree on this; *however,* I am not sure about my friends.
   You are looking in the wrong places; *therefore,* you will not find what you need.

3. Use a semicolon **between items in a series that has internal punctuation.**

   Example: I have visited New York, New York; Augusta, Maine; and Baltimore, Maryland.

Review Video: Semicolon Usage
Visit mometrix.com/academy and enter code: 370605

Colons

The colon is used to call attention to the words that follow it. A colon must come after a **complete independent clause**. The rules for colons are as follows:

1. Use a colon after an independent clause to **make a list.**

   Example: I want to learn many languages: Spanish, German, and Italian.

2. Use a colon for **explanations** or to **give a quote.**

   Examples:

   Quote: He started with an idea: "We are able to do more than we imagine."
   Explanation: There is one thing that stands out on your resume: responsibility.

3. Use a colon **after the greeting in a formal letter**, to **show hours and minutes,** and to **separate a title and subtitle.**

   Examples:

   Greeting in a formal letter: Dear Sir: | To Whom It May Concern:
   Time: It is 3:14 p.m.
   Title: The essay is titled "America: A Short Introduction to a Modern Country"

Review Video: Colons
Visit mometrix.com/academy and enter code: 868673

Parentheses

Parentheses are used for additional information. Also, they can be used to put labels for letters or numbers in a series. Parentheses should be not be used very often. If they are overused, parentheses can be a distraction instead of a help.

Examples:

> **Extra Information**: The rattlesnake (see Image 2) is a dangerous snake of North and South America.
>
> **Series**: Include in the email (1) your name, (2) your address, and (3) your question for the author.

Review Video: Parentheses
Visit mometrix.com/academy and enter code: 947743

Quotation Marks

Use quotation marks to close off **direct quotations** of a person's spoken or written words. Do not use quotation marks around indirect quotations. An indirect quotation gives someone's message without using the person's exact words. Use **single quotation marks** to close off a quotation inside a quotation.

> **Direct Quote**: Nancy said, "I am waiting for Henry to arrive."
>
> **Indirect Quote**: Henry said that he is going to be late to the meeting.
>
> **Quote inside a Quote**: The teacher asked, "Has everyone read 'The Gift of the Magi'?"

Quotation marks should be used around the titles of **short works**: newspaper and magazine articles, poems, short stories, songs, television episodes, radio programs, and subdivisions of books or websites.

Examples:

> "Rip Van Winkle" (short story by Washington Irving)
>
> "O Captain! My Captain!" (poem by Walt Whitman)

Although it is not standard usage, quotation marks are sometimes used to highlight **irony** or the use of words to mean something other than their dictionary definition. This type of usage should be employed sparingly, if at all.

Examples:

> The boss warned Frank that he was walking on "thin ice."
>
> (Frank is not walking on real ice. Instead, Frank is being warned to avoid mistakes.)
>
> The teacher thanked the young man for his "honesty."
>
> (In this example, the quotation marks around *honesty* show that the teacher does not believe the young man's explanation.)

Review Video: Quotation Marks
Visit mometrix.com/academy and enter code: 884918

Periods and commas are put **inside** quotation marks. Colons and semicolons are put **outside** the quotation marks. Question marks and exclamation points are placed inside quotation marks when they are part of a quote. When the question or exclamation mark goes with the whole sentence, the mark is left outside of the quotation marks.

Examples:

Period and comma: We read "The Gift of the Magi," "The Skylight Room," and "The Cactus."

Semicolon: They watched "The Nutcracker"; then, they went home.

Exclamation mark that is a part of a quote: The crowd cheered, "Victory!"

Question mark that goes with the whole sentence: Is your favorite short story "The Tell-Tale Heart"?

Apostrophes

An apostrophe is used to show **possession** or the **deletion of letters in contractions**. An apostrophe is not needed with the possessive pronouns *his, hers, its, ours, theirs, whose*, and *yours*.

Singular Nouns: David's car | a book's theme | my brother's board game

Plural Nouns with *-s*: the scissors' handle | boys' basketball

Plural Nouns without *-s*: Men's department | the people's adventure

Review Video: Apostrophes
Visit mometrix.com/academy and enter code: 213068

Review Video: Punctuation Errors in Possessive Pronouns
Visit mometrix.com/academy and enter code: 221438

Hyphens

Hyphens are used to **separate compound words**. Use hyphens in the following cases:

1. **Compound numbers** between 21 and 99 when written out in words
   Example: This team needs *twenty-five* points to win the game.

2. **Written-out fractions** that are used as **adjectives**
   Incorrect: *One-fourth* of the road is under construction.
   Correct: The recipe says that we need a *three-fourths* cup of butter.

3. Compound words used as **adjectives that come before a noun**
   Incorrect: The dog was *well-fed* for his nap.
   Correct: The *well-fed* dog took a nap.

4. Compound words that would be **hard to read** or **easily confused with other words**
   Examples: Semi-irresponsible | Anti-itch | Re-sort

Note: This is not a complete set of the rules for hyphens. A dictionary is the best tool for knowing if a compound word needs a hyphen.

Review Video: Hyphens
Visit mometrix.com/academy and enter code: 981632

Dashes

Dashes are used to show a **break** or a **change in thought** in a sentence or to act as parentheses in a sentence. When typing, use two hyphens to make a dash. Do not put a space before or after the dash. The following are the rules for dashes:

1. To set off **parenthetical statements** or an **appositive with internal punctuation**
   Example: The three trees—oak, pine, and magnolia—are coming on a truck tomorrow.

2. To show a **break or change in tone or thought**
   Example: The first question—how silly of me—does not have a correct answer.

Ellipsis Marks

The ellipsis mark has three periods (…) to show when **words have been removed** from a quotation. If a full sentence or more is removed from a quoted passage, you need to use four periods to show the removed text and the end punctuation mark. The ellipsis mark should not be used at the beginning of a quotation. The ellipsis mark should also not be used at the end of a quotation unless some words have been deleted from the end of the final sentence.

Example:

> "Then he picked up the groceries … paid for them … later he went home."

Brackets

There are two main reasons to use brackets:

1. When **placing parentheses inside of parentheses**
   Example: The hero of this story, Paul Revere (a silversmith and industrialist [see Ch. 4]), rode through towns of Massachusetts to warn of advancing British troops.

2. When adding **clarification or detail** to a quotation that is **not part of the quotation**
   Example:
   > The father explained, "My children are planning to attend my alma mater [State University]."

Common Errors

Word Confusion

Which, That, and Who

Which is used for things only.

Example: John's dog, *which is called Max,* is large and fierce.

That is used for people or things.

Example: Is this the only book *that Louis L'Amour wrote?*

Example: Is Louis L'Amour the author *that wrote Western novels?*

Who is used for people only.

Example: Mozart was the composer *who wrote those operas.*

Homophones

Homophones are words that sound alike (or similar), but they have different **spellings** and **definitions**.

To, Too, and Two

To can be an adverb or a preposition for showing direction, purpose, and relationship. See your dictionary for the many other ways to use *to* in a sentence.

Examples: I went to the store. | I want to go with you.

Too is an adverb that means *also, as well, very,* or *more than enough*.

Examples: I can walk a mile too. | You have eaten too much.

Two is the second number in the series of numbers (e.g., one (1), two, (2), three (3)...)

Example: You have two minutes left.

There, Their, and They're

There can be an adjective, adverb, or pronoun. Often, *there* is used to show a place or to start a sentence.

Examples: I went there yesterday. | There is something in his pocket.

Their is a pronoun that is used to show ownership.

Examples: He is their father. | This is their fourth apology this week.

They're is a contraction of *they are.*

Example: Did you know that they're in town?

Knew and New

Knew is the past tense of *know*.

Example: I knew the answer.

New is an adjective that means something is current, has not been used, or is modern.

Example: This is my new phone.

Then and Than

Then is an adverb that indicates sequence or order:

Example: I'm going to run to the library and then come home.

Than is special-purpose word used only for comparisons:

Example: Susie likes chips more than candy.

Its and It's

Its is a pronoun that shows ownership.

Example: The guitar is in its case.

It's is a contraction of *it is*.

Example: It's an honor and a privilege to meet you.

Note: The *h* in honor is silent, so the sound of the vowel *o* must have the article *an*.

Your and You're

Your is a pronoun that shows ownership.

Example: This is your moment to shine.

You're is a contraction of *you are*.

Example: Yes, you're correct.

Affect and Effect

There are two main reasons that *affect* and *effect* are so often confused: 1) both words can be used as either a noun or a verb, and 2) unlike most homophones, their usage and meanings are closely related to each other. Here is a quick rundown of the four usage options:

Affect (n): feeling, emotion, or mood that is displayed

Example: The patient had a flat *affect*. (i.e., his face showed little or no emotion)

Affect (v): to alter, to change, to influence

Example: The sunshine *affects* the plant's growth.

Effect (n): a result, a consequence

Example: What *effect* will this weather have on our schedule?

Effect (v): to bring about, to cause to be

Example: These new rules will *effect* order in the office.

The noun form of *affect* is rarely used outside of technical medical descriptions, so if a noun form is needed on the test, you can safely select *effect*. The verb form of *effect* is not as rare as the noun form of *affect*, but it's still not all that likely to show up on your test. If you need a verb and you can't decide which to use based on the definitions, choosing *affect* is your best bet.

Homographs

Homographs are words that share the same spelling, but have different meanings and sometimes different pronunciations. To figure out which meaning is being used, you should be looking for context clues. The context clues give hints to the meaning of the word. For example, the word *spot* has many meanings. It can mean "a place" or "a stain or blot." In the sentence "After my lunch, I saw a spot on my shirt," the word *spot* means "a stain or blot." The context clues of "After my lunch" and "on my shirt" guide you to this decision.

Bank

(noun): an establishment where money is held for savings or lending

(verb): to collect or pile up

Content

(noun): the topics that will be addressed within a book

(adjective): pleased or satisfied

(verb): to make someone pleased or satisfied

Fine

(noun): an amount of money that acts a penalty for an offense

(adjective): very small or thin

(adverb): in an acceptable way

(verb): to make someone pay money as a punishment

Incense

(noun): a material that is burned in religious settings and makes a pleasant aroma

(verb): to frustrate or anger

Lead

(noun): the first or highest position

(noun): a heavy metallic element

(verb): to direct a person or group of followers

(adjective): containing lead

Object

(noun): a lifeless item that can be held and observed

(verb): to disagree

Produce

(noun): fruits and vegetables

(verb): to make or create something

Refuse

(noun): garbage or debris that has been thrown away

(verb): to not allow

Subject

(noun): an area of study

(verb): to force or subdue

Tear

(noun): a fluid secreted by the eyes

(verb): to separate or pull apart

The Essay

Essay Structure

Introduction

An introduction announces the main point of the passage. Normally, the introduction ranges from 50 to 70 words (i.e., 3 or 4 sentences). The purpose of the introduction is to gain the reader's attention and conclude with the essay's main point. An introduction can begin with an interesting quote, question, or strong opinion that grabs the reader's attention. Your introduction should include a restatement of the prompt, a summary of the main points of your essay, and your position on the prompt (i.e., the thesis sentence/statement). Depending on the amount of available time, you may want to give more or less information on the main points of your essay. The important thing is to impress the audience with your thesis statement (i.e., your reason for writing the essay).

Thesis Statement

A thesis gives the main idea of the essay. A temporary thesis should be established early in the writing process because it will serve to keep the writer focused as ideas develop. This temporary thesis is subject to change as you continue to write.

The temporary thesis has two parts: a topic (i.e., the focus of your paper based on the prompt) and a comment. The comment makes an important point about the topic. A temporary thesis should be interesting and specific. Also, you need to limit the topic to a manageable scope. These three criteria are useful tools to measure the effectiveness of any temporary thesis:

1. Does the focus of my essay have enough interest to hold an audience?
2. Is the focus of my essay specific enough to generate interest?
3. Is the focus of my essay manageable for the time limit? Too broad? Too narrow?

The thesis should be a generalization rather than a fact because the thesis prepares readers for facts and details that support the thesis. The process of bringing the thesis into sharp focus may help in outlining major sections of the work. Once the thesis and introduction are complete, you can address the body of the work.

Review Video: Thesis Statements
Visit mometrix.com/academy and enter code: 691033

Supporting the Thesis

Throughout your essay, the thesis should be explained clearly and supported adequately by additional arguments. The thesis sentence needs to contain a clear statement of the purpose of your essay and a comment about the thesis. With the thesis statement, you have an opportunity to state what is noteworthy of this particular treatment of the prompt. Each sentence and paragraph should build on and support the thesis.

When you respond to the prompt, use parts of the passage to support your argument or defend your position. With supporting evidence from the passage, you strengthen your argument because readers can see your attention to the entire passage and your response to the details and facts within the passage. You can use facts, details, statistics, and direct quotations from the passage to uphold your position. Be sure to point out which information comes from the original passage and base your argument around that evidence.

PARAGRAPHS

Following the introduction, you will begin with body paragraphs. A paragraph should be unified around a main point. Normally, a good topic sentence summarizes the paragraph's main point. A topic sentence is a general sentence that gives an introduction to the paragraph. The sentences that follow are a support to the topic sentence. You may use the topic sentence as the final sentence to the paragraph if the earlier sentences give a clear explanation of the topic sentence. Overall, you need to stay true to the main point. This means that you need to remove unnecessary sentences that do not advance the main point.

The main point of a paragraph requires adequate development (i.e., a substantial paragraph that covers the main point). A paragraph of two or three sentences does not cover a main point. This is true when the main point of the paragraph gives strong support to the argument of the thesis. An occasional short paragraph is fine as a transitional device. However, you should aim to have six to seven sentences for each paragraph.

METHODS OF DEVELOPING PARAGRAPHS

A common method of development in your essay can be done with **examples**. These examples are the supporting details to the main idea of a paragraph or passage. When you write about something that your audience may not understand, you can provide an example to show your point. When you write about something that is not easily accepted, you can give examples to prove your point.

Illustrations are extended examples that require several sentences. Well selected illustrations can be a great way to develop a point that may not be familiar to your audience. With a time limit, you may have enough time to use one illustration. So, be sure that you use one that connects well with your main argument.

Analogies make comparisons between items that appear to have nothing in common. Analogies are employed by writers to provoke fresh thoughts about a subject. They may be used to explain the unfamiliar, to clarify an abstract point, or to argue a point. Although analogies are effective literary devices, they should be used carefully in arguments. Two things may be alike in some respects but completely different in others.

Cause and effect is an excellent device used when the cause and effect are accepted as true. One way of using cause and effect is to state the effect in the topic sentence of a paragraph and add the causes in the body of the paragraph. With this method, your paragraphs can have structure which always strengthens writing.

TYPES OF PARAGRAPHS

A **paragraph of narration** tells a story or a part of a story. Normally, the sentences are arranged in chronological order (i.e., the order that the events happened). However, you can include flashbacks (i.e., beginning the story at an earlier time).

A **descriptive paragraph** makes a verbal portrait of a person, place, or thing. When you use specific details that appeal to one or more of the senses (i.e., sight, sound, smell, taste, and touch), you give your readers a sense of being present in the moment.

A **process paragraph** is related to time order (i.e., First, you open the bottle. Second, you pour the liquid, etc.). Usually, this describes a process or teaches readers how to perform a process.

Comparing two things draws attention to their similarities and indicates a number of differences. When you contrast, you focus only on differences. Both comparisons and contrasts may be used point-by-point or in following paragraphs.

Reasons for starting a new paragraph include:

1. To mark off the introduction and concluding paragraphs
2. To signal a shift to a new idea or topic
3. To indicate an important shift in time or place
4. To explain a point in additional detail
5. To highlight a comparison, contrast, or cause and effect relationship

Conclusion

A good conclusion should leave readers satisfied and provide a sense of completeness. Many conclusions state the thesis in different words and give a summary of the ideas in the body paragraphs. Some writers find ways to conclude in a dramatic fashion. They may conclude with a vivid image or a warning and remind readers of the main point. The conclusion can be a few sentences because the body of the text has made the case for the thesis. A conclusion can summarize the main points and offer advice or ask a question. You should never introduce new ideas or arguments in a conclusion. Also, you need to avoid vague and aimless endings. Instead, close with a clear and specific paragraph.

Argumentative and Persuasive Writing Structure

Argumentative and persuasive writing takes a stand on a debatable issue, seeks to explore all sides of the issue, and finds the best possible solution. Argumentative and persuasive writing should not be combative or abusive. The word *argument* may remind you of two or more people shouting at each other and walking away in anger. However, an argumentative or persuasive essay should be a calm and reasonable presentation on your ideas for others to consider. When you write reasonable arguments, your goal is not to win or have the last word. Instead, you want to reveal current understanding of the question and suggest a solution to a problem. The purpose of argument and persuasion in a free society is to reach the best solution.

Introduction

The introduction of an essay that argues for or against an issue should end with a thesis sentence that gives a position (i.e., the side that you want to defend or oppose) on the prompt. The thesis should be supported by strong arguments that back up your position. The main points of your argument should have a growing effect which convinces readers that the thesis has merit. In your introduction, you should list the main points of your argument which will outline the entire argumentative essay.

Supporting Evidence

Evidence needs to be provided that supports the thesis and additional arguments. Most arguments must be supported by facts or statistics. Facts are something that is known with certainty and have been verified by several independent individuals. Examples and illustrations add an emotional component to arguments. With this component, you persuade readers in ways that facts and statistics cannot. The emotional component is effective when used with objective information that can be confirmed.

Counter Arguments

When you show both sides to the argument, you build trust with readers. The graders of your essay will be undecided or neutral. If you present only your side to the argument, your readers will be concerned at best. Showing the other side of the argument can take place anywhere in the essay, but one of the best places is after the thesis statement.

Building common ground with neutral or opposed readers can be appealing to skeptical readers. Sharing values with undecided readers can allow people to switch positions without giving up what they feel is important. For people who may oppose a position, they need to feel that they can change their minds without betraying who they are as a person. This appeal to having an open-mind can be a powerful tool in arguing a position without antagonizing other views. Objections can be countered on a point-by-point basis or in a summary paragraph. Be careful in how you point out flaws in counter arguments. If you are unfair to the other side of the argument, then you can lose trust with your audience.

Clearness in Writing

Coherence

A smooth flow of sentences and paragraphs without gaps or shifts is what is meant by coherent writing. When your writing is coherent, you give information in a way that helps your readers understand the connection between sentences or paragraphs. The ties between old and new information can be completed by several strategies.

Tips for Coherent Writing

Linking ideas clearly from the topic sentence to the body of the paragraph is essential for a smooth transition. The topic sentence states the main point, and this should be followed by specific details, examples, and illustrations that support the topic sentence.

The **repetition of key words** adds coherence to a paragraph. You can avoid overuse of a keyword by using synonyms of the key word.

Changing verb tenses in a paragraph can be confusing for your readers. Try to minimize shifting sentences from one verb tense to another. These shifts affect the smooth flows of words and can disrupt the coherence of the paragraph.

Transitions

Transitions are bridges between what has been read and what is about to be read. Transitions smooth the reader's path between sentences and inform readers of connections to new ideas in the essay. When you think about the appropriate phrase for a transition, you need to consider the previous and upcoming sentences or paragraphs. Thus, transitional phrases should be used with care. Tone should be considered when you want to use a transitional phrase. For example, *in summary* would be preferable to the informal *in short*. Consider these transitions:

Restatement: He wanted to walk the trails at the park, *namely* Yosemite National Park.

Contrast: This could be the best option. *On the other hand*, this option may lead to more damage.

Review Video: Transitions in Writing
Visit mometrix.com/academy and enter code: 233246

Avoid Unclear Words and Phrases

Clichés

Clichés are phrases that have been overused to the point that the phrase has no importance or has lost the original meaning. The phrases have no originality and add very little to your writing. Therefore, you should try to avoid the use of clichés. The best revision for clichés is to delete them. If this does not seem possible, then a cliché can be changed so that it is not predictable and empty of meaning.

Examples:

When life gives you lemons, make lemonade.

Every cloud has a silver lining.

Euphemisms

Euphemisms are acceptable words which replace language that seems too harsh or ugly. Normally, people use a euphemism when they speak about subjects such as death and bodily functions.

Examples:

My grandmother *passed away* this weekend.

He had to go to the *mens' room*.

These acceptable words can be unclear or misunderstood. If you are trying to decide between using a euphemism or avoiding a euphemism, then you should choose to avoid talking about the subject altogether. You want the graders of your work to understand your entire essay.

Jargon

Jargon is a specialized vocabulary that is used among members of a trade or profession. Since jargon is understood by a small audience, you should not use such vocabulary in your essay. Jargon includes exaggerated language that tries to impress rather than inform. Sentences filled with jargon are not precise and difficult to understand.

Examples:

"He is going to *toenail* these frames for us." (Toenail is construction jargon for nailing at an angle.)

"They brought in a *kip* of material today." (Kip refers to 1000 pounds in architecture and engineering.)

Slang

Slang is an informal and sometimes private language that is understood by some individuals. Slang has some usefulness, but the language can have a small audience. Again, you should avoid this in your writing. While the grader of your exam may be aware of the word, he or she may not understand the use of the word as you do.

Examples:

"Yes, the event was a blast!" (In this sentence, *blast* means that the event was a great experience.)

"That attempt was an epic fail." (By *epic fail*, the speaker means that his or her attempt was not a success.)

Reviewing the Essay

Revisions

A writer's choice of words is a signature of their style. Careful thought about the use of words can improve a piece of writing. When you pay attention to the use of specific nouns rather than general ones, you can make your essay an exciting piece to read.

Example:

General: His kindness will never be forgotten.

Specific: His thoughtful gifts and bear hugs will never be forgotten.

Think about the kind of verbs that you use in your sentences. Active verbs (e.g., run, swim) should be about an action. Whenever possible, trade a linking verb for an active verb to provide clear examples for your arguments and to strengthen your essay overall.

Example:

Passive: The winners were called to the stage by the judges.

Active: The judges called the winners to the stage.

Revising sentences is done to make writing more effective. Editing sentences is done to correct any errors. Sentences are the building blocks of writing, and they can be changed by paying attention to sentence length, sentence structure, and sentence openings. You should add variety to sentence length, structure, and openings so that the essay does not seem boring or repetitive. A careful analysis of a piece of writing will expose these stylistic problems, and they can be corrected before you finish your essay. Changing up your sentence structure and sentence length can make your essay more inviting and appealing to readers.

Recursive Writing Process

The recursive writing process is not as difficult as the phrase appears to you. Simply put, the recursive writing process means that the steps in the writing process occur in no particular order. For example, planning, drafting, and revising (all a part of the writing process) take place at about the same time and you may not notice that all three happen so close together. Truly, the writing process is a series of moving back and forth between planning, drafting, and revising. Then, more planning, more drafting, and more revising until your essay is complete.

Review Video: Recursive Writing Process
Visit mometrix.com/academy and enter code: 951611

Economics

Basics of Economics

Economics is the study of the ways specific societies allocate resources to individuals and groups within that society. Also important are the choices society makes regarding what efforts or initiatives are funded and which are not. Since resources in any society are finite, allocation becomes a vivid reflection of that society's values.

In general, the economic system that drives an individual society is based on:

- What goods are produced
- How those goods are produced
- Who acquires the goods or benefits from them

Economics consists of two main categories, macroeconomics, which studies larger systems, and microeconomics, which studies smaller systems.

Money

Money is used in three major ways:

1. As an accounting unit
2. As a store of value
3. As an exchange medium

In general, money must be acceptable throughout a society in exchange for debts or to purchase goods and services. Money should be relatively scarce, its value should remain stable, and it should be easily carried, durable, and easy to divide up.

There are three basic types of money: commodity, representative and fiat. Commodity money includes gems or precious metals. Representative money can be exchanged for items such as gold or silver which have inherent value. Fiat money, or legal tender, has no inherent value but has been declared to function as money by the government. It is often backed by gold or silver, but not necessarily on a one-to-one ratio.

Money in the US is not just currency. When economists calculate the amount of money available, they must take into account other factors such as deposits that have been placed in checking accounts, debit cards and "near moneys" such as savings accounts, that can be quickly converted into cash. Currency, checkable deposits and traveler's checks, referred to as M1, are added up, and then M2 is calculated by adding savings deposits, CDs and various other monetary deposits. The final result is the total quantity of available money.

Monetary Policy and the Role of the Federal Reserve System

The Federal Reserve System, also known as the Fed, implements all monetary policy in the US. Monetary policy regulates the amount of money available in the American banking system. The Fed can decrease or increase the amount of available money for loans, thus helping regulate the national economy.

Monetary policies implemented by the Fed are part of expansionary or contractionary monetary policies that help counteract inflation or unemployment. The Discount Rate is an interest rate charged by the Fed when banks borrow money from them. A lower discount rate leads banks to borrow more money, leading to increased spending. A higher discount rate has the opposite effect.

BANKS

Banks earn their income by loaning out money and charging interest on those loans. If less money is available, fewer loans can be made, which affects the amount of spending in the overall economy. While banks function by making loans, they are not allowed to loan out all the money they hold in deposit. The amount of money they must maintain in reserve is known as the reserve ratio. If the reserve ratio is raised, less money is available for loans and spending decreases. A lower reserve ratio increases available funds and increases spending. This ratio is determined by the Federal Reserve System.

MARKET ECONOMY AND PLANNED ECONOMY

A market economy is based on supply and demand. Demand has to do with what customers want and need, as well as how quantity those consumers are able to purchase based on other economic factors. Supply refers to how much can be produced to meet demand, or how much suppliers are willing and able to sell. Where the needs of consumers meet the needs of suppliers is referred to as a market equilibrium price. This price varies depending on many factors, including the overall health of a society's economy, overall beliefs and considerations of individuals in society, and other factors.

In a market economy, supply and demand are determined by consumers.

In a planned economy, a public entity or planning authority makes the decisions about what resources will be produced, how they will be produced, and who will be able to benefit from them. The means of production, such as factories, are also owned by a public entity rather than by private interests.

In market socialism, the economic structure falls somewhere between the market economy and the planned economy. Planning authorities determine allocation of resources at higher economic levels, while consumer goods are driven by a market economy.

Review Video: Basics of Market Economy
Visit mometrix.com/academy and enter code: 791556

Markets

Classifying Various Markets

The conditions prevailing in a given market are used to classify markets. Conditions considered include:

- Existence of competition
- Number and size of suppliers
- Influence of suppliers over price
- Variety of available products
- Ease of entering the market

Once these questions are answered, an economist can classify a certain market according to its structure and the nature of competition within the market.

Review Video: Classification of Markets
Visit mometrix.com/academy and enter code: 904798

Market Failure

When any of the elements for a successfully competitive market are missing, this can lead to a market failure. Certain elements are necessary to create what economists call "perfect competition." If one of these factors is weak or lacking, the market is classified as having "imperfect competition." Worse than imperfect competition, though, is a market failure. There are five major types of market failure:

- Competition is inadequate
- Information is inadequate
- Resources are not mobile
- Negative externalities, or side effects
- Failure to provide public goods

Externalities are side effects of a market that affect third parties. These effects can be either negative or positive.

Review Video: Market Failure
Visit mometrix.com/academy and enter code: 889023

Microeconomics

While economics generally studies how resources are allocated, microeconomics focuses on economic factors such as the way consumers behave, how income is distributed, and output and input markets. Studies are limited to the industry or firm level, rather than an entire country or society.

Among the elements studied in microeconomics are factors of production, costs of production, and factor income. These factors determine production decisions of individual firms, based on resources and costs.

Review Video: Microeconomics
Visit mometrix.com/academy and enter code: 779207

Production

Every good and service requires certain resources, or inputs. These inputs are referred to as factors of production. Every good and service requires four factors of production:

- Labor
- Land
- Capital
- Entrepreneurship

These factors can be fixed or variable and can produce fixed or variable costs. Examples of fixed costs include land and equipment. Variable costs include labor. The total of fixed and variable costs makes up the costs of production.

Factor Income

Factors of production all have an associated factor income. Factors that earn income include:

- Labor—earns wages
- Capital—earns interest
- Land—earns rent
- Entrepreneurs—earn profit

Each factor's income is determined by its contribution. In a market economy, this income is not guaranteed to be equal. How scarce the factor is and the weight of its contribution to the overall production process determines the final factor income.

Market Structures in an Output Market

Perfect competition—all existing firms sell an identical product. The firms are not able to control the final price. In addition, there is nothing that makes it difficult to become involved in or leave the industry. Anything that would prevent entering or leaving an industry is called a barrier to entry. An example of this market structure is agriculture.

Monopoly—a single seller controls the product and its price. Barriers to entry, such as prohibitively high fixed cost structures, prevent other sellers from entering the market.

Monopolistic competition—a number of firms sell similar products, but they are not identical, such as different brands of clothes or food. Barriers to entry are low.

Oligopoly—only a few firms control the production and distribution of products, such as automobiles. Barriers to entry are high, preventing large numbers of firms from entering the market.

Monopolies

Four types of monopolies are:

- Natural monopoly—a single supplier has a distinct advantage over the others.
- Geographic monopoly—only one business offers the product in a certain area.
- Technological monopoly—a single company controls the technology necessary to supply the product.
- Government monopoly—a government agency is the only provider of a specific good or service.

Control by the US Government

The US government has passed several acts to regulate businesses, including:

- Sherman Antitrust Act (1890)—this prohibited trusts, monopolies, and any other situations that eliminated competition.
- Clayton Antitrust Act (1914)—this prohibited price discrimination.
- Robinson-Patman Act (1936)—this strengthened provisions of the Clayton Antitrust Act, requiring businesses to offer the same pricing on products to any customer.

The government has taken other actions to protect competition and requirements for public disclosure. The Securities and Exchange Commission (SEC) makes companies that provide public stock also provide financial reports on a regular basis. Banks have more rules and requirements because of their kind of business. So, banks have to provide other types of information to the government.

Macroeconomics

Macroeconomics examines economies on a much larger level than microeconomics. While microeconomics studies economics on a firm or industry level, macroeconomics looks at economic trends and structures on a national level. Variables studied in macroeconomics include:

- Output
- Consumption
- Investment
- Government spending
- Net exports

The overall economic condition of a nation is defined as the Gross Domestic Product, or GDP. GDP measures a nation's economic output over a limited time period, such as a year.

Consumer Behavior as Defined in Macroeconomics

Marginal propensity to consume defines the tendency of consumers to increase spending in conjunction with increases in income. In general, individuals with greater income will buy more. As individuals increase their income through job changes or growth of experience, they will also increase spending.

Utility is a term that describes the satisfaction experienced by a consumer in relation to acquiring and using a good or service. Providers of goods and services will stress utility to convince consumers they want the products being presented.

Measuring the Gross Domestic Product of a Country

1. The expenditures approach calculates the GDP based on how much money is spent in each individual sector.
2. The income approach calculates based on how much money is earned in each sector.

Both methods yield the same results and both of these calculation methods are based on four economic sectors that make up a country's macro economy:

- Consumers
- Business
- Government
- Foreign sector

Calculating GDP Using the Income Approach

Several factors must be considered in order to accurately calculate the GDP using the incomes approach. Income factors are:

- Wages paid to laborers, or Compensation of Employees
- Rental income derived from land
- Interest income derived from invested capital
- Entrepreneurial income

Entrepreneurial income consists of two forms. Proprietor's Income is income that comes back to the entrepreneur himself. Corporate Profit is income that goes back into the corporation as a whole. Corporate profit is divided by the corporation into corporate profits taxes, dividends, and retained earnings. Two other figures must be subtracted in the incomes approach. These are indirect business taxes, including property and sales taxes, and depreciation.

Population of a Country and the Gross Domestic Product (GDP)

Changes in population can affect the calculation of a nation's GDP, particularly since GDP and GNP are generally measure per capita. If a country's economic production is low, but the population is high, the income per individual will be lower than if the income is high and the population is lower. Also, if the population grows quickly and the income grows slowly, individual income will remain low or even drop drastically.

Population growth can also affect overall economic growth. Economic growth requires both consumers to purchase goods and workers to produce them. A population that does not grow quickly enough will not supply enough workers to support rapid economic growth. Populations are studied by size, rates of growth due to immigration, the overall fertility rate, and life expectancy. For example, though the population of the United States is considerably larger than it was two hundred years ago, the rate of population growth has decreased greatly, from about three percent per year to less than one percent per year.

Ideal Balance to be Obtained in an Economy

Ideally, an economy functions efficiently, with the aggregate supply, or the amount of national output, equal to the aggregate demand, or the amount of the output that is purchased. In these cases, the economy is stable and prosperous.

However, economies more typically go through phases. These phases are:

- Boom—GDP is high and the economy prospers
- Recession—GDP falls, unemployment rises
- Trough—the recession reaches its lowest point
- Recovery—Unemployment lessens, prices rise, and the economy begins to stabilize again

These phases happen often, in cycles that are not necessarily predictable or regular.

Unemployment and Inflation

When demand outstrips supply, prices are driven artificially high, or inflated. This occurs when too much spending causes an imbalance in the economy. In general, inflation occurs because an economy is growing too quickly.

When there is too little spending and supply has moved far beyond demand, a surplus of product results. Companies cut back on production, reduce the number of workers they employ, and unemployment rises as people lose their jobs. This imbalance occurs when an economy becomes sluggish.

In general, both these economic instability situations are caused by an imbalance between supply and demand. Government intervention is often necessary to stabilize an economy when either inflation or unemployment becomes too serious.

Forms of Unemployment

There are five different forms of unemployment. Any of these factors can increase unemployment in certain sectors.

- **Frictional**—when workers change jobs and are unemployed while waiting for a new job.
- **Structural**—when economical shifts reduce the need for workers.
- **Cyclical**—when natural business cycles bring about loss of jobs.
- **Seasonal**—when seasonal cycles reduce the need for certain jobs.
- **Technological**—when advances in technology reduce the need for workers.

Inflation

Inflation is categorized by the overall rate at which it occurs.

- **Creeping inflation**—an inflation rate of about one to three percent annually.
- **Galloping inflation**—a high inflation rate of 100 to 300 percent annually.
- **Hyperinflation**—an inflation rate over 500 percent annually. Hyperinflation usually leads to complete monetary collapse in a society. Individuals are unable to have enough income to purchase their needed goods.

Government Intervention Policies

When an economy becomes too imbalanced, either due to excessive spending or not enough spending, government intervention often becomes necessary to put the economy back on track. Government Fiscal Policy can take several forms, including:

- Monetary policy
- Contractionary policies
- Expansionary policies

Contractionary policies help counteract inflation. These include increasing taxes and decreasing government spending to slow spending in the overall economy. Expansionary policies increase government spending and lower taxes in order to reduce unemployment and increase the level of spending in the economy overall. Monetary policy can take several forms, and affects the amount of funds available to banks for making loans.

Open Market Operations

The Federal Reserve System can also expand or contract the overall money supply through Open Market Operations. In this case, the Fed can buy or sell bonds it has purchased from banks, or from individuals. When they buy bonds, more money is put into circulation, creating an expansionary situation to stimulate the economy. When the Fed sells bonds, money is withdrawn from the system, creating a contractionary situation to slow an economy suffering from inflation.

Because of international financial markets, however, American banks often borrow and lend money in markets outside the US. By shifting their attention to international markets, domestic banks and other businesses can circumvent whatever contractionary policies the Fed may have put into place in order to help a struggling economy.

International Trade

International trade can take advantage of broader markets, bringing a wider variety of products within easy reach. By contrast, it can also allow individual countries to specialize in particular products that they can produce easily, such as those for which they have easy access to raw materials. Other products, more difficult to make domestically, can be acquired through trade with other nations.

International trade requires efficient use of native resources as well as sufficient disposable income to purchase native products and imported products. Many countries in the world engage extensively in international trade, but others still face major economic challenges.

Modern Trends in International Business

There have been many trends in international business. Much of the manufacturing has moved internationally to areas where the cost of labor is lower. China has emerged as a significant exporter, with many of the goods in the United States and other countries coming from there. Multinational businesses have a great impact on the growth and health of the economy, especially given their size. They add a lot to the growth of the GDP.

Trade also plays a large part in economic growth, both in the United States and other countries. There have also been some trends in the United States. The country has increased the importation of oil. Approximately half of the oil import originates from the Western Hemisphere. Also, the United States currently has a negative balance of trade, also known as a trade deficit. This means the United States is importing more than it is exporting.

Economy and Developing Nations

Characteristics of a Developing Nation

1. Low GDP
2. Rapid growth of population
3. Economy that depends on subsistence agriculture
4. Poor conditions, including high infant mortality rates, high disease rates, poor sanitation, and insufficient housing
5. Low literacy rate

Developing nations often function under oppressive governments that do not provide private property rights and withhold education and other rights from women. They also often feature an extreme disparity between upper and lower classes, with little opportunity for lower classes to improve their position.

Economic Development

Economic development occurs in three stages that are defined by the activities that drive the economy:

- Agricultural stage
- Manufacturing stage
- Service sector stage

In developing countries, it is often difficult to acquire the necessary funding to provide equipment and training to move into the advanced stages of economic development. Some can receive help from developed countries via foreign aid and investment or international organizations such as the International Monetary Fund or the World Bank. Having developed countries provide monetary, technical, or military assistance can help developing countries move forward to the next stage in their development.

Developing Nations and Economic Growth

Developing nations typically struggle to overcome obstacles that prevent or slow economic development. Major obstacles can include:

- Rapid, uncontrolled population growth
- Trade restrictions
- Misused resources, often perpetrated by the nation's government
- Traditional beliefs that can slow or reject change

Corrupt, oppressive governments often hamper the economic growth of developing nations, creating huge economic disparities and making it impossible for individuals to advance, in turn preventing overall growth. Governments sometimes export currency, called capital flight, which is detrimental to a country's economic development. In general, countries are more likely to experience economic growth if their governments encourage entrepreneurship and provide private property rights.

Problems with Swift Industrialization

Rapid growth throughout the world leaves some nations behind, and sometimes spurs their governments to move forward too quickly into industrialization and artificially rapid economic growth. While slow or nonexistent economic growth causes problems in a country, overly rapid industrialization carries its own issues.

Four major problems encountered due to rapid industrialization are:

- Use of technology not suited to the products or services being supplied
- Poor investment of capital
- Lack of time for the population to adapt to new paradigms
- Lack of time to experience all stages of development and adjust to each stage

Economy and Modern Technology

E-Commerce

The growth of the Internet has brought many changes to our society, not the least of which is the ways we do business. Where supply channels used to have to move in certain ways, many of these channels are now bypassed as e-commerce makes it possible for nearly any individual to set up a direct market to consumers, as well as direct interaction with suppliers. Competition is fierce. In many instances e-commerce can provide nearly instantaneous gratification, with a wide variety of products. Whoever provides the best product most quickly often rises to the top of a marketplace.

How this added element to the marketplace will affect the economy in the near and not-so-near future remains to be seen. Many industries are still struggling with the best ways to adapt to the rapid, continuous changes.

Knowledge Economy

The knowledge economy is a growing sector in the economy of developed countries, and includes the trade and development of:

- Data
- Intellectual property
- Technology, especially in the area of communications

Knowledge as a resource is steadily becoming more and more important. What is now being called the Information Age may prove to bring about changes in life and culture as significant as those brought on by the Agricultural and Industrial Revolutions.

Cybernomics

Related to the knowledge economy is what has been dubbed "cybernomics," or economics driven by e-commerce and other computer-based markets and products. Marketing has changed drastically with the growth of cyber communication, allowing suppliers to connect one-on-one with their customers. Other issues coming to the fore regarding cybernomics include:

- Secure online trade
- Intellectual property rights
- Rights to privacy
- Bringing developing nations into the fold

As these issues are debated and new laws and policies developed, the face of many industries continues to undergo drastic change. Many of the old ways of doing business no longer work, leaving industries scrambling to function profitably within the new system.

Marketing

Marketing consists of all of the activity necessary to convince consumers to acquire goods. One major way to move products into the hands of consumers is to convince them that any single product will satisfy a need. The ability of a product or service to satisfy the need of a consumer is called utility.

There are four types of utility:

- Form utility—a product's desirability lies in its physical characteristics.
- Place utility—a product's desirability is connected to its location and convenience.
- Time utility—a product's desirability is determined by its availability at a certain time.
- Ownership utility—a product's desirability is increased because ownership of the product passes to the consumer.

Marketing behavior will stress any or all of the types of utility to the consumer to which the product is being marketed.

Marketing Plan

1. Product—any elements pertaining directly to the product, including packaging, presentation, or services to include along with it.
2. Price—calculates cost of production, distribution, advertising, etc. as well as the desired profit to determine the final price.
3. Place—what outlets will be used to sell the product, whether traditional outlets such as brick and mortar stores or through direct mail or Internet marketing.
4. Promotion—ways to let consumers know the product is available, through advertising and other means.

Once these elements have all been determined, the producer can proceed with production and distribution of his product.

Review Video: Marketing Plan
Visit mometrix.com/academy and enter code: 983409

Determining a Product's Market

Successful marketing depends not only on convincing customers they need the product, but also on focusing the marketing towards those who have a need or desire for the product. Before releasing a product into the general marketplace, many producers will test markets to determine which will be the most receptive to the product.

There are three steps usually taken to evaluate a product's market:

- Market research—researching a market to determine if the market will be receptive to the product.
- Market surveys—a part of market research, market surveys ask specific questions of consumers to help determine the marketability of a product to a specific group.
- Test marketing—releasing the product into a small geographical area to see how it sells. Often test marketing is followed by wider marketing if the product does well.

Distribution Channels

Distribution channels determine the route a product takes on its journey from producer to consumer, and can also influenced the final price and availability of the product. There are two major forms of distributions: wholesale and retail. A wholesale distributor buys in large quantities and then resells smaller amounts to other businesses. Retailers sell directly to the consumers rather than to businesses.

In the modern marketplace, additional distribution channels have grown up with the rise of markets such as club warehouse stores as well as purchasing through catalogs or over the Internet. Most of these newer distribution channels bring products more directly to the consumer, eliminating the need for middlemen.

Distribution of Income and Poverty

Distribution of income in any society lies in a range from poorest to richest. In most societies, income is not distributed evenly. To determine income distribution, family incomes are ranked, lowest to highest. These rankings are divided into sections called quintiles, which are compared to each other. The uneven distribution of income is often linked to higher levels of education and ability in the upper classes, but can also be due to other factors such as discrimination and existing monopolies. The income gap in America continues to grow, largely due to growth in the service industry, changes in the American family unit and reduced influence of labor unions.

Poverty is defined by comparing incomes to poverty guidelines. Poverty guidelines determine the level of income necessary for a family to function. Those below the poverty line are often eligible for assistance from government agencies.

Management

Management Skills and Functions

Basic Skills

- Planning skills: outline and analysis of goals, charting of specific objectives, creation of schedules, assessment of resources, and identification of individual responsibilities.
- Decision-making skills: assessments and evaluation of available options, followed by the making of well-considered choices.
- Meeting management skills: selection of the right participants, development of agendas, efficient time management, and effective meeting guidance.
- Delegation skills: effective distribution of tasks to those employees capable of performing them and comprehensive oversight of the delegated tasks

Essential Functions

- Planning: the establishment of long-term goals and the specific objectives that must be reached on the way to these goals.
- Organizing: the creation of the departments and structures for the accomplishment of goals; a manager may need to hire specific employees in order to accomplish goals.
- Leading: promotion of positive thinking and morale in an organization; good managers are able to inspire and encourage their employees.
- Controlling: oversight and evaluation of professional performance; the establishment of rules and procedures for conduct and task performance.

Performance Objectives

Established quality and time goals for the accomplishment of tasks are known as performance objectives. An effective manager establishes clear performance objectives so that employees will understand what is expected of them. Furthermore, it is a great idea to include employees in the creation of performance objectives. Employees, for instance, could be asked to create a first draft of the objectives, and then to modify the draft in consultation with the manager. This kind of system increases the employees' personal investment in performance objectives. In any case, performance objectives need to be directly related to job description. Employees should not be asked to perform tasks for which they have not been trained.

Delegation

Delegation is the distribution of responsibility and authority to subordinates. For instance, an upper manager might delegate the responsibility of running a meeting to a competent middle manager. Delegation occurs up and down the vertical hierarchy of an organization. In order for delegation to be effective, the subordinate employee must understand and be capable of completing the delegated task. This means that the employee should have enough authority to make the decisions required for task completion.

Once the delegated task is complete, the manager who delegated it should be capable of evaluating the report of the subordinate. In most organizations, final responsibility for a task lies with the manager who delegated it, rather than the subordinate who completed it.

When tasks are delegated, a manager has more time to devote to other, perhaps more important duties. Also, the subordinate who is assigned the task may improve his or her performance by gaining experience with new and more difficult tasks. Indeed, one way of determining whether employees deserve promotion is to evaluate their performance with delegated tasks. Research suggests that delegation can increase employee loyalty and innovation. Delegation can be viewed as a form of on-the-job training, which in the long run will empower employees.

Before a project can be effectively delegated, it must be defined in detail. The manager needs to be capable of fully explaining the task to the assigned employee. Also, the manager needs to be good at delegating tasks to those employees who are skilled and experienced enough to complete them. If there is any question about the employee's competence, the manager should be prepared to oversee the delegated task closely. Oftentimes, it is a good idea to ask the opinion of the subordinate before delegating the task. When a task is delegated, a manager should ensure that the employee has sufficient resources and time to complete it. The subordinate employee may need access to special equipment or to other employees. Regardless, the manager should check with the subordinate frequently, to see if any problems or questions have arisen.

Leadership

Leadership is the development of an organizational vision, as well as the day-to-day guidance that encourages the team to work toward that vision. In business, a leader's vision is likely to include financial return for investors, quality products or services for customers, and efficient work within the organization. The theorists James Kouzes and Barry Posner outlined five important behaviors in a leader:

- Leaders question conventional beliefs and techniques.
- Leaders inspire others to a collective vision.
- Leaders provide their subordinates with information and autonomy.
- Leaders model the organizational vision in their own behavior.
- Leaders reward and appreciate their subordinates.

Leadership and management are similar, though management tends to be concerned with daily operations, while leadership has more to do with overall vision. Leaders establish the general direction of the organization, while managers create plans and budgets. Of course, the leader and the manager may be the same person. Nevertheless, a person in a leadership role needs to take a long-term, detached perspective. A manager, on the other hand, has to engage with the details of operations. Leadership can be described as supervisory or strategic. Supervisory leadership entails daily direction, support, and feedback. Strategic leadership, on the other hand, is more concerned with creating a climate of motivation and optimism within a company.

Leaders and Followers

Managers have to be both leaders and followers, insofar as they direct the actions of subordinates and report to upper managers or executives. Some of the characteristics that make a good follower are also those that make a good leader. Both leaders and followers need to understand their job tasks, have some autonomy, and understand their position in the organization. Leaders are successful when their followers can manage themselves and enhance their own importance. In order for followers to improve themselves, they need feedback and training by managers. Performance evaluations are a good venue for this sort of improvement. Over time, leaders and followers will learn better how to deal with one another to create positive change.

Types of Power

Legitimate power: the authority of a manager to issue commands to subordinates. In most organizations, the legitimate power of a manager is limited, so that he or she is only responsible for a defined range of employees and tasks.

Reward power: the authority of a manager to offer and distribute incentives, such as raises and bonuses.

Coercive power: the authority of a manager to discipline and punish subordinates.

Referent power: the authority of a manager that derives from his or her charisma, style, and other personal qualities.

Expert power: the authority of managers that derives from his or her exceptional training or knowledge of a certain subject.

Managerial Decisions

Decision-Making Process

The first step in the decision-making process is to identify the problem to be solved. Next, a manager should make note of all the criteria related to the problem, as for instance the time, resources, and priority. The manager should place these decision criteria in order. Then, he or she can begin to generate options. Once the list is complete, all of the available options should be surveyed objectively, with due attention to advantages and disadvantages. After all of this information has been weighed, the manager should make the decision that creates the best possible outcome. The decision will then be implemented, after which point the manager should receive feedback and evaluate the success of his or her decision.

Individual Decision-Making

Individual decision-making depends on a number of different factors. Some of these enhance decision-making, while others are obstacles to effective choices:

- Individual values: for instance, aesthetic, political, ethical, economic, or religious.
- Personality, gender, and social status: in some cases, a person's background can skew his or her perspective.
- Risk tolerance: the degree to which a manager can afford to make a risky decision. The assessment of risk will depend on the manager's evaluation of advantages and disadvantages.
- Cognitive dissonance: the difference between the situation as it is and the manager's perception of the situation. When there is a great degree of cognitive dissonance, decision-making tends to be poor.

Decision-Making Styles

Just as managers all have different personalities, so do they have different decision-making styles. For instance, analytical decision-makers take a rational, measured approach. The focus of such a decision-maker is always obtaining as much information as possible. A directive decision-maker, on the other hand, assembles important information but emphasizes the necessity of making a quick decision. A directive decision-maker is not afraid to take risk. A conceptual decision-maker tends to create a mental model of the situation, and then to base his or her decision on this model's predictions. Finally, a behavioral decision-maker concentrates on the effects of the decisions of other people. This kind of decision-maker is likely to ask for the opinions of others before making a decision.

Managerial Decision-Making

In general, managers find that they make better decisions when they have access to more information. However, it is also important for a manager to bring creativity, experience, and knowledge to the process of decision-making. Managers often draw a distinction between tactical decisions, which relate to the short term, and strategic decisions, which relate to the longer term. A particular decision may be characterized by certainty, uncertainty, or risk. That is, the decision-maker may have all of the necessary information, little of the necessary information, or some information but no guarantee of success.

One of the common characteristics of decisions made by managers is a lack of predetermined structure. In other words, managers are often called upon to solve problems without easy solutions. Many of the decisions made in an organization have preprogrammed answers, but managers are often required to create innovative solutions. For this reason, managerial decision-making entails a high degree of uncertainty. Managers are always at risk of making bad decisions. The best a manager can expect to do is minimize the amount of risk. A manager can expect to feel conflicted internally when making a difficult decision, and can expect negative feedback from others when making an unpopular decision.

Intuitive Decision-Making

When a manager bases a decision on his or her beliefs or emotions, he or she is engaging in intuitive decision-making. Often, experienced managers make correct decisions without exactly knowing why. They just have a certain intuition derived from long interaction with a given set of variables. It can be difficult to make a case in support of such a decision, however. There are certain personality issues that can lead to poor intuitive decision-making. For instance, a manager might become overly convinced of his or her intuition, to the extent that he or she ignores obvious counterarguments. A manager might become addicted to making risky decisions. On the other hand, a manager might be afraid to make controversial decisions because of a fear of failure.

Systematic Decision-Making

A manager who weighs the various alternatives before coming to a decision is engaging in a systematic decision-making process. One of the prerequisites for systematic decision-making is access to all relevant information. A manager needs to be able to isolate the information directly related to the decision, and must have access to employees who know a lot about the subject. A manager must be able to evaluate both sides of the issue and obtain more information when necessary. The manager should be able to construct logical counterarguments for his or her final decision. Also, the manager should know when to draw on the expertise of colleagues.

Models of Decision

Rational Decision Model

In the rational decision model, the decision-maker uses all of the available data to select the most logical option. Of course, this is an idealized scenario; in real life, managers are always working with incomplete information. The rational decision model is most appropriate for programmed decisions and situations in which there is very little risk. Rational decision-making works better when decisions are made by a single person rather than a group. So long as the situation is predictable and all the advantages and disadvantages of various alternatives are clear, the rational decision model is the best.

Administrative Decision Model

Unlike other models of decision-making, the administrative model is more descriptive than prescriptive. According to the administrative model, perfect information is never available and no person is perfect at analysis. For this reason, decision-making is a process of inevitable risk. This decision-making model seems most appropriate for complex and uncertain decisions. It also seems to be a better descriptor of group decision-making than unitary executive decision-making. A manager is charged with making a satisfactory decision, not necessarily the best decision.

Political Decision Model

In the political decision model, the primary determinant is the anticipated reaction from those affected by the decision. The political decision model is most appropriate for decisions that need to create a consensus and minimize conflict. According to the political decision model, the best decision is not necessarily that which will achieve the best results. In political life, sometimes the best decision is impossible because of the attitudes of constituents. This decision model takes into account the necessity of popular support for some decisions. This model is considered most appropriate for situations with ambiguous information and large groups of stakeholders.

Judgment Errors in Decision-Making

Managers who become experienced at making decisions may develop some bad habits. For instance, managers often develop shortcuts, known as heuristics, which simplify the decision-making process. These are often helpful, but sometimes may lead to error. In the availability heuristic, for instance, a manager relies on his or her own memory rather than available information. The representative heuristic, on the other hand, is the use of similar precedents to determine a decision, rather than attention to the facts as they are. Some decision-makers rely on an anchoring and adjustment model, in which obtained information becomes the foundation for future decision-making. Finally, some managers tend to stick by their decisions even when the evidence suggests they should do otherwise. This is known as the escalation of commitment to heuristic.

Barriers to Effective Decision-Making

There a number of psychological biases that can negatively impact decision-making. For instance, some managers have an illusion of control, which leads them to believe they have influence over uncontrollable factors. If a manager is suffering from the solution, he or she will be unlikely to adequately assess risk. Sometimes, a manager consistently makes bad decisions because he or she frames them incorrectly. In other words, the way information is presented can be as influential to decision-making as the content of the information. Some managers err by discounting the future, or overemphasizing short-term advantages at the expense of long-term factors. Finally, if a manager feels rushed, he or she is unlikely to make the best possible decision.

Hiring and Employment

Recruitment and Selection

Businesses use recruiting tactics to attract job applicants and manage their personnel needs. Large businesses need to plan hiring long in advance, so they hire special human resources employees to manage applications, interviews, and evaluations. The first step in the hiring process is a preliminary screening, during which candidates may be interviewed over the phone and resumes are reviewed. The next step is likely to be an in-person interview, which may be unstructured, semi-structured, or structured. A semi-structured interview uses some standard questions, while a structured interview uses a standard set of questions for all applicants.

Some businesses also administer aptitude, psychological, or personality tests. Next, a business will likely check the references of the remaining applicants, and may perform drug tests and background checks. Finally, candidates for management positions may be asked to participate in special leadership evaluations before hiring decisions are made.

The Workplace and the Employee

Compensation

Employee compensation is usually thought of in monetary terms, as some compensation is not directly financial. For instance, vacation days, use of company resources, and insurance are all forms of indirect financial compensation. Compensation is handled differently depending on the employee's position: some employees receive a flat rate for the amount of time they work, while other employees are paid based on what they produce. Some employees receive a combination of a flat rate and an incentive rate.

Companies whose employees are members of a union typically receive a high flat rate established through collective bargaining. When employees are paid according to individual incentive, they get a certain amount for each unit produced. A straight piecework wage consists of an hourly rate plus a little more for each unit produced.

In a differential piece rate payment, the employer pays one rate for a low level of production, and a higher rate for greater production. In a production bonus system, the employee is given a flat rate payment and a bonus whenever their production is greater than a certain amount. Finally, a gain-sharing incentive plan gives employees a bonus when their group exceeds expectations.

Workplace Benefits

The United States mandates that companies pay unemployment insurance, Social Security, and workers' compensation benefits. However, companies may also pay for vacation days, other forms of insurance, child care, and employee pensions. A pension plan is meant to supply retirement income. Some companies opt to contribute to an individual retirement account or 401(k) rather than a pension plan. Also, many companies pledge to match the employee's contribution to the retirement or pension plan. In a cafeteria or flexible benefit plan, employees agreed to set aside a portion of their wage they will spend on things like insurance or child care. This money is not entered into yearly total wages and is therefore not taxed as income.

Training and Development

Companies receive a number of benefits from continuously training and improving the skills of their employees. Production and efficiency tend to go up, and businesses often discover that some employees are capable of taking on more responsibility, which leads to less money spent on oversight. There's a slight distinction between training and development: training is learning how to perform a job for the first time, while development is learning how to perform an existing job better. Before training begins, employees are often given a needs assessment, so that their existing knowledge and skills can be assessed. Sometimes, performance on the needs assessment dictates the style of training. Businesses often provide basic orientation for new employees and diversity training so that employees harmoniously cooperate with colleagues from different cultures. For prospective managers, interpersonal training may be necessary. Some businesses have managers lead the training in what is known as coaching.

Evaluating Work Performance

Performance evaluations may use graphic rating scales, ranking methods, or descriptive essays. They detail the strengths and weaknesses of an employee's work. Performance evaluations are used to determine employee placement, compensation, and training. Many managers use performance evaluations to motivate their employees, and this can be effective so long as the evaluations are perceived as fair. In a graphic rating scale, employee performance is assigned a rating from outstanding to poor. This descriptive method works best with small numbers of employees. Another way of expressing performance evaluations is with descriptive essays, but these are often hard to compare. It is easy for a manager's prejudice or particular judgments to skew an evaluation. For this reason, managers should be trained in the organization's particular methods. As much as possible, the performance evaluations should strive for specificity.

Managing a Reinforcement and Punishment Program

In order to be consistent and effective, managers need to define the behaviors to be reinforced, rewarded, punished, and extinguished. All too often, a manager reinforces bad behavior by failing to identify successful deeds that were accomplished in the wrong way. The reinforcements should be appropriate to the individual employee. Money is not the only reinforcement in the workplace: managers can also use increased autonomy, personal recognition, and benefits to reward employee performance. Of course, managers and employees will inevitably make mistakes. If these mistakes are made in good faith, punishment should not be severe. Nevertheless, managers should implement disincentives and ensure that mistakes are dealt with constructively. The best way to run a reinforcement and punishment program is with consistent, detailed feedback.

"Big Five" Personality Traits Work Behavior

The so-called "Big Five" personality traits related to work behavior are

1. Extraversion
2. Emotional stability
3. Openness to new experience
4. Conscientiousness
5. Agreeableness

The extent to which an employee will take responsibility for himself or herself is tied to his or her locus of control, which is his or her perception of personal determination. An "internal" is a person who believes he or she has control, while an "external" is a person who believes he or she has little control. An external tends to need more supervision. Employees can also be classified by whether they are Type A or Type B. A Type A personality feels the need to be superior to others, and tends to be aggressive. A Type B, on the other hand, is more mellow and inclined to wait and see. The Myers-Briggs personality classification system divides people into four cognitive styles: sensation-thinking, intuition-thinking, sensation-feeling, and intuition-feeling. The system also classifies people in terms of extroversion-introversion and a tendency towards judgment or perception.

Employment Opportunities and the Law

Fair Labor Standards Act (1938): divided employees into exempt, who could not receive overtime pay, and non-exempt, who could.

Equal Pay Act (1963): outlawed pay discrimination based on gender.

Civil Rights Act (1964): outlawed employment discrimination based on race, sex, ethnicity, nationality, or religion; Title VII outlawed discrimination in recruiting, hiring, termination, promotion, compensation, and training.

Age Discrimination in Employment Act (1967): outlawed employment discrimination against those over 40 and limited mandatory retirement.

Vocational Rehabilitation Act (1973): enforced affirmative action for federal employers and contractors with respect to disability.

Americans with Disabilities Act (1990): outlawed employment discrimination against the disabled; definition of disability expanded to include cancer patients in remission, those afflicted with AIDS, alcoholics, and drug abusers.

Civil Rights Act (1991): strengthened anti-discriminatory legislation and redefined punishments for violators.

Family and Medical Leave Act (1991): asserted that employees with medical or family needs should receive twelve weeks unpaid leave without threat of termination.

U.S. Labor Laws

National Labor Relations Act, otherwise known as the Wagner Act (1935): legalized labor unions, outlawed several employer practices related to labor, and created the National Labor Relations Board. This act basically unionized the country overnight and enabled collective bargaining to begin winning victories for workers, such as minimum wage and maternity leave.

Labor-Management Relations Act, otherwise known as the Taft-Hartley Act (1947): protected management by outlawing some labor union practices, allowing workers to decertify their union, and reinforcing free speech rights.

Labor-Management Reporting and Disclosure Act, otherwise known as the Landrum-Griffin Act (1959): created a bill of rights for union members, including union reporting requirements and control over union dues.

Compensation and Benefits

Fair Labor Standards Act (FLSA), 1938: categorized exempt and non-exempt employees and established minimum wage, child labor, and maximum hour laws.

Equal Pay Act (EPA), 1963: outlawed pay discrimination based on gender, but allowed it in relation to merit, incentive systems, market demand, seniority, etc.

Comparable-worth doctrine: a woman who does work of equal worth to that of a man deserves to be paid as well as the man. There are no statutes requiring comparable-worth compensation, but some laws support this doctrine.

Employee Retirement Income Security Act (ERISA), 1974: employees who have earned the right to draw retirement benefits must be given them; bankrupt and defaulting companies will have their employee pensions paid by the government.

Pregnancy Discrimination Act (1978): categorized pregnancy as a disability and entitled pregnant women to the benefits afforded other disabled people.

Health and Safety

The Occupational Safety and Health Act (OSHA) asserts rules for workplace safety, as for instance mandatory onsite inspections and record-keeping related to deaths and injuries. Many professions remain dangerous. Coal miners, for instance, still die every year, although the numbers are greatly diminished from the hundreds of casualties suffered during the 1960s. To maintain workplace safety, it is essential for employees to speak up. There is legislation to protect workers who blow the whistle on unsafe working conditions. For instance, it is not legal for these employees to be fired for alerting authorities to conditions that could result in injury or death.

Evaluating a Work Environment

Job Enrichment

When employees feel that they do not have enough responsibility, are not growing professionally, and are not being recognized for their performance, they are more likely to perform below capacity or leave a job entirely. Job enrichment aims to reduce these occurrences by giving employees more autonomy and a broader set of skills. A job enrichment program can be expensive, however, so it is a good idea to determine whether an employee is willing before initiating one. An effective enrichment program will emphasize the following core areas:

- Skill variety: the employee is given a broader range of tasks to accomplish.
- Task identity: the employee is given charge of a task from its inception to its completion.
- Task significance: the employee is given more consequential tasks.
- Autonomy: the employee is given more freedom to pursue alternate methods.
- Feedback: the employee is given more response, both positive and negative, to his or her work.

Job Analysis, Design, and Redesign

Job analysis precedes job design. The fundamental point of job analysis is to determine how a particular job meshes with the organization as a whole. The job analyst will make a list of all the activities associated with a particular job, as well as the skills required to perform it. From this summary will come an outline of job descriptions and job specifications. Job design is the conscious construction of a professional role, with the aim of increasing employee satisfaction and efficiency. During job design, the designer is focused on specialization, range, and depth. Job redesign is the refinement of an already-existing job. It may involve the use of flex time, rotation, enlargement, or enrichment. More specialized jobs tend to have less range and depth, and vice versa.

Plan, Do, Check, Act (PDCA) Cycle

One of the most common quality planning cycles used in business is called the plan, do, check, act (PDCA) cycle. As the title indicates, the PDCA cycle has four steps. First, the organization identifies the quality improvement changes that need to be made. Then, the organization tests these changes with a small sample run. Next, the employees determine whether the implemented changes had the desired effect. Finally, if the small sample run indicates that the changes were positive, the changes are implemented across the full range of production. Often, businesses will use the PDCA cycle in one production area to inspire changes in another.

Strategic Planning Process

The first step of the strategic planning process is to identify explicitly the purpose, mission, and values of the organization. Next, the planners need to determine goals and objectives for both the short and the long term. In doing this, the planners should identify the organization's core competencies and available resources, so that it can maximize their potential. Next, the planners should perform a detailed analysis of the business environment. After this, they can create a strategy for all departments and for the organization as a whole. The strategy should include performance expectations and target outcomes. The next step is to implement the plan and review the outcomes, for instance in terms of market share, product quality, and financial performance.

SWOT Analysis

One simple tool for assessing the current health of a business is the SWOT analysis. SWOT stands for strengths, weaknesses, opportunities, and threats. The strengths of a business could be its resources, whether human or material. Experience and excellent training could be the strengths of a business. On the other hand, these same areas can be sources of weakness for a business. A lack of expertise in the production area is a definite weakness. The opportunities of a business are the ways in which it could improve its position. The threats to a business are all of the potential problems, such as malfeasance or a general decline in customer demand.

Psychology

Psychology studies human behavior and how the mind works. Some psychologists pursue scientific psychology, while others focus on applied psychology. Psychology correlates human behavior and can make use of this data to predict behavior or determine why a particular behavior has occurred. Psychologists also help work with people who have specific problems with relationships or with how they perceive the world. By observing patterns and recording them in detail, psychologists can apply these patterns to predictions about human behavior in individuals, groups, cultures, and even countries.

Important Influencers on Psychology

Importance of Aristotle

Aristotle is often cited as founding the science of psychology through his overall interest in the working of the human mind. His beliefs stated that the mind was part of the body, while the psyche functioned as a receiver of knowledge. He felt psychology's major focus was to uncover the soul. Later philosophers and scientists built on these ideas to eventually develop the modern science of psychology.

19TH Century Intellectuals

Johannes P. Muller and Hermann L.F. von Hemholtz, both German, conducted scientific, organized studies of sensation and perception. As the first psychologists to attempt this kind of study, they showed that it was possible to study actual physical processes that work to produce mental activity.

William James was the founder of the world's first psychology laboratory. William Wundt, also German, published the first experimental psychology journal. Together, James and Wundt helped bring psychology into its own, separating it from philosophy. The method of psychological study called introspection grew out of their work.

Sigmund Freud

An Austrian doctor, Freud developed a number of theories regarding human mental processes and behavior. He believed the subconscious to hold numerous repressed experiences and feelings that drove behavior without the individual being aware of it, and that these subconscious motivators could lead to severe personality problems and disorders. He particularly stressed sexual desire as a motivating force. He developed the method of psychoanalysis to help discover the hidden impulses driving individual behavior.

Freud's psychoanalytic theory proposed three major components to an individual's psychological makeup:

- Id—driven by instinct and basic drives.
- Ego—most conscious and producing self-awareness.
- Superego—strives for perfection and appropriate behavior.

The ego acts as mediator between the id and superego, which function in opposition to each other.

Carl Jung

A student of Freud, Jung eventually developed different theories regarding the workings of the human mind. With an intense interest in both Eastern and Western philosophy, he incorporated ideas from both into his psychological explorations. He developed the theories of extroversion and introversion, as well as proposing the existence of the collective unconscious and the occurrence of synchronicity.

Ivan Pavlov and B.F. Skinner

Ivan Pavlov and B.F. Skinner both built on the theories of John B. Watson, who developed the idea of behaviorism. This work came about largely as a counter to the growing importance of introspective techniques to psychological study.

Believing environment strongly influenced individual behavior, Pavlov and Skinner searched for connections between outside stimuli and behavioral patterns. Pavlov's experiments proved the existence of conditioned response. His most famous experiment conditioned dogs to salivate at the sound of a ringing bell.

Skinner went on to build further on these ideas, developing the "Skinner Box," a device used to develop and study conditioned response in rats.

Gestalt Psychology, Social Psychology, and Modern Psychology

- Gestalt psychology is a theory developed by Max Wertheimer. In Gestalt theory, events are not considered individually, but as part of a larger pattern.
- Social psychology is the study of how social conditions affect individuals.
- Modern psychology, as it has developed, combines earlier schools of psychology, including Freudian, Jungian, behaviorism, cognitive, humanistic and stimulus-response theories.

Nativism

Nativism is a theory that states that there is a certain body of knowledge all people are born with. This knowledge requires no learning or experience on the part of the individual. Rene Descartes, a French philosopher, developed this concept. He believed the body and mind affected each other profoundly, largely because they are separate from each other. The physical site of this interaction took place in the pineal gland according to his theory. The pineal gland is a small gland in the brain. Descartes developed several theories in the field of philosophy and psychology that are still studied in modern universities.

Empiricism

Empiricism was in direct opposition to Descartes' theory of nativism. Nativism states that people are born with a certain body of knowledge that they do not have to learn. Empiricism theorizes that all knowledge is acquired through life experience, impressing itself on a mind and brain that are blank at the time of birth. Major proponents of empiricism were Thomas Hobbes, John Locke, David Hume and George Berkeley.

Behaviorism

John B. Watson, an American, developed the idea of behaviorism. In his theory, growth, learning and training would always win out over any possible inborn tendencies. He believed that any person, regardless of origin, could learn to perform any type of art, craft or enterprise with sufficient training and experience.

Divisions of the Human Lifespan used to Classify Behavior and Growth

Development psychologists divide the human lifespan into stages, and list certain developmental milestones that generally take place during these stages.

1. Infancy and childhood—the most rapid period of human development during which, the child learns to experience its world, relate to other people, and perform tasks necessary to function in its native culture. Debate exists as to what characteristics are inborn and what are learned.

2. Adolescence—this period represents the shift from child to adult. Changes are rapid and can involve major physical and emotional shifts.
3. Adulthood—individuals take on new responsibilities, become self-sufficient, and often form their own families and other social networks.
4. Old age—priorities shift again as children become adults and no longer require support and supervision.

Types of Learning for Psychologists

Psychologists define learning as a permanent change in behavior. They divide types of learning into three basic categories, depending upon on how the behavioral change is acquired.

1. Classical conditioning—a learning process in which a specific stimulus is associated with a specific response over time.
2. Operant conditioning—a learning process in which behavior is punished or rewarded, leading to a desired long-term behavior.
3. Social learning—learning based on observation of others and modeling others' behavior.

These three learning processes work together to produce the wide variety of human behavior.

Factors Involved in Social Psychology

Social psychology studies the ways in which people interact as well as why and how they decide who to interact with. The ways people react with each other are defined in several ways, including:

1. Social perception—how we perceive others and their behavior as we make judgments based on our own experiences and prejudices.
2. Personal relationships—close relationships developed among people for various reasons, including the desire to reproduce and form a family unit.
3. Group behavior—people gather into groups with similar beliefs, needs, or other characteristics. Sometimes group behavior differs greatly from behavior that would be practiced by individuals alone.
4. Attitudes—individual attitudes toward others develop over time based on individual history, experience, knowledge, and other factors. Attitudes can change over time, but some are deeply ingrained and can lead to prejudice.

Important Terms

Affirmative action: a strategy for increasing the presence of minorities and underrepresented groups in business, by giving special preference to them in hiring.

Chain of command: the paths of authority in an organization, consisting of a series of superior-subordinate relationships.

Customer departmentalization: the process of sorting jobs according to the customers they serve, for instance, some manufacturers have different departments for dealing with corporate and private customers.

Departmentalization: the process of placing jobs in categories according to their customer base, geographical location, or function.

Equal employment opportunity (EEO): a foundation of business ethics in the United States, whereby all people are guaranteed an equal chance for employment, regardless of race, religion, gender, etc.

Functional departmentalization: the process of placing jobs in categories according to their function, such as marketing, manufacturing, and sales.

Geographic departmentalization: the sorting of jobs according to the geographical region served; this process is especially useful for very large international corporations.

Human resource management: the set of processes devoted to the hiring, training, and retention of employees, including preparation of compensation packages, performance evaluations, employee discipline, collective bargaining, arbitration, and terminations.

Human resource planning: process of predicting and planning for employee needs.

Job depth: the latitude or autonomy granted to a particular employee.

Job description: explicit verbal summary of the necessary skills, tasks, and equipment related to a job.

Job enlargement: an increase in the range of tasks performed by a single employee.

Job range: the span of different tasks to be performed by the same employee.

Job rotation: the movement of employees from position to position within an organization. Often, this strategy is employed to improve the skill base of each employee.

Job specialization: the degree to which an employee must perform different tasks; less-specialized jobs tend to have more range and depth.

Job specification: printed outline of the required knowledge and skills for a job.

Line position: any position within the chain of command that directly contributes to the completion of the organizational goals.

Product departmentalization: the process of sorting jobs according to their product line.

Staff position: any position that leads, assists, or supports the line positions.

Mathematics and Statistics

Operations and Number Sense

Numbers are the basic building blocks of mathematics. Specific features of numbers are identified by the following terms:

Integer – any positive or negative whole number, including zero. Integers do not include fractions $\left(\frac{1}{3}\right)$, decimals (0.56), or mixed numbers $\left(7\frac{3}{4}\right)$.

Prime number – any whole number greater than 1 that has only two factors, itself and 1; that is, a number that can be divided evenly only by 1 and itself.

Composite number – any whole number greater than 1 that has more than two different factors; in other words, any whole number that is not a prime number. For example: The composite number 8 has the factors of 1, 2, 4, and 8.

Even number – any integer that can be divided by 2 without leaving a remainder. For example: 2, 4, 6, 8, and so on.

Odd number – any integer that cannot be divided evenly by 2. For example: 3, 5, 7, 9, and so on.

Decimal number – any number that uses a decimal point to show the part of the number that is less than one. Example: 1.234.

Decimal point – a symbol used to separate the ones place from the tenths place in decimals or dollars from cents in currency.

Decimal place – the position of a number to the right of the decimal point. In the decimal 0.123, the 1 is in the first place to the right of the decimal point, indicating tenths; the 2 is in the second place, indicating hundredths; and the 3 is in the third place, indicating thousandths.

The decimal, or base 10, system is a number system that uses ten different digits (0, 1, 2, 3, 4, 5, 6, 7, 8, 9). An example of a number system that uses something other than ten digits is the binary, or base 2, number system, used by computers, which uses only the numbers 0 and 1. It is thought that the decimal system originated because people had only their 10 fingers for counting.

Rational numbers include all integers, decimals, and fractions. Any terminating or repeating decimal number is a rational number.

Irrational numbers cannot be written as fractions or decimals because the number of decimal places is infinite and there is no recurring pattern of digits within the number. For example, pi (π) begins with 3.141592 and continues without terminating or repeating, so pi is an irrational number.

Real numbers are the set of all rational and irrational numbers.

Review Video: Numbers and Their Classifications
Visit mometrix.com/academy and enter code: 461071

Rational Numbers from Least to Greatest

Example

Order the following rational numbers from least to greatest: 0.55, 17%, $\sqrt{25}$, $\frac{64}{4}$, $\frac{25}{50}$, 3.

Recall that the term *rational* simply means that the number can be expressed as a ratio or fraction. The set of rational numbers includes integers and decimals. Notice that each of the numbers in the problem can be written as a decimal or integer:

$$17\% = 0.17$$

$$\sqrt{25} = 5$$

$$\frac{64}{4} = 16$$

$$\frac{25}{50} = \frac{1}{2} = 0.5$$

So, the answer is 17%, $\frac{25}{50}$, 0.55, 3, $\sqrt{25}$, $\frac{64}{4}$.

Rational Numbers from Greatest to Least

Example

Order the following rational numbers from greatest to least: 0.3, 27%, $\sqrt{100}$, $\frac{72}{9}$, $\frac{1}{9}$. 4.5

Recall that the term *rational* simply means that the number can be expressed as a ratio or fraction. The set of rational numbers includes integers and decimals. Notice that each of the numbers in the problem can be written as a decimal or integer:

$$27\% = 0.27$$

$$\sqrt{100} = 10$$

$$\frac{72}{9} = 8$$

$$\frac{1}{9} \approx 0.11$$

So, the answer is $\sqrt{100}$, $\frac{72}{9}$, 4.5, 0.3, 27%, $\frac{1}{9}$.

Fractions

A fraction is a number that is expressed as one integer written above another integer, with a dividing line between them ($\frac{x}{y}$). It represents the quotient of the two numbers "x divided by y." It can also be thought of as x out of y equal parts.

The top number of a fraction is called the numerator, and it represents the number of parts under consideration. The 1 in $\frac{1}{4}$ means that 1 part out of the whole is being considered in the calculation. The bottom number of a fraction is called the denominator, and it represents the total number of equal parts. The 4 in $\frac{1}{4}$ means that the whole consists of 4 equal parts. A fraction cannot have a denominator of zero; this is referred to as "undefined."

Fractions can be manipulated by multiplying or dividing (but not adding or subtracting) both the numerator and denominator by the same number, without changing the value of the fraction. If you divide both numbers by a common factor, you are reducing or simplifying the fraction. Two fractions that have the same value, but are expressed differently are known as equivalent fractions. For example, $\frac{2}{10}, \frac{3}{15}, \frac{4}{20}$, and $\frac{5}{25}$ are all equivalent fractions. They can also all be reduced or simplified to $\frac{1}{5}$.

When two fractions are manipulated so that they have the same denominator, this is known as finding a common denominator. The number chosen to be that common denominator should be the least common multiple of the two original denominators. Example: $\frac{3}{4}$ and $\frac{5}{6}$; the least common multiple of 4 and 6 is 12. Manipulating to achieve the common denominator: $\frac{3}{4} = \frac{9}{12}; \frac{5}{6} = \frac{10}{12}$.

A fraction whose denominator is greater than its numerator is known as a proper fraction, while a fraction whose numerator is greater than its denominator is known as an improper fraction. Proper fractions have values less than one and improper fractions have values greater than one.

A mixed number is a number that contains both an integer and a fraction. Any improper fraction can be rewritten as a mixed number. Example: $\frac{8}{3} = \frac{6}{3} + \frac{2}{3} = 2 + \frac{2}{3} = 2\frac{2}{3}$. Similarly, any mixed number can be rewritten as an improper fraction. Example: $1\frac{3}{5} = 1 + \frac{3}{5} = \frac{5}{5} + \frac{3}{5} = \frac{8}{5}$.

A fraction that contains a fraction in the numerator, denominator, or both is called a *Complex Fraction*. These can be solved in a number of ways; with the simplest being by following the order of operations as stated earlier. For example, $\left(\frac{4}{7}\right) / \left(\frac{5}{8}\right) = 0.571 / 0.625 = 0.914$. Another way to solve this problem is to multiply the fraction in the numerator by the recipricol of the fraction in the denominator. For example, $\left(\frac{4}{7}\right) / \left(\frac{5}{8}\right) = \frac{4}{7} \times \frac{8}{5} = \frac{32}{35} = 0.914$.

Review Video: Fractions
Visit mometrix.com/academy and enter code: 262335

Decimals

Decimal Illustration

Use a model to represent the decimal: 0.24. Write 0.24 as a fraction.

The decimal 0.24 is twenty-four hundredths. One possible model to represent this fraction is to draw 100 pennies, since each penny is worth 1 one hundredth of a dollar. Draw one hundred circles to represent one hundred pennies. Shade 24 of the pennies to represent the decimal twenty-four hundredths.

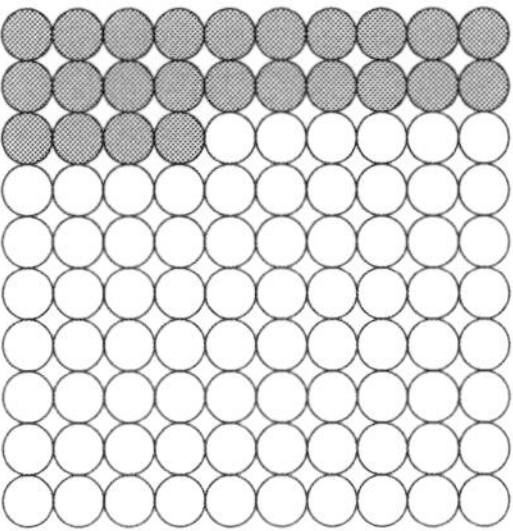

To write the decimal as a fraction, write a fraction: $\frac{\#\,shaded\ spaces}{\#\,total\ spaces}$. The number of shaded spaces is 24, and the total number of spaces is 100, so as a fraction 0.24 equals $\frac{24}{100}$. This fraction can then be reduced to $\frac{6}{25}$.

Basic Mathematical Operations

There are four basic mathematical operations:

Addition increases the value of one quantity by the value of another quantity. Example: 2 + 4 = 6; 8 + 9 = 17. The result is called the sum. With addition, the order does not matter. 4 + 2 = 2 + 4.

Subtraction is the opposite operation to addition; it decreases the value of one quantity by the value of another quantity. Example: 6 – 4 = 2; 17 – 8 = 9. The result is called the difference. Note that with subtraction, the order does matter. 6 – 4 ≠ 4 – 6.

Review Video: Addition and Subtraction
Visit mometrix.com/academy and enter code: 521157

Multiplication can be thought of as repeated addition. One number tells how many times to add the other number to itself. Example: 3 × 2 (three times two) = 2 + 2 + 2 = 6. With multiplication, the order does not matter. 2 × 3 (or 3 + 3) = 3 × 2 (or 2 + 2 + 2).

Division is the opposite operation to multiplication; one number tells us how many parts to divide the other number into. Example: 20 ÷ 4 = 5; if 20 is split into 4 equal parts, each part is 5. With division, the order of the numbers does matter. 20 ÷ 4 ≠ 4 ÷ 20.

Review Video: Multiplication and Division
Visit mometrix.com/academy and enter code: 643326

Order of Operations

Order of Operations is a set of rules that dictates the order in which we must perform each operation in an expression so that we will evaluate it accurately. If we have an expression that includes multiple different operations, Order of Operations tells us which operations to do first. The most common mnemonic for Order of Operations is PEMDAS, or "Please Excuse My Dear Aunt Sally." PEMDAS stands for Parentheses, Exponents, Multiplication, Division, Addition, Subtraction. It is important to understand that multiplication and division have equal precedence, as do addition and subtraction, so those pairs of operations are simply worked from left to right in order.

Example: Evaluate the expression $5 + 20 \div 4 \times (2 + 3)^2 - 6$ using the correct order of operations.

P: Perform the operations inside the parentheses, $(2 + 3) = 5$.

E: Simplify the exponents, $(5)^2 = 25$.

The equation now looks like this: $5 + 20 \div 4 \times 25 - 6$.

MD: Perform multiplication and division from left to right, $20 \div 4 = 5$; then $5 \times 25 = 125$.

The equation now looks like this: $5 + 125 - 6$.

AS: Perform addition and subtraction from left to right, $5 + 125 = 130$; then $130 - 6 = 124$.

Review Video: Order of Operations
Visit mometrix.com/academy and enter code: 259675

Exponents and Parentheses

An exponent is a superscript number placed next to another number at the top right. It indicates how many times the base number is to be multiplied by itself. Exponents provide a shorthand way to write what would be a longer mathematical expression. Example: $a^2 = a \times a$; $2^4 = 2 \times 2 \times 2 \times 2$. A number with an exponent of 2 is said to be "squared," while a number with an exponent of 3 is said to be "cubed."

The value of a number raised to an exponent is called its power. So, 8^4 is read as "8 to the 4th power," or "8 raised to the power of 4." A negative exponent is the same as the reciprocal of a positive exponent. Example: $a^{-2} = 1/a^2$.

Review Video: Exponents
Visit mometrix.com/academy and enter code: 600998

Parentheses are used to designate which operations should be done first when there are multiple operations. Example: $4 - (2 + 1) = 1$; the parentheses tell us that we must add 2 and 1, and then subtract the sum from 4, rather than subtracting 2 from 4 and then adding 1 (this would give us an answer of 3).

Laws of Exponents

The laws of exponents are as follows:

1. Any number to the power of 1 is equal to itself: $a^1 = a$.
2. The number 1 raised to any power is equal to 1: $1^n = 1$.
3. Any number raised to the power of 0 is equal to 1: $a^0 = 1$.
4. Add exponents to multiply powers of the same base number: $a^n \times a^m = a^{n+m}$.
5. Subtract exponents to divide powers of the same number: $a^n \div a^m = a^{n-m}$.
6. Multiply exponents to raise a power to a power: $(a^n)^m = a^{n \times m}$.
7. If multiplied or divided numbers inside parentheses are collectively raised to a power, this is the same as each individual term being raised to that power: $(a \times b)^n = a^n \times b^n$; $(a \div b)^n = a^n \div b^n$.

Note: Exponents do not have to be integers. Fractional or decimal exponents follow all the rules above as well. Example: $5^{\frac{1}{4}} \times 5^{\frac{3}{4}} = 5^{\frac{1}{4}+\frac{3}{4}} = 5^1 = 5$.

OPERATIONS WITH FRACTIONS

If two fractions have a common denominator, they can be added or subtracted simply by adding or subtracting the two numerators and retaining the same denominator. Example: $\frac{1}{2}+\frac{1}{4}=\frac{2}{4}+\frac{1}{4}=\frac{3}{4}$. If the two fractions do not already have the same denominator, one or both of them must be manipulated to achieve a common denominator before they can be added or subtracted.

Review Video: Adding and Subtracting Fractions
Visit mometrix.com/academy and enter code: 378080

Two fractions can be multiplied by multiplying the two numerators to find the new numerator and the two denominators to find the new denominator. Example: $\frac{1}{3}\times\frac{2}{3}=\frac{1\times 2}{3\times 3}=\frac{2}{9}$.

Two fractions can be divided flipping the numerator and denominator of the second fraction and then proceeding as though it were a multiplication. Example: $\frac{2}{3}\div\frac{3}{4}=\frac{2}{3}\times\frac{4}{3}=\frac{8}{9}$.

Review Video: Multiplying and Dividing Fractions
Visit mometrix.com/academy and enter code: 473632

OPERATIONS WITH DECIMALS

ADDING AND SUBTRACTING DECIMALS

When adding and subtracting decimals, the decimal points must always be aligned. Adding decimals is just like adding regular whole numbers. Example: 4.5 + 2 = 6.5.

If the problem-solver does not properly align the decimal points, an incorrect answer of 4.7 may result. An easy way to add decimals is to align all of the decimal points in a vertical column visually. This will allow one to see exactly where the decimal should be placed in the final answer. Begin adding from right to left. Add each column in turn, making sure to carry the number to the left if a column adds up to more than 9. The same rules apply to the subtraction of decimals.

Review Video: Adding and Subtracting Decimals
Visit mometrix.com/academy and enter code: 381101

MULTIPLYING DECIMALS

A simple multiplication problem has two components: a multiplicand and a multiplier. When multiplying decimals, work as though the numbers were whole rather than decimals. Once the final product is calculated, count the number of places to the right of the decimal in both the multiplicand and the multiplier. Then, count that number of places from the right of the product and place the decimal in that position.

For example, 12.3 × 2.56 has three places to the right of the respective decimals. Multiply 123 × 256 to get 31488. Now, beginning on the right, count three places to the left and insert the decimal. The final product will be 31.488.

Review Video: Multiplying Decimals
Visit mometrix.com/academy and enter code: 731574

DIVIDING DECIMALS

Every division problem has a divisor and a dividend. The dividend is the number that is being divided. In the problem 14 ÷ 7, 14 is the dividend and 7 is the divisor. In a division problem with decimals, the divisor must be converted into a whole number. Begin by moving the decimal in the divisor to the right until a whole number is created. Next, move the decimal in the dividend the same number of spaces to the right. For example, 4.9 into 24.5 would become 49 into 245. The decimal was moved one space to the right to create a whole number in the divisor, and then the same was done for the dividend. Once the whole numbers are created, the problem is carried out normally: $245 \div 49 = 5$.

Review Video: Dividing Decimals
Visit mometrix.com/academy and enter code: 560690

Operations with Positive & Negative Numbers

Addition

When adding signed numbers, if the signs are the same simply add the absolute values of the addends and apply the original sign to the sum. For example, $(+4) + (+8) = +12$ and $(-4) + (-8) = -12$. When the original signs are different, take the absolute values of the addends and subtract the smaller value from the larger value, then apply the original sign of the larger value to the difference. For instance, $(+4) + (-8) = -4$ and $(-4) + (+8) = +4$.

Subtraction

For subtracting signed numbers, change the sign of the number after the minus symbol and then follow the same rules used for addition. For example, $(+4)-(+8) = (+4) + (-8) = -4$.

Multiplication

If the signs are the same the product is positive when multiplying signed numbers. For example, $(+4) \times (+8) = +32$ and $(-4) \times (-8) = +32$. If the signs are opposite, the product is negative. For example, $(+4) \times (-8) = -32$ and $(-4) \times (+8) = -32$. When more than two factors are multiplied together, the sign of the product is determined by how many negative factors are present. If there are an odd number of negative factors then the product is negative, whereas an even number of negative factors indicates a positive product. For instance, $(+4) \times (-8) \times (-2) = +64$ and $(-4) \times (-8) \times (-2) = -64$.

Division

The rules for dividing signed numbers are similar to multiplying signed numbers. If the dividend and divisor have the same sign, the quotient is positive. If the dividend and divisor have opposite signs, the quotient is negative. For example, $(-4) \div (+8) = -0.5$.

Percentages

Percentages can be thought of as fractions that are based on a whole of 100; that is, one whole is equal to 100%. The word percent means "per hundred." Fractions can be expressed as percents by finding equivalent fractions with a denomination of 100. Example: $\frac{7}{10} = \frac{70}{100} = 70\%$; $\frac{1}{4} = \frac{25}{100} = 25\%$.

To express a percentage as a fraction, divide the percentage number by 100 and reduce the fraction to its simplest possible terms. Example: $60\% = \frac{60}{100} = \frac{3}{5}$; $96\% = \frac{96}{100} = \frac{24}{25}$.

Converting decimals to percentages and percentages to decimals is as simple as moving the decimal point. To convert from a decimal to a percent, move the decimal point two places to the right. To convert from a percent to a decimal, move it two places to the left. Example: 0.23 = 23%; 5.34 = 534%; 0.007 = 0.7%; 700% = 7.00; 86% = 0.86; 0.15% = 0.0015.

It may be helpful to remember that the percentage number will always be larger than the equivalent decimal number.

A percentage problem can be presented three main ways: (1) Find what percentage of some number another number is. Example: What percentage of 40 is 8? (2) Find what number is some percentage of a given number. Example: What number is 20% of 40? (3) Find what number another number is a given percentage of. Example: What number is 8 20% of? The three components in all of these cases are the same: a whole (W), a part (P), and a percentage (%). These are related by the equation: P = W × %. This is the form of the equation you would use to solve problems of type (2). To solve types (1) and (3), you would use these two forms: % = P/W and W = P/%.

The thing that frequently makes percentage problems difficult is that they are most often also word problems, so a large part of solving them is figuring out which quantities are what. Example: In a school cafeteria, 7 students choose pizza, 9 choose hamburgers, and 4 choose tacos. Find the percentage that chooses tacos. To find the whole, you must first add all of the parts: 7 + 9 + 4 = 20. The percentage can then be found by dividing the part by the whole (% = P/W): $\frac{4}{20} = \frac{20}{100} = 20\%$.

Review Video: Percentages
Visit mometrix.com/academy and enter code: 141911

Factors and Multiples

Factors are numbers that are multiplied together to obtain a product. For example, in the equation 2 × 3 = 6, the numbers 2 and 3 are factors. A prime number has only two factors (1 and itself), but other numbers can have many factors.

A common factor is a number that divides exactly into two or more other numbers. For example, the factors of 12 are 1, 2, 3, 4, 6, and 12, while the factors of 15 are 1, 3, 5, and 15. The common factors of 12 and 15 are 1 and 3.

A prime factor is also a prime number. Therefore, the prime factors of 12 are 1, 2, and 3. For 15, the prime factors are 1, 3, and 5.

Review Video: Factors
Visit mometrix.com/academy and enter code: 920086

The *greatest common factor* (GCF) is the largest number that is a factor of two or more numbers. For example, the factors of 15 are 1, 3, 5, and 15; the factors of 35 are 1, 5, 7, and 35. Therefore, the greatest common factor of 15 and 35 is 5.

The least common multiple (LCM) is the smallest number that is a multiple of two or more numbers. For example, the multiples of 3 include 3, 6, 9, 12, 15, etc.; the multiples of 5 include 5, 10, 15, 20, etc. Therefore, the least common multiple of 3 and 5 is 15.

Review Video: Multiples
Visit mometrix.com/academy and enter code: 626738

Ratios

A ratio is a comparison of two quantities in a particular order. Example: If there are 14 computers in a lab, and the class has 20 students, there is a student to computer ratio of 20 to 14, commonly written as 20:14.

Two more comparisons used frequently in algebra are ratios and proportions. A *Ratio* is a comparison of two quantities, expressed in a number of different ways. Ratios can be listed as "a to b", "a:b", or "a/b". Examples of ratios are miles per hour (miles/hour), meters per second (meters/second), miles per gallon (miles/gallon), etc.

Review Video: Ratios
Visit mometrix.com/academy and enter code: 996914

Proportions and Cross Products

A proportion is a relationship between two quantities that dictates how one changes when the other changes. A direct proportion describes a relationship in which a quantity increases by a set amount for every increase in the other quantity, or decreases by that same amount for every decrease in the other quantity. Example: For every 1 sheet cake, 18 people can be served cake. The number of sheet cakes, and the number of people that can be served from them is directly proportional.

A statement of two equal ratios is a *Proportion*, such as $\frac{m}{b} = \frac{w}{z}$. If Fred travels 2 miles in 1 hour and Jane travels 4 miles in 2 hours, their speeds are said to be proportional because $\frac{2}{1} = \frac{4}{2}$. In a proportion, the product of the numerator of the first ratio and the denominator of the second ratio is equal to the product of the denominator of the first ratio and the numerator of the second ratio. Using the previous example, we see that $m \times z = b \times w$, thus $2 \times 2 = 1 \times 4$.

Review Video: Proportions
Visit mometrix.com/academy and enter code: 505355

Inverse proportion is a relationship in which an increase in one quantity is accompanied by a decrease in the other, or vice versa. Example: the time required for a car trip decreases as the speed increases, and increases as the speed decreases, so the time required is inversely proportional to the speed of the car.

Roots and Square Roots

A root, such as a square root, is another way of writing a fractional exponent. Instead of using a superscript, roots use the radical symbol ($\sqrt{\ }$) to indicate the operation. A radical will have a number underneath the bar, and may sometimes have a number in the upper left: $\sqrt[n]{a}$, read as "the nth root of a."

The relationship between radical notation and exponent notation can be described by this equation: $\sqrt[n]{a} = a^{1/n}$. The two special cases of n = 2 and n = 3 are called square roots and cube roots. If there is no number to the upper left, it is understood to be a square root (n = 2). Nearly all of the roots you encounter will be square roots. A square root is the same as a number raised to the one-half power. When we say that a is the square root of b ($a = \sqrt{b}$), we mean that a multiplied by itself equals b: ($a \times a = b$).

A perfect square is a number that has an integer for its square root. There are 10 perfect squares from 1 to 100: 1, 4, 9, 16, 25, 36, 49, 64, 81, 100 (the squares of integers 1 through 10).

Coefficients and the Distributive Property

Coefficients

A coefficient is a number or symbol that is multiplied by a variable. For example, in the expression 2(ab), the number 2 is the coefficient of (ab). The expression can be written in other ways to have a different coefficient. For example, the expression can be 2a(b). This means that 2a is the coefficient of (b).

Distributive Property

The distributive property can be used to multiply each addend in parentheses. Then, the products are added to reach the result. The formula for the distributive property looks like this: $a(b+c) = ab+ac$.

Example: 6(2+4)

First, multiply 6 and 2. The answer is 12.

Then, multiply 6 and 4. The answer is 24.

Last, we add 12 and 24. The final answer is 36.

Scientific Notation

Scientific notation is a way of writing long numbers in a shorter form. The form $a \times 10^n$ is used in scientific notation. This form means that *a* is greater than or equal to 1 but less than 10. Also, *n* is the number of places the decimal must move to get from the original number to *a*.

Example: The number 230,400,000 is long to write. To see this value in scientific notation, place a decimal point between the first and second numbers. This includes all digits through the last non-zero digit (a = 2.304).

To find the correct power of 10, count the number of places the decimal point had to move (n = 8). The number is positive if the decimal moved to the left. Thus, the number is negative if it moved to the right. So, 230,400,000 can be written as 2.304×10^8.

Now, let's look at the number 0.00002304. We have the same value for *a*. However, this time the decimal moved 5 places to the right (n = -5). So, 0.00002304 can be written as 2.304×10^{-5}. This notation makes it easy to compare very large or very small numbers. By comparing exponents, you can see that 3.28×10^4 is smaller than 1.51×10^5 because 4 is less than 5.

Addition and Subtraction

To add and subtract numbers in scientific notation, you need the numbers to have the same power of 10. Next, you can add the constants. Then, you can use the power of 10 with the result.

If the constant is greater than 10 or less than 1, you need to move the decimal place. For constants less than 1, the decimal is moved to the right. For constants greater than 10, the decimal is moved to the left. Also, the power of 10 needs to change as you move the decimal place.

Example 1

In the problem $(4.8 \times 10^4) + (2.2 \times 10^4)$, the numbers have the same power of 10. So, add 4.8 and 2.2. So, you have 7 as the result. Now, the number can be written as (7×10^4).

Example 2

In the problem $(3.1 \times 10^8) - (2.4 \times 10^8)$, the numbers have the same power of 10. So, subtract 3.1 and 2.4, and you'll have 0.7 as the result. Remember that you cannot have a constant that is less than 1. So, you need to move the decimal place one time to the right: (7×10^8). Also, the power of 10 has to change. Now, the number can be written as (7×10^{-1}).

The power of 10 is -1 because we moved the decimal place one time to the right. Now you have $(7 \times 10^{-1}) \times 10^8$. The reason is that we still have the power of 10 as 8. Now, you can add the -1 to the +8 for an answer of (7×10^7).

Example 3

In the problem$(5.3 \times 10^6) + (2.7 \times 10^7)$, the numbers do not have the same power of 10. So, you need one of the terms to have the same power. So, take (5.3×10^6) and change it to (0.53×10^7). Now, you can add 0.53 and 2.7. So, the number can be written as (3.23×10^7).

Multiplication

In the problem $(2.4 \times 10^3) \times (5.7 \times 10^5)$, you need to multiply 2.4 and 5.7. Then, you need to add the powers of 10 which are 3 and 5 for this example. So, you have (13.68×10^8). Remember that this cannot be an answer for scientific notation. The 13.68 for a constant is higher than 10. So, move the decimal to the left one time and change the exponent. Now, you have (1.368×10^9) as the answer.

Division

In the problem $(5.6 \times 10^6) \div (2.3 \times 10^2)$, you need to divide 5.6 and 2.3. Then, you need to subtract the powers of 10 which are 6 and 2 for this example. So, you have (2.43×10^4).

Algebra

Important Concepts

Substitute an Integer

Polynomial Expressions

Solve the expression $(x^2+4)+(3x^2+4x+2)$, when x=5.

First, substitute in 5 for each occurrence of x: $(5^2 + 4) + (3(5)^2 + 4(5) + 2) =$

Second, solve the parentheses: $(29) + (97) =$

Third, add 29 and 97: $29 + 97 = 126$

Linear Expressions

Solve the expression $(x - 4) + (4x + 10)$, when x=6.

First, put in 6 for every x: $(6 - 4) + (4(6) + 10)$

Second, solve the parentheses: $(2) + (34) =$

Third, add 2 and 34: $(2) + (34) = 36$

Rational Expressions

Solve the expression: $\frac{x+7}{10-x}$, when x=9

First, put in 9 for every x: $\frac{9+7}{10-9}$

Second, solve the numerator and the denominator: $\frac{16}{1}$

Third, divide 16 and 1: $\frac{16}{1}$=16.

Writing an Expression from Word-to-Symbol

To write an expression, you must first put variables with the unknown values in the problem. Then, translate the words and phrases into expressions that have numbers and symbols.

Inequalities

To write out an inequality, you may need to translate a sentence into an inequality. This translation is putting the words into symbols. When translating, choose a variable to stand for the unknown value. Then, change the words or phrases into symbols. For example, the sum of 2 and a number is at most 12. So, you would write: $2 + b \leq 12$.

Example: A farm sells vegetables and dairy products. One third of the sales from dairy products plus half of the sales from vegetables should be greater than the monthly payment (*P*) for the farm.

Let *d* stand for the sales from dairy products. Let *v* stand for the sales from vegetables. One third of the sales from dairy products is the expression $\frac{d}{3}$. One half of the sales from vegetables is the expression $\frac{v}{2}$. The sum of these expressions should be greater than the monthly payment for the farm. An inequality for this is $\frac{d}{3} + \frac{v}{2} > P$.

Rational Expressions

John and Luke play basketball every week. John can make 5 free throws per minute faster than Luke can make three-point shots. On one day, John made 30 free throws in the same time that it took Luke to make 20 three-point shots. So, how fast are Luke and John scoring points?

First, set up what you know. You know that John made 30 free throws, and he had a rate of 5 free throws per minute faster than Luke's three-point shots: $\frac{30}{x+5}$. The x is for Luke's speed. Also, you know that Luke made 20 three-point shots in the same amount of time that John scored his free throws: $\frac{20}{x}$. So, we can set up proportions because their times are equal.

$$\frac{30}{x+5} = \frac{20}{x}$$

Cross factor the proportion: $30x = 20(x + 5)$

Then distribute the 20 across the values in the parentheses: $30x = 20x + 100$

Now you can subtract 20x from both sides of the equation, and you are left with: $10x = 100$

Divide both sides by 10: $\frac{10x}{10} = \frac{100}{10}$

Now you are left with: $x = 10$. So Luke's speed was 10 three-point shots per minute and John's speed was 15 free throws per minute.

Review Video: Rational Expressions
Visit mometrix.com/academy and enter code: 415183

Polynomial Expressions

Fred buys some CDs for $12 each. He also buys two DVDs. The total that Fred spent is $60. Write an equation that shows the connection between the number of CDs and the average cost of a DVD.

Let *c* stand for the number of CDs that Fred buys. Also, let *d* stand for the average cost of one of the DVDs that Fred buys. The expression $12c$ gives the cost of the CDs and the expression $2d$ gives the cost of the DVDs. So the equation $12c + 2d = 60$ states the number of CDs and the average cost of a DVD.

Solve Equations in One Variable

Manipulating Equations

Sometimes you will have variables missing in equations. So, you need to find the missing variable. To do this, you need to remember one important thing: whatever you do to one side of an equation, you need to do to the other side. If you subtract 100 from one side of an equation, you need to subtract 100 from the other side of the equation. This will allow you to change the form of the equation to find missing values.

Example

Ray earns $10 an hour. This can be given with the expression $10x$, where *x* is equal to the number of hours that Ray works. This is the independent variable. The independent variable is the amount that can change. The money that Ray earns is in *y* hours. So, you would write the equation: $10x = y$. The variable *y* is the dependent variable. This depends on *x* and cannot be changed. Now, let's say that Ray makes $360. How many hours did he work to make $360?

$$10x = 360$$

Now, you want to know how many hours that Ray worked. So, you want to get x by itself. To do that, you can divide both sides of the equation by 10.

$$\frac{10x}{10} = \frac{360}{10}$$

So, you have: $x = 36$. Now, you know that Ray worked 36 hours to make $360.

Solving One Variable Linear Equations

Another way to write an equation is $ax + b = 0$ where $a \neq 0$. This is known as a *One Variable Linear Equation*. A solution to an equation is called a *Root*.

Example: $5x + 10 = 0$

If we solve for x, the solution is $x = -2$. In other words, the root of the equation is -2.

The first step is to subtract 10 from both sides. This gives $5x = -10$.

Next, divide both sides by the coefficient of the variable. For this example, that is 5. So, you should have $x = -2$. You can make sure that you have the correct answer by placing -2 back into the original equation. So, the equation now looks like this: $(5)(-2) + 10 = -10 + 10 = 0$.

The *Solution Set* is the set of all solutions to an equation. In the last example, the solution set would be -2. If there were more solutions, then they would also be included in the solution set. Usually, there are more solutions in multivariable equations. When an equation has no true solutions, this is known as an *Empty Set*. Equations with identical solution sets are *Equivalent Equations*. An *Identity* is a term whose value or determinant is equal to 1.

To solve a *Radical Equation*, start by placing the radical term on one side of the equation by itself. Then, move all other terms to the other side of the equation. Look at the index of the radical symbol. Remember, if no number is given, then you have a square root. Raise both sides of the equation to the power equal to the index of the radical. Solve the equation as you would a normal polynomial equation. When you have found the roots, you must check them in the original problem to remove any remaining roots.

Data Interpretation

Statistics

Statistics is the branch of mathematics that deals with collecting, recording, interpreting, illustrating, and analyzing large amounts of data. The following terms are often used in the discussion of data and statistics:

- **Data**: the collective name for pieces of information (singular is datum).
- **Quantitative data**: measurements (such as length, mass, and speed) that provide information about quantities in numbers
- **Qualitative data**: information (such as colors, scents, tastes, and shapes) that cannot be measured using numbers
- **Discrete data**: information that can be expressed only by a specific value, such as whole or half numbers; For example, since people can be counted only in whole numbers, a population count would be discrete data.
- **Continuous data**: information (such as time and temperature) that can be expressed by any value within a given range
- **Primary data**: information that has been collected directly from a survey, investigation, or experiment, such as a questionnaire or the recording of daily temperatures; Primary data that has not yet been organized or analyzed is called raw data.
- **Secondary data**: information that has been collected, sorted, and processed by the researcher
- **Ordinal data**: information that can be placed in numerical order, such as age or weight
- **Nominal data**: information that cannot be placed in numerical order, such as names or places.

Measures of Central Tendency

The quantities of mean, median, and mode are all referred to as measures of central tendency. They can each give a picture of what the whole set of data looks like with just a single number. Knowing what each of these values represents is vital to making use of the information they provide.

The mean, also known as the arithmetic mean or average, of a data set is calculated by summing all of the values in the set and dividing that sum by the number of values. For example, if a data set has 6 numbers and the sum of those 6 numbers is 30, the mean is calculated as $30/6 = 5$.

The median is the middle value of a data set. The median can be found by putting the data set in numerical order, and locating the middle value. In the data set (1, 2, 3, 4, 5), the median is 3. If there is an even number of values in the set, the median is calculated by taking the average of the two middle values. In the data set, (1, 2, 3, 4, 5, 6), the median would be $(3 + 4)/2 = 3.5$.

The mode is the value that appears most frequently in the data set. In the data set (1, 2, 3, 4, 5, 5, 5), the mode would be 5 since the value 5 appears three times. If multiple values appear the same number of times, there are multiple values for the mode. If the data set were (1, 2, 2, 3, 4, 4, 5, 5), the modes would be 2, 4, and 5. If no value appears more than any other value in the data set, then there is no mode.

Measures of Dispersion

The standard deviation expresses how spread out the values of a distribution are from the mean. Standard deviation is given in the same units as the original data and is represented by a lower-case sigma (σ). A high standard deviation means that the values are very spread out. A low standard deviation means that the values are close together.

If every value in a distribution is increased or decreased by the same amount, the mean, median, and mode are increased or decreased by that amount, but the standard deviation stays the same. If every value in a distribution is multiplied or divided by the same number, the mean, median, mode, and standard deviation will all be multiplied or divided by that number.

The range of a distribution is the difference between the highest and lowest values in the distribution. For example, in the data set (1, 3, 5, 7, 9, 11), the highest and lowest values are 11 and 1, respectively. The range then would be calculated as 11 – 1 = 10.

The three quartiles are the three values that divide a data set into four equal parts. Quartiles are generally only calculated for data sets with a large number of values. As a simple example, for the data set consisting of the numbers 1 through 99, the first quartile (Q1) would be 25, the second quartile (Q2), always equal to the median, would be 50, and the third quartile (Q3) would be 75. The difference between Q1 and Q3 is known as the interquartile range.

PROBABILITY

Probability is a branch of statistics that deals with the likelihood of something taking place. One classic example is a coin toss. There are only two possible results: heads or tails. The likelihood, or probability, that the coin will land as heads is 1 out of 2 (1/2, 0.5, 50%). Tails has the same probability. Another common example is a 6-sided die roll. There are six possible results from rolling a single die, each with an equal chance of happening, so the probability of any given number coming up is 1 out of 6.

Review Video: Intro to Probability
Visit mometrix.com/academy and enter code: 212374

Terms frequently used in probability:

Event: a situation that produces results of some sort (a coin toss)

Compound event: event that involves two or more items (rolling a pair of dice; taking the sum)

Outcome: a possible result in an experiment or event (heads, tails)

Desired outcome (or success): an outcome that meets a particular set of criteria (a roll of 1 or 2 if we are looking for numbers less than 3)

Independent events: two or more events whose outcomes do not affect one another (two coins tossed at the same time)

Dependent events: two or more events whose outcomes affect one another (two cards drawn consecutively from the same deck)

Certain outcome: probability of outcome is 100% or 1

Impossible outcome: probability of outcome is 0% or 0

Mutually exclusive outcomes: two or more outcomes whose criteria cannot all be satisfied in a single outcome (a coin coming up heads and tails on the same toss)

Theoretical probability is the likelihood of a certain outcome occurring for a given event. It can be determined without actually performing the event. It is calculated as P (probability of success) = (desired outcomes)/(total outcomes).

Example:

There are 20 marbles in a bag and 5 are red. The theoretical probability of randomly selecting a red marble is 5 out of 20, (5/20 = 1/4, 0.25, or 25%).

Most of the time, when we talk about probability, we mean theoretical probability. Experimental probability, or relative frequency, is the number of times an outcome occurs in a particular experiment or a certain number of observed events.

While theoretical probability is based on what *should* happen, experimental probability is based on what *has* happened. Experimental probability is calculated in the same way as theoretical, except that actual outcomes are used instead of possible outcomes.

Theoretical and experimental probability do not always line up with one another. Theoretical probability says that out of 20 coin tosses, 10 should be heads. However, if we were actually to toss 20 coins, we might record just 5 heads. This doesn't mean that our theoretical probability is incorrect; it just means that this particular experiment had results that were different from what was predicted.

Review Video: Theoretical and Experimental Probability
Visit mometrix.com/academy and enter code: 444349

DISPLAYING DATA

BAR GRAPH

A bar graph is a graph that uses bars to compare data, as if each bar were a ruler being used to measure the data. The graph includes a scale that identifies the units being measured.

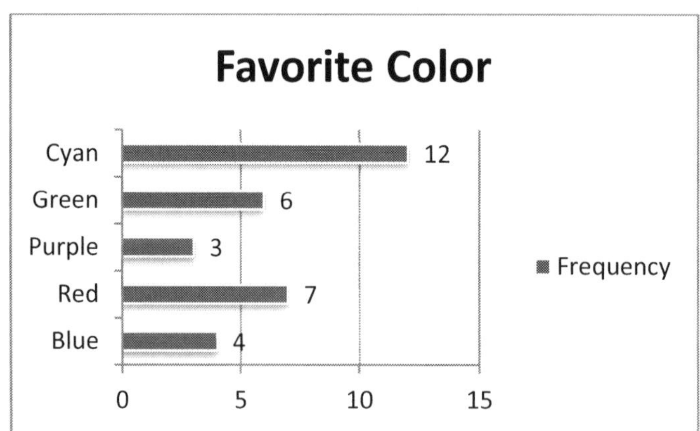

LINE GRAPH

A line graph is a graph that connects points to show how data increases or decreases over time. The time line is the horizontal axis. The connecting lines between data points on the graph are a way to more clearly show how the data changes.

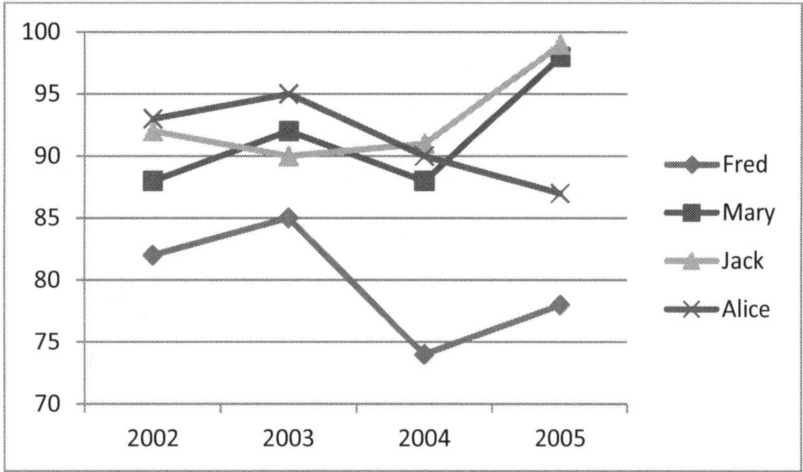

PIE CHART

A pie chart or circle graph is a diagram used to compare parts of a whole. The full pie represents the whole, and it is divided into sectors that each represent something that is a part of the whole. Each sector or slice of the pie is either labeled to indicate what it represents, or explained on a key associated with the chart. The size of each slice is determined by the percentage of the whole that the associated quantity represents. Numerically, the angle measurement of each sector can be computed by solving the proportion: $x/360 = \text{part/whole}$.

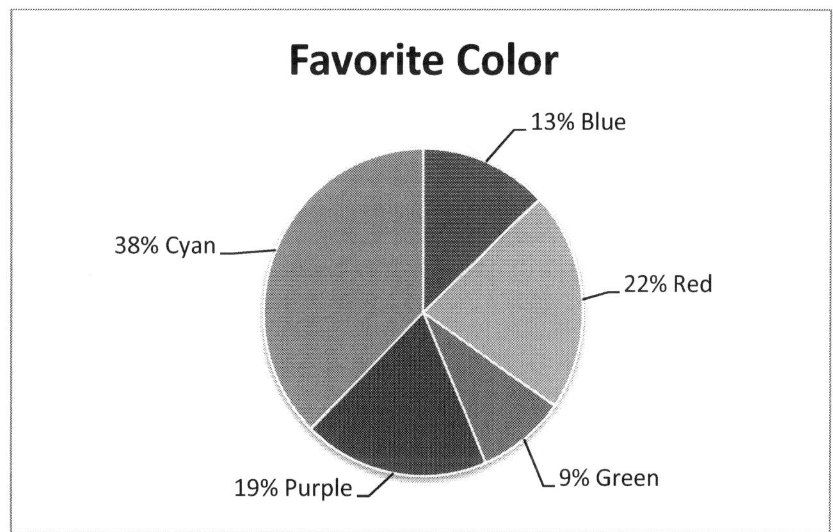

HISTOGRAM

A histogram is a special type of bar graph where the data are grouped in intervals (for example 20–29, 30–39, 40–49, etc.). The frequency, or number of times a value occurs in each interval, is indicated by the height of the bar. The intervals do not have to be the same amount but usually are (all data in ranges of 10 or all in ranges of 5, for example). The smaller the intervals, the more detailed the information.

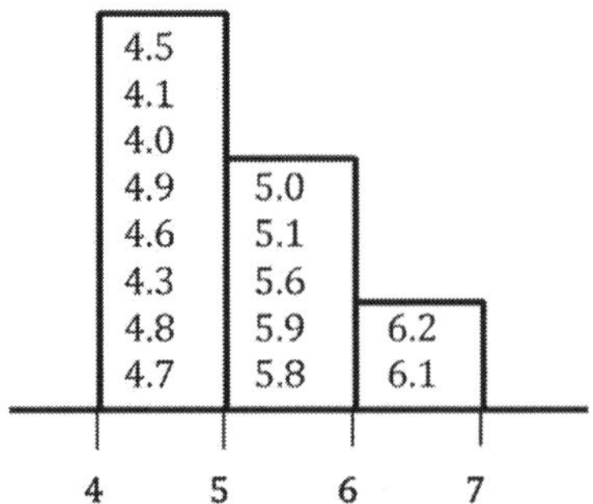

Stem and Leaf Plot

A *Stem and Leaf Plot* can outline groups of data that fall into a range of values. Each piece of data is split into two parts: the first, or left, part is called the stem. The second, or right, part is called the leaf. Each stem is listed in a column from smallest to largest. Each leaf that has the common stem is listed in that stem's row from smallest to largest.

For example, in a set of two-digit numbers, the digit in the tens place is the stem. So, the digit in the ones place is the leaf. With a stem and leaf plot, you can see which subset of numbers (10s, 20s, 30s, etc.) is the largest. This information can be found by looking at a histogram. However, a stem and leaf plot also lets you look closer and see which values fall in that range. Using all of the test scores from the line graph, we can put together a stem and leaf plot:

Test Scores									
7	4	8							
8	2	5	7	8	8				
9	0	0	1	2	2	3	5	8	9

Again, a stem-and-leaf plot is similar to histograms and frequency plots. However, a stem-and-leaf plot keeps all of the original data. In this example, you can see that almost half of the students scored in the 80s. Also, all of the data has been maintained. These plots can be used for larger numbers as well. However, they work better for small sets of data.

Scatter Plots

Scatter Plots are useful for knowing the types of functions that are given with the data. Also, they are helpful for finding the simple regression. A simple regression is a regression that uses an independent variable.

A regression is a chart that is used to predict future events. Linear scatter plots may be positive or negative. Many nonlinear scatter plots are exponential or quadratic. Below are some common types of scatter plots:

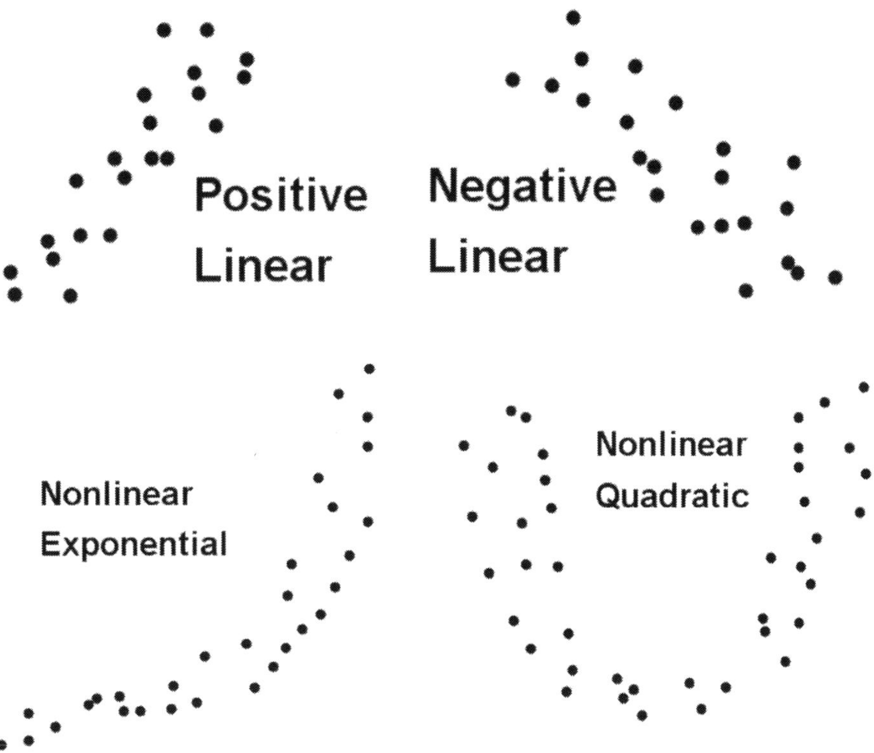

INTERPRETATION OF GRAPHS

EXAMPLE 1

The following graph shows the ages of five patients a nurse is caring for in the hospital:

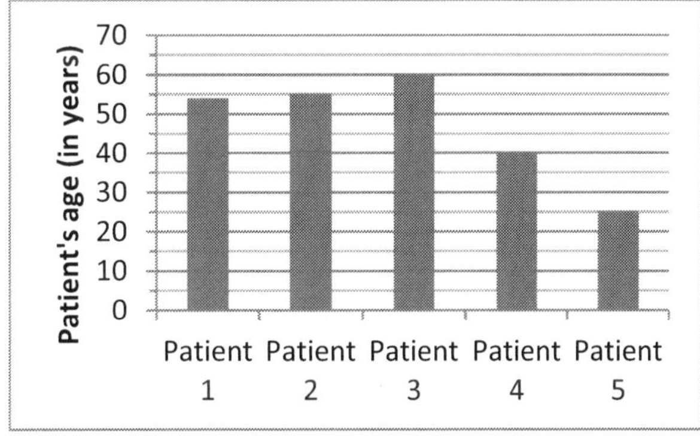

Use this graph to determine the age range of the patients for which the nurse is caring.

Use the graph to find the age of each patient: Patient 1 is 54 years old; Patient 2 is 55 years old; Patient 3 is 60 years old; Patient 4 is 40 years old; and Patient 5 is 25 years old. The age range is the age of the oldest patient minus the age of the youngest patient. In other words, 60 – 25 = 35. The age range is 35 years.

Example 2

Following is a line graph representing the heart rate of a patient during the day. Use the graph to answer the following questions:

The patient's minimum measured heart rate occurred at what time? The patient's maximum measured heart rate occurred at what time? At what times during the day did the patient have the same measured heart rate? What trends, if any, can you find about the patient's heart rate throughout the day?

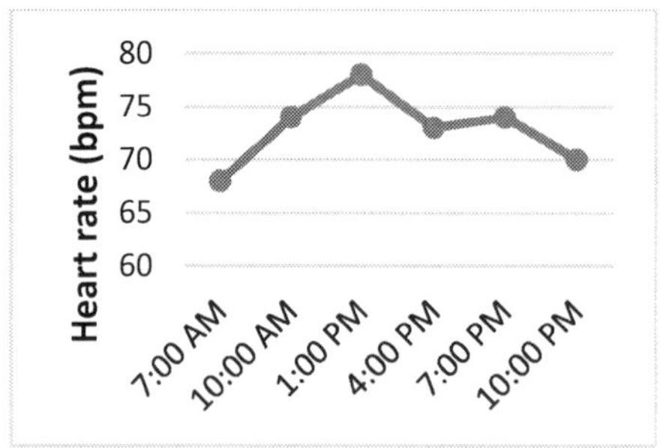

The patient's minimum measured heart rate occurred at the lowest data point on the graph, which is 68 bpm at 7:00 AM. The patient's maximum measured heart rate occurred at the highest data point on the graph, which is 78 bpm at 1:00 PM. The patient had the same measured heart rate of 74 bpm at 10:00 AM and 7:00 PM. The patient's heart rate increased through the morning to early afternoon, and generally declined as the afternoon progressed.

Data Organization

Example:

A nurse found the heart rates of eleven different patients to be 76, 80, 90, 86, 70, 76, 72, 88, 88, 68, and 88 beats per minute. Organize this information in a table.

There are several ways to organize data in a table. The table below is an example.

Patient Number	1	2	3	4	5	6	7	8	9	10	11
Heart Rate (bpm)	76	80	90	86	70	76	72	88	88	68	88

When making a table, be sure to label the columns and rows appropriately.

Consistency between Studies

Example:

In a drug study containing 100 patients, a new cholesterol drug was found to decrease low-density lipoprotein (LDL) levels in 25% of the patients. In a second study containing 50 patients, the same drug administered at the same dosage was found to decrease LDL levels in 50% of the patients. Are the results of these two studies consistent with one another?

Even though in both studies 25 people (25% of 100 is 25 and 50% of 50 is 25) showed improvements in their LDL levels, the results of the studies are inconsistent. The results of the second study indicate that the drug has a much higher efficacy (desired result) than the results of the first study. Because 50 out of 150 total patients showed improvement on the medication, one could argue that the drug is effective in one third (or approximately 33%) of patients. However, one should be wary of the reliability of results when they're not reproducible from one study to the next and when the sample size is fairly low.

Independent and Dependent Variables

A variable is a symbol, usually an alphabetic character, designating a value that may change within the scope of a given problem. Variables can be described as either independent or dependent variables. An independent variable is an input into a system that may take on values freely. Dependent variables are those that change as a consequence of changes in other values in the equation.

Example

A patient told a doctor she feels fine after running one mile but that her knee starts hurting after running two miles. Her knee throbs after running three miles and swells after running four. Identify the independent and dependent variables with regard to the distance she runs and her level of pain.

An independent variable is one that does not depend on any other variables in the situation. In this case, the distance the patient runs would be considered the independent variable. The dependent variable would be her level of pain because it depends on how far she runs.

Bivariate Data

Bivariate Data is data from two different variables. The prefix *bi-* means *two.* In a *Scatter Plot*, each value in the set of data is put on a grid. This is similar to the Cartesian plane where each axis represents one of the two variables.

When you look at the pattern made by the points on the grid, you may know if there is a relationship between the two variables. Also, you may know what that relationship is and if it exists.

The variables may be directly proportionate, inversely proportionate, or show no proportion. Also, you may be able to see if the data is linear. If the data is linear, you can find an equation to show the two variables. The following scatter plot shows the relationship between preference for brand "A" and the age of the consumers surveyed.

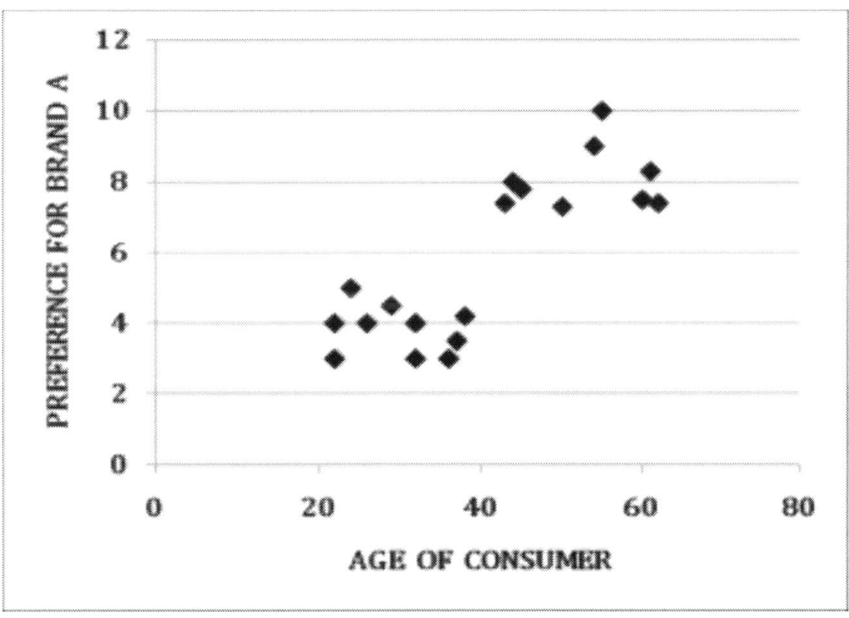

Shape of Data Distribution

Symmetry and Skewness

Symmetry is a characteristic of the shape of the plotted data. Specifically, it refers to how well the data on one side of the median mirrors the data on the other side.

A skewed data set is one that has a distinctly longer or fatter tail on one side of the peak or the other. A data set that is skewed left has more of its values to the left of the peak, while a set that is skewed right has more of its values to the right of the peak. When actually looking at the graph, these names may seem counterintuitive since, in a left-skewed data set, the bulk of the values seem to be on the right side of the graph, and vice versa. However, if the graph is viewed strictly in relation to the peak, the direction of skewness makes more sense.

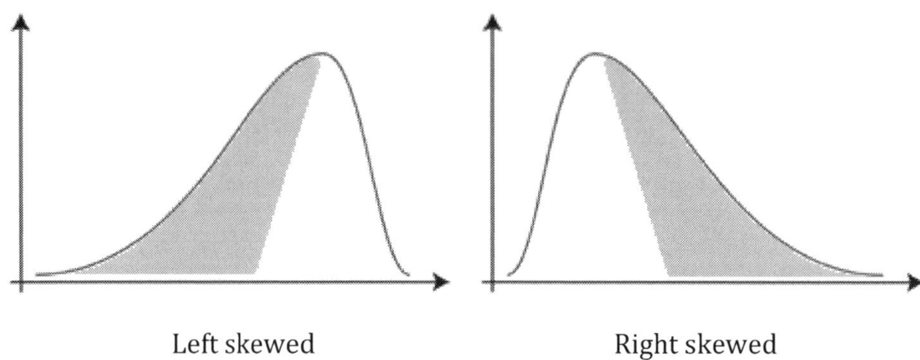

Left skewed Right skewed

Unimodal vs. Bimodal

If a distribution has a single peak, it would be considered unimodal. If it has two discernible peaks it would be considered bimodal. Bimodal distributions may be an indication that the set of data being considered is actually the combination of two sets of data with significant differences.

Uniformity

A uniform distribution is a distribution in which there is no distinct peak or variation in the data. No values or ranges are particularly more common than any other values or ranges.

United States Government

Political Study

Political Science

Political science focuses on studying different governments and how they compare to each other, general political theory, ways political theory is put into action, how nations and governments interact with each other, and a general study of governmental structure and function. Other elements of political science include the study of elections, governmental administration at various levels, development and action of political parties, and how values such as freedom, power, justice and equality are expressed in different political cultures.

Political science also encompasses elements of other disciplines, including:

- History—how historical events have shaped political thought and process
- Sociology—the effects of various stages of social development on the growth and development of government and politics
- Anthropology—the effects of governmental process on the culture of an individual group and its relationships with other groups
- Economics—how government policies regulate distribution of products and how they can control and/or influence the economy in general

Theories on the Origin of the State

Evolutionary—the state evolved from the family, with the head of state the equivalent of the family's patriarch or matriarch.

Force—one person or group of people brought everyone in an area under their control, forming the first government.

Divine Right—certain people were chosen by the prevailing deity to be the rulers of the nation, which is itself created by the deity or deities.

Social Contract—there is no natural order. The people allow themselves to be governed to maintain social order, while the state in turn promises to protect the people they govern. If the government fails to protect its people, the people have the right to seek new leaders.

Philosophers on Politics

Ancient Greek philosophers Aristotle and Plato believed political science would lead to order in political matters, and that this scientifically organized order would create stable, just societies.

Thomas Aquinas adapted the ideas of Aristotle to a Christian perspective. His ideas stated that individuals have certain rights, but also certain duties, and that these rights and duties should determine the type and extent of government rule. In stating that laws should limit the role of government, he laid the groundwork for ideas that would eventually become modern constitutionalism.

Niccolò Machiavelli, author of *The Prince*, was a proponent of politics based solely on power.

Thomas Hobbes and John Locke

Thomas Hobbes, author of *Leviathan* (1651), believed that individual's lives were focused solely on a quest for power, and that the state must work to control this urge. Hobbes felt that people were completely unable to live harmoniously without the intervention of government.

John Locke wrote *Two Treatises of Civil Government* in 1690. This work argued against the ideas of Thomas Hobbes. He put forth the theory of *tabula rasa*—that people are born with minds that are a blank slate. Experience molds individual minds, not innate knowledge or intuition. He also believed that all men are essentially good, as well as independent and equal. Many of Locke's ideas found their way into the Constitution of the United States.

Montesquieu and Rousseau

These two French philosophers heavily influenced the French Revolution (1789-1815). They believed government policies and ideas should change to alleviate existing problems, an idea referred to as "liberalism." Rousseau in particular directly influenced the Revolution with writings such as *The Social Contract* (1762), *Declaration of the Rights of Man,* and *The Citizen* (1789). Other ideas Rousseau and Montesquieu espoused included:

- Individual freedom and community welfare are of equal importance
- Man's innate goodness leads to natural harmony
- Reason develops with the rise of civilized society
- Individual citizens carry certain obligations to the existing government

18th and 19th Century Philosophers

Hume and Bentham believed politics should have as its main goal maintaining "the greatest happiness of the greatest number." Hume also believed in empiricism, or that ideas should not be believed until the proof has been observed. He was a natural skeptic, as well, and always sought out the truth of matters himself rather than believing what he was told.

John Stuart Mill, a British philosopher as well as an economist, believed in progressive policies such as women's suffrage, emancipation, and the development of labor organizations and farming cooperatives. Fichte and Hegel were eighteenth century German philosophers who supported a form of liberalism grounded largely in socialism and a sense of nationalism.

Types of Government

Anarchism, Communism and Dictatorship

Anarchists believe that all government should be eliminated and that individuals should rule themselves. Historically, anarchists have used violence and assassination to further their beliefs.

Communism is based on class conflict, revolution and a one-party state. Ideally, a communist government would involve a single government for the entire world. Communist government controls the production and flow of goods and services rather than leaving this to companies or individuals.

Dictatorship involves rule by a single individual. If rule is enforced by a small group, this is referred to as an oligarchy. Few benevolent dictatorships have existed. Dictators tend to rule with a violent hand, using a highly repressive police force to ensure control over the populace.

Fascism and Monarchy

Fascism centers on a single leader and is, ideologically, an oppositional belief to Communism. Fascism includes a single party state and centralized control. The power of the fascist leader lies in the "cult of personality," and the fascist state often focuses on expansion and conquering of other nations.

Monarchy was the major form of government for Europe through most of its history. A monarchy is led by a king or a queen. This position is hereditary, and the rulers are not elected. In modern times, constitutional monarchy has developed, where the king and queen still exist but most of the governmental decisions are made by democratic institutions such as a parliament.

Presidential System and Socialism

A Presidential System, like a parliamentary system, has a legislature and political parties, but there is no difference between the head of state and the head of government. Instead of separating these functions, an elected president performs both. Election of the president can be direct or indirect, and the president may not necessarily belong to the largest political party.

In Socialism, the state controls production of goods, though it does not necessarily own all means of production. The state also provides a variety of social services to citizens and helps guide the economy. A democratic form of government often exists in socialist countries.

Totalitarian and Authoritarian Systems of Government

A totalitarian system believes everything should be under the control of the government, from resource production to the press to religion and other social institutions. All aspects of life under a totalitarian system must conform to the ideals of the government.

Authoritarian governments practices widespread state authority, but do not necessarily dismantle all public institutions. If a church, for example, exists as an organization but poses no threat to the authority of the state, an authoritarian government might leave it as it is. While all totalitarian governments are by definition authoritarian, a government can be authoritarian without becoming totalitarian.

> **Review Video: Totalitarianism vs. Authoritarianism**
> Visit mometrix.com/academy and enter code: 104046

Parliamentary and Democratic Systems of Government

In a parliamentary system, government involves a legislature and a variety of political parties. The head of government, usually a Prime Minister, is typically the head of the dominant party. A head of state can be elected, or this position can be taken by a monarch, such as in Great Britain's constitutional monarchy system.

In a democratic system of government, the people elect their government representatives. The term democracy is a Greek term that means "for the rule of the people." There are two forms of democracy—direct and indirect. In a direct democracy, each issue or election is decided by a vote where each individual is counted separately. An indirect democracy employs a legislature that votes on issues that affect large number of people whom the legislative members represent. Democracy can exist as a Parliamentary system or a Presidential system. The US is a presidential, indirect democracy.

Realism, Liberalism, Institutionalism, and Constructivism

The theory of realism states that nations are by nature aggressive, and work in their own self-interest. Relations between nations are determined by military and economic strength. The nation is seen as the highest authority.

Liberalism believes states can cooperate, and that they act based on capabilities rather than power. This term was originally coined to describe Woodrow Wilson's theories on international cooperation.

In institutionalism, institutions provide structure and incentive for cooperation among nations. Institutions are defined as a set of rules used to make international decisions. These institutions also help distribute power and determine how nations will interact.

Constructivism, like liberalism, is based on international cooperation, but recognizes that perceptions countries have of each other can affect their relations.

Principles of U.S. Government

Important Terms

Federalism: the power of the government does not belong entirely to the national government, but is divided between national and state governments.

Popular sovereignty: the government is determined by the people, and gains its authority and power from the people.

Separation of powers: the government is divided into three branches, executive, legislative and judicial, with each branch having its own set of powers.

Judicial review: courts at all levels of government can declare laws invalid if they contradict the constitutions of individual states, or the US Constitution, with the Supreme Court serving as the final judicial authority on decisions of this kind.

Checks and balances: no single branch can act without input from another, and each branch has the power to "check" any other, as well as balance other branches' powers.

Limited government: governmental powers are limited and certain individual rights are defined as inviolable by the government.

Federalism

Debate on how federalism should function in practice has gone on since the period when the Constitution was being written. There were—and still are—two main factions regarding this issue:

1. States' rights—those favoring the states' rights position feel that the state governments should take the lead in performing local actions to manage various problems.
2. Nationalist—those favoring a nationalist position feel the national government should take the lead to deal with those same matters.

The flexibility of the Constitution has allowed US government to shift and adapt as the needs of the country have changed. Power has often shifted from the state governments to the national government and back again, and both levels of government have developed various ways to influence each other.

Federalism has three major effects on public policy in the US.

1. Determining whether the local, state or national government originates policy
2. Affecting how policies are made
3. Ensuring policy-making functions under a set of limitations

Federalism also influences the political balance of power in the US by:

1. making it difficult if not impossible for a single political party to seize total power.
2. ensuring that individuals can participate in the political system at various levels.
3. making it possible for individuals working within the system to be able to affect policy at some level, whether local or more widespread.

Powers Delegated to the National Government by the US Constitution

The structure of the US government divides powers between national and state governments. Powers delegated to the national government by the Constitution are:

1. Expressed powers—powers directly defined in the Constitution, including power to declare war, regulate commerce, make money, and collect taxes.
2. Implied powers—powers the national government must have in order to carry out the expressed powers.
3. Inherent powers—powers inherent to any government. These powers are not expressly defined in the constitution.

Some of these powers, such as collection and levying of taxes, are also granted to the individual state governments.

Branches of the US Federal Government

Legislative Branch

The Legislative Branch consists of the two Houses of Congress: the House of Representatives and the Senate. All members of the Legislative Branch are elected officials. The Legislative Branch is largely concerned with law-making. All laws must be approved by Congress before they go into effect. They are also responsible for regulating money and trade, approving presidential appointments, and establishing organizations like the postal service and federal courts. Congress can also propose amendments to the Constitution, and can impeach, or bring charges against, the president. Only Congress can declare war.

Executive Branch

The Executive Branch consists of the President, Vice President, presidential advisors, and other various cabinet members. These advisors are appointed by the President, but must be approved by Congress. The Executive Branch carries out laws, treaties, and war declarations enacted by Congress. The President can also veto bills approved by Congress, and serves as commander-in-chief of the US military. The president appoints cabinet members, ambassadors to foreign countries, and federal judges.

Judicial Branch

The Judicial Branch is made up of the federal court system, headed by the Supreme Court. The Judicial Branch makes decisions on challenges as to whether laws passed by Congress meet the requirements of the US Constitution. The Supreme Court may also choose to review decisions made by lower courts to determine their constitutionality.

Supreme Court

When the Founding Fathers wrote in the Declaration of Independence that "all men are created equal," they meant "men," and, in fact, defined citizens as white men who owned land. However, as the country has developed and changed, the definition has expanded to more wholly include all people. "Equality" does not mean all people are inherently the same, but it does mean they all should be granted the same rights and should be treated the same by the government. Amendments to the Constitution have granted citizenship and voting rights to all Americans. The Supreme Court evaluates various laws and court decisions to determine if they properly represent the idea of equal protection. One sample case was Brown v. Board of Education, in 1954, which declared separate-but-equal to be unconstitutional.

Citizenship and the Bill of Rights

QUALIFICATIONS OF A U.S. CITIZEN

Anyone born in the US, born abroad to a US citizen, or who has gone through a process of naturalization to become a citizen, is considered a citizen of the United States. It is possible to lose US citizenship as a result of conviction of certain crimes such as treason. Citizenship may also be lost if a citizen pledges an oath to another country or serves in the military of a country engaged in hostilities with the US. A US citizen can also choose to hold dual citizenship, work as an expatriate in another country without losing US citizenship, or even to renounce citizenship if he or she so chooses.

RIGHTS, DUTIES, AND RESPONSIBILITIES OF CITIZENS OF THE UNITED STATES

Citizens are granted certain rights under the US government. The most important of these are defined in the Bill of Rights, and include freedom of speech, religion, assembly, and a variety of other rights the government is not allowed to remove.

Duties of a US citizen include:

1. Paying taxes
2. Loyalty to the government, though the US does not prosecute those who criticize or seek to change the government
3. Support and defend the Constitution
4. Serve in the Armed Forces as required by law
5. Obeying laws as set forth by the various levels of government.

Responsibilities of a US citizen include:

1. Voting in elections
2. Respecting one another's rights and not infringing upon them
3. Staying informed about various political and national issues
4. Respecting one another's beliefs

CIVIL LIBERTIES AND CIVIL RIGHTS

While the terms civil liberties and civil rights are often used synonymously, in actuality their definitions are slightly different. The two concepts work together, however, to define the basics of a free state.

1. "Civil liberties" define the constitutional freedoms guaranteed to citizens. Examples include freedoms such as free speech, privacy, or free thought.
2. "Civil rights" are guarantees of or protections of civil liberties. One comparison can be found in the case of freedom of religion. The civil liberty is that one has the freedom to practice the religion of his or her choice, whereas the civil right would protect that individual from being denied a job on the basis of their religion.

CURRENT POLITICAL DISCUSSIONS ON CIVIL LIBERTY CHALLENGES

The civil rights movements of the 1960s and ongoing struggle for women's rights and rights of other minorities have led to challenges to existing law. In addition, debate has raged over how much information the government should be required to divulge to the public. Major issues in today's political climate include:

- Continued debate over women's rights, especially as regards equal pay for equal work
- Debate over affirmative action to encourage hiring of minorities
- Debate over civil rights of homosexuals, including marriage and military service
- Decisions as to whether any minorities should be compensated for past discriminatory practices
- Balance between the public's right to know and the government's need to maintain national security
- Balance between the public's right to privacy and national security

Suffrage and Franchise

Suffrage and franchise are both terms referring to the right to vote. Which individuals actually have the right to vote has changed as the US has developed as a nation.

In the early years, only white male landowners were granted suffrage. By the nineteenth century, most states had franchised, or granted the right to vote to, all adult white males. The Fifteenth Amendment of 1870 granted suffrage to former slaves. The Nineteenth Amendment gave women the right to vote, and in 1971 the Twenty-sixth Amendment expanded voting rights to include any US citizen over the age of eighteen. However, those who have not been granted full citizenship and citizens who have committed certain crimes do not have voting rights.

Bill of Rights

The first ten amendments of the US Constitution are known as the Bill of Rights. These amendments prevent the government from infringing upon certain freedoms that the founding fathers felt were natural rights that already belonged to all people. These rights included freedom of speech, freedom of religion, right to bear arms, and freedom of assembly. Many of the rights were formulated in direct response to the way the colonists felt they had been mistreated by the British government.

The first ten amendments were passed by Congress in 1789. Three-fourths of the existing thirteen states had ratified them by December of 1791, making them official additions to the Constitution.

- First Amendment—grants freedom of religion, speech, freedom of the press, and the right to assemble.
- Second Amendment—right to bear arms.
- Third Amendment—Congress cannot force individuals to house troops.
- Fourth Amendment—protection from unreasonable search and seizure.
- Fifth Amendment—no individual is required to testify against himself, and no individual may be tried twice for the same crime.
- Sixth Amendment—right to criminal trial by jury, right to legal counsel.
- Seventh Amendment—right to civil trial by jury.
- Eighth Amendment—no excessive bail, no cruel and unusual punishment.
- Ninth Amendment—prevents the absence of rights not explicitly named in the Constitution from being interpreted as a reason to have them taken away.
- Tenth Amendment—any rights not directly delegated to the national government, or not directly prohibited, belong to the states or to the people.

Rights of Those Accused of Crimes

The US Constitution makes allowances for the rights of criminals, or anyone who has transgressed established laws. There must be laws to protect citizens from criminals, but those accused of crimes must also be protected and their basic rights as individuals preserved. In addition, the Constitution protects individuals from the power of authorities who act in case of transgressions to prevent police forces and other enforcement organizations from becoming oppressive.

The Fourth, Fifth, Sixth and Eighth amendments specifically address these issues:

- No unreasonable search and seizure (Fourth Amendment)
- No self-incrimination or double jeopardy—being tried for the same crime more than once (Fifth Amendment)
- Right to trial by jury and right to legal counsel (Sixth Amendment)
- No cruel or unusual punishment (Eighth Amendment)

Instances for Restrictions on First Amendment Freedoms

In some cases, the government restricts certain elements of First Amendment rights. Some examples include:

- Freedom of religion—when a religion espouses activities that are otherwise illegal, the government often restricts these forms of religious expression. Examples include polygamy, animal sacrifice, and use of illicit drugs or illegal substances.
- Freedom of speech—can be restricted if exercise of free speech endangers other people.
- Freedom of the press—laws prevent the press from publishing falsehoods.

In emergency situations such as wartime, stricter restrictions are sometimes placed on these rights, especially rights to free speech and assembly, and freedom of the press, in order to protect national security.

Elections in the United States

Political Parties

George Washington was adamantly against the establishment of political parties, based on the abuses perpetrated by such parties in Britain. However, political parties developed in US politics almost from the beginning. Major parties throughout US History have included:

- Federalists and Democratic-Republicans—formed in the late 1700s and disagreed on the balance of power between national and state government
- Democrats and Whigs—developed before the Civil War, based on disagreements about various issues such as slavery
- Democrats and Republicans—developed after the Civil War, with issues centering on the treatment of the post-war South

While third parties sometimes enter the picture in US politics, the government is basically a two-party system, dominated by the Democrats and Republicans.

Different types and numbers of political parties can have a significant effect on how a government is run. If there is a single party, or a one-party system, the government is defined by that one party, and all policy is based on that party's beliefs. In a two-party system, two parties with different viewpoints compete for power and influence. The US is basically a two-party system, with checks and balances to make it difficult for one party to gain complete power over the other. There are also multi-party systems, with three or more parties. In multiparty systems, various parties will often come to agreements in order to form a majority and shift the balance of power.

Political parties form organizations at all levels of government. Activities of individual parties include:

- Recruiting and backing candidates for offices
- Discussing various issues with the public, increasing public awareness
- Working toward compromise on difficult issues
- Staffing government offices and providing administrative support

At the administrative level, parties work to ensure that viable candidates are available for elections and that offices and staff are in place to support candidates as they run for office and afterwards, when they are elected.

Political Orientations

Liberal—believes government should work to increase equality, even at the expense of some freedoms. Government should assist those in need of help. Focus on enforced social justice and free education for everyone.

Conservative—believes government should be limited in most cases. Government should allow its citizens to help one another and solve their own problems rather than enforcing solutions. Business should not be overregulated, allowing a free market.

Moderate—incorporates some liberal and some conservative values, generally falling somewhere in between in overall belief.

Libertarian—believes government's role should be limited to protecting the life and liberty of citizens. Government should not be involved in any citizen's life unless that citizen is encroaching upon the rights of another.

Free Press and the Media

The right to free speech guaranteed in the first amendment to the Constitution allows the media to report on government and political activities without fear of retribution. Because the media has access to information about the government, its policies and actions, as well as debates and discussions that occur in Congress, it can ensure that the people are informed about the inner workings of the government. The media can also draw attention to injustices, imbalances of power, and other transgressions the government or government officials might commit.

However, media outlets may, like special interest groups, align themselves with certain political viewpoints and skew their reports to fit that viewpoint. The rise of the Internet has made media reporting even more complex, as news can be found from an infinite variety of sources, both reliable and unreliable.

Processes of Selecting Political Candidates

Historically, in the quest for political office, a potential candidate has followed one of the following four processes:

1. Nominating conventions—an official meeting of the members of a party for the express purpose of nominating candidates for upcoming elections. The Democratic National Convention and the Republican National Convention, convened to announce candidates for presidency, are examples of this kind of gathering.
2. Caucuses—a meeting, usually attended by a party's leaders. Some states still use caucuses, but not all.
3. Primary elections—the most common method of choosing candidates today, the primary is a publicly held election to choose candidates.
4. Petitions—signatures are gathered to place a candidate on the ballot. Petitions can also be used to place legislation on a ballot.

Participating in the Political Process

In addition to voting for elected officials, American citizens are able to participate in the political process through several other avenues. These include:

- Participating in local government
- Participating in caucuses for large elections
- Volunteering to help political parties
- Running for election to local, state, or national offices

Individuals can also donate money to political causes, or support political groups that focus on specific causes such as abortion, wildlife conservation or women's rights. These groups often make use of representatives who lobby legislators to act in support of their efforts.

FUNDING FOR POLITICAL CAMPAIGNS

Political campaigns are very expensive ventures. In addition to the basic necessities of a campaign office, including office supplies, office space, etc., a large quantity of the money that funds a political campaign goes toward advertising. Television advertising in particular is quite costly.

Money to fund a political campaign can come from several sources including:

- The candidate's personal funds
- Donations by individuals
- Special interest groups

The most significant source of campaign funding is special interest groups. Groups in favor of certain policies will donate money to candidates they believe will support those policies. Special interest groups also do their own advertising in support of candidates they endorse.

Foreign Policy

Foreign policy is a set of goals, policies and strategies that determine how an individual nation will interact with other countries. These strategies shift, sometimes quickly and drastically, according to actions or changes occurring in the other countries. However, a nation's foreign policy is often based on a certain set of ideals and national needs. Examples of US foreign policy include isolationism versus internationalism. In the 1800s, the US leaned more toward isolationism, exhibiting a reluctance to become involved in foreign affairs. The World Wars led to a period of internationalism, as the US entered these wars in support of other countries and joined the United Nations.

Today's foreign policy tends more toward interdependence, or globalism, recognizing the widespread effects of issues like economic health. US foreign policy is largely determined by Congress and the president, influenced by the secretary of state, secretary of defense, and the national security adviser. Executive officials actually carry out policies. The main departments in charge of these day-to-day issues are the US Department of State, also referred to as the State Department. The Department of State carries out policy, negotiates treaties, maintains diplomatic relations, assists citizens traveling in foreign countries, and ensures that the president is properly informed of any international issues. The Department of Defense, the largest executive department in the US, supervises the armed forces and provides assistance to the president in his role as commander in chief.

Diplomats

Diplomats are individuals who reside in foreign countries in order to maintain communications between that country and their home country. They help negotiate trade agreements, environmental policies, and convey official information to foreign governments. They also help resolve conflicts between the countries, often working to sort out issues without making the conflicts official in any way. Diplomats, or ambassadors, are appointed in America by the president. Appointments must be approved by Congress.

International Organizations

Intergovernmental organizations (IGOs). These organizations are made up of members from various national governments. The UN is an example of an intergovernmental organization. Treaties among the member nations determine the functions and powers of these groups.

Nongovernmental organizations (NGOs). An NGO lies outside the scope of any government and are usually supported through private donations. An example of an NGO is the International Red Cross, which works with governments all over the world when their countries are in crisis, but is formally affiliated with no particular country or government.

United Nations

The United Nations (UN) helps form international policies by hosting representatives of various countries who then provide input into policy decisions. Countries who are members of the UN must agree to abide by all final UN resolutions, but this is not always the case in practice, as dissent is not uncommon. If countries do not follow UN resolutions, the UN can decide on sanctions against those countries, often economic sanctions, such as trade restriction. The UN can also send military forces to problem areas, with "peace keeping" troops brought in from member nations. An example of this function is the Korean War, the first war in which an international organization played a major role.

United States History

European Settlement

Age of Exploration

The Age of Exploration is also called the Age of Discovery. It is generally considered to have begun in the early fifteenth century, and continued into the seventeenth century. Major developments of the Age of Exploration included technological advances in navigation, mapmaking and shipbuilding.

These advances led to expanded European exploration of the rest of the world. Explorers set out from several European countries, including Portuguese, Spain, France and England, seeking new routes to Asia. These efforts led to the discovery of new lands, as well as colonization in India, Asia, Africa, and North America.

Technological Advances in Navigation and Seafaring

For long ocean journeys, it was important for sailors to be able to find their way home even when their vessels sailed far out to sea, well out of sight of land. A variety of navigational tools enabled them to launch ambitious journeys over long distances. The compass and astrolabe were particularly important advancements. The magnetic compass had been used by Chinese navigators for some time, and knowledge of the astrolabe came to Europe from Arab navigators and traders who had refined designs developed by the ancient Greeks.

The Portuguese developed a ship called a caravel in the 1400s that incorporated navigational advancements with the ability to make long sea journeys. Equipped with this advanced vessel, the Portuguese achieved a major goal of the Age of Exploration by discovering a sea route from Europe to Asia in 1498.

Christopher Columbus

In 1492, Columbus, a Genoan explorer, obtained financial backing from King Ferdinand and Queen Isabella of Spain to seek a sea route to Asia. He sought a trade route with the Asian Indies to the west. With three ships, the *Niña*, the *Pinta* and the *Santa Maria*, he eventually landed in the West Indies. While Columbus failed in his effort to discover a western route to Asia, he is credited with the discovery of the Americas.

Review Video: Christopher Columbus
Visit mometrix.com/academy and enter code: 496598

Colonization of the Americas

Initial French colonies were focused on expanding the fur trade. Later, French colonization led to the growth of plantations in Louisiana which brought numerous African slaves to the New World. Spanish colonists came to look for wealth, and to converting the natives to Christianity. For some, the desire for gold led to mining in the New World, while others established large ranches. The Dutch were also involved in the fur trade, and also imported slaves as the need for laborers increased. British colonists arrived with various goals. Some were simply looking for additional income, while others were fleeing Britain to escape religious persecution.

British Colonies

New England Colonies

The New England colonies were: New Hampshire, Connecticut, Rhode Island and Massachusetts.

The colonies in New England were founded largely to escape religious persecution in England. The beliefs of the Puritans, who migrated to America in the 1600s, significantly influenced the development of these colonies.

Situated in the northeast coastal areas of America, the New England colonies featured numerous harbors as well as dense forest. The soil, however, is rocky and, with a very short growing season, was not well suited for agriculture.

The economy of New England during the colonial period centered around fishing, shipbuilding and trade along with some small farms and lumber mills. Although some groups congregated in small farms, life centered largely on towns and cities where merchants largely controlled the trade economy. Coastal cities such as Boston grew and thrived.

Middle Atlantic Colonies

The Middle or Middle Atlantic Colonies were: New York, New Jersey, Pennsylvania and Delaware. Unlike the New England colonies, where most colonists were from England and Scotland, the Middle Colonies founders were from various countries including the Netherlands, Holland and Sweden. Various factors led these colonists to America.

More fertile than New England, the Middle Colonies became major producers of crops included rye, oats, potatoes, wheat, and barley. Some particularly wealthy inhabitants owned large farms and/or businesses. Farmers in general were able to produce enough to have a surplus to sell. Tenant farmers also rented land from larger land owners.

Southern Colonies

The Southern Colonies were Maryland, Virginia, North Carolina, South Carolina and Georgia. Of the Southern Colonies, Virginia was the first permanent English colony and Georgia the last. The warm climate and rich soil of the south encouraged agriculture, and the growing season was long. As a result, economy in the south was based largely on labor-intensive plantations. Crops included tobacco, rice and indigo, all of which became valuable cash crops. Most land in the south was controlled by wealthy plantation owners and farmers. Labor on the farms came in the form of indentured servants and African slaves. The first of these African slaves arrived in Virginia in 1619, starting a long, unpleasant history of slavery in the American colonies.

Navigation Acts

Enacted in 1651, the Navigation Acts were an attempt by Britain to dominate international trade. Aimed largely at the Dutch, the Acts banned foreign ships from transporting goods to the British colonies, and from transporting goods to Britain from elsewhere in Europe. While the restrictions on trade angered some colonists, these Acts were helpful to other American colonists who, as members of the British Empire, were legally able to provide ships for Britain's growing trade interests and use the ships for their own trading ventures. By the time the French and Indian War had ended, one-third of British merchant ships were built in the American colonies. Many colonists amassed fortunes in the shipbuilding trade.

Triangular Trade

Triangular trade began in the Colonies with ships setting off for Africa carrying rum. In Africa, the rum was traded for gold or slaves. Ships then went from Africa to the West Indies, trading slaves for sugar, molasses, or money. To complete the triangle, the ships returned to the colonies with sugar or molasses to make more rum, as well as stores of gold and silver.

This trade triangle violated the Molasses Act of 1733, which required the colonists to pay high duties to Britain on molasses acquired from French, Dutch, and Spanish colonies. The colonists ignored these duties, and the British government adopted a policy of salutary neglect by not enforcing them.

Review Video: Triangular Trade
Visit mometrix.com/academy and enter code: 415470

French and Indian Wars

The British defeat of the Spanish Armada in 1750 led to the decline of Spanish power in Europe. This in turn led the British and French into battle over several wars between 1689 and 1748. These wars were:

- King William's War, or the Nine Years War, 1689-1697. This war was fought largely in Flanders.
- The War of Spanish Succession, or Queen Anne's War, 1702-1713
- War of Austrian Succession, or King George's War, 1740-1748

The fourth and final, the French and Indian War, was fought largely in the North American territory, and resulted in the end of France's reign as a colonial power in North America. Although the French held many advantages, including more cooperative colonists and numerous Indian allies, the strong leadership of William Pitt eventually led the British to victory. Costs incurred during the wars eventually led to discontent in the colonies. This helped spark the American Revolution.

Review Video: French and Indian War
Visit mometrix.com/academy and enter code: 502183

The French and Indian War created circumstances for which the British desperately needed more revenue. These included:

- The need to pay off the war debt.
- The need for funds to defend the expanding empire
- The need for funds to govern Britain's thirty-three far-flung colonies, including the American colonies

These needs led the British to pass additional laws to increase revenues from the colonies. Because they had spent so much money to defend the American colonies, the British felt it was appropriate to collect considerably higher taxes from them. The colonists felt this was unfair, and many were led to protest the increasing taxes. Eventually, protest led to violence.

American Revolution

EFFECTS OF NEW LAWS ON BRITISH COLONIES

While earlier revenue-generating acts such as the Navigation Acts brought money to the colonists, the new laws after 1763 required colonists to pay money back to Britain. The British felt this was fair since the colonists were British subjects and since they had incurred debt protecting the Colonies. The colonists felt it was not only unfair, but illegal.

The development of local government in America had given the colonists a different view of the structure and role of government. This made it difficult for the British to understand colonist's protests against what the British felt was a fair and reasonable solution to the mother country's financial problems.

DISCONTENT IN THE AMERICAN COLONIES

More and more colonists had been born on American soil, decreasing any sense of kinship with the far away British rulers. Their new environment had led to new ideas of government and a strong view of the colonies as a separate entity from Britain.

Colonists were allowed to self-govern in domestic issues, but Britain controlled international issues. In fact, the American colonies were largely left to form their own local government bodies, giving them more freedom than any other colonial territory. This gave the colonists a sense of independence which led them to resent control from Britain.

Threats during the French and Indian War led the colonists to call for unification in order to protect themselves.

IMPORTANT MOMENTS LEADING TO THE AMERICAN REVOLUTION

As new towns and other legislative districts developed in America, the colonists began to practice representative government. Colonial legislative bodies were made up of elected representatives chosen by male property owners in the districts. These individuals represented interests of the districts from which they had been elected.

By contrast, in Britain the Parliament represented the entire country. Parliament was not elected to represent individual districts. Instead, they represented specific classes. Because of this drastically different approach to government, the British did not understand the colonists' statement that they had no representation in the British Parliament.

The Quartering Act, 1765. This act required colonists to provide accommodations and supplies for British troops. In addition, colonists were prohibited from settling west of the Appalachians until given permission by Britain.

The Sugar Act, 1764. This act not only required taxes to be collected on molasses brought into the colonies, but gave British officials the right to search the homes of anyone suspected of violating it.

The Stamp Act, 1765. The Stamp Act taxed printed materials such as newspapers and legal documents. Protests led the Stamp Act to be repealed in 1766, but the repeal also included the Declaratory Act, which stated that Parliament had the right to govern the colonies.

The Townshend Acts, 1767. These acts taxed paper, paint, lead and tea that came into the colonies. Colonists led boycotts in protest, and in Massachusetts leaders like Samuel and John Adams began to organize resistance against British rule.

Boston Massacre

With the passage of the Stamp Act, nine colonies met in New York to demand its repeal. Elsewhere, protest arose in New York City, Philadelphia, Boston and other cities. These protests sometimes escalated into violence, often targeting ruling British officials.

The passage of the Townshend Acts in 1767 led to additional tension in the colonies. The British sent troops to New York City and Boston. On March 5, 1770, protesters began to taunt the British troops, throwing snowballs. The soldiers responded by firing into the crowd. This clash between protesters and soldiers led to five deaths and eight injuries, and was christened the Boston Massacre. Shortly thereafter, Britain repealed the majority of the Townshend Acts.

Tea Act and the Boston Tea Party

The majority of the Townshend Acts were repealed after the Boston Massacre in 1770, but Britain kept the tax on tea. In 1773, the Tea Act was passed. This allowed the East India Company to sell tea for much lower prices, and also allowed them to bypass American distributors, selling directly to shopkeepers instead. Colonial tea merchants saw this as a direct assault on their business. In December of 1773, 150 merchants boarded ships in Boston Harbor and dumped 342 chests of tea into the sea in protest of the new laws. This act of protest came to be known as the Boston Tea Party.

Coercive Acts

The Coercive Acts passed by Britain in 1774 were meant to punish Massachusetts for defying British authority. The four Coercive Acts:

1. Shut down ports in Boston until the city paid back the value of the tea destroyed during the Boston Tea Party.
2. Required that local government officials in Massachusetts be appointed by the governor rather than being elected by the people.
3. Allowed trials of British soldiers to be transferred to Britain rather than being held in Massachusetts.
4. Required locals to provide lodging for British soldiers any time there was a disturbance, even if lodging required them to stay in private homes.

These Acts led to the assembly of the First Continental Congress in Philadelphia on September 5, 1774. Fifty-five delegates met, representing 12 of the American colonies. They sought compromise with England over England's increasingly harsh efforts to control the colonies.

First Continental Congress

The First Continental Congress met in Philadelphia on September 5, 1774. Their goal was to achieve a peaceful agreement with Britain. Made up of delegates from 12 of the 13 colonies, the Congress affirmed loyalty to Britain and the power of Parliament to dictate foreign affairs in the colonies. However, they demanded that the Intolerable Acts be repealed, and instituted a trade embargo with Britain until this came to pass.

In response, George III of Britain declared that the American colonies must submit or face military action. The British sought to end assemblies opposing their policies. These assemblies gathered weapons and began to form militias. On April 19, 1775, the British military was ordered to disperse a meeting of the Massachusetts Assembly. A battle ensued on Lexington Common as the armed colonists resisted. The resulting battles became the Battle of Lexington and Concord—the first battles of the American Revolution.

Second Continental Congress

The Second Continental Congress met in Philadelphia on May 10, 1775, a month after Lexington and Concord. Their discussions centered on defense of the American colonies and how to conduct the growing war, as well as local government. The delegates also discussed declaring independence from Britain, with many members in favor of this drastic move. They established an army, and on June 15, named George Washington as its commander in chief.

By 1776, it was obvious that there was no turning back from full-scale war with Britain. The colonial delegates of the Continental Congress drafted the Declaration of Independence on July 4, 1776.

Review Video: The First and Second Continental Congress
Visit mometrix.com/academy and enter code: 835211

Declaration of Independence

Penned by Thomas Jefferson and signed on July 4, 1776, the Declaration of Independence stated that King George III had violated the rights of the colonists and was establishing a tyrannical reign over them.

Many of Jefferson's ideas of natural rights and property rights were shaped by seventeenth century philosopher John Locke. Jefferson focused on natural rights, as demonstrated by the assertion of people's rights to "life, liberty and the pursuit of happiness." Locke's comparable idea asserted "life, liberty, and private property." Both felt that the purpose of government was to protect the rights of the people, and that individual rights were more important than individuals' obligations to the state.

Review Video: Declaration of Independence
Visit mometrix.com/academy and enter code: 256838

Revolutionary War

1. The Battle of Lexington and Concord (April, 1775) is considered the first engagement of the Revolutionary War.
2. The Battle of Bunker Hill, in June of 1775, was one of the bloodiest of the entire war. Although American troops withdrew, about half the British army was lost. The colonists proved they could stand against professional British soldiers. In August, Britain declared that the American colonies were officially in a state of rebellion.
3. The first colonial victory occurred in Trenton, New Jersey, when Washington and his troops crossed the Delaware River on Christmas Day, 1776 for a December 26, surprise attack on British and Hessian troops.
4. The Battle of Saratoga effectively ended a plan to separate the New England colonies from their Southern counterparts. The surrender of British general John Burgoyne led to France joining the war as allies of the Americans, and is generally considered a turning point of the war.
5. On October 19, 1781, General Cornwallis surrendered after a defeat in the Battle of Yorktown, Virginia, ending the Revolutionary War.

Review Video: The Revolutionary War
Visit mometrix.com/academy and enter code: 935282

Treaty of Paris

The Treaty of Paris was signed on September 3, 1783, bringing an official end to the Revolutionary War. In this document, Britain officially recognized the United States of America as an independent nation. The treaty established the Mississippi River as the country's western border. The treaty also restored Florida to Spain, while France reclaimed African and Caribbean colonies seized by the British in 1763. On November 24, 1783, the last British troops departed from the newly born United States of America.

Early Formation of United States

U.S. Constitution

Articles of Confederation

A precursor to the Constitution, the Articles of Confederation represented the first attempt of the newly independent colonies to establish the basics of independent government. The Continental Congress passed the Articles on November 15, 1777. They went into effect on March 1, 1781, following ratification by the thirteen states.

The Articles prevented a central government from gaining too much power, instead giving power to a Congressional body made up of delegates from all thirteen states. However, the individual states retained final authority. Without a strong central executive, though, this weak alliance among the new states proved ineffective in settling disputes or enforcing laws. The idea of a weak central government needed to be revised. Recognition of these weaknesses eventually led to the drafting of a new document, the Constitution.

Review Video: Articles of Confederation
Visit mometrix.com/academy and enter code: 927401

Development of Bicameral Legislature

Delegates from twelve of the thirteen states (Rhode Island was not represented) met in Philadelphia in May of 1787, initially intending to revise the Articles of Confederation. However, it quickly became apparent that a simple revision would not provide the workable governmental structure the newly formed country needed.

After vowing to keep all the proceedings secret until the final document was completed, the delegates set out to draft what would eventually become the Constitution of the United States of America. By keeping the negotiations secret, the delegates were able to present a completed document to the country for ratification, rather than having every small detail hammered out by the general public.

Virginia Plan, the New Jersey Plan, and the Great Compromise

The delegates agreed that the new nation required a strong central government, but that its overall power should be limited. The various branches of the government should have balanced power, so that no one group could control the others. Final power belonged with the citizens who voted officials into office based on who would provide the best representation.

Disagreement immediately occurred between delegates from large states and those from smaller states. The governor of Virginia, Edmond Randolph, felt that representation in Congress should be based on state population. This was the Virginia Plan. The New Jersey Plan, presented by William Paterson, from New Jersey, proposed each state have equal representation.

Finally, Roger Sherman from Connecticut formulated the Connecticut Compromise, also called the Great Compromise. The result was the familiar structure we have today. Each state has the equal representation of two Senators in the Senate, with the number of representatives in the House of Representatives based on population. This is called a bicameral Congress. Both houses may draft bills, but financial matters must originate in the House of Representatives.

Three-Fifths Compromise

During debate on the U.S. Constitution, a disagreement arose between the Northern and Southern states involving how slaves should be counted when determining a state's quota of representatives. In the South large numbers of slaves were commonly used to run plantations. Delegates wanted slaves to be counted to determine the number of representatives, but not counted to determine the amount of taxes the states would pay. The Northern states wanted exactly the opposite arrangement. The final decision was to count three-fifths of the slave population both for tax purposes and to determine representation. This was called the three-fifths compromise.

Commerce Compromise

The Commerce Compromise also resulted from a North/South disagreement. In the North the economy was centered on industry and trade. The Southern economy was largely agricultural. The Northern states wanted to give the new government the ability to regulate exports as well as trade between the states. The South opposed this plan. Another compromise was in order. In the end, Congress received regulatory power over all trade, including the ability to collect tariffs on exported goods. In the South, this raised another red flag regarding the slave trade, as they were concerned about the effect on their economy if tariffs were levied on slaves. The final agreement allowed importing slaves to continue for twenty years without government intervention. Import taxes on slaves were limited, and after the year 1808, Congress could decide whether to allow continued imports of slaves.

Initial Concerns for the Constitution

Once the Constitution was drafted, it was presented for approval by the states. Nine states needed to approve the document for it to become official. However, debate and discussion continued. Major concerns included:

- The lack of a bill of rights to protect individual freedoms.
- States felt too much power was being handed over to the central government.
- Voters wanted more control over their elected representatives.

Discussion about necessary changes to the Constitution divided roughly into two camps: Federalists and Anti-Federalists. Federalists wanted a strong central government. Anti-Federalists wanted to prevent a tyrannical government from developing if a central government held too much power.

Federalists and Jeffersonian Republicans

Major Federalist leaders included Alexander Hamilton, John Jay and James Madison. They wrote a series of letters, called the Federalist Papers, aimed at convincing the states to ratify the Constitution. These were published in New York papers.

Anti-Federalists included Thomas Jefferson and Patrick Henry. They argued against the Constitution as it was originally drafted in arguments called the Anti-Federalist Papers.

The final compromise produced a strong central government controlled by checks and balances. A Bill of Rights was also added, becoming the first ten amendments to the Constitution. These amendments protected rights such as freedom of speech, freedom of religion, and other basic rights. Aside from various amendments added throughout the years, the United States Constitution has remained unchanged.

The First Administration

George Washington was elected as the first President of the United States in 1789. John Adams, who finished second in the election, became the first Vice President. Thomas Jefferson was appointed by Washington as Secretary of State. Alexander Hamilton was also appointed Secretary of the Treasury.

Alien and Sedition Acts

When John Adams became president, a war was raging between Britain and France. While Adams and the Federalists backed the British, Thomas Jefferson and the Republican Party supported the French. The United States nearly went to war with France during this time period, while France worked to spread its international standing and influence under the leadership of Napoleon Bonaparte. The Alien and Sedition Acts grew out of this conflict, and made it illegal to speak in a hostile fashion against the existing government. They also allowed the president to deport anyone in the U.S. who was not a citizen and who was suspected of treason or treasonous activity.

When Jefferson became the third president in 1800, he repealed these four laws and pardoned anyone who had been convicted under them.

War of 1812 and Era of Good Feelings

The Orders in Council (1807)

The British had two major objections to America's continued trade with France. First, they saw the US as helping France's war effort by providing supplies and goods. Second, the United States had grown into a competitor, taking trade and money away from British ships and tradesmen.

In its attempts to end American trade with France, the British put into effect the Orders in Council, which made any and all French-owned ports off-limits to American ships. They also began to seize American ships and conscript their crews, a practice greatly offensive to the U.S.

War of 1812

The War of 1812 grew out of the continuing tension between France and Great Britain. Napoleon continued to strive to conquer Britain, while the U.S. continued trade with both countries, but favoring France and the French colonies. Because of what Britain saw as an alliance between America and France, they determined to bring an end to trade between the two nations.

With the British preventing U.S. trade with the French and the French preventing trade with the British, James Madison's presidency introduced acts to regulate international trade. If either Britain or France removed their restrictions, America would not trade with the other. Napoleon acted first, and Madison prohibited trade with England. England saw this as the U.S. formally siding with the French, and war ensued in 1812.

Two major naval battles, at Lake Erie and Lake Champlain, kept the British from invading the U.S. via Canada. American attempts to conquer Canadian lands were not successful. In another memorable British attack, the British invaded Washington DC and burned the White House. Legend has it that Dolly Madison, the First Lady, salvaged the American flag from the fire. The War of 1812 has been called the Second American Revolution. It established the superiority of the U.S. naval forces and reestablished U.S. independence from Britain and Europe.

On Christmas Eve, 1814, the Treaty of Ghent officially ended the war. However, Andrew Jackson, unaware that the war was over, managed another victory at New Orleans on January 8, 1815. This victory upped American morale and led to a new wave of nationalism and national pride known as the "Era of Good Feelings."

Developments After the War of 1812

Monroe Doctrine

On December 2, 1823, President Monroe delivered a message to Congress in which he introduced the Monroe Doctrine. In this address, he stated that any attempts by European powers to establish new colonies on the North American continent would be considered interference in American politics. The U.S. would stay out of European matters, and expected Europe to offer America the same courtesy. This approach to foreign policy stated in no uncertain terms that America would not tolerate any new European colonies in the New World, and that events occurring in Europe would no longer influence the policies and doctrines of the U.S.

The American System

Spurred by the trade conflicts of the War of 1812, and supported by Henry Clay and others, the American System set up tariffs to help protect American interests from competition with products from overseas. Reducing competition led to growth in employment and an overall increase in American industry. The higher tariffs also provided funds for the government to pay for various improvements. Congress passed high tariffs in 1816 and also chartered a federal bank. The Second Bank of the United States was given the job of regulating America's money supply.

Major Ideas on American Foreign Policy

Isolationism – the early US government did not intend to establish colonies, though they did plan to grow larger within the bounds of North America.

No entangling alliances – both George Washington and Thomas Jefferson were opposed to forming any permanent alliances with other countries or becoming involved in other countries' internal issues.

Nationalism –a positive patriotic feeling about the United States blossomed quickly among its citizens, particularly after the War of 1812, when the U.S. once again defeated Britain. The Industrial Revolution also sparked increased nationalism by allowing even the most far-flung areas of the U.S. to communicate with each other via telegraph and the expanding railroad.

Development of Political Parties in Early U.S. Government

Many in the U.S. were against political parties after seeing the way parties, or factions, functioned in Britain. The factions in Britain were more interested in personal profit than the overall good of the country, and they did not want this to happen in the U.S.

However, the differences of opinion between Thomas Jefferson and Alexander Hamilton led to formation of political parties. Hamilton favored a stronger central government, while Jefferson felt more power should remain with the states. Jefferson was in favor of strict Constitutional interpretation, while Hamilton believed in a more flexible approach. As various others joined the separate camps, Hamilton backers began to term themselves Federalists while those supporting Jefferson became identified as Democratic-Republicans.

Whig Party, the Democratic Party, and the Republican Party

Thomas Jefferson was elected president in 1800 and again in 1804. The Federalist Party began a decline, and its major figure, Alexander Hamilton, died in a duel with Aaron Burr in 1804. By 1816, the Federalist Party virtually disappeared.

New parties sprang up to take its place. After 1824, the Democratic-Republican Party suffered a split. The Whigs arose, backing John Quincy Adams and industrial growth. The new Democratic Party formed, in opposition to the Whigs, and their candidate, Andrew Jackson, was elected as president in 1828.

By the 1850s, issues regarding slavery led to the formation of the Republican Party, which was anti-slavery, while the Democratic Party of the time, with a larger interest in the South, favored slavery. This Republican/Democrat division formed the basis of today's two-party system.

Important Cases for the First Supreme Court

Marbury v. Madison

The main duty of the Supreme Court today is judicial review. This power was largely established by Marbury v. Madison. This case set precedent for the Supreme Court to nullify laws it found to be unconstitutional.

When John Adams was voted out of office in 1800, he worked, during his final days in office, to appoint Federalist judges to Supreme Court positions, knowing Jefferson, his replacement, held opposing views. As late as March 3, the day before Jefferson was to take office, Adams made last-minute appointments referred to as "Midnight Judges."

One of the late appointments was William Marbury. The next day, March 4, Jefferson ordered his Secretary of State, James Madison, not to deliver Marbury's commission. This decision was backed by Chief Justice Marshall, who determined that the Judiciary Act of 1789, which granted the power to deliver commissions, was illegal in that it gave the Judicial Branch powers not granted in the Constitution.

Review Video: Marbury v. Madison
Visit mometrix.com/academy and enter code: 573964

McCulloch v Maryland

Judicial review was further exercised by the Supreme Court in McCulloch v Maryland. When Congress chartered a national bank, the Second Bank of the United States, Maryland voted to tax any bank business dealing with banks chartered outside the state, including the federally chartered bank. Andrew McCulloch, an employee of the Second Bank of the US in Baltimore, refused to pay this tax. The resulting lawsuit from the State of Maryland went to the Supreme Court for judgment.

John Marshall, Chief Justice of the Supreme Court, stated that Congress was within its rights to charter a national bank. In addition, the State of Maryland did not have the power to levy a tax on the federal bank or on the federal government in general. In cases where state and federal government collided, precedent was set for the federal government to prevail.

Economic Overview of Parts of U.S. in Late 19th Century

In the Northeast, the economy mostly depended on manufacturing, industry and industrial development. This led to a dichotomy between rich business owners and industrial leaders and the much poorer workers who supported their businesses.

The South continued to depend on agriculture, especially large-scale farms or plantations worked mostly by slaves and indentured servants.

In the West, where new settlement had begun to develop, the land was largely wild. Growing communities were essentially agricultural; growing crops and raising livestock. The differences between regions led each to support different interests both politically and economically.

Manifest Destiny

In the 1800s, many believed America was destined by God to expand west, bringing as much of the North American continent as possible under the umbrella of U.S. government. With the Northwest Ordinance and the Louisiana Purchase, over half of the continent became American. However, the rapid and relentless expansion brought conflict with the Native Americans, Great Britain, Mexico and Spain.

One result of "Manifest Destiny" was the Mexican-American War, which occurred from 1846-1848. By the end of the war, Texas, California and a large portion of what is now the American Southwest joined the growing nation. Conflict also arose over the Oregon country, shared by the US and Britain. In 1846, President James Polk resolved this problem by compromising with Britain, establishing a U.S. boundary south of the 49th parallel.

Review Video: Manifest Destiny
Visit mometrix.com/academy and enter code: 957409

Louisiana Purchase

With tension still high between France and Britain, Napoleon was in need of money to support his continuing war efforts. To secure necessary funds, he decided to sell the Louisiana Territory to the U.S. At the same time President Thomas Jefferson wanted to buy New Orleans, feeling U.S. trade was made vulnerable to both Spain and France at that port. Instead, Napoleon sold him the entire territory for the bargain price of fifteen million dollars. The Louisiana Territory was larger than all the rest of the United States put together, and it eventually became fifteen additional states.

Federalists in Congress were opposed to the purchase. They feared that the Louisiana Purchase would extend slavery, and that further western growth would weaken the power of the northern states.

Review Video: The Louisiana Purchase
Visit mometrix.com/academy and enter code: 920513

Lewis and Clark Expedition

The purchase of the Louisiana Territory from France in 1803 more than doubled the size of the United States. President Thomas Jefferson wanted to have the area mapped and explored, since much of the territory was wilderness. He chose Meriwether Lewis and William Clark to head an expedition into the Louisiana Territory. After two years, Lewis and Clark returned, having traveled all the way to the Pacific Ocean. They brought maps, detailed journals, and various types of knowledge and information about the wide expanse of land they had traversed. The Lewis and Clark Expedition opened up the west in the Louisiana Territory and beyond for further exploration and settlement.

Review Video: The Lewis and Clark Expedition
Visit mometrix.com/academy and enter code: 570657

Moving into Native American Lands

After the Revolutionary War, the Treaty of Paris, which outlined the terms of surrender of the British to the Americans, granted large parcels of land to the U.S. that were occupied by Native Americans. The new government attempted to claim the land, treating the natives as a conquered people. This approached proved unenforceable.

Next, the government tried purchasing the land from the Indians via a series of treaties as the country expanded westward. In practice, however, these treaties were not honored, and Native Americans were simply dislocated and forced to move farther and farther west as American expansion continued, often with military action.

Indian Removal Act of 1830 and the Treaty of New Echota

The Indian Removal Act of 1830 gave the new American government power to form treaties with Native Americans. In theory, America would claim land east of the Mississippi in exchange for land west of the Mississippi, to which the natives would relocate voluntarily. In practice, many tribal leaders were forced into signing the treaties, and relocation at times occurred by force.

The Treaty of New Echota was supposedly a treaty between the US government and Cherokee tribes in Georgia. However, the treaty was not signed by tribal leaders, but rather by a small portion of the represented people. The leaders protested by refusing to be removed, but President, Martin Van Buren, enforced the treaty by sending soldiers. During their forced relocation, more than 4,000 Cherokee Indians died on what became known as the Trail of Tears.

Native Americans in the Late 19th Century

America's westward expansion led to conflict and violent confrontations with Native Americans such as the Battle of Little Bighorn. In 1876, the American government ordered all Indians to relocate to reservations. Lack of compliance led to the Dawes Act in 1887, which ordered assimilation rather than separation. This act remained in effect until 1934. Reformers also forced Indian children to attend Indian Boarding Schools, where they were not allowed to speak their native language and were forced to accept Christianity. Children were often abused in these schools, and were indoctrinated to abandon their identity as Native Americans.

In 1890, the massacre at Wounded Knee, accompanied by Geronimo's surrender, led the Native Americans to work to preserve their culture rather than fight for their lands.

Jacksonian Democracy

Jacksonian Democracy is largely seen as a shift from politics favoring the wealthy to politics favoring the common man. All free white males were given the right to vote, not just property owners, as had been the case previously. Jackson's approach favored the patronage system, Laissez faire economics, and relocation of the Indian tribes from the Southeast portion of the country. Jackson opposed the formation of a federal bank, and allowed the Second Band of the United States to collapse by vetoing a bill to renew the charter.

Jackson also faced the challenge of the "null and void" or nullification theory when South Carolina claimed that it could ignore or nullify any federal law it considered unconstitutional. Jackson sent troops to the state to enforce the protested tariff laws, and a compromise engineered by Henry Clay in 1833 settled the matter for the time being.

Mexican-American War

Spain had held colonial interests in America since the 1540s—earlier even than Great Britain. In 1821, Mexico revolted against Spain and became a free nation. Likewise, this was followed by Texas, who after an 1836 revolution declared its independence.

In 1844, the Democrats pressed President Tyler to annex Texas. Unlike his predecessor, Andrew Jackson, Tyler agreed to admit Texas into the Union. In 1845, Texas became a state.

During Mexico's war for independence, they had incurred $4.5 million in war debts to the U.S. Polk offered to forgive the debts in return for New Mexico and Upper California, but Mexico refused. In 1846, war was declared in response to a Mexican attack on American troops along the southern border of Texas.

Additional conflict arose in Congress over the Wilmot Proviso, which stated that slavery was prohibited in any territory the U.S. acquired from Mexico as a result of the Mexican-American war. The war ended in 1848.

Review Video: The Mexican-American War
Visit mometrix.com/academy and enter code: 271216

GADSDEN PURCHASE

After the Mexican-American war, a second treaty in 1853 determined hundreds of miles of America's southwest borders. In 1854, the Gadsden Purchase was finalized, providing even more territory to aid in the building of the transcontinental railroad. This purchase added what would eventually become the southernmost regions of Arizona and New Mexico to the growing nation. The modern outline of the United States was by this time nearly complete.

19th Century Developments

Education in the Early Nineteenth Century

Horace Mann, among others, felt that public schooling could help children become better citizens, keep them away from crime, prevent poverty, and help American society become more unified. His *Common School Journal* brought his ideas of the importance of education into the public consciousness. Increased literacy led to increased awareness of current events, Western expansion, and other major developments of the time period. Public interest and participation in the arts and literature also increased. By the end of the 19th century, all children had access to a free public elementary education.

Developments in Transportation

As America expanded its borders, it also developed new technology to travel the rapidly growing country. Roads and railroads traversed the nation, with the Transcontinental Railroad eventually allowing travel from one coast to the other. Canals and steamboats simplified water travel and made shipping easier and less expensive. The Erie Canal (1825) connected the Great Lakes with the Hudson River. Other canals connected other major water ways, further facilitating transportation and the shipment of goods.

With growing numbers of settlers moving into the West, wagon trails developed, including the Oregon Trail, California Trail and the Santa Fe Trail. The most common vehicles seen along these westbound trails were covered wagons, also known as prairie schooners.

Industrial Activity and Labor Movements

During the eighteenth century, goods were often manufactured in houses or small shops. With increased technology allowing for the use of machines, factories began to develop. In factories a large volume of salable goods could be produced in a much shorter amount of time. Many Americans, including increasing numbers of immigrants, found jobs in these factories, which were in constant need of labor.

Another major invention was the cotton gin, which significantly decreased the processing time of cotton, and was a major factor in the rapid expansion of cotton production in the South.

Development of Labor Movements

In 1751, a group of bakers held a protest in which they stopped baking bread. This was technically the first American labor strike. In the 1830s and 1840s, labor movements began in earnest. Boston's masons, carpenters and stoneworkers protested the length of the workday, fighting to reduce it to ten hours. In 1844, a group of women in the textile industry also fought to reduce their workday to ten hours, forming the Lowell Female Labor Reform Association. Many other protests occurred and organizations developed through this time period with the same goal in mind.

Second Great Awakening

Led by Protestant evangelical leaders, the Second Great Awakening occurred between 1800 and 1830. Several missionary groups grew out of the movement, including the American Home Missionary Society, which formed in 1826. The ideas behind the Second Great Awakening focused on personal responsibility, both as an individual and in response to injustice and suffering. The American Bible Society and the American Tract Society provided literature, while various traveling preachers spread the word. New denominations arose, including the Latter-Day Saints and Seventh-Day Adventists.

Another movement associated with the Second Great Awakening was the temperance movement, focused on ending the production and use of alcohol. One major organization behind the temperance movement was the Society for the Promotion of Temperance, formed in 1826 in Boston, Massachusetts.

WOMEN'S RIGHTS MOVEMENT

The women's rights movement began in the 1840s with leaders including Elizabeth Cady Stanton, Ernestine Rose and Lucretia Mott. Later, in 1869, the National Woman Suffrage Association, fighting for women's right to vote, came into being. It was led by Susan B. Anthony, Ernestine Rose and Elizabeth Cady Stanton.

Review Video: Elizabeth Cady Stanton
Visit mometrix.com/academy and enter code: 987734

In 1848 in Seneca Falls, the first women's rights convention was held, with about three hundred attendees. The Seneca Falls Convention brought to the floor the issue that women could not vote or run for office. The convention produced a "Declaration of Sentiments" which outlined a plan for women to attain the rights they deserved. Frederick Douglass supported the women's rights movement, as well as the abolition movement. In fact, women's rights and abolition movements often went hand-in-hand through this time period.

Civil War and Reconstruction

North and South Conflict

The conflict between North and South coalesced around the issue of slavery, but other elements contributed to the growing disagreement. Though most farmers in the South worked small farms with little or no slave labor, the huge plantations run by the South's rich depended on slaves or indentured servants to remain profitable. They had also become more dependent on cotton, with slave populations growing in concert with the rapid increase in cotton production.

In the North, a more diverse agricultural economy and the growth of industry made slaves rarer. The abolitionist movement grew steadily, with Harriet Beecher Stowe's *Uncle Tom's Cabin* giving many an idea to rally around. A collection of anti-slavery organizations formed, with many actively working to free slaves in the South, often bringing them North.

Anti-Slavery Organizations

1. American Colonization Society—protestant churches formed this group, aimed at returning black slaves to Africa. Former slaves subsequently formed Liberia, but the colony did not do well, as the region was not well-suited for agriculture.
2. American Anti-Slavery Society—William Lloyd Garrison, a Quaker, was the major force behind this group and its newspaper, *The Liberator.*
3. Female Anti-Slavery Society—a women-only group formed by Margaretta Forten because women were not allowed to join the Anti-Slavery Society formed by her father.
4. Anti-Slavery Convention of American Women—This group continued meeting even after pro-slavery factions burned down their original meeting place.
5. Female Vigilant Society—an organization that raised funds to help the Underground Railroad, as well as slave refugees.

Missouri Compromise

By 1819, the United States had developed a tenuous balance between slave and free states, with exactly twenty-two senators in Congress from each faction. However, Missouri was ready to join the union as a state. As a slave state, it would tip the balance in Congress. To prevent this imbalance, the Missouri Compromise brought the northern part of Massachusetts into the union as Maine, established as a free state. Maine's admission balanced the admission of Missouri as a slave state, maintaining the status quo. In addition, the remaining portion of the Louisiana Purchase was to remain free north of latitude 36° 30'. Since cotton did not grow well this far north, this limitation was acceptable to congressmen representing the slave states.

However, the proposed Missouri constitution presented a problem, as it outlawed immigration of free blacks into the state. Another compromise was in order, this time proposed by Henry Clay. Clay earned his title of the Great Compromiser by stating that the U.S. Constitution overruled Missouri's.

Review Video: Missouri Compromise
Visit mometrix.com/academy and enter code: 848091

Popular Sovereignty and the Compromise of 1850

In addition to the pro-slavery and anti-slavery factions, a third group rose who felt that each individual state should decide whether to allow or permit slavery within its borders. This idea was referred to as popular sovereignty.

When California applied to join the union in 1849, the balance of congressional power was again threatened. The Compromise of 1850 introduced a group of laws meant to bring an end to the conflict.

These laws included:

- California being admitted as a free state.
- Slave trade in Washington, D.C. being outlawed.
- An increase in efforts to capture escaped slaves.
- New Mexico and Utah territories would decide individually whether or not to allow slavery.

In spite of these measures, debate raged each time a new state prepared to enter the union.

Kansas-Nebraska Act

With the creation of the Kansas and Nebraska territories in 1854, another debate began. Congress allowed popular sovereignty in these territories, but slavery opponents argued that the Missouri Compromise had already made slavery illegal in this region. In Kansas, two separate governments arose, one pro- and one anti-slavery. Conflict between the two factions rose to violence, leading Kansas to gain the nickname of "Bleeding Kansas."

Dred Scott Decision

Abolitionist factions coalesced around the case of Dred Scott, using his case to test the country's laws regarding slavery. Scott, a slave, had been taken by his owner from Missouri, which was a slave state. He then traveled to Illinois, a free state, then on to the Minnesota Territory, also free based on the Missouri Compromise. Then, he returned to Missouri. The owner subsequently died. Abolitionists took Scott's case to court, stating that Scott was no longer a slave but free, since he had lived in free territory. The case went to the Supreme Court.

Review Video: Dred Scott Act
Visit mometrix.com/academy and enter code: 364838

The Supreme Court stated that, because Scott, as a slave, was not a U.S. citizen, his time in free states did not change his status. He also did not have the right to sue. In addition, the Court determined that the Missouri Compromise was unconstitutional, saying Congress had overstepped its bounds by outlawing slavery in the territories.

Harper's Ferry and John Brown

John Brown, an abolitionist, had participated in several anti-slavery actions, including killing five pro-slavery men in retaliation, after Lawrence, Kansas, an anti-slavery town, was sacked. He and other abolitionists also banded together to pool their funds and build a runaway slave colony.

In 1859, Brown seized a federal arsenal in Harper's Ferry, located in what is now West Virginia. Brown intended to seize guns and ammunition and lead a slave rebellion. Robert E. Lee captured Brown and 22 followers, who were subsequently tried and hanged. While Northerners took the executions as an indication that the government supported slavery, Southerners were of the opinion that most of the North supported Brown and were, in general, anti-slavery.

PRESIDENTIAL ELECTION OF 1860

The 1860 Presidential candidates represented four different parties, each with a different opinion on slavery.

- John Breckenridge, representing the Southern Democrats, was pro-slavery.
- Abraham Lincoln, of the Republican Party, was anti-slavery.
- Stephen Douglas, of the Northern Democrats, felt that the issue should be determined locally, on a state-by-state basis.
- John Bell, of the Constitutional Union Party, focused primarily on keeping the Union intact.

In the end, Abraham Lincoln won both the popular and electoral election. Southern states, who had sworn to secede from the Union if Lincoln was elected did so, led by South Carolina. Shortly thereafter, the Civil War began when shots were fired on Fort Sumter in Charleston.

EMANCIPATION PROCLAMATION

The Emancipation Proclamation, issued by President Lincoln in 1863, freed all slaves in Confederate States that did not return to the Union by the beginning of the year. While the original proclamation did not free any slaves actually under Union control, it did set a precedent for the emancipation of slaves as the war progressed.

The Emancipation Proclamation worked in the Union's favor as many freed slaves and other black troops joined the Union Army. Almost 200,000 blacks fought in the Union army, and over 10,000 served in the navy. By the end of the war, over 4 million slaves had been freed, and in 1865 slavery was banned by Constitutional amendment.

Review Video: Emancipation Proclamation
Visit mometrix.com/academy and enter code: 181778

ADVANTAGES OF THE NORTH AND SOUTH IN THE CIVIL WAR

The Northern states had significant advantages, including:

- Larger population. The North consisted of 24 states to the South's 11.
- Better transportation and finances. With railroads primarily in the North, supply chains were much more dependable, as was trade coming from overseas.
- More raw materials. The North held the majority of America's gold, as well as iron, copper and other minerals vital to wartime.

The South's advantages included:

- Better-trained military officers. Many of the Southern officers were West Point trained and had commanded in the Mexican and Indian wars.
- More familiar with weapons. The climate and lifestyle of the South meant most of the people were well versed in both guns and horses. The industrial North had less extensive experience.
- Defensive position. The South felt victory was guaranteed, since they were protecting their own lands, while the North would be invading.
- Well-defined goals. The South was fighting a war to be allowed to govern themselves and preserve their way of life.

Major Battles of the Civil War

The Battle of Bull Run, July 21, 1861. The First Battle of Bull Run, was the first major land battle of the war. Observers, expecting to enjoy an entertaining skirmish, set up picnics nearby. Instead, they found themselves witness to a bloodbath. Union forces were defeated, and the battle set the course of the Civil War as long, bloody and costly.

The Capture of Fort Henry by Ulysses S. Grant. This battle in February of 1862 marked the Union's first major victory.

The Battle of Gettysburg, July 1-3, 1863. Often seen as the turning point of the war, Gettysburg also saw the largest number of casualties of the war, with over 50,000 dead. Robert E. Lee was defeated, and the Confederate army, significantly crippled, withdrew.

The Overland Campaign, 1864. Grant, now in command of all the Union armies, led this high casualty campaign that eventually positioned the Union for victory.

Sherman's March to the Sea. William Tecumseh Sherman, in May of 1864, conquered Atlanta. He then continued to Savannah, destroying indiscriminately as he went.

Following Lee's defeat at the Appomattox Courthouse, General Grant accepted Lee's surrender in the home of Wilmer McLean, Appomattox, Virginia on April 9, 1865.

Lincoln's Assassination

The Civil War ended with the surrender of the South on April 9, 1865. Five days later, Lincoln and his wife, Mary, went to the play *Our American Cousin* at the Ford Theater. John Wilkes Booth, who did not know that the war was over, did his part in a plot to help the Confederacy by shooting Lincoln. Booth was tracked down and killed by Union soldiers twelve days later. Lincoln was carried from the theater to a nearby house, where he died the next morning.

Review Video: Civil War
Visit mometrix.com/academy and enter code: 239557

Thirteenth, Fourteenth and Fifteenth Amendments

The Thirteenth Amendment was passed on December 18, 1865. This amendment prohibited slavery in the United States.

Review Video: The 13th Amendment
Visit mometrix.com/academy and enter code: 800185

The Fourteenth Amendment overturned the Dred Scott decision, and was ratified July 9, 1868. American citizenship was redefined, with all citizens guaranteed equal legal protection by all states. It also guaranteed citizens the right to file a lawsuit or serve on a jury.

Review Video: The 14th Amendment
Visit mometrix.com/academy and enter code: 851325

The Fifteenth Amendment was ratified February 3, 1870. It states that no citizen of the United States can be denied the right to vote based on race, color, or previous status as a slave.

Review Video: The 15th Amendment
Visit mometrix.com/academy and enter code: 287199

Reconstruction and the Freedmen's Bureau

In the aftermath of the Civil War, the South was left in chaos. From 1865 to 1877, government on all levels worked to help restore order to the South, ensure civil rights to the freed slaves, and bring the Confederate states back into the Union. In 1866, Congress passed the Reconstruction Acts, putting former Confederate states under military rule.

The Freedmen's Bureau was formed to help freedmen and give assistance to whites in the South who needed basic necessities like food and clothing. Many in the South felt the Freedmen's Bureau worked to set freed slaves against their former owners. The Bureau was intended to help former slaves become self-sufficient, and to keep them from falling prey to those who would take advantage of them.

Phases of Reconstruction

Presidential Reconstruction – largely driven by President Andrew Johnson's policies, the Presidential phase of Reconstruction was lenient on the South and allowed continued discrimination against and control over blacks.

Congressional Reconstruction – Congress, controlled largely by Radical Republicans, took a different stance, providing a wider range of civil rights for blacks and greater control over Southern government. Congressional Reconstruction is marked by military control of the former Confederate States.

Redemption – Gradually, the Confederate states were readmitted into the union. During this time, white Democrats took over the government of most of the South. Troops finally departed the South in 1877.

Review Video: Reconstruction Era
Visit mometrix.com/academy and enter code: 790561

Radical and Moderate Republicans

The Radical Republicans wished to treat the South quite harshly after the war. Thaddeus Stephens, the House Leader, suggested that the Confederate States be treated as if they were territories again, with ten years of military rule and territorial government before they would be readmitted. They also wanted to give all black men the right to vote. Former Confederate soldiers would be required to swear they had not fought against the Union in order to be granted full rights as American citizens.

By contrast, the moderate Republicans wanted only black men who were literate or who had served as Union troops to be able to vote. All Confederate soldiers except troop leaders would also be able to vote. Before his death, Lincoln had favored a more moderate approach to Reconstruction, hoping this approach might bring some states back into the Union before the end of the war.

Black Codes and the Civil Rights Bill

The Black Codes were proposed to control freed slaves. They would not be allowed to bear arms, assemble, serve on juries, or testify against whites. Schools would be segregated, and unemployed blacks could be arrested and forced to work.

The Civil Rights bill countered these codes, providing much wider rights for the freed slaves.

Andrew Johnson, who became president after Lincoln's death, supported the Black Codes, and vetoed the Civil Rights bill. Congress overrode his veto and impeached Johnson, the culmination of tensions between Congress and the president. He came within a single vote of being convicted.

Carpetbaggers and Scalawags

The chaos in the south attracted a number of people seeking to fill the power vacuums and take advantage of the economic disruption.

Scalawags were southern Whites who aligned with Freedmen to take over local governments. Many in the South who could have filled political offices refused to take the necessary oath required to grant them the right to vote, leaving many opportunities for Scalawags and others.

Carpetbaggers were northerners who traveled to the South for various reasons. Some provided assistance, while others sought to make money or to acquire political power during this chaotic period.

Gilded Age

The time period from the end of the Civil War to the beginning of the First World War is often referred to as the Gilded Age, or the Second Industrial Revolution. The U.S. was changing from an agriculturally based economy to an industrial economy, with rapid growth accompanying the shift. In addition, the country itself was expanding, spreading into the seemingly unlimited West.

This time period saw the beginning of banks, department stores, chain stores, and trusts—all familiar features of our modern-day landscape. Cities also grew rapidly, and large numbers of immigrants arrived in the country, swelling the urban ranks.

Transcontinental Railroad

In 1869, the Union Pacific Railroad completed the first section of a planned transcontinental railroad. This section went from Omaha, Nebraska to Sacramento, California. With the rise of the railroad, products were much more easily transported across country. While this was positive overall for industry throughout the country, it was often damaging to family farmers, who found themselves paying high shipping costs for smaller supply orders while larger companies received major discounts.

Ninety percent of the workers constructing the railroad were Chinese, working in very dangerous conditions for very low pay.

Immigration Limits in the 19th Century

In 1870, the Naturalization Act put limits on U.S. citizenship, allowing full citizenship only to whites and those of African descent. The Chinese Exclusion Act of 1882 put limits on Chinese immigration. The Immigration Act of 1882 taxed immigrants, charging fifty cents per person. These funds helped pay administrative costs for regulating immigration. Ellis Island opened in 1892 as a processing center those arriving in New York. 1921 saw the Emergency Quota Act passed, also known as the Johnson Quota Act, which severely limited the number of immigrants allowed into the country.

Agriculture

Technological Advances

During the mid-1800s, irrigation techniques improved significantly. Advances occurred in cultivation and breeding, as well as fertilizer use and crop rotation. In the Great Plains, also known as the Great American Desert, the dense soil was finally cultivated with steel plows. In 1892, gasoline-powered tractors arrived, and were widely used by 1900.

Other advancements in agriculture's tool set included barbed wire fences, combines, silos, deep-water wells, and the cream separator.

Major Legislation

The Department of Agriculture came into being in 1862, working for the interests of farmers and ranchers across the country.

The Morrill Land-Grant Acts were passed in 1862, allowing land-grant colleges.

In conjunction with land-grant colleges, the Hatch Act of 1887 brought agriculture experimental stations into the picture, helping discover new farming techniques.

In 1914, the Smith-Lever Act provided cooperative programs to help educate people about food, home economics, community development and agriculture. Related agriculture extension programs helped farmers increase crop production to feed the rapidly growing nation.

Major Inventors from the 1800s

1. Alexander Graham Bell—the telephone
2. Orville and Wilbur Wright—the airplane
3. Richard Gatling—the machine gun
4. Walter Hunt, Elias Howe and Isaac Singer—the sewing machine
5. Nikola Tesla—alternating current
6. George Eastman—the camera
7. Thomas Edison—light bulbs, motion pictures, the phonograph
8. Samuel Morse—the telegraph
9. Charles Goodyear—vulcanized rubber
10. Cyrus McCormick—the reaper
11. George Westinghouse—the transformer, the air brake

This was an active period for invention, with about 700,000 patents registered between 1860 and 1900.

Populist Party

A major recession struck the United States during the 1890s, with crop prices falling dramatically. Drought compounded the problems, leaving many American farmers in crippling debt. The Farmers Alliance formed, drawing the rural poor into a single political entity.

Recession also affected the more industrial parts of the country. The Knights of Labor, formed in 1869 by Uriah Stephens, was able to unite workers into a union to protect their rights. Dissatisfied by views espoused by industrialists, these two groups, the Farmers Alliance and the Knights of Labor, joined to form the Populist Party.

Some of the elements of the party's platform included:

- National currency
- Income tax
- Government ownership of railroads, telegraph and telephone systems
- Secret ballot for voting
- Immigration restriction
- Term limits for President and Vice-President

The Populist Party was in favor of decreasing elitism and making the voice of the common man more easily heard in the political process.

Growth of the Labor Movement

The first large, well-organized strike occurred in 1892. Called the Homestead Strike, it occurred when the Amalgamated Association of Iron and Steel Works struck against the Carnegie Steel Company. Gunfire ensued, and Carnegie was able to eliminate the plant's union.

In 1894, workers, led by Eugene Debs, initiated the Pullman Strike after the Pullman Palace Car Co. cut their wages by 28 percent. President Grover Cleveland called in troops to break up the strike on the grounds that it interfered with mail delivery.

Mary Harris Jones, also known as Mother Jones, organized the Children's Crusade to protest child labor. A protest march proceeded to the home of President Theodore Roosevelt in 1902. Jones also worked with the United Mine Workers of America, and helped found the Industrial Workers of the World.

Panic of 1893

Far from a U.S.-centric event, the Panic of 1893 was an economic crisis that affected most of the globe. As a response to the Panic, President Grover Cleveland repealed the Sherman Silver Purchase Act, afraid it had caused the downturn rather than boosting the economy as intended.

The Panic led to bankruptcies, with railroads going under and factory unemployment rising as high as 25 percent. In the end, the Republican Party regained power due to the economic crisis.

Progressive Era

From the 1890s to the end of the First World War, Progressives set forth an ideology that drove many levels of society and politics. The Progressives were in favor of workers' rights and safety, and wanted measures taken against waste and corruption. They felt science could help improve society, and that the government could—and should—provide answers to a variety of social problems.

Progressives came from a wide variety of backgrounds, but were united in their desire to improve society.

Review Video: The Progressive Era
Visit mometrix.com/academy and enter code: 722394

Muckrakers

"Muckrakers" was a term used to identify aggressive investigative journalists who brought to light scandals, corruption, and many other wrongs being perpetrated in late nineteenth century society. Among these intrepid writers were:

- Ida Tarbell—he exposed the Standard Oil Trust.
- Jacob Riis—a photographer, he helped improve the lot of the poor in New York.
- Lincoln Steffens—he worked to expose political corruption.
- Upton Sinclair—his book *The Jungle* led to reforms in the meat packing industry.

Through the work of these journalists, many new policies came into being, including workmen's compensation, child labor laws, and trust-busting.

Federal Trade Commission

Muckrakers such as Ida Tarbell and Lincoln Steffens brought to light the damaging trend of trusts—huge corporations working to monopolize areas of commerce and so control prices and distribution. The Sherman Act and the Clayton Antitrust Act set out guidelines for competition among corporations and set out to eliminate these trusts. The Federal Trade Commission was formed in order to enforce antitrust measures and ensure companies were operated fairly and did not create controlling monopolies.

Constitutional Amendments: 16th, 17th, 18th, and 19th

The early twentieth century saw several amendments made to the U.S. Constitution. These included:

- Sixteenth Amendment, 1913 established a graduated income tax.
- Seventeenth Amendment, 1913 allowed direct election of Senators.
- Eighteenth Amendment, 1919 prohibited the sale, production and importation of alcohol. This amendment was later repealed by the Twenty-first Amendment.
- Nineteenth Amendment, 1920 gave women the right to vote.

These amendments largely grew out of the Progressive Era, as many citizens worked to improve American society.

Spanish-American War

Spain had controlled Cuba since the fifteenth century. Over the centuries, the Spanish had quashed a variety of revolts. In 1886, slavery ended in Cuba, and another revolt was rising.

In the meantime, the US had expressed interest in Cuba, offering Spain $130 million for the island in 1853, during Franklin Pierce's presidency. In 1898, the Cuban revolt was underway. In spite of various factions supporting the Cubans, the US President, William McKinley, refused to recognize the rebellion, preferring negotiation over involvement in war. Then The Maine, a US battleship in Havana Harbor, was blown up, costing nearly 300 lives. The US declared war two months later, and the war ended four months later with a Spanish surrender.

The Spanish-American war, 1898-1902, saw a number of Native Americans serving with Teddy Roosevelt in the Rough Riders. Apache scouts accompanied General John J. Pershing to Mexico, hoping to find Pancho Villa. More than 17,000 Native Americans were drafted into service for World War I, though at the time they were not considered as legal citizens. In 1924, Indians were finally granted official citizenship by the Indian Citizenship Act.

After decades of relocation, forced assimilation and outright genocide the number of Native Americans in the U.S. has greatly declined. Though many Native Americans have chosen—or have been forced—to assimilate, about 300 reservations exist today, with most of their inhabitants living in abject poverty.

Panama Canal

Initial work began on the Panama Canal in 1880, though the idea had been discussed since the 1500s. The Canal greatly reduces the length and time needed to sail from one ocean to the other by connecting the Atlantic to the Pacific through the Isthmus of Panama, which joins South America to North America. Before the Canal was built, travelers had to sail all the way around South America to reach the West Coast of the US.

The French began the work in 1880, after successfully completing the Suez Canal, connecting the Mediterranean Sea to the Red Sea. However, their efforts quickly fell apart. The US moved in to take over, completing the complex canal in 1914.

The Panama Canal was constructed as a lock-and-lake canal, with ships actually lifted on locks to travel from one lake to another over the rugged, mountainous terrain. In order to maintain control of the Canal Zone, the US assisted Panama in its battle for independence from Columbia.

Roosevelt's "Big Stick Diplomacy"

Theodore Roosevelt's famous quote, "Speak softly and carry a big stick," is supposedly of African origins, at least according to Roosevelt. He used this proverb to justify expanded involvement in foreign affairs during his tenure as President. The US military was deployed to protect American interests in Latin America. Roosevelt also worked to maintain an equal or greater influence in Latin America than those held by European interests.

As a result, the US Navy grew larger, and the US generally became more involved in foreign affairs. Roosevelt felt that if any country was left vulnerable to control by Europe, due to economic issues or political instability, the US had not only a right to intervene, but was obligated to do so. This led to US involvement in Cuba, Nicaragua, Haiti and the Dominican Republic over several decades leading into the First and Second World Wars.

William Howard Taft's "Dollar Diplomacy"

During William Howard Taft's presidency, Taft instituted "Dollar Diplomacy." This approach was used as a description of American efforts to influence Latin America and East Asia through economic rather than military means. Taft saw past efforts in these areas to be political and warlike, while his efforts focused on peaceful economic goals. His justification of the policy was to protect the Panama Canal, which was vital to US trade interests.

In spite of Taft's assurance that Dollar Diplomacy was a peaceful approach, many interventions proved violent. During Latin American revolts, such as those in Nicaragua, the US sent troops to settle the revolutions. Afterwards, bankers moved in to help support the new leaders through loans. Dollar Diplomacy continued until 1913, when Woodrow Wilson was elected President.

International Diplomacy of Woodrow Wilson

Turning away from Taft's "Dollar Diplomacy", Wilson instituted a foreign policy he referred to as "moral diplomacy." This approach still influences American foreign policy today.

Wilson felt that representative government and democracy in all countries would lead to worldwide stability. Democratic governments, he felt, would be less likely to threaten American interests.

He also saw the US and Great Britain as the great role models in this area, as well as champions of world peace and self-government. Free trade and international commerce would allow the US to speak out regarding world events.

Main elements of Wilson's policies included:

1. Maintaining a strong military
2. Promoting democracy throughout the world
3. Expanding international trade to boost the American economy

First World War and the 1920s

The First World War occurred from 1914 to 1918 and was fought largely in Europe. Triggered by the assassination of Austrian Archduke Francis Ferdinand, the war rapidly escalated. At the beginning of the conflict, Woodrow Wilson declared the US neutral.

Events Leading to US Involvement

Sinking of the Lusitania

The British passenger liner RMS Lusitania was sunk by a German U-boat in 1915. Among the 1,000 civilian victims were 100 Americans. Outraged by this act, many Americans began to push for US involvement in the war, using the Lusitania as a rallying cry.

German U-Boat Aggression

Wilson continued to keep the US out of the war, with his 1916 reelection slogan, "He kept us out of war." While he continued to work toward an end of the war, German U-boats began to indiscriminately attack American and Canadian merchant ships carrying supplies to Germany's enemies in Europe.

Zimmerman Note

The final event that brought the US into World War I was the interception of the Zimmerman Note. In this telegram, Germany communicated with the Mexican government its intentions to invade the US with Mexico's assistance.

Review Video: WWI Overview
Visit mometrix.com/academy and enter code: 659767

U.S. Support in World War I

American railroads came under government control in December 1917. The widespread system was consolidated into a single system, with each region assigned a director. This greatly increased the efficiency of the railroad system, allowing the railroads to supply both domestic and military needs. Control returned to private ownership in 1920. In 1918, telegraph, telephone and cable services also came under Federal control, to be returned to private management the next year.

The American Red Cross supported the war effort by knitting clothes for Army and Navy troops. They also helped supply hospital and refugee clothing and surgical dressings. Over eight million people participated in this effort.

To generate wartime funds, the US government sold Liberty Bonds. In four issues, they sold nearly $25 billion—more than one fifth of Americans purchased them. After the war, Liberty Bonds were replaced with Victory Bonds.

Wilson's Fourteen Points

President Woodrow Wilson proposed Fourteen Points as the basis for a peace settlement to end the war. Presented to the US Congress in January 1918, the Fourteen Points included:

- Five points outlining general ideals
- Eight points to resolve immediate problems of political and territorial nature
- One point proposing an organization of nations with the intent of maintaining world peace

In November of that same year, Germany agreed to an armistice, assuming the final treaty would be based on the Fourteen Points. However, during the peace conference in Paris 1919, there was much disagreement, leading to a final agreement that punished Germany and the other Central Powers much more than originally intended. Henry Cabot Lodge, who had become the Foreign Relations Committee chairman in 1918, wanted an unconditional surrender from Germany.

A League of Nations was included in the Treaty of Versailles at Wilson's insistence. The Senate rejected the Treaty of Versailles, and in the end, Wilson refused to concede to Lodge's demands. As a result, the US did not join the League of Nations.

Review Video: Woodrow Wilson's 14 Points
Visit mometrix.com/academy and enter code: 335789

America in the 1920s

The post-war '20s saw many Americans moving from the farm to the city, with growing prosperity in the US. The Roaring Twenties, or the Jazz Age, was driven largely by growth in the automobile and entertainment industries. Individuals like Charles Lindbergh, the first aviator to make a solo flight cross the Atlantic Ocean, added to the American admiration of individual accomplishment. Telephone lines, distribution of electricity, highways, the radio, and other inventions brought great changes to everyday life.

The Harlem Renaissance saw a number of African American artists settling in Harlem, New York City. This community produced a number of well-known artists and writers, including Langston Hughes, Nella Larson, Zora Neale Hurston, Claude McKay, Countee Cullen and Jean Toomer.

The growth of jazz, also largely driven by African Americans, defined the Jazz Age. Its unconventional, improvisational style matched the growing sense of optimism and exploration of the decade. Originating as an offshoot of the blues, jazz began in New Orleans. Some significant jazz musicians were Duke Ellington, Louis Armstrong and Jelly Roll Morton.

Social Tension in 20th Century America

National Origins Act of 1924

The National Origins Act (Johnson-Reed Act) placed limitations on immigration. The number of immigrants allowed into the US was based on the population of each nationality of immigrants who were living in the country in 1890. Only two percent of each nationality's 1890 population numbers were allowed to immigrate. This led to great disparities between immigrants from various nations, and Asian immigration was not allowed at all.

Some of the impetus behind the Johnson-Reed Act came as a result of paranoia following the Russian Revolution. Fear of communist influences in the US led to a general fear of immigrants.

Red Scare

World War I created many jobs, but after the war ended these jobs disappeared, leaving many unemployed. In the wake of these employment changes the International Workers of the World and the Socialist Party, headed by Eugene Debs, became more and more visible. Workers initiated strikes in an attempt to regain the favorable working conditions that had been put into place before the war. Unfortunately, many of these strikes became violent, and the actions were blamed on "Reds," or Communists, for trying to spread their views into America. With the Bolshevik Revolution being recent news in Russia, many Americans feared a similar revolution might occur here. The Red Scare ensued, with many individuals jailed for supposedly holding communist, anarchist or socialist beliefs.

Growth of Civil Rights for African Americans

Marcus Garvey founded the Universal Negro Improvement Association, which became a large and active organization focused on building black nationalism. In 1911, the National Association for the Advancement of Colored People (NAACP) came into being, working to defeat Jim Crow laws. The NAACP also helped prevent racial segregation from becoming federal law, fought against lynchings, helped black soldiers in WWI become officers, and helped defend the Scottsboro Boys, who were unjustly accused of rape.

Ku Klux Klan

In 1866, Confederate Army veterans came together to fight against Reconstruction in the South, forming a group called the Ku Klux Klan (KKK). With white supremacist beliefs, including anti-Semitism, nativism, anti-Catholicism, and overt racism, this organization relied heavily on violence to get its message across. In 1915, they grew again in power, using a film called *The Birth of a Nation*, by D.W. Griffith, to spread their ideas. In the 1920s, the reach of the KKK spread far into the North and Midwest, and members controlled a number of state governments. Its membership and power began to decline during the Great Depression, but experienced a major resurgence later.

American Civil Liberties Union

The American Civil Liberties Union (ACLU), founded in 1920, grew from the American Union Against Militarism. This former organization helped conscientious objectors avoid going to war during WWI, and also helped those being prosecuted under the Espionage Act (1917) and the Sedition Act (1918), many of whom were immigrants. Their major goals were to protect immigrants and other citizens who were threatened with prosecution for their political beliefs, and to support labor unions, which were also under threat by the government during the Red Scare.

Anti-Defamation League

In 1913, the Anti-Defamation League was formed to prevent anti-Semitic behavior and practices. Its actions also worked to prevent all forms of racism, and to prevent individuals from being discriminated against for any reason involving their race. They spoke against the Ku Klux Klan, as well as other racist or anti-Semitic organizations. This organization still exists, and still works to fight discrimination against minorities of all kinds.

The Great Depression and World War II

Great Depression

The Great Depression, which began in 1929 with the Stock Market Crash, grew out of several factors that had developed over the previous years including:

- Growing economic disparity between the rich and middle-class, with the rich amassing wealth much more quickly than the lower classes
- Disparity in economic distribution in industries
- Growing use of credit, leading to an inflated demand for some goods
- Government support of new industries rather than providing additional support for agriculture
- Risky stock market investments, leading to the stock market crash

Additional factors contributing to the Depression also included the Labor Day Hurricane in the Florida Keys (1935) and the Great Hurricane of 1938, in Long Island, along with the Dust Bowl in the Great Plains, which destroyed crops and resulted in the displacement of as many as 2.5 million people.

Review Video: The Great Depression
Visit mometrix.com/academy and enter code: 635912

Franklin D. Roosevelt's "New Deal"

Franklin D. Roosevelt was elected president in 1932 with his promise of a "New Deal" for Americans. His goals were to provide government work programs to provide jobs, wages and relief to numerous workers throughout the beleaguered US. Congress gave Roosevelt almost free rein to produce relief legislation.

The goals of this legislation were:

- Relief: Accomplished largely by creating jobs
- Recovery: Stimulate the economy through the National Recovery Administration
- Reform: Pass legislation to prevent future similar economic crashes

The Roosevelt Administration also passed legislation regarding ecological issues, including the Soil Conservation Service, aimed at preventing another Dust Bowl.

The administration passed several laws and established several institutions to initiate the "reform" portion of the New Deal, including:

- Glass-Steagall Act—separated investment from the business of banking.
- Securities Exchange Commission (SEC)—helped regulate Wall Street investment practices, making them less dangerous to the overall economy.
- Wagner Act—provided worker and union rights to improve relations between employees and employers. This act was later amended by the Taft-Hartley Act of 1947 and the Landrum Griffin Act of 1959, which further clarified certain elements.
- Social Security Act of 1935—provided pensions as well as unemployment insurance.
- Davis-Bacon Act (1931)—provided fair compensation for contractors and subcontractors.
- Walsh-Healey Act (1936)—established a minimum wage, child labor laws, safety standards, and overtime pay.

Other actions focused on insuring bank deposits and adjusting the value of American currency. Most of these regulatory agencies and government policies and programs still exist today.

Roosevelt's "Alphabet Organizations"

So-called alphabet organizations set up during Roosevelt's administration included:

- Civilian Conservation Corps (CCC)—provided jobs in the forestry service
- Agricultural Adjustment Administration (AAA)—increased agricultural income by adjusting both production and prices.
- Tennessee Valley Authority (TVA)—organized projects to build dams in the Tennessee River for flood control and production of electricity, resulting in increased productivity for industries in the area, and easier navigation of the Tennessee River
- Public Works Administration (PWA) and Civil Works Administration (CWA)—initiated over 34,000 projects, providing employment
- Works Progress Administration (WPA)—helped unemployed persons to secure employment on government work projects or elsewhere

Interventionism and Isolationism

When war broke out in Europe in 1939, President Roosevelt stated that the US would remain neutral. However, his overall approach was considered "interventionist," as he was willing to provide any necessary aid to the Allies short of actually entering the conflict. Thus, the US supplied a wide variety of war materials to the Allied nations.

Isolationists believed the US should not provide any aid to the Allies, including supplies. They felt Roosevelt, by assisting the Allies, was leading the US into a war for which it was not prepared. Led by Charles A. Lindbergh, the Isolationists believed any involvement in the European conflict endangered the US by weakening its national defense.

United States Entrance into World War II

In 1937, Japan invaded China, prompting the US to halt all exports to Japan. Roosevelt also did not allow Japanese interests to withdraw money held in US banks. In 1941, General Tojo rose to power as the Japanese Premier. Recognizing America's ability to bring a halt to Japan's expansion, he authorized the bombing of Pearl Harbor on December 7, of that year. The US responded by declaring war on Japan. Because of the Tipartite Pact among the Axis Powers, Germany and Italy then declared war on the US, followed by Bulgaria and Hungary.

Minorities and Women in World War II

Minorities

The 442nd Regimental Combat Team consisted of Japanese Americans fighting in Europe for the US. The most highly decorated unit per member in US history, they suffered a 93 percent casualty rate during the war.

The Tuskegee Airmen were African American aviators, the first black Americans allowed to fly for the military. In spite of not being eligible to become official navy pilots, they flew over 15,000 missions and were highly decorated.

The Navajo Code Talkers were native Navajo who used their traditional language to transmit information among Allied forces. Because Navajo is a language and not simply a code, the Axis powers were never able to translate it. Use of Navajo Code Talkers to transmit information was instrumental in the taking of Iwo Jima and other major victories of the war.

Women

Women served widely in the military during WWII, working in numerous positions, including the Flight Nurses Corps. Women also moved into the workforce while men were overseas, leading to over 19 million women in the US workforce by 1944. Rosie the Riveter stood as a symbol of these women and a means of recruiting others to take needed positions. Women, as well as their families left behind during wartime, also grew Victory Gardens to help provide food.

War Relocation Camps

In 1940, the US passed the Alien Registration Act, which required all aliens older than fourteen to be fingerprinted and registered. They were also required to report changes of address within five days.

Tension between whites and Japanese immigrants in California, which had been building since the beginning of the century, came to a head with the bombing of Pearl Harbor in 1941. Believing that even those Japanese living in the US were likely to be loyal to their native country, the president ordered numerous Japanese to be arrested on suspicion of subversive action isolated in exclusion zones known as War Relocation Camps. Over 120,000 Japanese Americans, two thirds of them citizens of the US, were sent to these camps during the war.

Atomic Bomb

The atomic bomb, developed during WWII, was the most powerful bomb ever invented. A single bomb, carried by a single plane, held enough power to destroy an entire city. This devastating effect was demonstrated with the bombing of Hiroshima and Nagasaki in 1945 in what later became a controversial move, but ended the war. The bombings resulted in as many as 200,000 immediate deaths and many more as time passed after the bombings, mostly due to radiation poisoning.

Whatever the arguments against the use of "The Bomb", the post WWII era saw many countries develop similar weapons to match the newly expanded military power of the US. The impact of those developments and use of nuclear weapons continues to haunt international relations today.

Surrender of Axis Powers

Surrender of Germany

In 1941, Hitler violated the non-aggression pact he had signed with Stalin in 1939 by invading the USSR. Stalin then joined the Allies. Stalin, Roosevelt and Winston Churchill planned to defeat Germany first, then Japan, bringing the war to an end.

Starting in 1942 through 1943, the Allies drove Axis forces out of Africa. In addition, the Germans were soundly defeated at Stalingrad.

Between July 1943 and May 1945, Allied troops liberated Italy. June 6, 1944, known as D-Day, the Allies invaded France at Normandy. Soviet troops moved on the eastern front at the same time, driving German forces back. April 25, 1945, Berlin was surrounded by Soviet troops. On May 7, Germany surrendered.

Surrender of Japan

War continued with Japan after Germany's surrender. Japanese forces had taken a large portion of Southeast Asia and the Western Pacific, all the way to the Aleutian Islands in Alaska. General Doolittle bombed several Japanese cities while American troops scored a victory at Midway. Additional fighting in the Battle of the Coral Sea further weakened Japan's position. As a final blow, the US dropped two atomic bombs, one on Hiroshima and the other on Nagasaki, Japan. This was the first-time atomic bombs had ever been used in warfare, and the devastation was horrific and demoralizing. Japan surrendered on September 2, 1945.

Yalta Conference and the Potsdam Conference

In February 1945, Joseph Stalin, Franklin D. Roosevelt and Winston Churchill met in Yalta to discuss the post-war treatment of Europe, particularly Germany. Though Germany had not yet surrendered, its defeat was imminent. After Germany's official surrender, Clement Attlee, Harry Truman and Joseph Stalin met to formalize those plans. This meeting was called the Potsdam Conference.

Basic provisions of these agreements included:

- Dividing Germany and Berlin into four zones of occupation
- Demilitarization of Germany
- Poland remaining under Soviet control
- Outlawing the Nazi Party
- Trials for Nazi leaders
- Relocation of numerous German citizens
- The USSR joined the United Nations, established in 1945
- Establishment of the United Nations Security Council, consisting of the US, the UK, the USSR, China and France

Peace Treaty with Japan

General Douglas MacArthur directed the American military occupation of Japan after the country surrendered. The goals the US occupation included removing Japan's military and making the country a democracy. A 1947 constitution removed power from the emperor and gave it to the people, as well as granting voting rights to women. Japan was no longer allowed to declare war, and a group of 25 government officials were tried for war crimes. In 1951, the US finally signed a peace treaty with Japan. This treaty allowed Japan to rearm itself for purposes of self-defense, but stripped the country of the empire it had built overseas.

State of the US after World War II

Following WWII, the US became the strongest political power in the world, becoming a major player in world affairs and foreign policies. The US determined to stop the spread of Communism, naming itself the "arsenal of democracy."

In addition, America had emerged with a greater sense of itself as a single, integrated nation, with many regional and economic differences diminished. The government worked for greater equality and the growth of communications increased contact among different areas of the country.

Both the aftermath of the Great Depression and the necessities of WWII had given the government greater control over various institutions as well as the economy. This also meant the American government took on greater responsibility for the well-being of its citizens, both in the domestic arena, such as providing basic needs, and in protecting them from foreign threats. This increased role of providing basic necessities for all Americans has been criticized by some as "the welfare state."

Review Video: World War II
Visit mometrix.com/academy and enter code: 759402

Technological Advances following the Second World War

Numerous technological advances after the Second World War led to more effective treatment of diseases, more efficient communication and transportation, and new means of generating power. Advances in medicine increased the lifespan of people in developed countries, and near-instantaneous communication began to make the world a much smaller place.

- Discovery of penicillin (1928)
- Supersonic air travel (1947)
- First commercial airline flight (1948)
- Nuclear power (1951)
- Orbital leading to manned space flight (Sputnik—1957)
- First man on the moon (1969)

United States Policy toward Immigrants after World War II

Prior to WW II, the US had been limiting immigration for several decades. After WW II, policy shifted slightly to accommodate political refugees from Europe and elsewhere. So many people were displaced by the war that in 1946, The UN formed the International Refugee Organization to deal with the problem.

In 1948, the US Congress passed the Displaced Persons Act, which allowed over 400,000 European refugees to enter the US, most of them concentration camp survivors and refugees from Eastern Europe. In 1952, the President's Escapee Program allowed refugees from Communist Europe to enter the US, as did the Refugee Relief Act, passed in 1953.

At the same time, however, the Internal Security Act of 1950 allowed deportation of declared Communists, and Asians were subjected to a quota based on race, rather than country of origin. Later changes included:

- 1962—Migration and Refugee Assistance Act—helped assist refugees in need.
- 1965—Immigration Act—ended quotas based on nation of origin.
- 1986—Immigration Reform and Control Act—prohibited the hiring of illegal immigrants, but also granted amnesty to about three million illegals already in the country.

Progress and Protest: 1948 - 1975

Civil Rights Movement

In the 1950s, post-war America was experiencing a rapid growth in prosperity. However, African Americans found themselves left behind. Following the lead of Mahatma Gandhi, who lead similar class struggles in India; African Americans began to demand equal rights.

Major Figures

Rosa Parks—often called the "mother of the Civil Rights Movement," her refusal to give up her seat on the bus to a white man served as a seed from which the movement grew.

Martin Luther King, Jr.—the best-known leader of the movement, King drew on Gandhi's beliefs and encouraged non-violent opposition. He led a march on Washington in 1963, received the Nobel Peace Prize in 1968, and was assassinated in 1968.

Malcolm X—espousing less peaceful means of change, Malcolm X became a Black Muslim, and supported black nationalism.

Stokely Carmichael—Carmichael invented the term "Black Power" and served as head of the Student Nonviolent Coordinating Committee. He believed in black pride and black culture, and felt separate political and social institutions should be developed for blacks.

Clayton Powell—chairman of the Coordinating Committee for Employment, he led rent strikes and other actions, as well as a bus boycott, to increase the hiring of blacks.

Jesse Jackson—Jackson was selected to head the Chicago Operation Breadbasket in 1966 by Martin Luther King, Jr., and went on to organize boycotts and other actions. He also had an unsuccessful run for President.

Major Events

Montgomery Bus Boycott—in 1955, Rosa Parks refused to give her seat on the bus to a white man. As a result, she was tried and convicted of disorderly conduct and of violating local ordinances. A 381-day boycott ensued, protesting segregation on public buses.

Desegregation of Little Rock—In 1957, after the Supreme Court decision on Brown vs. Board of Education, which declared "separate but equal" unconstitutional, the Arkansas school board voted to desegregate their schools. Even though Arkansas was considered progressive, its governor brought in the National Guard to prevent nine black students from entering Central High School in Little Rock. President Eisenhower responded by federalizing the National Guard and ordering them to stand down.

Birmingham Campaign—Protestors organized a variety of actions such as sit-ins and an organized march to launch a voting campaign. When the City of Birmingham declared the protests illegal, the protestors, including Martin Luther King, Jr., persisted and were arrested and jailed.

Legislation Influenced by the Civil Rights Movement

1. Brown vs. Board of Education (1954)—the Supreme Court declared that "separate but equal" accommodations and services were unconstitutional.
2. Civil Rights Act of 1964—declared discrimination illegal in employment, education, or public accommodation.
3. Voting Rights Act of 1965—ended various activities practiced, mostly in the South, to bar blacks from exercising their voting rights. These included poll taxes and literacy tests.

Harry S. Truman

Harry S. Truman took over the presidency from Franklin D. Roosevelt near the end of WW II. He made the final decision to drop atomic bombs on Japan, and he played a major role in the final decisions regarding treatment of post-war Germany.

On the domestic front, Truman initiated a 21-point plan known as the Fair Deal. This plan expanded Social Security, provided public housing, and made the Fair Employment Practices Act permanent. Truman helped support Greece and Turkey, under threat from the USSR, supported South Korea against communist North Korea, and helped with recovery in Western Europe. He also participated in the formation of NATO, the North Atlantic Treaty Organization.

Dwight D. Eisenhower

Eisenhower carried out a middle-of-the-road foreign policy and brought about several steps forward in equal rights. He worked to minimize tensions during the Cold War, and negotiated a peace treaty with Russia after the death of Stalin. He enforced desegregation by sending troops to Little Rock, Arkansas when the schools there were desegregated, and also ordered the desegregation of the military. Organizations formed during his administration included the Department of Health, Education and Welfare, and the National Aeronautics and Space Administration (NASA).

Korean War

The Korean War began in 1950 and ended in 1953. For the first time in history, a world organization—the United Nations—played a military role in a war. North Korea sent Communist troops into South Korea, seeking to bring the entire country under Communist control. The UN sent out a call to member nations, asking them to support South Korea. Truman sent troops, as did many other UN member nations. The war ended three years later with a truce rather than a peace treaty, and Korea remains divided at 38 degrees North Latitude, with Communist rule remaining in the North and a democratic government ruling the South.

John F. Kennedy

Although cut short by his assassination, during his term JFK instituted economic programs that led to a period of continuous expansion in the US unmatched since before WW II. He formed the Alliance for Progress and the Peace Corps, organizations intended to help developing nations. He also oversaw the passage of new civil rights legislation, and drafted plans to attack poverty and its causes, along with support of the arts. Kennedy's presidency ended when he was assassinated by Lee Harvey Oswald in 1963.

Cuban Missile Crisis

The Cuban Missile Crisis occurred in 1962, during John F. Kennedy's presidency. Russian Premier Nikita Khrushchev decided to place nuclear missiles in Cuba to protect the island from invasion by the US. American U-2 planes flying over the island photographed the missile bases as they were being built. Tensions rose, with the US concerned about nuclear missiles so close to its shores, and the USSR concerned about American missiles that had been placed in Turkey. Eventually, the missile sites were removed, and a US naval blockade turned back Soviet ships carrying missiles to Cuba. During negotiations, the US agreed to remove their missiles from Turkey and agreed to sell surplus wheat to the USSR. A telephone hot line between Moscow and Washington was set up to allow instant communication between the two heads of state to prevent similar incidents in the future.

LYNDON B. JOHNSON

Kennedy's Vice President, Lyndon Johnson, assumed the presidency after Kennedy's assassination. He supported civil rights bills, tax cuts, and other wide-reaching legislation that Kennedy had also supported. Johnson saw America as a "Great Society," and enacted legislation to fight disease and poverty, renew urban areas, support education and environmental conservation. Medicare was instituted under his administration. He continued Kennedy's supported of space exploration, and he is also known, although less positively, for his handling of the Vietnam War.

THE SPACE RACE

The Space Race was a technological rivalry between the Soviet Union and the United Space on the subject of outer space travel and exploration. Each country aimed to achieve certain space exploration landmarks first, including sending the first unmanned satellite into space, sending the first human into space, and putting the first human beings on the moon. The technology for such endeavors advanced rapidly in each country's efforts to win the "race."

Both sides achieved substantial victories: the Soviet Union won the unmanned satellite race with Sputnik 1 on October 4, 1957 and the first man in space race with Yuri Gagarin on April 12, 1961, while the United States won the race to put a man on the moon with Apollo 11 and Neil Armstrong on July 21, 1969.

VIETNAM WAR

After World War II, the US pledged, as part of its foreign policy, to come to the assistance of any country threatened by Communism. When Vietnam was divided into a Communist North and democratic South, much like Korea before it, the eventual attempts by the North to unify the country under Communist rule led to intervention by the US.

On the home front, the Vietnam War became more and more unpopular politically, with Americans growing increasingly discontent with the inability of the US to achieve the goals it had set for the Asian country. When President Richard Nixon took office in 1969, his escalation of the war led to protests at Kent State in Ohio, during which several students were killed by National Guard troops.

Protests continued, eventually resulting in the end of the compulsory draft in 1973. In that same year, the US departed Vietnam. In 1975, the south surrendered, and Vietnam became a unified country under Communist rule.

The Cold War

COLD WAR FOREIGN POLICY ACTS OF UNITED STATES

Marshall Plan—sent aid to war-torn Europe after WW II, largely focusing on preventing the spread of communism.

Containment—proposed by George F. Kennan, Containment focused on containing the spread of Soviet communism.

Truman Doctrine—Harry S. Truman stated that the US would provide both economic and military support to any country threatened by Soviet takeover.

National Security Act—passed in 1947, this act created the Department of Defense, the Central Intelligence Agency, and the National Security Council.

The combination of these acts led to the cold war, with Soviet communists attempting to spread their influence and the US and other countries trying to contain or stop this spread.

NATO, THE WARSAW PACT, AND THE BERLIN WALL

NATO, the North Atlantic Treaty Organization, came into being in 1949. It essentially amounted to an agreement among the US and Western European countries that an attack on any one of these countries was to be considered an attack against the entire group.

Under the influence of the Soviet Union, the Eastern European countries of USSR, Bulgaria, East Germany, Poland, Romania, Albania, Poland and Czechoslovakia responded with the Warsaw Pact, which created a similar agreement among those nations. In 1961, a wall was built to separate Communist East Berlin from democratic West Berlin. A similar, though metaphorical, wall lay between east and west, as well, and was referred to as the Iron Curtain.

NUCLEAR ARMS RACE

After the war, major nations, particularly the US and USSR, rushed to develop the atomic bomb, and later the hydrogen bomb, as well as many other highly advanced weapons systems. These countries seemed determined to outpace each other with the development of numerous, deadly weapons. These weapons were expensive and extremely dangerous, and it is possible that the war between US and Soviet interests remained "cold" due to the fear that one side or the other would use these terrifyingly powerful weapons.

END OF THE COLD WAR

In the late 1980s, Mikhail Gorbachev ruled the Soviet Union. He introduced a series of reform programs. Also, during this period, the Berlin Wall came down, ending the separation of East and West Germany. The Soviet Union relinquished its power over the various republics in Eastern Europe, and they became independent nations with their own individual governments. With the end of the USSR, the cold war also came to an end.

Review Video: The Cold War Resolution
Visit mometrix.com/academy and enter code: 278032

The Presidency: 1970s to Present Day

Richard Nixon

Richard Nixon is best known for illegal activities during his presidency, but other important events marked his tenure as president, including:

- Vietnam War comes to an end
- Improved diplomatic relations between the US and China, and the US and the USSR
- National Environmental Policy Act passed, providing for environmental protection
- Compulsory draft ended
- Supreme Court legalizes abortion in Roe v Wade
- Watergate

The Watergate scandal of 1972 ended Nixon's presidency, when he resigned rather than face impeachment and removal from office.

Gerald Ford

Gerald Ford was appointed to the vice presidency after Nixon's vice president Spiro Agnew resigned under charges of tax evasion. With Nixon's resignation, Ford became president.

Ford's presidency saw negotiations with Russia to limit nuclear arms, as well as struggles to deal with inflation, economic downturn, and energy shortages. Ford's policies sought to reduce governmental control of various businesses and reduce the role of government overall. He also worked to prevent escalation of conflicts in the Middle East.

Jimmy Carter

Jimmy Carter was elected president in 1976. Faced with a budget deficit, high unemployment, and continued inflation, Carter also dealt with numerous matters of international diplomacy including:

- Panama Canal Treaties
- Camp David Accords—negotiations between Anwar el-Sadat, the president of Egypt, and Menachem Begin, the Israeli Prime Minister, leading to a peace treaty between the two nations.
- Strategic Arms Limitation Talks (SALT) and resulting agreements and treaties
- Iran Hostage Crisis—when the Shah of Iran was deposed, an Islamic cleric, the Ayatollah Ruholla Khomeini, came into power. Fifty-three American hostages were taken and held for 444 days in the US Embassy.

Ronald Reagan

Ronald Reagan, at 69, became the oldest American president. The two terms of his administration included notable events such as:

- Reaganomics, also known as supply-side or trickle-down economics, involving major tax cuts in the upper income brackets
- Economic Recovery Tax Act of 1981
- First female justice appointed to the Supreme Court, Sandra Day O'Connor
- Massive increase in the national debt—increased from $600 billion to $3 trillion
- Reduction of nuclear weapons via negotiations with Mikhail Gorbachev

- Loss of the space shuttle Challenger
- Iran-Contra scandal—cover-up of US involvement in revolutions in El Salvador and Nicaragua
- Deregulation of savings and loan industry

George H. W. Bush

Reagan's presidency was followed by a term under his former Vice President, George H. W. Bush. His run for president included the famous "thousand points of light" speech, which was instrumental in increasing his standing in the election polls.

During Bush's presidency, numerous major international events took place, including:

- Fall of the Berlin wall and Germany's unification
- Panamanian dictator Manuel Noriega captured and tried on drug and racketeering charges
- Dissolution of the Soviet Union
- Gulf War, or Operation Desert Storm, triggered by Iraq's invasion of Kuwait
- Tiananmen Square Massacre in Beijing, China
- Ruby Ridge
- The arrival of the World Wide Web

Bill Clinton

William Jefferson Clinton was the second president in US history to be impeached, but he was not convicted, and maintained high approval ratings in spite of the impeachment. Major events during his presidency included:

- Family and Medical Leave Act
- Don't Ask Don't Tell, a compromise position regarding homosexuals serving in the military
- North American Free Trade Agreement, or NAFTA
- Defense of Marriage Act
- Oslo Accords
- Siege at Waco, Texas, involving the Branch Davidians led by David Koresh
- Bombing of the Murrah Federal Building in Oklahoma City, Oklahoma
- Troops sent to Haiti, Bosnia and Somalia to assist with domestic problems in those areas

George W. Bush

Amidst controversy, George W. Bush, son of George Herbert Walker Bush, became president after William Clinton. The election was tightly contested, and though he did not win the popular vote, he won the electoral vote. In the end a Supreme Court ruling was necessary to resolve the issue. His second term was also tightly contested. However, in the election for his second term, Bush won both the popular and the electoral vote.

On 9/11/2001, during his first year in office, Bush's presidency was challenged by the first terrorist attack on American soil when al-Qaeda terrorists flew planes into the World Trade Center, destroying it, and into the Pentagon, causing major damage. This event led to major changes in security in the US, especially regarding airline travel. It also led to US troops being deployed in Afghanistan.

Later, Bush initiated war in Iraq with the claim that the country held weapons of mass destruction. On March 20, 2003, the US, along with troops from more than 20 other countries, invaded Iraq.

The last months of Bush's administration saw a serious economic meltdown in the US and worldwide. Dramatic increases in oil prices resulted in extreme increases of gasoline prices. This, along with the meltdown of the mortgage industry, created serious and overwhelming economic issues for the Bush administration.

BARACK OBAMA

In 2008, Barack Obama, a Senator from Illinois, became the first African-American US president. His administration has focused on improving the lot of a country suffering from a major recession. His major initiatives included:

- Economic bailout packages
- Improvements in women's rights
- Moves to broaden LGBT rights
- Health care reform legislation
- Reinforcement of the war in Afghanistan

DONALD TRUMP

In 2016, Donald Trump, previously a real estate developer and television personality, was elected 45th president after a tumultuous election in which he won the electoral college but lost the popular vote. Marked by tension between the administration and domestic media, Trump's initiatives included:

- Appointing two Supreme Court Justices: Neil Gorsuch and Brett Kavanaugh
- Passing a major tax reform bill
- Enacting travel and emigration restrictions on eight nations: Iran, Libya, Syria, Yemen, Somalia, Chad, North Korea, and Venezuela
- Recognizing Jerusalem, rather than Tel Aviv, as the capital of Israel
- Responding to the novel coronavirus (SARS-CoV-2) outbreak

Almost completely along party lines, Donald Trump was impeached by the House on charges of abuse of power and obstruction of Congress; he was acquitted by the Senate.

Geography

Europe

The geographic realm of Europe is made up of five geographic regions (Western Europe, the British Isles, Northern Europe, Southern [Mediterranean] Europe, and Eastern Europe). It is home to one of the largest population clusters in the world. Despite the relatively small size of its territory, Europe's people and their actions have affected (and continue to affect) all the world's realms. Technological innovations, political revolutions, and vast empires have influenced the behaviors of people on each continent. European colonial endeavors have established communities and impacted the formation of ideologies the world over. Europe's natural and human resources have helped the realm to survive and grow throughout the years. For approximately the last 50 years, Europe has been engaged in a unification program known as the European Union. Currently, 27 of the realm's 48 nation-states are members of the Union.

Economic Geography

The economy of Europe is dominated by the European Union, which, if considered as a whole, has the largest economy in the world. Though the functional region of Western Europe has historically been the hub of economic activity in the realm, this situation is changing with the development of other core regions, productive complementarities, and interregional/international trade markets. Levels of economic development tend to decline as one moves from west to east across the realm; this too is changing with the growth of the economies of former member countries of the Soviet Union, and their increasing interactions with other regions and realms. Europe's agricultural and fishing sectors are highly developed, and still center on Western Europe. Europe's manufacturing sector is also quite developed. While many of the realm's industries are concentrated in Western Europe, deindustrialization in the region has resulted in the outsourcing of labor to areas such as Eastern Europe and China. Financial activity in the realm is concentrated in several cities, with London as the largest.

Russia

Russia, the largest territorial state on Earth, is an example of a geographic realm which has undergone tremendous amounts of change throughout its existence. Tsars conquered and dominated Russian territory, which was subsequently inhabited by Soviets, who then shaped the domain and its peoples into the Soviet Union. Though World War II tested the empire, it also validated the U.S.S.R.'s status as a global superpower, which it retained until the late 1980's. Internal factors (such as mismanagement of a communist government) and external factors (including the Second World War, pressure from anti-communist leaders, and the global decline of colonialism) eventually led to the dissolution of the Soviet Union in 1991. Consequent cultural, economic, and social diversity have given rise to the establishment of four geographical regions (each of which contains subregions): the Russian Core, the Eastern Frontier, Siberia, and the Far East.

Economic Geography

The economic geography of Russia is highly varied, and characterized by discrete core and peripheral regions of economic activity. Despite the presence of substantial natural resources (such as gas and oil) and a well-educated labor force, the effects of the transition from a failed centrally-planned economy during the Soviet Era to a free market continue to hinder the development of the economies in certain regions. In the agricultural sector, production has decreased drastically with attempts at the privatization of collective farms and restructuring of the economy. Also, the harsh climate in the realm has had an effect on agricultural production. The levels of meat, milk, vegetables, and grains have decreased yearly since 1989. This has had negative ramifications in a country that is largely dependent on its own food production. The inefficiencies and inadequacies held over from the Soviet Union continue to disturb Russia's industrial sector, particularly in the extraction of raw materials and the distribution of goods. Still, Russia is the most industrialized of all the former Soviet republics.

North America

Geography

The geographic realm of North America is home to two countries, Canada and the United States (which is currently considered a global superpower). This realm is characterized by pluralistic (diverse) societies which, unfortunately, are often plagued by social inequalities. It is also a postindustrial realm, which means that the economies of Canada and the United States each experienced increases in the amount of available information technology and rapid expansions of the tertiary (service) sector of industry after the industrialization processes in those countries. The eight regions of North America (many of which stretch across the U.S.-Canada boundary) are largely differentiated by differences in the various economic activities practiced in different areas. These regions include the Continental Core, the South, the Southwest, the West Coast, the Agricultural Heartland, French Canada, the New England/Maritime Provinces, and the Marginal Interior.

Economic Geography

United States

As a current superpower, the United States has one of the most advanced economies in the world. Like Canada, the United States contains many deposits of natural resources. For instance, the North American realm has more coal reserves than any other. The spatial organization of regional agricultural production in the United States exists within the framework of a modified Von Thunen model, with the "megalopolis" of New England at its center, and belts of specialized activity extending westward. Though the manufacturing sector is less important in a postindustrial economy, this type of activity is still practiced in the United States, and tends to cluster around several urban-industrial nodes, especially within the Manufacturing Belt (located in the Northeast United States). Increased mechanization and advancements in technology have eliminated many "blue-collar" jobs in this region. Most laborers in the U.S. workforce are employed in quaternary economic activity. States offering noneconomic amenities (such as weather and proximity to urban centers and universities) have experienced higher levels of growth than other regions.

Canada

As one of the world's wealthiest nations, Canada has a largely postindustrial economy, with employment concentrated in the service sector (particularly retail). However, unlike many developed countries, primary economic activities (specifically logging and oil production) are important aspects of the country's economy. Canada has a large and varied (though regionally variable) supply of natural resources, such as oil, nickel, and lead. Canadian agricultural products (especially wheat and grains) are exported in high levels to the United States, Europe, and East Asia. Another unusual aspect of Canada's economy (as compared to those of other highly-developed nations) is the historical secondary status of the manufacturing sector of industry. Though it is certainly not unimportant, manufacturing has never been as vital to the nation's economy as primary or tertiary activities. Many of Canada's industrial firms are branches of U.S. companies.

Regional disparities in wealth and economy strength have increased regionalism throughout the region.

Central and South America

Geography

Central America

The geographic realm of Central America, which is sometimes referred to as Middle America, covers the territory between southern North America and the boundary between Panama and Colombia. The exact demarcations of the realm vary from source to source; however, the economic subregion recognized by the United Nations includes all mainland states of North America south of the U.S.-Mexico border in the realm. Basically, this definition counts Mexico and Belize as members of the Central America realm, while other definitions assign these countries to the North American realm. Due to the influence of Spanish and Portuguese colonialism in Central America, this realm and South America are often jointly referred to as Latin America. Central America is divided into four regions: Mexico, the seven states of Central America (Belize, Costa Rica, El Salvador, Guatemala, Honduras, Nicaragua, and Panama), the larger islands of the Caribbean (the Greater Antilles), and the smaller islands of the Caribbean (the Lesser Antilles).

South America

The geographic realm of South America is made up of four regions: Brazil, the Northeastern countries, the West, and the Southern Cone.

South America and Central America are often collectively referred to as Latin America, due to the enduring cultural and social influences of former Spanish and Portuguese colonial presences in these areas. These influences are most visible in the languages, architecture, music, and visual arts of the peoples of South America. Roman Catholicism and traditional systems relating to land ownership, also transmitted from European countries, continue to be major factors in the evolution of South American societies. In addition, the cultural practices and beliefs of Native Americans have been and continue to be vital shaping forces in the realm.

Economic Geography

Central America

The economic geography of Central America includes the least developed territories in the Americas, with the exception of Mexico. Under the Mainland-Rimland framework, Central America is divided into a Euro-Amerindian Mainland (made up of mainland Middle America from Mexico to Panama, excluding parts of the Caribbean coast) and a Euro-African rimland (consisting of the coastal zone and the Caribbean islands). Economic activity on the Mainland has historically been oriented around haciendas (privately-owned estates maintained more for prestige and self-sufficiency than maximum production), and is therefore less dependent on trade with other nations. Governmental and social pressures have led to the forced specialization of productive activity in or the parceling out of haciendas in this area. The Rimland's economy has traditionally focused on plantation production, characterized by efficient production of one crop specifically for export and the importation of labor. The Rimland's economy is thus more dependent on the fluctuating global market. Plantation systems, like hacienda systems, continue to metamorphose under internal and external pressures; still, their effects remain visible in the region.

South America

The economic geography of South America is characterized by high levels of regional disparity. In many of the realm's countries (such as Brazil, Bolivia, and Venezuela), the richest 20% of the population may control over 60% of the nation's wealth, while the poorest 20% may own less than 5% of that wealth. Although several South American nations have become involved in the mining of oil, coal, and valuable minerals in high amounts, the realm's main economic focus is agriculture. The South American realm is unusual, because subsistence farming and commercial farming exist side by side; generally, a geographic realm is dominated by one or the other. Commercial farmers in this area tend to be involved in cattle ranching, wheat farming, grain farming (in a "Corn Belt" zone similar to that in the United States), or plantation-type agriculture. Commercial agricultural endeavors tend to be located near the coasts of the South American continent, with small pockets of activity in the interior. Subsistence-level farming takes place on all other arable land.

Africa

Geography

North Africa/Southwest Asia

The size and geographic diversity of the geographic realm of North Africa/Southwest Asia have spawned a number of different labels for the region, none of which are completely satisfactory. These labels include the Islamic realm, the Arab World, the dry world, Africa, and Asia. Though Islam and aridity do dominate the religious and climatic aspects of the realm, which domination is not complete, and the heterogeneity within these groups alone makes a difficulty with the notion of referring to the realm by a single characteristic. The use of relative location is seen as less divisive. The North Africa realm is composed of three regions (Egypt, North Africa, and the Southwest), and Southwest Asia is composed of four (the Middle East [this label is also disputed, due to what some see as the pejorative connotations of the term], the Arabian Peninsula, the North, and the East).

Sub-Saharan Africa

The geographic realm of Sub-Saharan Africa is composed of the territory between the southern border of the Sahara Desert and the southernmost coast of the country of South Africa. The boundary between the North Africa realm and the Sub-Saharan realm is a prime example of a transition zone; several states straddle this hypothetical divide. This area of the globe constitutes a fairly distinctive cultural realm, due to a fusion of traditional African beliefs and cultures with the influences of European colonialism.

Many countries in this realm exhibit export-oriented transport systems and European concepts of political geography while retaining their traditional languages, religions, and social practices. The realm of Sub-Saharan Africa is the least developed realm in the world, and the majority of its residents engage in agricultural production. This realm is made up of four regions: West Africa, East Africa, Equatorial Africa, and Southern Africa.

Economic Geography

North Africa/Southwest Asia

The economic geography of the realm of North Africa/Southwest Asia is primarily agricultural. Through much of the fertile farmland associated with Mesopotamia and the Fertile Crescent (another ancient culture hearth characterized by its advanced agricultural activity) has dried up, many residents of this realm continue to produce resilient crops (particularly cereals), mostly at subsistence levels. Another important aspect of the economic geography of this realm is the vast oil reserves located on the southern Arabian Peninsula, in North Africa, and near the Caspian Sea. While oil is considered one of the most important natural resources on our planet, its presence in North Africa/Southwest Asia has improved the quality of life for only a small portion of the population. This realm exhibits a large gap between the rich and the poor.

Sub-Saharan Africa

The economic geography of the realm of Sub-Saharan Africa is primarily agricultural. Though many raw materials useful to industrialized countries (such as oil and diamonds) are located within this realm, most residents of Sub-Saharan Africa have little or no access to the technology needed to extract these resources, or to the world economy. Agriculturalists in this realm generally produce at the subsistence level (partially due to the harsh physical conditions—hot, dry weather—of the realm). Grain crops are produced more easily in drier areas, while root crops are grown in relatively wetter areas. Peoples in Sub-Saharan Africa also depend on pastoralism (especially the raising of goats, cattle, and chicken) and fishing for their livelihoods. Though this realm is the least developed in the world, farmers are attempting to better their situations by introducing cash crops to their land. Still, many in the area (which has the highest rate of population growth in the world) remain malnourished.

Asia

Geography

South Asia

The geographic realm of South Asia, which is one of the world's largest population agglomerations, has India at its center. This realm is delineated by natural boundaries: the Himalayan Mountains to the north and east, and the Arabian Sea and the Bay of Bengal to the south. India was once the cornerstone of civilization, and later a key part of the British colonial empire. Violent conflicts over the control of territory within South Asia have culminated in the creation of six states. This realm, with its many languages and variety of religious affiliations, contains deep cultural divisions. It contains five regions: the Ganges Plain, Pakistan, the mountainous North, Bangladesh, and the Dravidian South (including the island of Sri Lanka).

East Asia

The geographic realm of East Asia has China at its center; this realm houses the largest concentration of human population in the world. Culturally, the 1.3 billion Chinese people dominate this realm, while the Japanese dominate economically. In fact, the economic activity and success of Japan have recently led to the tentative identification of the Pacific Rim region, a functional region with Japan as its anchor. The conceptualization of this region, as well as its practical development in the real world, continue to affect several realms and regions facing the Pacific Ocean. East Asia contains five regions: China Proper (eastern and northeastern China), which includes (somewhat precariously) North Korea, the mountains and plateaus of Xizang (the former Tibet), the deserts of Xinjiang, Mongolia, and the Pacific Rim (including Japan, Taiwan, South Korea, Thailand, and sometimes Malaysia), most of which was formerly referred to as the Jakota Triangle.

Southeast Asia

The geographic realm of Southeast Asia contains ethnic and linguistic groups that are particularly diverse. The high occurrence of conflicts for territory and/or power in this realm throughout history has led some to refer to the realm as "the Eastern Europe of Asia." Some use the term Indochina synonymously with Southeast Asia, which is appropriate because it conveys the identities of the two major cultural contributors to the realm. The ethnic affinities of those in this realm tend to lie with China, while cultural influences (specifically religious) arrived in the region from India. The two major regions of Southeast Asia are differentiated by their spatial separation. Indochina is the eastern, mainland part of the region; the archipelagoes of the Philippines and Indonesia make up the other region.

Economic Geography

South Asia

The economic geography of South Asia is low-income, as the area continues to experience the effects of former British colonization. When they came to South Asia, European powers changed trade patterns in the realm; Europe replaced India as the provider of manufactured goods for the realm. This caused a decrease in South Asian industry. Colonialists also exploited raw materials in the realm. Today, each of the states in South Asia has a low-income economy, due largely to the fact that these economies tend to center on inefficient and relatively less productive agricultural methods. Most residents of this region live in villages and survive directly on their parcels of land (often measuring less than an acre). Low-technology production methods keep crop yields (both per acre and per worker) at the subsistence level. Also, local traditions of inheritance often subdivide already undersized plots, preventing the organization of progressive measures, such as cooperative farming and shared irrigation in many states. The lack of a strong official agricultural development policy at the state and federal levels also inhibits the maturation of agricultural production.

East Asia

The economic geography of East Asia is highly variable: Japan is one of the most developed countries on the globe, while Mongolia is one of the least developed. The wide inter- and intraregional variations in this realm's development level, therefore, demonstrate that it is inappropriate to label entire realms as "developed" or "underdeveloped." Agriculturalists in the realm tend to inhabit the fertile basins of the great rivers of the east, and produce grains such as wheat. East Asia is also home to large deposits of raw materials such as coal and natural gas. Economic development in the nations of the Jakota Triangle (Japan, South Korea, and Taiwan) is thought to presage the future growth and modernization of the other political entities in the region. Japan, in particular, has experienced rapid growth in all industrial sectors, and possesses long-established trading relationships with nations across the globe. China, the other giant of the realm, has developed a mixed-market economy that displays both capitalistic and communistic characteristics.

Southeast Asia

The economic geography of Southeast Asia resembles that of East Asia. It is a study in economic contrasts; like Eastern Europe, this realm is a shatter belt. Singapore, for example, has the second-busiest port in the world, and is a major banking and financial center. Indonesia, Thailand, and the Philippines have grown from foreign direct investments (a manner of transferring capital across political boundaries, in which the investor exercises control over the acquired asset) in local industries. Also, the islands of Southeast Asia contain large petroleum reserves. Countries such as Vietnam and Cambodia, on the other hand, are some of the least developed countries in the world. This is partially due to the effects of the transition from a planned economy to a market economy. Levels of unemployment tend to be high in both urban and rural areas, as masses of people leave their farmlands (typically rice and/or grains) for crowded cities with limited job opportunities. The lack of a cohesive infrastructure, coupled with political instability, continue to cause issues with economic growth in these countries.

Oceania

GEOGRAPHY

AUSTRALIA

The geographic realm of Australia is formed by the regions of Australia and New Zealand. This realm is distinguished from other areas of the world by its continental isolation and the strong influence of Western culture among its peoples, who are demographically unique. Today, the furthest northwestern points of Australia may be considered part of the Pacific Rim region of East Asia. Australia is anomalous alongside Southeast Asia and the regions of the Pacific, due to its relatively high level of economic development. Still, some of the peoples of New Zealand remain traditional societies. The realm of Australia is made up of four regions. Australia the state is divided into an urbanized core and an arid interior, and New Zealand is made up of two large islands that are physically and culturally distinct.

PACIFIC REALM

The geographic realm of the Pacific is made up of the thousands of islands (large and small) that are situated in the Pacific Ocean, between Asia and Australia to the west and the Americas to the east. This geographic realm is more fragmented than any other; it is also culturally heterogeneous. The Pacific Realm is traditionally subdivided into three regions: Melanesia (the most populous Pacific region), which is associated with New Guinea; Micronesia (so named for the small sizes of this region's constituent islands), which is located to the north; and Polynesia, which extends from the Hawaiian archipelago southward to Easter Island and southwestward to New Zealand. The regions of Melanesia and Polynesia meet in New Zealand (the residents of which are descended from Polynesian peoples) and Australia (whose indigenous population is Melanesian).

ECONOMIC GEOGRAPHY

AUSTRALIA

The economic geography of Australia, as well as New Zealand, relies principally on the exportation of livestock products; Australia also participates in farming (especially wheat) and mining activities. Dependence on a constantly fluctuating world market places this realm's economy in a precarious position. Despite the plethora of advantages enjoyed by residents of the realm (plentiful farmlands, diverse mineral deposits, access to waterways, and underground water resources, as well as political stability), the Australian economy's growth has declined. Though it is considered one of the most developed realms in the world, Australia must now compete with the emerging Pacific Rim for trade opportunities. Australia has attempted to integrate itself into the Pacific Rim by exporting raw materials to countries in that region. Agriculturalists in this realm produce grains, rice, and certain fruits, while pastoralists produce wool and meat raising sheep. Manufacturing in Australia remains oriented to local domestic markets, partially due to the high costs of shipping and transportation to and from the relatively isolated realm.

PACIFIC REALM

The economic geography of the Pacific Realm is based on tourism. Though this realm covers a larger total area than any other, it possesses the least land area. Coral atolls, ancient volcanoes, open sea, and tropical vegetation offer travelers one spectacular view after another. The region of Melanesia produces valuable export items such as palm oil, coffee, and cocoa, in addition to the subsistence-level production of root crops and bananas. Melanesia also houses large mineral deposits. Micronesia is also involved in agriculture; fertile soils in this region help to diversify crop production. Polynesia, the region that includes the Hawaiian Islands, has a highly developed tourism economy. Most states in the Pacific Realm have high or upper-middle income economies.

World History

Early Civilization and Mesopotamia

Human development has been divided into several phases:

- Lower Paleolithic or Old Stone Age, about one million years ago—early humans used tools like needles, hatchets, awls, and cutting tools.
- Upper Paleolithic or New Stone Age, 6,000-8,000 BCE—also known as the Neolithic, textiles and pottery are developed. Humans of this era discovered the wheel, began to practice agriculture, made polished tools, and had some domesticated animals.
- Bronze Age, 3,000 BCE—metals are discovered and the first civilizations emerge as humans become more technologically advanced.
- Iron Age, 1,200-1,000 BCE—metal tools replace stone tools as humans develop knowledge of smelting.

Civilization

Civilizations are defined as having the following characteristics:

- Use of metal to make weapons and tools
- Written language
- A defined territorial state
- A calendar

The earliest civilizations developed in river valleys where reliable, fertile land was easily found, including:

- Nile River valley in Egypt
- Mesopotamia
- Indus River
- Hwang Ho in China

The very earliest civilizations developed in the Tigris-Euphrates valley in Mesopotamia, which is now part of Iraq, and in Egypt's Nile valley. These civilizations arose between 4,000 and 3,000 BCE. The area where these civilizations grew is known as the Fertile Crescent. There, geography and the availability of water made large-scale human habitation possible.

The earliest civilizations are also referred to as fluvial civilizations because they were founded near rivers. Rivers and the water they provide were vital to these early groupings, offering:

- Water for drinking and cultivating crops
- A gathering place for wild animals that could be hunted
- Easily available water for domesticated animals
- Rich soil deposits as a result of regular flooding

Irrigation techniques helped direct water where it was most needed, to sustain herds of domestic animals and to nourish crops of increasing size and quality.

FERTILE CRESCENT

James Breasted, an archeologist from the University of Chicago, coined the term Fertile Crescent to describe the area in Southwest Asia and Mediterranean basin where the earliest civilizations arose. The region includes modern day Iraq, Syria, Lebanon, Israel/Palestine and Jordan. It is bordered on the south by the Arabian Desert, the west by the Mediterranean Sea, and to the north and east by the Taurus and Zagros Mountains respectively. This area not only provided the raw materials for the development of increasingly advanced civilizations, but also saw waves of migration and invasion, leading to the earliest wars and genocides as groups conquered and absorbed each other's cultures and inhabitants.

CIVILIZATIONS OF MESOPOTAMIA

The major civilizations of Mesopotamia, in what is now called the Middle East, were the Sumerians, the Amorites, the Hittites, the Assyrians, the Chaldeans, and the Persians. These cultures controlled different areas of Mesopotamia during various time periods, but were similar in that they were autocratic. This meant a single ruler served as the head of the government and often, the main religious ruler, as well. These, often tyrannical, militaristic leaders, controlled all aspects of life, including law, trade, and religious activity. Portions of the legacies of these civilizations remain in cultures today. These include mythologies, religious systems, mathematical innovations and even elements of various languages.

EGYPTIAN CULTURE

The Egyptians were one of the most advanced ancient cultures, having developed construction methods to build the great pyramids, as well as a form of writing known as hieroglyphics. Their religion was highly developed and complex, and included advanced techniques for the preservation of bodies after death. They also made paper by processing papyrus, a plant commonly found along the Nile, invented the decimal system, devised a solar calendar, and advanced overall knowledge of arithmetic and geometry.

Review Video: Egyptians
Visit mometrix.com/academy and enter code: 398041

SUMERIAN CULTURE

Sumer, located in the southern part of Mesopotamia, consisted of a dozen city-states. Each city-state had its own gods, and the leader of each city-state also served as the high priest. Cultural legacies of Sumer include:

- The invention of writing
- Invention of the wheel
- The first library—established in Assyria by Ashurbanipal
- The Hanging Gardens of Babylon—one of the Seven Wonders of the Ancient World
- First written laws—Ur-Nammu's Codes and the Codes of Hammurabi
- The *Epic of Gilgamesh*—the first epic story in history

The Sumerians were the first to invent the wheel, and also brought irrigation systems into use. Their cuneiform writing was simpler than Egyptian hieroglyphs, and they developed the timekeeping system we still use today.

Review Video: Early Mesopotamia: The Sumerians
Visit mometrix.com/academy and enter code: 939880

Hittite Empire

The Hittites were centered in what is now Turkey, but their empire extended into Palestine and Syria. They conquered the Babylonian civilization, but adopted their religion and their system of laws. Overall, the Hittites tended to tolerate other religions, unlike many other contemporary cultures, and absorbed foreign gods into their own belief systems rather than forcing their religion onto peoples they conquered. The Hittite Empire reached its peak in 1600-1200 BCE. After a war with Egypt, which weakened them severely, they were eventually conquered by the Assyrians in 700 BCE.

Babylonian Civilization

After the Sumerian civilization declined, the next dominant civilization was Babylon. The Babylonians conquered the Sumerians and established a city on the Euphrates River in approximately 1,750 B.C. One of the most famous Babylonian rulers was Hammurabi, who established the famous Code, an extremely detailed set of laws. This marked the first time that a set of rules governing every aspect of social life was applied to an entire people. The Babylonians are also known for their construction of ziggurats, long pyramid-like structures that were used as religious temples. Over time, the Babylonians acquired a reputation as a sensuous and hedonistic people, and the name Babylon has come to stand for any debauched civilization.

Review Video: Early Mesopotamia: The Babylonians
Visit mometrix.com/academy and enter code: 340325

Hebrew Culture

The Hebrew or ancient Israelite culture developed the monotheistic religion that eventually developed into modern Judaism, Christianity, and Islam.

Review Video: Early Mesopotamia: The Jews
Visit mometrix.com/academy and enter code: 899354

Judaism was founded in the 20th century B.C. by a man named Abraham, who was chosen to enter into a covenant with God, whereby he would receive special treatment in exchange for obedience and worship. Abraham then moved to Canaan (present-day Lebanon). Later, his descendants would move to Egypt and be enslaved, before being eventually liberated by God through the leader Moses and reconquering Canaan. Moses received from God a set of strict laws, known as the Ten Commandments. All of this is described in the Torah, the essential Jewish Scripture. There are also several other important books, including the Talmud, and many important commentaries by learned Jewish theologians.

Ancient Civilizations

African Kingdoms

Kushite Culture

Kush, or Cush, was located south of ancient Egypt, and the earliest existing records of this civilization were found in Egyptian texts. At one time, Kush was the largest empire on the Nile River, surpassing even Egypt. In Neolithic times, Kushites lived in villages, with buildings made of mud bricks. They were settled rather than nomadic, and practiced hunting and fishing, cultivated grain, and also herded cattle. Kerma, the capitol, was a major center of trade.

Kush determined leadership through matrilineal descent of their kings, as did Egypt. Their heads of state, the Kandake or Kentake, were female. Their polytheistic religion included the primary Egyptian gods as well as regional gods, including a lion god, which is commonly found in African cultures. Kush was conquered by Nubia in 800 BCE.

Mali

Today, Mali is the largest nation in west Africa. Indeed, throughout African history Mali has been a major power. Until the 11th century, it was a part of the empire of Ghana, a wealthy trading nation. Mali would eventually rise to prominence in its own right. The economy of Mali was based upon the rich mineral resources (especially gold) of the region. Mali reached its highest prominence during the reign of Mansa Musa (A.D. 1312-7). This ruler introduced Islam to his people, which at this time lived as far north as Morocco. The city of Timbuktu became a cultural center for the region, as well as a crossroads for trade routes that stretched across the Sahara. Over time, internal disputes would divide Mali into several smaller kingdoms.

Ancient Indian Civilization

The Indus River Valley is an area bordered by the Himalayan Mountains in what is now Pakistan. The two great cities of this civilization were Harappa and Mohenjo-Daro, though there were also a large number of smaller communities in the area. The people of this region developed a system of writing, as well as systems of weight and measurement which were useful in trade. They exchanged goods with the people of Mesopotamia in the west as well as with the people of Tibet in the east. The Aryans invaded this region and brought with them iron technology and the Sanskrit language. The introduction of iron tools made it possible to cultivate the forests of the Ganges River Valley in what is now India.

Mauryan Empire

The Mauryan Empire lasted approximately between the years 321 and 185 B.C. in India. It was established by the powerful leader Chandragupta Maurya, and featured a strong military and an efficient bureaucracy. The Mauryan empire eventually spread as far west as the Indus River as present-day Afghanistan. At its greatest expansion, the Mauryan empire comprised almost the entirety of what is now India. The leader Ashoka (c. 272-232 B.C.) converted to Buddhism, and his rule was prosperous for rich and poor alike. After the death of Ashoka, however, the Mauryan Empire splintered, as the southern lands sought autonomy and the northern lands were subject to constant foreign invasions.

Caste System

The Hindu caste system is a means of organizing society. It divides the populace into four groups, each associated with a part of the body of the Hindu god Parusha. The highest class is the brahmins, associated with the mouth of the god. In the original system, the brahmin class was made up of priests. The second caste is the kshatriyas, made up of rulers and soldiers; this caste is associated with the arms of Parusha. Next are the vaishyas, associated with the legs of the god. This caste was composed of landowners, merchants, and artisans. The last group is the shudras, associated with the feet of the god. This caste was composed of servants and slaves. Women do not have a place in the traditional Hindu caste system.

Hinduism

Hinduism is the traditional religion of India. It is expressed in an individual's philosophy and behavior, rather than in the performance of any specific rituals. Hinduism does not claim a founder, but has evolved slowly over thousands of years; the first Hindu writings date back to the third millennium B.C. There are a few concepts that are common to all permutations of Hinduism, such as the Vedas, which are considered to be the sacred texts of the religion. The chief aim in life for a Hindu is to liberate himself from the cycle of suffering and rebirth. Hindus believe in reincarnation and that a person's conduct in this life will affect his or her position in the next (karma). Although Hinduism is frequently associated with the caste system, the two are actually unrelated.

Earliest Civilizations in China

The earliest civilizations in what would become China flourished along the banks of the Huang He (Yellow) River before the year 2,000 B.C. The first Chinese dynasty was the Xia (Hsia), succeeded by the Shang dynasty. In this period, the rulers established an intricate system of government and a comprehensive judiciary. The basic components of this system would be preserved in Chinese civilization for centuries. The distinctive Chinese style of writing also developed during this period. Like Egyptian hieroglyphs, the Chinese pictographs are meant to resemble their definition. Over time, though, the Chinese characters have come to resemble their definitions less and less.

Development and Growth of the Chinese Empires

In China, history was divided into a series of dynasties. The most famous of these, the Han Dynasty, existed from 206 BCE to 220 CE. Accomplishments of the Chinese Empires included:

- Building the Great Wall of China
- Numerous inventions, including paper, paper money, printing, and gunpowder
- High level of artistic development
- Silk production

The Chinese Empires were comparable to Rome as far as their artistic and intellectual accomplishments, as well as the size and scope of their influence.

Buddhism

Buddhism was created by Gautama Siddhartha (otherwise known as Buddha) in about 528 B.C. It was in part a response to Hinduism, which Buddha felt had become bloated with worldliness and politics. Traditional Buddhism is based upon the Four Noble Truths: existence is suffering, suffering is caused by desire, an end of suffering will come with Nirvana, and Nirvana will come with the practice of the Eightfold Path. The steps of the Eightfold Path are: right views; right resolve; right speech; right action; right livelihood; right effort; right mindfulness; and right concentration. Buddhism has no deities. Buddhism did not receive any official sanction for a long time, but eventually spread and took hold in India, China, Japan, and elsewhere.

Ancient Cultures of the Americas

Less is known of ancient American civilizations since less was left behind. Those we know something of include:

- The Norte Chico civilization in Peru, an agricultural society of 20 individual communities, that existed over 5,000 years ago. This culture is also known as Caral-Supe, and is the oldest known civilization in the Americas.
- The Anasazi, or Ancient Pueblo People, in what is now the southwestern United States. Emerging about 1200 BCE, the Anasazi built complex adobe dwellings, and were the forerunners of later Pueblo Indian cultures.
- The Maya emerged in southern Mexico and northern Central America as early as 2,600 BCE. They developed a written language and a complex calendar.

Mayans

The Mayans were based in the Mexico's Yucatan Peninsula, Tabasco, and Chiapas, as well as in what is now Guatemala and Honduras. Between the years A.D. 200 and 950, they developed a sophisticated civilization, with complex religions, architecture, arts, engineering, and astronomy. The Mayans did have a form of hieroglyphic writing, but most of their history and folklore was preserved orally. The Mayans are responsible for creating an extremely accurate calendar and for first conceiving of the number zero. The Mayan civilization was supported by agriculture, but it was run by a class of priests and warriors. In the 9th century, the Mayans were overrun by Toltecs from the north, who created the legend of the feathered serpent Quetzalcoatl.

Incas

The Incas inhabited a huge area, from present-day Ecuador to central Chile to the eastern side of the Andes Mountains. The Incas territory expanded especially after the 14th century A.D. The Incas were engaged in frequent conflicts with rival groups, and they frequently enslaved the groups that they defeated. They eventually formed a permanent underclass to ensure that the lands of the military leaders would be cultivated. Incas typically dispersed rival groups. The Incan religion contained a god in heaven, a cult of ancestors, and a number of sacred objects and places. The Incas called themselves the children of the Sun.

Classical Civilization of the Mediterranean

HELLENISTIC AGE

ATHENS

Ancient Greece was dominated by two city-states, Athens and Sparta. These two had very distinct cultures. Athens was a coastal city with a democratic form of government which amassed wealth by trading overseas. Athens is also known as the city that gave life to philosophy and the arts. Socrates engaged in his famous dialogues in the streets of Athens, and though he was eventually executed by the Athenian government for supposedly corrupting the youth, his thoughts achieved immortality in the writings of his student Plato. In turn, Plato's student Aristotle developed a strict form of reasoning that has formed the basis of much subsequent Western thought. Athens is also renowned for the architectural marvel that is the Parthenon.

SPARTA

While Athens was known for its devotion to the arts and its democratic form of government, its rival city-state Sparta was devoted to agriculture and the military. Sparta was not located on the coast, and therefore the Spartans had little contact with distant peoples. Spartan society was governed by a strict class system. Most people (helots) worked the land of other people as virtual serfs. In the upper classes, participation in military training was compulsory. Indeed, Spartan youths left their families to begin military training at a young age. The Spartans did not produce any noteworthy philosophers, but as a culture they stressed the good of the group over that of the individual. This is in stark contrast to most Athenian thought, which celebrates the achievements of the individual.

PERICLEAN AGE

The Periclean Age in Greece, so named because Pericles was the leader of Athens during the period, took place in the fifth century B.C. It was during this period that most of the great contributions to Western culture were made, including the philosophy of Socrates, the medical work of Hippocrates, and the great dramatic works of Aeschlyus, Sophocles, and Euripides. The Hellenistic Age (4th century B.C.), on the other hand, is more commonly known for the military conquests made by Alexander the Great. If it were not for the conquests of Alexander during the Hellenistic Age, many of the innovations and achievements of the Periclean Age may not have had such a great influence on the West. It should be noted that the Hellenistic Age was not without its own great thinkers; in fact, Alexander studied as a boy under Aristotle.

During the Age of Pericles, an alliance of Greek city-states was challenged by the mighty Persians. Miraculously, the outnumbered Greeks were able to defeat the Persians at Thermopylae and Marathon, and staved off conquest. The war with the Persians impoverished the Greeks, however, and increased rivalries among the city-states. In Athens, the requirements for citizenship were loosened, though slavery remained. Conflict between Sparta and Athens culminated in the Peloponnesian War, won by Sparta. Eventually, the whole of Greece would be conquered by Philip of Macedon, who allowed the Greeks to maintain their culture and traditions. Alexander the Great was the son of Philip and became the master of an empire larger than any the world had ever seen. During his reign, he united many disparate peoples through a common law and exchange policy. He died at the age of 33, and his empire was divided into three parts amongst his generals.

Impact of Ancient Greece on Modern Society

Ancient Greece made numerous major contributions to cultural development, including:

- Theater—Aristophanes and other Greek playwrights laid the groundwork for modern theatrical performance.
- Alphabet—the Greek alphabet, derived from the Phoenician alphabet, developed into the Roman alphabet, and then into our modern-day alphabet.
- Geometry—Pythagoras and Euclid pioneered much of the system of geometry still taught today. Archimedes made various mathematical discoveries, including the value of pi.
- Historical writing—much of ancient history doubles as mythology or religious texts. Herodotus and Thucydides made use of research and interpretation to record historical events.
- Philosophy—Socrates, Plato, and Aristotle served as the fathers of Western philosophy. Their work is still required reading for philosophy students.

Review Video: Ancient Greece
Visit mometrix.com/academy and enter code: 800829

Persian Wars

The Persian Empire, ruled by Cyrus the Great, encompassed an area from the Black Sea to Afghanistan, and beyond into Central Asia. After the death of Cyrus, Darius became king in 522 BCE. The empire reached its zenith during his reign.

From 499-448 BCE, the Greeks and Persians fought in the Persian Wars. Battles of the Persian Wars included:

- The Battle of Marathon, in which heavily outnumbered Greek forces managed to achieve victory.
- The Battle of Thermopylae, in which a small band of Spartans held off a throng of Persian troops for several days.
- The Battle of Salamis, a naval battle that again saw outnumbered Greeks achieving victory.
- The Battle of Plataea, another Greek victory, but one in which they outnumbered the Persians.

The Persian Wars did not see the end of the Persian Empire, but discouraged additional attempts to invade Greece.

Roman Republic and Empire

ROMAN REPUBLIC

Roman civilization dates from the founding of the city in 753 B.C. until the defeat of the last Emperor, Romulus Augustus, in A.D. 476. The republic itself lasted from the overthrow of the monarchy in 509 B.C. until the empowering of the first Emperor, Octavian Augustus, in 27 B.C. The area along the Tiber River where Rome would be built was previously inhabited by a group known as the Etruscans. Rome took its name from the legendary Romulus, who is said to have founded it after triumphing over his brother Remus.

ROMAN SOCIETY STRUCTURE

The basic structure of Roman society consisted of patricians at the top of the social hierarchy, who were descendants of the founders of the republic and often wealthy. Beneath the patricians were the plebeians, which consisted of all other freemen. Finally, at the bottom of the social hierarchy were slaves. Women were not included in most social or economic business, although a Roman woman's rights were often significantly preferable to her contemporaries in other civilizations. The Roman Republic, which was the first political arrangement of Rome, was led by two consuls who were chosen annually. The Consuls presided over the Senate, made up of a permanent group of those who had been previously elected to a high-ranking magistracy (originally primarily patrician in composition); and the Assembly, which was solely for the plebeians. Rome had extensive laws covering individual and property rights.

Review Video: Roman Republic Part One
Visit mometrix.com/academy and enter code: 360192

JULIUS CAESAR

As Rome continued to expand, class conflicts developed between the nobility and the poor. In this era of unrest, it became possible for individual leaders to claim more power than the law had allowed previously. In 60 B.C., the famous general Julius Caesar formed a three-person alliance (often mis-termed the "First Triumvirate") to govern Rome. The other two members were Gnaeus Pompey Magnus and Marcus Licinius Crassus. During this period, Caesar led a successful campaign against the Gauls (a people in modern-day France) and made himself richer than the entire Roman State on the proceeds from his conquest. After Crassus was killed in battle, Caesar pushed Pompey out and assumed total control of Rome, crowning himself dictator-for-life. Though Caesar was very popular with the mob, his decision to claim lifelong power alienated him from the nobility in the Senate. He was assassinated by a group of senators, led by Marcus Iunius Brutus, in 44 B.C.

THE TRIUMVIRATE

After the assassination of Caesar in 44 B.C., Rome was mired in chaos. Those who had conspired to kill Caesar had hoped to return to the republican form of government, but instead another trio of leaders came to the fore, this time as a governmental commission of "three men for reconstituting the Republic," known as the Triumvirate. The Triumvirate was composed of Marc Antony, one of Caesar's greatest generals and a Consul at the time; Octavius, the nephew and testamentary heir of Caesar; and Marcus Aemilius Lepidus, a third wheel who was quickly made a non-entity.

While Octavius stayed in Rome, Antony left for Egypt, where he stayed for a time as the guest and lover of Cleopatra. Eventually, infighting between Octavius and Antony led the former to mount a campaign against Egypt. When they realized that they were defeated, Antony and Cleopatra committed suicide to avoid the shame of being paraded in Octavian's triumph. Lepidus, having been marginalized, Octavius (now known as Augustus) became the first Emperor.

Review Video: Roman Republic Part Two
Visit mometrix.com/academy and enter code: 881514

Roman Empire

After the ascension of Augustus, Rome entered a period of relative tranquility. Augustus dubbed this era, which lasted about forty years, the Pax Romana. Rome remained an empire, although the conquered peoples were able to obtain Roman citizenship without having to forfeit their native customs. It was at this period that Rome reached its greatest geographic proportions, stretching all the way from to present-day Scotland to the Middle East. This was also the greatest period for Roman artistic achievement; both Virgil and Ovid were active during the Pax Romana, and, indeed, the Aeneid of Virgil was written in part to glorify Augustus. It was at this time that the polytheist religion of Rome was challenged first by the Judaism of the conquered Hebrews, and later by the early Christians.

Christianity in the Roman Empire

Early Christianity was a mass of competing doctrines, including various groups such as the Gnostics and Arians who all sought to have their view legitimized as the truth. Eventually, the orthodox church through an ecumenical council of bishops created in the fourth century A.D. the canon of New Testament texts which exists today. The apostles had created a hierarchy of bishops, priests, and deacons who stressed obedience to duly constituted church authority. By the middle of the second century, Christianity began to attract intellectuals in the Roman Empire. Although Christians were still liable to be persecuted in the farther reaches of the empire, many turned to the Church as the empire crumbled, as the Church was all that was left of civilization, and would rebuild Europe over the next millennium.

Constantine

The Roman Emperor Constantine, in response to the inconvenient vastness of his dominion, established an eastern capital: Constantinople, in A.D. 330. Having received a sign in the heavens which promised him victory over his rivals for the office of Emperor should he convert to Christianity, Constantine famously issued the Edict of Milan, in which he called for the end of the persecution of Christians, after a sound victory as promised. After this act, Christianity flourished in the Roman Empire and became the official religion of the state. A movement called monasticism developed within the religion, advocating the renunciation of worldly goods in favor of contemplation and prayer. After the death of Constantine, the empire once again proved unwieldy for one man, and therefore it split as it had previously, with the western half being governed from Rome, and the eastern half from Constantinople. This arrangement would prove untenable, however; a Germanic tribe of barbarians eventually sacked Rome, and the western Roman capital fell in A.D. 476.

The Huns and Attila

One of the major barbarian tribes to challenge the Roman Empire in its decline were the Huns. The Huns were a nomadic people who moved east across central Asia during the 4th century A.D. The Huns were divided into several branches: the White Huns overran the Sasanian Empire and conquered many cities in the northern part of the Indian subcontinent; another group roamed eastern Europe and established a strong empire on the Hungarian Plain around A.D. 400. The Huns were known for their amazing horsemanship and for being aggressive on the battlefield. It was under the guidance of Attila (440s) that the Huns reached their highest level of prominence. During this period, they collected tribute from many of the areas within the Roman Empire. Soon after the death of Attila, however, the Huns became complacent and lost most of their territory.

Byzantine Empire

In the early fourth century, the Roman Empire split, with the eastern portion becoming the Eastern Empire, or the Byzantine Empire. In 330 CE, Constantine founded the city of Constantinople, which became the center of the Byzantine Empire. Its major influences came from Mesopotamia and Persia, in contrast to the Western Empire, which maintained traditions more closely linked to Greece and Carthage.

After the fall of Rome and the western Roman Empire, a series of Emperors, including the Emperor Justinian, led the Byzantine Empire from Constantinople and even managed to successfully reconquer large parts of the former western empire for a number of years. The Justinian era is especially remembered for the contributions to law and religious art work, in particular the development of mosaics. In the years after the fall of Rome, the Catholic Christian Church gradually rose to fill the power vacuum. In what had been the western Roman Empire, the Church acted completely independent of any political body, while even in the Byzantine Empire the Church was increasing in power. Only the influence of the Byzantine Emperor kept the Church from being the most powerful group in Europe.

Nicene Creed

The Byzantine Empire was Christian-based but incorporated Greek language, philosophy and literature and drew its law and government policies from Rome. However, there was as yet no unified doctrine of Christianity, as it was a relatively new religion that had spread rapidly and without a great deal of organization.

In 325, the First Council of Nicaea addressed this issue. From this conference came the Nicene Creed, addressing the Trinity and other basic Christian beliefs. The Council of Chalcedon in 451 stated that any rejection of the Trinity was blasphemy.

The Medieval Age

Feudalism

A major element of the social and economic life of Europe, feudalism developed as a way to ensure European rulers would have the wherewithal to quickly raise an army when necessary. Vassals swore loyalty and promised to provide military service for lords, who in return offered a fief, or a parcel of land, for them to use to generate their livelihood. Vassals could work the land themselves, have it worked by peasants or serfs—workers who had few rights and were little more than slaves—or grant the fief to someone else. The king legally owned all the land, but in return promised to protect the vassals from invasion and war. Vassals returned a certain percentage of their income to the lords, who in turn passed a portion of their income on to the king.

A similar practice was manorialism, in which the feudal system was applied to a self-contained manor. These manors were often owned by the lords who ran them, but were usually included in the same system of loyalty and promises of military service that drove feudalism.

> **Review Video: The Middle Ages: Feudalism**
> Visit mometrix.com/academy and enter code: 165907

Religion in the Middle Ages

Influence of the Roman Catholic Church

The Roman Catholic Church extended significant influence both politically and economically throughout medieval society. The church supplied education, as there were no established schools or universities. To a large extent, the church had filled a power void left by various invasions throughout the former Roman Empire, leading it to exercise a role that was far more political than religious. Kings were heavily influenced by the Pope and other church officials, and churches controlled large amounts of land throughout Europe.

Roman Catholic and Eastern Orthodox

Emperor Leo III ordered the destruction of all icons throughout the Byzantine Empire. Images of Jesus were replaced with a cross, and images of Jesus, Mary or other religious figures were considered blasphemy on grounds of idolatry.

The current Pope, Gregory II, called a synod to discuss the issue. The synod declared that destroying these images was heretical, and that strong disciplinary measures would result for anyone who took this step. Leo's response was an attempt to kidnap Pope Gregory, but this plan ended in failure when his ships were destroyed by a storm.

Development of Christianity

Surprising though it may seem, one of the best things that happened to Christian thought during the Middle Ages was its contact with Islam. The complex philosophies of Muslim scholars helped spur the evolution of Christian theology. These in addition to the rediscovery of ancient philosophers such as Aristotle led Christians to begin to glorify reason as the God-given tool for investigating religious faith. Many assertions made by the new rational theologians, however, were dubbed heresy by many Church leaders, as more and more Christian thinkers were bemoaning the materialistic ways of the Church leaders. One of the leading Christian thinkers of the Middle Ages was St. Thomas Aquinas, whose Summa Theologica outlined rational explanations for the belief in God and in the miracles of Christianity.

The rapid evolution in Christian thought that took place during the Middle Ages gave rise to the formation of the first universities. For the first time in Western Europe, young men would move to large cities to study theology, law, and medicine at formal institutions. In addition to this trend, the academic method known as scholasticism was developed, in which scholars would use logic and deductive reasoning in order to analyze a work or determine something of an abstract nature. Among the so-called scholastics, two schools of thought developed: those scholars who adhered to the ideas of Plato were known as realists, and those who followed Aristotle were known as nominalists. The word "realist" is somewhat confusing when used to refer to the work of Plato, who believed that our perceptions of objects were merely perceptions of the barest shadows of their reality. Another development of Christianity in this period was mysticism; Christian mystics believed that they could achieve union with God through self-denial, contemplative prayer, and alms-giving.

ISLAM

Born in 570 CE, Mohammed became prominent in 610, leading his followers in a new religion called Islam, which means submission to God's will. Before this time, the Arabian Peninsula was inhabited largely by Bedouins, nomads who battled amongst each other and lived in tribal organizations. But by the time Mohammed died in 632, most of Arabia had become Muslim to some extent.

Mohammed conquered Mecca, where a temple called the Kaaba had long served as a center of the nomadic religions. He declared this temple the most sacred of Islam, and Mecca as the holy city. His writings became the Koran, or Qur'an, divine revelations he said had been delivered to him by the angel Gabriel.

Review Video: Islam
Visit mometrix.com/academy and enter code: 359164

Mohammed's teachings gave the formerly tribal Arabian people a sense of unity that had not existed in the area before. After his death, the converted Muslims of Arabia conquered a vast territory, creating an empire and bringing advances in literature, technology, science and art just as Europe was declining under the scourge of the Black Death. Literature from this period includes the *Arabian Nights* and the *Rubaiyat* of Omar Khayyam.

Later in its development, Islam split into two factions, the Shiite and the Sunni Muslims. Conflict continues today between these groups.

THE MAGNA CARTA

England, unlike many of the other regions of Western Europe, had been accustomed to a strong monarchy. This tradition was challenged in A.D. 1215, when noblemen forced King John to sign the Magna Carta, a document which gave feudal rights back to the nobles and extended the rule of law to the middle-class burghers. The Magna Carta made the formation of the Houses of Parliament possible. Over time, Parliament would evolve into a two-house structure: the House of Lords which contained nobles and clergy and the House of Commons which contained knights and burghers. The House of Lords was mainly occupied with legal questions, while the House of Commons dealt mainly in economic issues.

BLACK DEATH

The Black Death, believed to be bubonic plague, came to Europe probably brought by fleas carried on rats that were regular passengers on sailing vessels. It killed in excess of a third of the entire population of Europe and effectively ended feudalism as a political system. Many who had formerly served as peasants or serfs found different work, as a demand for skilled labor grew. Nation-states grew in power, and in the face of the pandemic, many began to turn away from faith in God and toward the ideals of ancient Greece and Rome for government and other beliefs.

Crusades

The Crusades began in the eleventh century and progressed well into the twelfth. The major goal of these various military ventures was to slow the progression of Muslim forces into Europe and to expel them from the Holy Land, where they had taken control of Jerusalem and Palestine.

Alexius I, the Eastern emperor, called for helped from Pope Urban II when Palestine was taken. In 1095, the Pope, hoping to reunite Eastern and Western Christian influences, encouraged all Christians to help the cause. Amidst great bloodshed, this Crusade recaptured Jerusalem, but over the next centuries, Jerusalem and other areas of the Holy Land changed hands numerous times.

The Second Crusade, in 1145, consisted of an unsuccessful attempt to retake Damascus. The Third Crusade, under Pope Gregory VIII, attempted to recapture Jerusalem, but failed. The Fourth Crusade, under Pope Innocent III, attempted to come into the Holy Land via Egypt.

The Crusades led to greater power for the Pope and the Catholic Church in general and also opened numerous trading and cultural routes between Europe and the East.

Explorations, Renaissance, and Reformation

Age of Exploration

At the same time that the Renaissance was reinvigorating European cultural life, a desire to explore the world abroad was growing. Indeed, the ability to make long voyages was facilitated by the advances in navigational technology made around this time. The main reason for exploration, though, was economic. Europeans had first been introduced to eastern goods during the Crusades, and the exploits of Marco Polo in the 13th century had further whetted the western appetite for contact with distant lands. This increasing focus on exploration and trade caused a general shift in the balance of power in Europe. Land-locked countries, like Germany, found that they were excluded from participating in the lucrative new economy. On the other hand, those countries which bordered the Atlantic (England, France, Spain, and Portugal) were the most powerful players.

The Explorers

Italian Exploration

Christopher Columbus

Before 1400, few Europeans knew anything about the world. When Christopher Columbus read of the exploits of the Italian Marco Polo, however, he was inspired to seek out new trade routes. Also, Prince Henry of Portugal established a navigation institute that encouraged sailors to explore. For a long time, extended sea voyages were restricted by a lack of navigational and seafaring technology; the inventions of the compass, astrolabe, and caravel remedied this situation. There was also a high cost associated with long travels; around 1400, however, new monarchs in France, England, Spain, and Portugal decided that they were willing to pay a high price to get a piece of the spice trade. Finally, the question of a motive for exploration was answered by the increasing fervor for missionary work, as well as the economic necessity of developing new trade routes.

Amerigo Vespucci

Amerigo Vespucci, from whose name the word "America" was derived, mapped the Atlantic coast of South America and was able to convince stubborn Europeans that these lands were not a part of India.

Portugese Exploration

As exploration created new opportunities for amassing wealth, Portugal enjoyed special favor because of its excellent location and cordial relations with many of the Muslim nations of North Africa. The ruler of Portugal at this time was even known as Prince Henry "the Navigator" (1394-1460).

In order to solidify trade arrangements, European rulers began to think about colonizing foreign lands. In order to fund these expensive trips, a new kind of business known as the joint-stock company was developed. In a joint-stock company, a group of merchants would combine their resources to pay for the passage of a vessel. These groups would later be influential in securing colonial charters for many of their agents. One of the most powerful examples was the Muscovy Company of England, which controlled almost all trade with Russia.

Vasco da Gama

Vasco da Gama was the first European to sail around the Cape of Good Hope, on the southern tip of what is now South Africa. This made it possible to reach Asia by boat. Balboa explored Central America, and was the first European to view the Pacific Ocean.

Ferdinand Magellan

Magellan is remembered as the first to circumnavigate the globe. Cortes was a powerful commander who subjugated the Aztecs in what is now Mexico; he used great brutality to achieve his ends. Pizarro, like Cortes, was a conquistador; he conquered the Incas in what is now Peru.

Spanish Exploration

Cortez

Hernán Cortez (1485-1547) was a Spanish conquistador. He assisted in the conquest of Cuba, and lived there until 1518, when he was assigned to lead an expedition into Mexico. He and 700 men landed on the Mexican shore and he promptly had his ships burnt, in order to indicate his sincerity about establishing a foothold in the country. Cortez then led his troops into Tenochtitlan, the capital of the Aztec Empire. They were received graciously by the Aztec ruler, Montezuma, whom they immediately enslaved. The Aztecs tried to revolt against the Spanish influence, but Cortez formed a coalition with other anti-Aztec groups and brutally eliminated the Aztec uprising. Cortez went on to rule "New Spain" for a number of years.

Mercantilism

As foreign trade became the most important part of every nation's economy, the economic theory of mercantilism became popular. According to mercantilism, a nation should never import more than it exports. Of course, it is impossible for every country to achieve this goal at the same time, and so European countries were in fierce competition at all times. The solution that most nations pursued was to establish colonies, because these could supply resources for export by the mother country without really being considered imports. This rush to colonize had disastrous consequences for the indigenous peoples of the Americas and Africa. Europeans often looted the Native Americans for anything of value, and their need for cheap labor to cultivate the land there spawned the African slave trade.

Renaissance

Renaissance literally means "rebirth." After the darkness of the Dark Ages and the Black Plague, interest rose again in the beliefs and politics of ancient Greece and Rome. Art, literature, music, science, and philosophy all burgeoned during the Renaissance. Many of the ideas of the Renaissance began in Florence, Italy, spurred by the Medici family. Education for the upper classes expanded to include law, math, reading, writing, and classical Greek and Roman works. As the Renaissance progressed, the world was presented through art and literature in a realistic way that had never been explored before. This realism drove culture to new heights.

Artists of the Renaissance included Leonardo da Vinci, also an inventor, Michelangelo, also an architect, and others who focused on realism in their work. In literature, major contributions came from the humanist, authors like Petrarch, Erasmus, Sir Thomas More, and Boccaccio, who believed man should focus on reality rather than on the ethereal. Shakespeare, Cervantes and Dante followed in their footsteps, and their works found a wide audience thanks to Gutenberg's development of the printing press.

Scientific developments of the Renaissance included the work of Copernicus, Galileo and Kepler, who challenged the geocentric philosophies of the church by proving the earth was not the center of the solar system.

Review Video: Renaissance
Visit mometrix.com/academy and enter code: 123100

Scientific Revolution

In addition to holding power in the political realm, church doctrine also governed scientific belief. During the Scientific Revolution, astronomers and other scientists began to amass evidence that challenged the church's scientific doctrines. Major figures of the Scientific Revolution included:

- Nicolaus Copernicus—wrote *Revolutions of the Celestial Spheres*, arguing that the Earth revolved around the sun.
- Tycho Brahe—catalogued astronomical observations.
- Johannes Kepler—developed Laws of Planetary Motions.
- Galileo Galilei—defended the heliocentric theories of Copernicus and Kepler, discovered four moons of Jupiter, and died under house arrest by the Church, charged with heresy.
- Isaac Newton—discovered gravity, studied optics, calculus and physics, and believed the workings of nature could be observed, studied, and proven through observation.

Review Video: The Scientific Revolution
Visit mometrix.com/academy and enter code: 974600

Reformation Period

The Reformation consisted of the Protestant Revolution and the Catholic Reformation. The Protestant Revolution rose in Germany when Martin Luther protested abuses of the Catholic Church. John Calvin led the movement in Switzerland, while in England King Henry VIII made use of the Revolution's ideas to further his own political goals.

Review Video: The Reformation: Martin Luther
Visit mometrix.com/academy and enter code: 691828

The Catholic Reformation occurred in response to the Protestant Revolution, leading to various changes in the Catholic Church. Some provided wider tolerance of different religious viewpoints, but others actually increased the persecution of those deemed to be heretics.

Review Video: The Counter Reformation
Visit mometrix.com/academy and enter code: 950498

From a religious standpoint, the Reformation occurred due to abuses by the Catholic Church such as indulgences and dispensations, religious offices being offered up for sale, and an increasingly dissolute clergy. Politically, the Reformation was driven by increased power of various ruling monarchs, who wished to take all power to themselves rather than allowing power to remain with the church. They also had begun to chafe at papal taxes and the church's increasing wealth. The ideas of the Protestant Revolution removed power from the Catholic Church and the Pope himself, playing nicely into the hands of those monarchs, such as Henry VIII, who wanted out from under the church's control.

Review Video: The Reformation: The Protestants
Visit mometrix.com/academy and enter code: 583582

Enlightenment and Revolution

The rapid advance in learning known as the Scientific Revolution was a product of the systematic form of inquiry known as the scientific method. With the scientific method, learning is incremental: a question is posed, a hypothetical solution is offered, observations are made, and the hypothesis is either supported or refuted. The consistency of the method made it easy for scientific discoveries to be transferred from one country to another. Along with a standardized form of measurement, the development of the scientific method gave scientists a common language. Scientists also benefited from the development of powerful telescopes and microscopes.

After Copernicus startled the world by challenging the geocentric (that is, earth-centered) model for the universe, the Italian Galileo Galilei supplied scientific experiments that proved the accuracy of Copernicus' theory. One of the philosophical heroes of the Scientific Revolution was the Frenchman Rene Descartes, who attempted to base his beliefs about the world upon empirical and provable facts: most famously, "I think, therefore I am." Francis Bacon was an English intellectual who wrote copiously on the possibilities for science to improve the human condition. Sir Isaac Newton excelled in many fields, but is best known for his theories of motion and gravitation. Newton helped create the general idea that objects in the world behave in regular and predictable ways.

Between the years 1600 and 1770, political and social philosophy in Europe underwent a tremendous change, known collectively as the Enlightenment. Just as Northern Italy had been the center of the Renaissance, so now Paris was the hub of progressive thought. The collection of philosophes, who sought to bring every subject under the authority of reason, included both deists (those who believed in God) and atheists (those who did not). The study known as political science first emerged during this period. Intellectuals began to question the divine right that had been claimed by absolute monarchs in the past; they sought to determine which was the best form of government for all the citizens of the country.

Major philosophers of the Enlightenment included:

- Rene Descartes—"I think, therefore I am." He believed strongly in logic and rules of observation.
- David Hume—pioneered empiricism and skepticism, believing that truth could only be found through direct experience, and that what others said to be true was always suspect.
- Immanuel Kant—believed in self-examination and observation, and that the root of morality lay within human beings.
- Jean-Jacques Rousseau—developed the idea of the social contract, that government existed by the agreement of the people, and that the government was obligated to protect the people and their basic rights. His ideas influenced John Locke and Thomas Jefferson.

Review Video: Age of Enlightenment
Visit mometrix.com/academy and enter code: 143022

American Revolution and the French Revolution

Both the American and French Revolution came about as a protest against the excesses and overly controlling nature of their respective monarchs. In America, the British colonies had been left mostly self-governing until the British monarchs began to increase control, leading the colonies to revolt. In France, the nobility's excesses had led to increasingly difficult economic conditions, with inflation, heavy taxation and food shortages creating horrible burdens on the people. Both revolutions led to the development of republics to replace the monarchies that were displaced.

However, the French Revolution eventually led to the rise of the dictator Napoleon Bonaparte, while the American Revolution produced a working republic from the beginning.

Review Video: The Revolutionary War
Visit mometrix.com/academy and enter code: 935282

Events of the French Revolution

In 1789, King Louis XVI, faced with a huge national debt, convened parliament. The Third Estate, or Commons, a division of the French parliament, then claimed power, and the king's resistance led to the storming of the Bastille, the royal prison.

Review Video: The French Revolution: The Estates General
Visit mometrix.com/academy and enter code: 805480

Review Video: The French Revolution: The National Assembly
Visit mometrix.com/academy and enter code: 338451

The people established a constitutional monarchy. When King Louis XVI and Marie Antoinette attempted to leave the country, they were executed on the guillotine. From 1793 to 1794, Robespierre and extreme radicals, the Jacobins, instituted a Reign of Terror, executing thousands of nobles as well as anyone considered an enemy of the Revolution. Robespierre was then executed, as well, and the Directory came into power.

This governing body proved incompetent and corrupt, allowing Napoleon Bonaparte to come to power in 1799, first as a dictator, then as emperor. While the French Revolution threw off the power of a corrupt monarchy, its immediate results were likely not what the original perpetrators of the revolt had intended.

Review Video: The French Revolution: Napoleon Bonaparte
Visit mometrix.com/academy and enter code: 876330

19th Century Developments

Industrial Revolution

The Industrial Revolution began in Great Britain, bringing coal- and steam-powered machinery into widespread use. Industry began a period of rapid growth with these developments. Goods that had previously been produced in small workshops or even in homes were produced more efficiently and in much larger quantities in factories. Where society had been largely agrarian based, the focus swiftly shifted to an industrial outlook.

As electricity and internal combustion engines replaced coal and steam as energy sources, even more drastic and rapid changes occurred. Western European countries in particular turned to colonialism, taking control of portions of Africa and Asia to assure access to the raw materials needed to produce factory goods. Specialized labor became very much in demand, and businesses grew rapidly, creating monopolies, increasing world trade, and creating large urban centers. Even agriculture changed fundamentally as the Industrial Revolution led to a second Agricultural Revolution as the addition of the new technologies advanced agricultural production.

The first phase of the Industrial Revolution took place from roughly 1750 to 1830. The textile industry experienced major changes as more and more elements of the process became mechanized. Mining benefited from the steam engine. Transportation became easier and more widely available as waterways were improved and the railroad came into prominence.

In the second phase, from 1830 to 1910, industries further improved in efficiency and new industries were introduced as photography, various chemical processes, and electricity became more widely available to produce new goods or new, improved versions of old goods. Petroleum and hydroelectric became major sources of power. During this time, the industrial revolution spread out of Western Europe and into the US and Japan.

The Industrial Revolution led to widespread education, a wider franchise, and the development of mass communication in the political arena.

Economically, conflicts arose between companies and their employees, as struggles for fair treatment and fair wages increased. Unions gained power and became more active. Government regulation over industries increased, but at the same time, growing businesses fought for the right to free enterprise.

In the social sphere, populations increased and began to concentrate around centers of industry. Cities became larger and more densely populated. Scientific advancements led to more efficient agriculture, greater supply of goods, and increased knowledge of medicine and sanitation, leading to better overall health.

Review Video: The Industrial Revolution
Visit mometrix.com/academy and enter code: 372796

19th Century Political Developments

Social Liberalism

Social liberalism developed in the late nineteenth century as an alternative to classical liberalism. Social liberalism declares that political problems can be solved by the work of liberal institutions in the government. Unlike the classical liberals, social liberals believe that the government should exercise some influence on the economy, and should extend some basic welfare services to the people. The aim of social liberalism was to improve life for the poor and disadvantaged. Social liberals were also very outspoken on issues of civil rights and individual liberties. Some of the most famous social liberals are Jeremy Bentham, John Stuart Mill, and John Dewey.

Nationalism

Nationalism, put simply, is a strong belief in, identification with, and allegiance to a particular nation and people. Nationalistic belief unified various areas that had previously seen themselves as fragmented which led to patriotism and, in some cases, imperialism. As nationalism grew, individual nations sought to grow, bringing in other, smaller states that shared similar characteristics such as language and cultural beliefs. Unfortunately, a major side effect of these growing nationalistic beliefs was often conflict and outright war.

In Europe, imperialism led countries to spread their influence into Africa and Asia. Africa was eventually divided among several European countries that needed the raw materials to be found there. Asia also came under European control, with the exception of China, Japan and Siam (now Thailand). In the US, Manifest Destiny became the rallying cry as the country expanded west. Italy and Germany formed larger nations from a variety of smaller states.

Review Video: Nationalism
Visit mometrix.com/academy and enter code: 865693

Communism and Socialism

At their roots, socialism and communism both focus on public ownership and distribution of goods and services. However, communism works toward revolution by drawing on what it sees to be inevitable class antagonism, eventually overthrowing the upper classes and the systems of capitalism. Socialism makes use of democratic procedures, building on the existing order. This was particularly true of the Utopian-Socialists, who saw industrial capitalism as oppressive, not allowing workers to prosper.

While socialism struggled between the World Wars, communism took hold, especially in Eastern Europe. After WW II, democratic socialism became more common. Later, capitalism took a stronger hold again, and today most industrialized countries in the world function under an economy that mixes elements of capitalism and socialism.

Review Video: Socialism
Visit mometrix.com/academy and enter code: 917677

Challenges of the Early 20th Century

Russian Revolution of 1905

In Russia, rule lay in the hands of the Czars, and the overall structure was feudalistic. Beneath the Czars was a group of rich nobles, landowners whose lands were worked by peasants and serfs. The Russo-Japanese War (1904-1905) made conditions much worse for the lower classes. When peasants demonstrated outside the Czar's Winter Palace, the palace guard fired upon the crowd. The demonstration had been organized by a trade union leader, and after the violent response, many unions as well as political parties blossomed and began to lead numerous strikes. When the economy ground to a halt, Czar Nicholas II signed a document known as the October Manifesto, which established a constitutional monarchy and gave legislative power to parliament. However, he violated the Manifesto shortly thereafter, disbanding parliament and ignoring the civil liberties granted by the Manifesto. This eventually led to the Bolshevik Revolution of 1917.

The Beginnings of the Great War

In the early years of the twentieth century, relations among the various European powers were complex. Ever since the Franco-Prussian War, won by Prussia, the two sides had been enemies. At the center of their conflict was the territory of Alsace-Lorraine, which each side claimed as its own. In order to bolster their position in the region, each side entered into networks of alliances. After years of negotiations, two main alliances contained the major European powers: the Triple Alliance (Germany, Austria, Italy) and the Triple Entente (France, Britain, Russia). These two alliances would end up being the opposing sides in the great war of the ensuing years.

In the years before the First World War, the Balkans were attempting to gain independence from the Hapsburg empire of Austria. This insurrection culminated in the assassination of Austrian Archduke Franz Ferdinand in 1914 by Gavrilo Princip, a member of a Serbian nationalist group. At this point, a chain reaction of war declarations (spurred by the comprehensive alliances of the time) ensued. Austria declared war against Serbia; Germany and Turkey joined with the Austrians; Russia declared war on these countries in support of Serbia; France joined with Russia; and Britain and Italy joined forces with France, even though Italy had been a member of the Triple Alliance.

World War I

Trench Warfare

Fighting during WW I took place largely in a series of trenches built along the Eastern and Western Fronts. These trenches added up to about 24,000 miles, each side having dug at least 12,000 miles' worth during the course of the war. This produced fronts that stretched nearly 400 miles, from the coast of Belgium to the border of Switzerland.

The Allies made use of straightforward open-air trenches with a front line, supporting lines, and communications lines. By contrast, the German trenches sometimes included well-equipped underground living quarters.

Western Front

The western front of World War I refers to the battles that took place in Belgium and France from 1914 to 1918. The German Army marched into Belgium on August 4, 1914, to make its way to France. The Belgians, however, were not willing to allow the Germans to march through Belgium unhindered, and they launched a series of attacks against the Germans that weakened and slowed down the German forces. This cost the Germans a large amount of time that was vital to the Schlieffen Plan, but the Germans continued their advance and made it to the edge of France by the beginning of September 1914. When the Germans reached France, a series of battles ensued between the French and the British forces that had arrived in France by the time Germany made its way through Belgium. These battles ultimately resulted in the deaths of hundreds of thousands of men on both sides, but they did very little to improve the position of either side throughout most of the war.

Eastern Front

The eastern front of World War I refers to the battles that took place in Austria, Germany, Hungary, Poland, Prussia, and Russia from 1914 to 1917. The First and Second Russian armies marched into East Prussia and Poland in mid-August 1914 to make their way to Austria and eventually Germany. The German forces stationed in East Prussia were able to force the First Russian Army to retreat, but the Second Russian Army was able to move into Poland and destroy the Austrian forces stationed there. The German forces, as a result, moved into Poland to force the Second Russian Army to retreat, and after a series of battles, the Germans eventually forced the Russians back into Russia. This allowed the Germans to advance farther and farther into Russia until the people of Russia finally revolted against the Russian government to end the chaos, famine, and death that the war was causing in Russia. This forced the Russian government to exit the war.

Overview

Despite the fact that almost every nation in Europe had entered into World War I, most Europeans thought the conflict would be brief. Instead, advances in weapons technology made the war bloody and excruciatingly slow. Much of the fighting was done from trenches, and some battles would see the deaths of thousands of soldiers at a time. The war was also slow because the sides were very evenly matched; that is, until 1917, when the United States entered on the side of Britain. Also, in 1917, the Russians exited the war via the Brest-Litovsk Treaty. Russia was basically exhausted after suffering through a Revolution in 1917 in which the Bolsheviks came to power. The entry of the US provided the British and French with supplies and troops, and Germany was soon forced to call for a truce.

Treaty of Versailles

The war left Europe deeply in debt, and particularly devastated the German economy. The ensuing Great Depression made matters worse, and economic devastation opened the door for Communist, Fascist and Socialist governments to gain power.

The Treaty of Versailles was a treaty that France, Germany, Great Britain, Italy, Japan, and the United States signed to end World War I. This treaty was specifically designed to establish the terms under which Germany surrendered, and it identified several concessions that the Germans had to make. The terms of the treaty specifically required Germany to surrender a large portion of land it acquired both before and during the war, required Germany to pay reparations for the damage that it caused in each of the Allied nations, required Emperor Wilhelm II of Germany and other members of the German Army to be tried as war criminals, required Germany to reduce the size of its army and navy, required Germany to allow the Allied powers to establish a demilitarized zone in the Rhineland, and required Germany to make many other similar concessions.

Interwar Years

In the years after the First World War, the general mood in Europe was one of wariness. Most nations were exhausted by the conflict, and few felt that the signing of the Treaty of Versailles and the formation of the League of Nations had created a permanent peace. In the 1920s, Britain, Germany, France, and the United States were all liberal democracies without a strong executive. Unlike the United States, however, even the victorious European nations suffered a profound economic depression. One nation that saw no diminution in nationalism was Italy. In part out of a fear of communism, Italians supported the rise of the fascist dictator Benito Mussolini. Fascism was a political philosophy that promised Italians a return to the glory days of Rome, when they were a mighty power ruled by a dominating executive. Of course, in order to maintain his authority Mussolini had to brutally suppress any opposition.

Still shell-shocked from the First World War, the nations of western Europe were slow to respond to the growing menace of Nazi Germany. In general, they pursued a policy of appeasement and isolation. The British prime minister Neville Chamberlain was especially committed to using diplomacy over war. Then, in 1936, Hitler sent troops to occupy the Rhineland, a strip of territory on the German border. At around the same time, Mussolini invaded Ethiopia; the two aggressors, Germany and Italy, entered into an agreement making them the Axis Powers. In 1938, Germany annexed Austria and indicated that it was about to attack Czechoslovakia. In response to these actions, Chamberlain brought together Mussolini and Hitler for the Munich Conference of 1938. These talks would only briefly suspend German aggression.

Great Depression

The Great Depression refers to a period from the late 1920s to the early 1940s in which the economy of almost every major nation began to decline rapidly. The beginning of this period is typically associated with the date that the stock market crashed (October 29, 1929), but the Great Depression actually resulted from a series of different problems in different nations at different times. In fact, the Great Depression was actually caused by so many different problems (industry changes, inadequate stock regulation, war relief costs, etc.) that it ultimately affected each nation in a different way. France, Germany, and Great Britain began to feel the effects of an economic decline in the early 1920s, but the conditions of the economies of each of these nations deteriorated almost immediately after the stock market crash. This led to the widespread closure of businesses throughout Europe, and the unemployment rate increased drastically in each of these nations as a result. Russia, on the other hand, was virtually unaffected because of its communist economy.

Rise of the Fascist Party

The Fascists were a group of radical political reformers who wanted to create a nation in which all the people in the nation were not treated as individuals but instead as parts of a greater whole who were each expected to respect the absolute authority of the government and work toward the ultimate glory of the nation. It is important to note, however, that fascism (in other words, a fascist government) doesn't typically allow an individual to have any rights at all.

Benito Mussolini was the leader of the National Fascist Party and later the Prime Minister of Italy during the mid-twentieth century. He is known for establishing the Fascist Party, helping the Fascist Party take control of Italy, and ultimately attempting to expand Italy's influence across Europe during World War II.

Rise of the Nazi Party

The Nazis, who were also known as the National Socialist German Workers' Party, were radical political reformers who wanted to create a nation in which the government was not only allowed to restrict the actions of its people without question, but a nation in which the government was actually expected to restrict the actions of its people (in other words, a totalitarian government). Adolf Hitler was the führer (a German term that literally means "leader") of the Nazi Party and later the führer of all Germany during the mid-twentieth century. He is known for establishing the Nazi Party, helping the Nazi Party take control of Germany, and ultimately being responsible for the actions that Germany took during World War II (including the Holocaust). He is also known for his book, Mein Kampf, in which he discussed his belief that Germany's problems could be traced back to the Jewish population.

World War II

German Invasion across Europe

The invasion of Poland in 1939 is often considered to be the official beginning of World War II. It is important to note, however, that the Axis powers (Germany, Italy, and Japan) were involved in several military actions immediately prior to the invasion of Poland. In fact, Japan, had sent forces to seize control of Manchuria in 1931 and then later sent troops to seize control of the rest of China in 1937. Japan was actually engaged in a series of battles with the Chinese throughout most of the 1930s. (These battles actually lasted until the end of World War II.) Italy, like Japan, attempted to expand its influence by sending forces into Ethiopia in 1935 and by later sending troops to seize control of Albania in 1939. Finally, Germany, who left the League of Nations in 1933 so that it could begin its massive expansion campaign, had sent forces to reclaim the Rhineland in 1936 and then later sent forces to claim Austria in 1938 and Czechoslovakia in 1939.

After Chamberlain had tried to forestall German aggression at the Munich Conference of 1938, Germany nevertheless invaded Czechoslovakia in 1939. It was also during this year that Hitler signed a secret agreement with Stalin pledging not to attack Russia so long as Russia stayed out of German affairs. Hitler then declared war on and conquered Poland. At this step, Great Britain and France were finally forced to declare war upon Germany.

Germany at this point was a dominating military adversary. New advances in motorized military vehicles made it possible for Germany to conquer large areas of land quickly in a new form of warfare called Blitzkrieg (lightning-war). The Axis powers conquered almost the entire European continent, including France, over the course of 1940. Only Great Britain remained in opposition, and the Nazis undertook a ferocious aerial assault on the British, who were by then led by Winston Churchill, but failed to do enough damage to make an invasion of the island country practical. Instead, Hitler turned East and decided to violate his truce with Stalin, invading Russia in 1941 and overwhelming much of the Soviet military and advancing deep into Russian territory in a huge surprise offensive.

Japan in World War II

The Japanese, like the Germans, became seduced by the notion of their own racial superiority during the 1930s. As in Germany, this inevitably led to a lust for territorial expansion. By 1941, Japan had conquered Korea, Manchuria, and parts of China. Japan was also threatening to invade American interests in the Philippines. The United States imposed economic sanctions on Japan making it difficult for the Japanese war industry to function. In response, the Japanese launched a surprise attack on the United States by bombing the US naval base of Pearl Harbor. After the attack on Pearl Harbor, the United States would declare war upon Japan (and Germany would in turn declare war on the United States).

The United States Joins the Allied Powers

Isolationism refers to the political belief that a country shouldn't interfere in the affairs of other nations and that a country should avoid any activity that would involve the country in the activities of another nation whenever possible. The United States and the nations of Europe began to move away from isolationism after World War I, but many nations still had a strong desire to avoid a conflict. Appeasement refers to a political tactic in which a country seeks to avoid a conflict by simply allowing another nation to conduct whatever activities it wants. Both tactics were used by countries prior to World War II and allowed Hitler to operate uncontested until his attack on Poland in 1939.

Battles in World War II

The tide turned against Hitler once the United States entered the war. The harsh Russian winter halted the German advance into Russia short of Moscow in 1941. The Germans made further gains in the summer of 1942, but were decisively beaten at the battle of Stalingrad and were slowly pushed back out of Russia from then on. American and British troops landed in North Africa in 1942 and used that as a springboard to invade Italy in 1943.

The Japanese made huge territorial gains before the US turned the tide at the Battles of Midway and Guadalcanal. The war in the Pacific would take much longer than the war in Europe due to the island-hopping nature of the fight. The Japanese unwillingness to surrender made it almost impossible for America to entirely vanquish them without enormous loss of life. So, the United States decided to drop atomic bombs on Hiroshima and Nagasaki to force Japan to surrender and finally end the war in the Pacific in August 1945.

Blitzkrieg

The blitzkrieg, or "lightning war," consisted of fast, powerful surprise attacks that disrupted communications, made it difficult if not impossible for the victims to retaliate, and demoralized Germany's foes. The "blitz," or the aerial bombing of England in 1940, was one example, with bombings occurring in London and other cities 57 nights in a row. The Battle of Britain, from 1940 to 1941, also brought intense raids by Germany's air force, the Luftwaffe, mostly targeting ports and British air force bases. Eventually, Britain's Royal Air Force blocked the Luftwaffe, ending Germany's hopes for conquering Britain.

D-Day

In 1944, the Americans and British opened yet another front with a massive invasion of northern France in the D-Day landings. Fighting numerically superior forces on multiple fronts, the Germans steadily lost ground and the Allies pushed into Germany from both East and West in 1945. Surrounded and with the war lost, Hitler committed suicide in his bunker in Berlin in April, 1945 and the remaining German forces surrendered shortly afterwards.

Battle of the Bulge

Following the D-Day Invasion, Allied forces gained considerable ground, and began a major campaign to push through Europe. In December of 1944, Hitler launched a counteroffensive, attempting to retake Antwerp, an important port. The ensuing battle became the largest land battle on the war's Western Front, and was known as the Battle of the Ardennes, or the Battle of the Bulge.

The battle lasted from December 16, 1944 to January 28, 1945. The Germans pushed forward, making inroads into Allied lines, but in the end the Allies brought the advance to a halt. The Germans were pushed back, with massive losses on both sides. However, those losses proved crippling to the German army.

Holocaust

As Germany sank deeper and deeper into dire economic straits, the tendency was to look for a person or group of people to blame for the problems of the country. With distrust of the Jewish people already ingrained, it was easy for German authorities to set up the Jews as scapegoats for Germany's problems.

Under the rule of Hitler and the Nazi party, the "Final Solution" for the supposed Jewish problem was devised. Millions of Jews, as well as Gypsies, homosexuals, Communists, Catholics, the mentally ill and others, simply named as criminals, were transported to concentration camps during the course of the war. At least six million were slaughtered in death camps such as Auschwitz, where horrible conditions and torture of prisoners were commonplace.

The Allies were aware of rumors of mass slaughter throughout the war, but many discounted the reports. Only when troops went in to liberate the prisoners was the true horror of the concentration camps brought to light.

The Holocaust resulted in massive loss of human life, but also in the loss and destruction of cultures. Because the genocide focused on specific ethnic groups, many traditions, histories, knowledge, and other cultural elements were lost, particularly among the Jewish and Gypsy populations.

After World War II, the United Nations recognized genocide as a "crime against humanity." The UN passed the Universal Declaration of Human Rights in order to further specify what rights the organization protected. Nazi war criminals faced justice during the Nuremberg Trials. There individuals, rather than their governments, were held accountable for war crimes.

Review Video: The Holocaust
Visit mometrix.com/academy and enter code: 350695

AFTERMATH OF WORLD WAR II

With millions of military and civilian deaths and over 12 million persons displaced, WW II left large regions of Europe and Asia in disarray. Communist governments moved in with promises of renewed prosperity and economic stability. The Soviet Union backed Communist regimes in much of Eastern Europe. In China, Mao Zedong led communist forces in the overthrow of the Chinese Nationalist Party and instituted a Communist government in 1949.

While the new Communist governments restored a measure of stability to much of Eastern Europe, it brought its own problems, with dictatorial governments and an oppressive police force. The spread of Communism also led to several years of tension between Communist countries and the democratic west, as the west fought to slow the spread of oppressive regimes throughout the world. With both sides in possession of nuclear weapons, tensions rose. Each side feared the other would resort to nuclear attack. This standoff lasted until 1989, when the Berlin Wall fell. The Soviet Union was dissolved two years later.

Modern Global Events

Cold War

After the defeat of the Axis powers in WWII, the United States and Russia entered into a long and often secret conflict, in which each side used diplomatic, economic, and occasionally military forces to try and assert itself as the dominant world power. The first issue on which these nations butted heads was the rebuilding of Europe. Germany was divided into an eastern and western section; the western half was democratic and looked to the US for guidance, while Eastern Germany became a communist nation in the USSR's sphere of influence. Russia worked to bring all of its neighbors (including Poland, Czechoslovakia, Hungary, Romania, and Bulgaria) under its control. The western borders of these nations formed what Churchill referred to as the iron curtain, dividing communist Eastern Europe from democratic Western Europe.

China was torn by civil strife all throughout the Second World War. At one point, the American government had to renounce its trade rights in China in order to persuade China not to sign a peace treaty with Japan while the US still needed Chinese support. Once Japan had been defeated, the Red Army under Mao moved into Manchuria (which had recently been vacated by the Soviets). The major cities were still occupied by Nationalist forces, supported by the Americans. In 1946, fighting resumed between the opposing factions, and the Nationalists under Chiang were eventually forced to abandon central China. In 1949, the Red Army forced Chiang Kai-shek to leave the mainland and find refuge on Taiwan. On October 1, 1949, the communists declared the official creation of the People's Republic of China.

Marshall Plan

In order to stop the spread of communism in Europe and elsewhere, the President Truman asserted his policy of "containment" in the so-called Truman Doctrine. This meant that the US would support the anticommunist governments throughout the world. The Marshall Plan advanced this policy by supplying aid to war-ravaged countries in Western Europe. When the Eastern Bloc countries prevented aid from reaching West Berlin, the US, England, and France organized the Berlin Airlift to overcome this obstacle. In 1949, the Western European and North American nations entered into a mutual defense treaty, NATO (North Atlantic Treaty Organization). As a response, the eastern Bloc nations joined with the Soviet Union in the Warsaw Pact.

Mutual Disarmament of Nuclear Weapons

During the Cold War, the United States and the Soviet Union each tried to deter an attack by the other by building up fantastic arsenals of nuclear missiles. The two nations would also expend considerable effort trying to be the first in space. Finally, in the late 60s and early 70s, the two nations would begin talks aimed at mutual disarmament. This occurred in part because relations between China and the USSR had cooled. Before this period of détente, however, there had been a couple of serious threats to global peace. In 1961, the US had financed an unsuccessful invasion of Cuba at the Bay of Pigs. This led the Soviet Union to establish missile bases on communist Cuba; the US and USSR almost declared war on one another during the Cuban Missile Crisis of 1962.

Fall of the Soviet Union

Over time, the leaders of the Soviet Union and United States began to realize the total annihilation that would ensue if nuclear war was declared, and it was agreed that both sides would disarm. The two treaties that were signed during the 1970s are known as the Strategic Arms Limitation Talks (SALT) I and II. When Mikhail Gorbachev came into power in the USSR in 1985, he established a policy of glasnost, or "openness." In response to US President Ronald Reagan's military build-up using the might of the US economy, Gorbachev understood that the Soviet Union could not economically compete militarily under a communist system and overcome the military might of the United States. He thus advocated perestroika, a gradual metamorphosis of the Soviet economy. In 1991, these reforms culminated in the disintegration of the ruling Communist party, and the disbanding of the Soviet Union. This occurred two years after the Berlin Wall, which for more than forty years had separated communist and anticommunist Germany, was finally torn down.

Post-Colonialism

In 1947, after years of peaceful protests led by Mahatma Gandhi, India was given its independence and partitioned into three states, India and Pakistan. The following year, Gandhi would be assassinated in India. In 1965, border disputes would flare into the Indo-Pakistani War. In 1971, Pakistan would fend off attacks from Bengali rebels, who sought to achieve independence. The next year, however, Bangladesh would be established as an independent state. In 1984, India had its own internal problems: after the Indian army occupied the Golden Temple sacred to the Sikhs, the Indian leader Indira Gandhi was assassinated by her Sikh bodyguards. Anti-Sikh riots resulted, and much blood was shed.

Establishment of Israel

After WWII, the United Nations announced that Palestine would be partitioned in order to make room for a new Jewish state. Israel was created in 1948. In 1951, the Iranian leader Mossadegh nationalized the oil interests, making his government extremely wealthy and powerful. This move would be emulated by future leaders. In 1967, in the Six Day War, Israel routed a coalition of Arab nations, seizing the West Bank, Sinai, and Jerusalem. In 1972, Palestinian terrorists murdered 12 Israeli athletes at the Olympics in Munich. In 1973, the oil-producing Arab nations placed an embargo on shipments to the West, causing major energy crises in the US and Europe. Also, in 1973, Israelis and Arabs battled again in the Yom Kippur War. In 1977, Egyptian leader Anwar Sadat became the first Arab leader to visit Israel.

Peace Talks at Camp David

In 1978, American President Jimmy Carter hosted successful peace talks between Egypt and Israel at Camp David. The next year, however, a fundamentalist Islamist regime would take power in Iran, and many Americans would be taken hostage, only released upon the election of Ronald Reagan. Between 1980 and 1988, Iran and Iraq engaged in a bloody and brutal war, begun when the Iraqi leader Saddam Hussein seized territory in western Iran. Also, during this period, Afghan rebels were engaged in a prolonged, ultimately successful fight for independence from the Soviets. In 1982, Israel attacked Lebanon, which was harboring the Palestinian leader Yasser Arafat. Lebanon would be forced to oust Arafat the next year. Israel would continue attacking Arafat and the Palestinian Liberation Organization, and the PLO would continue to sponsor terrorist activities against Israel.

Korean War

In 1910, Japan took control of Korea, and maintained this control until 1945, when Soviet and US troops occupied the country. The Soviet Union controlled North Korea, while the US controlled South Korea. In 1947, the UN ordered elections in Korea to unify the country but the Soviet Union refused to allow them to take place, instead setting up a communist government in North Korea. In 1950, the US withdrew troops, and the North Korean troops moved to invade South Korea.

The Korean War was the first war in which the UN—or any international organization—played a major role. The US, Australia, Canada, France, Netherlands, Great Britain, Turkey, China, USSR and other countries sent troops at various times, for both sides, throughout the war. In 1953, the war ended in a truce, but no peace agreement was ever achieved, and Korea remains divided.

Vietnam War

Vietnam had previously been part of a French colony called French Indochina.

The Vietnam War began with the French Indochina War from 1946-1954, in which France battled with the Democratic Republic of Vietnam, ruled by Ho Chi Minh.

In 1954, a siege at Dien Bien Phu ended in a Vietnamese victory. Vietnam was then divided into North and South, much like Korea. Communist forces controlled the North and the South was controlled by South Vietnamese forces, supported by the US. Conflict ensued, leading to a war. US troops eventually lead the fight, in support of South Vietnam. The war became a major political issue in the US, with many citizens protesting American involvement.

In 1976, South Vietnam surrendered, and Vietnam became the Socialist Republic of Vietnam.

Major Occurrences of Genocide in Modern History

Armenian genocide—occurred in the 1900s when the Young Turks, heirs to the Ottoman Empire, slaughtered over a million Armenians between 1915 and 1917. This constituted nearly half the Armenian population at the time.

Russian purges under Stalin—Scholars have attributed deaths between 3 and 60 million, both directly and indirectly, to the policies and edicts of Joseph Stalin's regime. The deaths took place from 1921 to 1953, when Stalin died. In recent years, many scholars have settled on a number of deaths near 20 million but this is still disputed today.

Rwandan Genocide—in 1994, hundreds of thousands of Tutsi and Hutu sympathizers were slaughtered during the Rwandan Civil War. The UN did not act or authorize intervention during these atrocities.

United Nations

The United Nations (UN) came into being toward the end of World War II. A successor to the less-than-successful League of Nations, formed after World War I, the UN built and improved on those ideas. Since its inception, the UN has worked to bring the countries of the world together for diplomatic solutions to international problems, including sanctions and other restrictions. It has also initiated military action, calling for peacekeeping troops from member countries to move against countries violating UN policies.

One example of UN involvement in an international conflict is the Korean War, the first war in which an international alliance of this kind was actively involved.

Decolonization

A rise of nationalism among European colonies led to many of them declaring independence. India and Pakistan became independent of Britain at this time, and numerous African and Asian colonies declared independence, as well. This period of decolonization lasted into the 1960s.

Some colonies moved successfully into independence but many, especially in Africa and Asia, struggled to create stable governments and economies, and suffered from ethnic and religious conflicts. Some of those countries still struggle today.

Terrorism

Terrorism is politically- motivated violence. It is invariably considered criminal activity. It can include such crimes as murder, assault and battery, destruction of property, airplane hijacking and kidnapping, as long as those crimes are performed with the intent of altering the political process in some way. It is rarely a direct attack on whatever political mechanism is meant to be affected, but on innocent victims with the intent of politically and ideologically influencing others. Terrorism has been around for centuries if not millennia. The most famous terrorist act of recent years was almost certainly the September 11, 2001, attacks in New York and Virginia.

GLOBALISM

In the modern era, globalism has emerged as a popular political ideology. Globalism is based in the idea that all people and all nations are interdependent. Each nation is dependent on one or more other nations for production of and markets for goods, and for income generation. Today's ease of international travel and communication, including technological advances such as the airplane, has heightened this sense of interdependence.

The global economy, and the general idea of globalism, has shaped many economic and political choices since the beginning of the twentieth century. Many of today's issues, including environmental awareness, economic struggles, and continued warfare, often require the cooperation of many countries if they are to be dealt with effectively.

With countries worldwide often seeking the same resources, some, particularly nonrenewable resources, have experienced high demand. At times this has resulted in wild price fluctuations. One major example is the demand for petroleum products such as oil and natural gas.

Increased travel and communication make it possible to deal with diseases in remote locations; however, it also allows diseases to be spread via travelers, as well.

A major factor contributing to increased globalization over the past few decades has been the Internet. By allowing instantaneous communication with anyone nearly anywhere on the globe, the Internet has led to interaction between far-flung individuals and countries, and an ever-increasing awareness of happenings all over the world.

ROLE OF THE MIDDLE EAST IN INTERNATIONAL RELATIONS AND ECONOMICS

Its location on the globe, with ease of access to Europe and Asia, and its preponderance of oil deposits, makes the middle eastern countries a crucial factor in many international issues both diplomatic and economic. Because of its central location, the Middle East has been a hotbed for violence since before the beginning of recorded history. Conflicts over land, resources, religious and political power continue in the area today, spurred by conflict over control of the area's vast oil fields as well as over territories that have been disputed for literally hundreds—and even thousands—of years.

FSOT Practice Test

Job Knowledge

1. What is the most efficient way to send another person a copy of an e-mail without letting the intended recipient know?

a. Add a cc.
b. Forward it.
c. Add a bcc.
d. Send it through postal mail.

2. An instructor lists all student grades on a particular test. The most popular grade is an 86, attained by 13 of the 22 students. What is 86 considered?

a. The mean
b. The average
c. The range
d. The mode

3. Where is the U.S. banking system regulated?

a. On the local level
b. On the state level
c. On the federal level
d. On both the state and the federal level

4. During which president's administration was Medicare and Medicaid started?

a. Lyndon Johnson
b. Franklin Roosevelt
c. Herbert Hoover
d. Theodore Roosevelt

5. What is the main way the U.S. government controls our money supply?

a. Changes in interest rates
b. Raising taxes
c. Striving for high economic growth
d. Regulating inflation

6. The economic systems of the United States and Russia are both most closely tied to:

a. the government
b. their geography
c. historical events
d. technology

7. The European Union's first treaties focused on building:

a. A common market
b. Environmental stability
c. Humanitarian values
d. Solidarity

8. How is a database best defined?

a. A tool for collecting and organizing information
b. An accounting program for keeping track of revenue and expenses
c. An index describing a company's departments
d. A listing of computer software

9. What is a true statement about motivating people?

a. People have to be self-motivated.
b. People are always motivated by money.
c. Fear of losing a job is a good long-term motivator.
d. All people are motivated by the same things.

10. An employer makes a rule that employees speak only English on the job. What law is this most likely to violate?

a. Immigration Reform and Control Act
b. Title VII
c. Civil Rights Act of 1991
d. Anti-Discrimination Act

11. Which is a true statement about noncitizens living in the United States?

a. They are illegally residing here.
b. They can receive Social Security benefits.
c. They are not eligible for food stamps.
d. They do not contribute to the U.S. economy.

12. Which two countries made efforts to curb overpopulation in their countries in the late 20th century?

a. Great Britain and Mexico
b. Nigeria and China
c. Iran and Great Britain
d. Nigeria and Great Britain

13. Who led Poland as president from 1990 to 1995?

a. Vaclav Havel
b. Nicolae Ceausescu
c. Lech Walesa
d. Helmut Kohl

14. Which group was responsible for a large part of the terrorism in Northern Ireland throughout most of the last half of the 20th century?

a. Al-Qaeda
b. Independent Muslims
c. IRA
d. Catholics

15. Weak organizational, financial, and political governments are at risk for:

a. Insurgency
b. Immigration
c. Failed states
d. Loss of military

16. Which 1992 treaty established the euro as the single currency for Europe?

a. General Agreement on Trade and Tariffs
b. European Union Treaty
c. Maastricht Treaty
d. World Trade Organization Agreement

17. In the 1980s, some Latin American countries took up neoliberalism. What was the main idea of this economic model?

a. Government dependence and monopolization
b. Free markets and privatization
c. Denationalization and taxation
d. Industrialization and regulation

18. Which country put the first satellite in space, in 1957?

a. Russia
b. United States
c. Germany
d. Korea

19. Which word is best defined as the unlimited power to govern?

a. Oligarchy
b. Communism
c. Absolutism
d. Patriarchy

20. How many Federal Reserve banks are in the United States?

a. 1
b. 2
c. 12
d. 27

21. Which phrase, coined during the Cold War, best describes a First World country?

a. A stateless nation
b. An impoverished and unstable country
c. An industrialized but not democratic country
d. An industrial democracy

22. In 2002, President George W. Bush cited certain countries as being part of an "axis of evil." Which country was not part of that description?

a. Iran
b. Iraq
c. North Korea
d. Afghanistan

23. What was the Patriot Act created to confront and work against?

a. Terrorism
b. Weapons of mass destruction
c. Free trade
d. Global warming

24. Which freedom is not covered by the First Amendment to the Constitution?

a. Freedom of the press
b. Freedom from cruel and unusual punishment
c. Freedom of assembly
d. Freedom to petition the government

25. Which amendment guarantees a speedy trial in the United States?

a. Fourth Amendment
b. Sixth Amendment
c. Eighth Amendment
d. Fourteenth Amendment

26. Which is a phrase used to describe irresponsible and inflammatory reporting by the press?

a. Propaganda
b. Penny press
c. Free speech
d. Yellow journalism

27. How long is the elected term for a member of the Senate?

a. 3 years
b. 4 years
c. 5 years
d. 6 years

28. What is a term used for a person who flees a nation for political freedom?

a. Prisoner of war
b. Nonresident alien
c. Immigrant
d. Refugee

29. Which is not a constitutional responsibility of the president of the United States?

a. Negotiating treaties with Senate approval
b. Recommending legislation
c. Choosing chairpersons for standing committees of Congress
d. Seeking counsel of cabinet secretaries

30. Which government body has the least influence on foreign policy?

a. Congress
b. State Department
c. Defense Department
d. National Security Council

31. Which factor is least likely to be considered to affect a country's gross domestic product (GDP)?

a. The size of its workforce
b. The amount of its capital
c. Technology in place
d. Education of its workforce

32. Most political theorists, regardless of ideology, believe that __________ benefits all countries economically.

a. Multistate structures
b. Population control
c. Free international trade
d. Interest groups

33. What is the most likely result when the minimum wage is raised?

a. A decrease in saving
b. A decrease in inflation
c. An increase in saving
d. An increase in inflation

34. What is the most important component to a successful market economy?

a. Price
b. Government
c. Banks
d. Demand

35. An athlete will buy the same amount of spinach each week regardless of its price. What can be said of spinach and the athlete?

a. The athlete's purchases are dependent on her income's elasticity.
b. The athlete considers spinach a low utility purchase.
c. The athlete has an inelastic demand for spinach.
d. The athlete has an unlimited demand for spinach.

36. Two drivers set out for a destination 150 miles away. Car A travels at an average speed of 75 miles per hour. Car B travels at an average speed of 60 miles per hour. How soon after Car A arrives at the destination will Car B show up?

a. 15 minutes
b. 30 minutes
c. 45 minutes
d. 60 minutes

37. A book retails for $35.00. A book store marks it 15% off, today only. Those with frequent buyer cards get an additional 10% off when they show their card at the register. What will the book cost a frequent buyer today?

a. $26.25
b. $26.78
c. $29.75
d. $31.50

38. Six people step onto an elevator with a weight limit of 1,500 pounds. One person weighs 325 pounds. What would the average weight of each of the other people need to be to be within the limit?

a. 195 pounds
b. 235 pounds
c. 250 pounds
d. 300 pounds

39. The check for a $10,000 lottery win has 32% deducted for taxes. What is the amount of the check?

a. $3,200
b. $6,800
c. $9,680
d. $9.968

40. A man makes a $25,000 loan at 6% interest to a friend. The man repays $5,000. How much is still owed?

a. $20,000
b. $21,500
c. $23,800
d. $26,410

41. A man spends one-fourth of his day at school, one-twelfth of his day eating and doing errands, and one-half of his day working at his family business. How much of his day is left for sleeping?

a. 4 hours
b. 5 hours
c. 6 hours
d. 8 hours

42. What is a true statement about the subject line in an email?

a. Most people do not bother reading it.
b. It should be just one or two words.
c. It is not necessary on most business emails.
d. It should convey what the message is about.

43. When speaking to a heterogeneous audience of adults, to whom should planned remarks be targeted?

a. To the middle part of the group
b. To the most educated of the group
c. To the least educated of the group
d. To the least educated for the first half, to the most educated for the remainder

44. Which leader was not part of the Allied Big Three who met for the Yalta Conference during World War II?

a. Winston Churchill
b. Franklin D. Roosevelt
c. Douglas MacArthur
d. Joseph Stalin

45. Which word describes a way to separate a computer network from viruses and outside networks?

a. Bug
b. Filter
c. Firewall
d. Encryption

46. Which country has the problem of trying to unify 250 different ethnic groups?

a. Nigeria
b. China
c. Iran
d. Mexico

47. Which part of a computer is considered to be its brain?

a. Central processing unit (CPU)
b. Random access memory (RAM)
c. Operating system (OS)
d. Universal resource locator (URL)

48. In order to add the fractions 5/7 and 3/8, what must first be found?

a. Lowest common denominator
b. The greatest common factor
c. A multiple of 5
d. The lowest factored numerator

49. What is a true statement about individual employees' goals?

a. They should be difficult for the employee to attain.
b. They should be aligned with the organization's goals.
c. They should be set up by a manager.
d. There should be consequences for not attaining them.

50. The Immigration Reform and Control Act (IRCA) of 1986 required employers to:

a. permit employees to speak their native language
b. give hiring preference to people born in the United States
c. verify that all employees can legally work in the United States
d. give hiring preference to individuals born outside the United States

Situational Judgment

1. Your supervisor asks you to perform a duty that you have never done before. You are confident that you can accomplish the task but are busy with other time-sensitive work. What should you do?

a. Tell your supervisor that you are busy right now but will get to the task later today.
b. Tell your supervisor that this request is outside of your scope of practice.
c. Tell your supervisor that you have not performed this task before and might have questions during the process.
d. Tell your supervisor that you will get started on it right away.

2. You notice that your coworker stays logged into her desktop computer with personal health and financial information visible to customers and colleagues passing by. The computer is in a high-traffic area, and when your coworker leaves for a break, the computer is unattended. What should you do?

a. Log your coworker out of the computer, and inform her of your actions when she returns.
b. When your coworker returns, talk with her about the security risk associated with staying logged into an unattended computer.
c. Immediately inform your supervisor of her transgression.
d. Close the visible customer information screen on the computer, and wait for your coworker to return.

3. You are the team leader for a new project in the workplace. Your teammates offer an idea on how to accomplish your latest task, but the plan is not achievable at this time due to current logistics. What should you do?

a. Tell your coworker that you appreciate his idea and will take it into consideration going forward.
b. Tell your coworker that the idea can't be implemented.
c. Tell your coworker that changes may need to be made before the idea can be implemented.
d. Tell your coworker that although you appreciate his enthusiasm, you are the leader, and you have to make all of the decisions.

4. Your supervisor implements a new policy that you do not agree with. You believe that the policy is detrimental to the department and business. What should you do?

a. Refuse to participate in the new policy, and voice your concerns immediately.
b. Stop by your supervisor's office to talk about your concerns privately.
c. Bring up your concerns at a department meeting where other coworkers can help debate the issue.
d. Follow the new policy without objection.

5. You are stationed in a foreign country that is experiencing civil unrest. You are unfamiliar with the culture of the community and want to meet some of the community members and learn about their culture. What should you do?

a. Schedule and meet-and-greet event between your team and the community.
b. Accept a volunteer community outreach position within your organization.
c. Read the local newspaper at watch the daily news.
d. Organize an open-house event when community members can visit your facility.

6. Your facility is hiring new employees, and you are called to conduct an interview with another manager. The other manager is asking the female applicant questions such as these: "Can you tell us about your personal life? Do you have any small children that will be a hindrance to your job performance?" What should you do?

a. Politely interject with a different line of questioning.
b. Whisper to the manager that he can't ask those kinds of questions.
c. Immediately ask to speak to the other manager outside the interview room.
d. Allow the other manager to continue, but don't record the applicant's answer.

7. You are the manager of a small group of individuals. You notice that morale is low in your department, with many staff members complaining of long hours and low pay. Several staff members are threatening to quit. What should you do first?

a. Organize a department meeting where staff members can discuss their issues.
b. Send a memo asking staff to email you with their problems and opinions.
c. Offer "take 5" meetings daily during which you can have real-time discussion with staff.
d. Tell the staff that you will reevaluate the current workflow and salary guidelines at the end of the fiscal year.

8. You are the manager of a small department, and you have the opportunity to promote one member of your staff to supervisor. Which of the following employees should be promoted first?

a. An employee with the most seniority in the department but is frequently tardy
b. An employee who is new to the company but is reliable and punctual
c. An employee who is a new graduate but has taken on extra responsibility and performed the job duties well
d. An employee who has worked for the department for several years and offers new ideas and solutions to problems

9. You are a team leader in your department. Your supervisor has added a significant number of tasks to your workload, all of which are time sensitive. What should you do?

a. Prioritize the tasks, and work on the most important ones first.
b. Delegate some of the tasks to your most responsible team members.
c. Tell your supervisor that you have too many projects due at once and you can't take on the new tasks.
d. Tell your supervisor that you may need an extension on the projects' due dates.

10. Your department is performing at a deficit due to wasteful allocation of funds and materials. Your current projects include a weekly newsletter sent to hundreds of customers, purchasing office supplies, and other general office work. Your manager asks you to look for ways to save money on supplies in your current projects. What should you do first?

a. Instead of sending paper newsletters to your customers, send email notices.
b. Decrease your newsletter release from weekly to twice per month.
c. Instead of printing important emails, scan them into your desktop computer.
d. Stop purchasing office supplies for the office, and ask employees to supply their own.
e. Evaluate other vendors for better pricing on office supplies.

11. A customer has waged a complaint against you for rudeness and aggression. You don't think that you did anything wrong as the customer was rude to you first and you responded in kind. What should you do?

a. Offer to apologize to the customer personally.
b. Apologize to your supervisor.
c. Make no efforts to apologize as the customer was rude to you first.
d. Tell your supervisor that the customer was rude to you and you lost your temper.

12. A customer group is coming into your office to learn about a new piece of equipment that your company is now producing. Your supervisor asks you to lead the presentation to the group. What should you do?

a. Use technological terms and scientific jargon.
b. Use lay terms for most of the presentation, but highlight any critical technical terminology.
c. Use lay terms for the entire presentation.
d. Offer a hands-on demonstration if possible.
e. Conduct a lecture-based demonstration with time for questions at the end.

13. You are responsible for paying the invoices in your department, and you've noticed that the printing costs for your department's promotional materials have increased significantly each month. You have used other printing companies at your previous employer that offer more competitive pricing. Your coworker, who is in charge of the printing account, says that your supervisor's family member works at the more expensive printing company, and that's why your company uses them. What should you do?

a. Report your supervisor for an ethics violation.
b. Present your supervisor with information about the other less-expensive printing companies.
c. Tell your supervisor that you've noticed an increase in printing costs and ask if you can investigate other options.
d. Continue paying the invoices without questioning the cost increase.

14. You are employed by a relief organization that offers daily living supplies to the community at a discounted price. A mother approaches you saying she can't afford the high price of your organization's baby supplies. She is $2 short on her purchase. What should you do?

a. Ask your supervisor if the customer can be offered credit or a discount.
b. Pay the $2 difference yourself.
c. Manually change the price of the item to $2 less than the sticker price as this is a small amount of money for essential items.
d. Apologize to the customer, and state that the price can't be changed.

15. Your department is undergoing diversity training as a facility-wide initiative. You don't see the value in diversity training as you have completed similar training at your previous employer just a few months ago. What should you do?

a. Don't attend the training session as it would be redundant to complete the training a second time.
b. Ask your supervisor if you may skip the training because you've already completed a similar course.
c. Attend the required diversity training.
d. Ask for more information on the diversity class curriculum.

16. You are in the break room having lunch with a group of coworkers. After a few minutes, some of the group starts speaking in a foreign language and laughing. You feel uncomfortable because you can't understand the conversation and worry that they are making fun of you or the rest of the group. What should you do?

a. Ignore the conversation.
b. Interrupt the conversation, and tell the coworkers that it is rude to speak in a language that the rest of the group doesn't understand.
c. Speak with one of the coworkers privately, and tell him or her that speaking in another language makes the rest of the group feel left out.
d. Start your own conversation with the remaining coworkers.

17. You are a new employee at a foreign embassy. Your job responsibility includes handling classified documents in a small office setting. You find your coworker looking over your shoulder, possibly attempting to read a classified national security-related document. What should you do first?

a. Quickly put away the document.
b. Tell your coworker that the document is classified.
c. Inform your supervisor of the possible security breach.
d. Report your coworker for a security violation.
e. Ask another coworker about the office's security policy.

18. Your facility has an equipment reprocessing room in which types of equipment are sanitized, tested, and prepared for future use. Hazardous chemicals are used to clean these machines, but you see that your coworker is not using any personal protective equipment. What should you do?

a. Tell your coworker that the cleaning chemicals can be hazardous and offer personal protective equipment to wear.
b. Ask your supervisor to post signs reminding employees to use personal protective equipment.
c. Offer to help, and put on your own protective equipment as an example of the proper procedure.
d. Allow the coworker to continue.

19. You are working in a government facility based in the United States. Part of your job includes transporting large pieces of equipment from one area to another. While pushing an exceptionally heavy machine around a corner, the machine's wheel breaks off, causing the machine to suddenly stop moving. The quick twisting motion, combined with the machine's sudden stop, causes pain in your back. What should you do first?

a. Report the equipment as inoperable, and send it to the repair ward.
b. Fill out an incident report, and give it to your supervisor.
c. Seek medical care for your injury.
d. Return to work and see if the pain improves later.
e. Go home and rest

20. Your team is asked to reorganize your department's equipment room. The equipment room is small and difficult to walk through due to pieces of equipment and boxes of supplies stored there. Your coworker begins to remove equipment and boxes from the room and piles them in front of the doorway to make more room for you to work. What should you do?

a. Work as quickly as possible so that you can clear the doorway sooner.
b. Immediately remove the equipment from the doorway.
c. Tell your coworker that you can't completely block a doorway, and remove one of the boxes to clear a small path.
d. Continue moving boxes as needed because it won't take more than a few minutes to complete your task.

21. You are employed in a facility that uses types of gasses that are stored in cylinders. While walking through another unit, you see pressurized E cylinders of oxygen propped against a wall, whereas others are laying on the ground. What should you do?

a. Leave the cylinders as they are.
b. Put the cylinders that are on the ground in a tank holder.
c. Find tank holders for all of the cylinders.
d. Inform your supervisor that some oxygen cylinders are unsecured.
e. Tell the unit's employees in that some of their cylinders need to be secured

22. You are the leader of a small team in a foreign embassy. Some of your team members practice a religion in which they must pray several times a day at specific intervals. You are shorthanded today and would prefer that these employees work without their usual prayer breaks. What should you do?

a. Tell the employees that you are too shorthanded today to take breaks.
b. Ask the employees if they could alter their prayer schedule so that not all employees are away at once.
c. Offer the employees a quiet place to pray that is close by so that they are not away for too long.
d. Allow the employees to take their usual prayer breaks with no modifications.

23. You are stationed at the front desk of a foreign embassy. Your job entails checking and recording visitors' and employees' identification information, logging their entrance and exit times, and giving directions as needed. A visitor, whom you've met several times before, is running late for his appointment and is irritated that you are stopping him for an identification check. What should you do?

a. Tell him that you do recognize him and wave him through.
b. Apologize for the inconvenience, and tell him that although you do remember him well, you are required to log his identifying information at every visit.
c. Tell him that your job requires you to log his identifying information, and you will report him if there is any further argument.
d. Record his identifying information, and then speak with your supervisor to ensure you are following proper procedure.

24. You work in an area that handles and disposes of hazardous chemicals. During orientation, you were instructed to wear gloves and a splash mask when handling the chemicals as they can be dangerous to your health. Lately, you've noticed that your department has not been stocking the protective equipment that you need to perform your job. You notified your supervisor, who stated that due to budget constraints in the department, she is trying to stop nonessential purchasing. She says the chemicals aren't that dangerous and to be careful. What should you do?

a. Bring personal protective equipment from home.
b. Continue to work while being extra cautious with the chemicals.
c. Tell your supervisor that you can't complete your job without the splash mask and gloves.
d. Report the issue to your facility's safety team.
e. Ask the supervisor in a neighboring department if you might use some of their personal protective equipment today since your department ran out.

25. You are working at the front desk of a foreign embassy when an employee enters. She looks ill and is sweating. She says she feels lightheaded and promptly loses consciousness. You can tell that she's hit her head from the sound of her falling to the floor. What should you do first?

a. Splash water on her face, and call for another employee's assistance.
b. Activate the emergency response system.
c. Move her out of the vestibule and over to a quieter area for further assessment.
d. Immediately call her supervisor to report the incident
e. Check to see if she is breathing and has a pulse.

26. You are a new employee stationed in a foreign country that is experiencing civil unrest. An act of terrorism is carried out with many casualties and injured civilians. You are called along with the rest of your facility to help assess and move victims into the medical tents. The situation is chaotic, and you have no specific instructions from your supervisor. What should you do?

a. Wait for specific instructions from the medical team.
b. Look for the most severely injured people, and move them to the medical tents first.
c. Move the people closest to you over to the medical tents first.
d. Ask a coworker with more seniority to help you assess victims.

27. You are a new member of your facility's disaster response team. You are on your way home when you receive an automated phone call from your facility's emergency response system. The call says that a mass casualty disaster has taken place at your facility, and you are asked to report back to the building immediately and meet in the front parking lot. Once you return to the building, what should you do first?

a. Report to the parking lot, and ask a coworker what needs to be done.
b. Report to the parking lot, and find your emergency coordinator.
c. Begin work immediately by assessing the situation and taking action.
d. Call your supervisor, and ask how you can help.

28. A new employee has reported for work, and your supervisor asks you to escort her to the department and make her feel welcome. What should you do?

a. Say hello to the employee and offer a handshake. Then introduce yourself and escort her to the department.
b. Greet the employee with a warm hug, and tell her you are delighted she's joining the team. Then take her to the department.
c. Say hello to the employee and wait for her to initiate a handshake. Then escort her to the department.
d. Greet the employee with a handshake and tell her you'd be happy to show her around.

29. You are called to work with a new customer at your facility. You are required to greet customers by last name, but you are unsure of how to pronounce the unfamiliar last name of this customer. What should you do?

a. Attempt to pronounce the last name, and apologize if you pronounced it wrong.
b. Refer to the customer by their first name.
c. Greet the customer, and ask how to pronounce the last name.
d. Apologize to the customer, and say that you are unsure of how to pronounce his or her last name.

30. You are a team leader attending a meeting conducted by your department director. As you sit in the audience, your coworker continues to chat with others around you and attempts to bring you into the conversation. What should you do?

a. "Shush" your teammates loudly so that others are aware of their rudeness.
b. Ignore your coworker when he or she talks to you, and then say, "I'm sorry, I'm concentrating on the presentation."
c. Quietly tell your teammates that you can't hear the presenter.
d. Sit quietly, and don't participate in the chatter.
e. Move your seat to a quieter section of the seating area.

31. You referred a former colleague to your current company, and he was hired as your department supervisor. You are now in contract negotiations with him, and you are hoping to persuade him to give you a raise in salary. You believe your contract should be renewed with a salary increase because you have taken on more responsibility this year, met all sales quotas, retained new business, and have been a dependable employee. How can you successfully negotiate this salary raise?

a. Remind your supervisor of his referral to this company, and tell him that because you did him a favor, he should do one for you.
b. Promise him that if he renews your contract at a higher salary, you will continue to search for new customers and ways to increase revenue.
c. Present him with testimonials from satisfied customers whom you've recruited and retained in the past year.
d. Present him with written documentation of your successes including retaining new business, increasing revenues, and sales quota reports.

32. You are called to speak with a new customer about her business. Your supervisor wants you to gather information about the culture of the business and determine how a partnership would benefit both of you. What should you do?

a. Do most of the talking, as you need to explain to the customer the needs of your company if she were to enter into a business partnership.
b. Let the customer do most of the talking as you need to learn as much as possible about the nature of her business.
c. Listen attentively to the customer as she describes her business model, and periodically interject with information about your company.
d. Ask open-ended questions about the culture of the customer's business, and then ask if she has questions about your business.

33. You are called to greet a new customer and conduct a meeting between the customer and your business associates. The customer arrives at the boardroom a few minutes late, and your team has other meetings to attend soon. What should you do?

a. Introduce yourself, and make pleasant small talk before beginning the meeting.
b. Shake the customer's hand and tell him that you have a lot to discuss and need to get started immediately.
c. Introduce yourself, and say that the team has been waiting for quite a while for him to arrive, and you hope he hasn't had trouble finding his way to the boardroom.
d. Introduce yourself and the other members of the team. Then state that you will have to cut your meeting short due to time constraints.

34. Your supervisor asks your team for volunteers to take on a new task. Your coworker, John, immediately volunteers. John always offers to take on more responsibility at work, consistently puts in longer hours than you do, and also works some hours on the weekends. You feel that John is making you look lazy, and you want to have some of the same opportunities that he has. What should you do?

a. Tell John that you appreciate his great work ethic but would like to have an opportunity to take on more responsibility, too.
b. Tell John that he is so quick to volunteer that others in the office are upset with him because they don't get the same opportunities.
c. Tell your supervisor that you'd like to take on some new responsibilities, and ask if there's anything you can help with.
d. Tell your supervisor that the department is unhappy with John because he takes on all the available projects before others can volunteer.
e. Next time your supervisor asks for volunteers, try to volunteer before John offers.

35. You are working in an American office with a group of colleagues stationed at a European office and must meet a deadline for an important project. Your European colleagues are taking a week off work for a holiday, which is a common occurrence for them this time of year. Last year, you fell behind on your project due to their absence, and you are worried you won't meet your deadline this year. What should you do?

a. Tell the colleagues that although a weeklong vacation might be common in their country, you are working on an American project that requires American work schedules.
b. Tell the colleagues that while they are on vacation, you will continue to work on the project and email them with any important updates.
c. Prior to their vacation, make a plan with your colleagues to expedite your tasks and accelerate your work so that there is less to catch up on when they return.
d. Accept this cultural difference, and work on the project without their help even if this results in the project being late.

36. Your supervisor has a hands-off management style. She rarely gives praise and does not offer to help others when they are busy. You and your coworkers find that taking your daily lunch break is difficult because there is no one to relieve you at your posts. What should you do?

a. Ask your supervisor for a private meeting, and tell her that your team needs more support. Ask her if she can help by relieving your team members for lunch.
b. Tell your supervisor that you noticed she doesn't like your team members, and ask what you can do to help change her mind.
c. Work with your coworkers to make a lunch break rotation schedule during which you relieve each other for lunch.
d. Work with your coworkers to make a list of areas in which you need extra help, and present it at the next department meeting.

37. You have been working independently on a project for several months, when your supervisor notifies you that the project has been cancelled. He asks you to join another team and help work on their ongoing project. What should you do?

a. Ask your supervisor if you can take on any other independent projects.
b. Ask your supervisor why your project was cancelled, when you were doing such a good job, and tell her you don't like to work in group settings.
c. Join the other team, and ask how you can help.
d. Join the other team, and wait for instruction.

38. A coworker has been on leave for several weeks. When she returns, she appears to be in good health, and you are curious about why she was out of work for so long. What should you do?

a. Tell your coworker you're glad to see her, and ask her how she is feeling today.
b. Tell your coworker that she looks well, and ask if she was on leave due to medical problems.
c. Ask other colleagues if they know why your coworker was on leave.
d. Don't ask any questions about her health or why she was on leave.

39. You are the leader of a small group of colleagues. Your supervisor assigns a new member to your team whom you haven't seen in several months. The colleague appears to have gained weight since you last saw him. You're concerned about his health and ability to perform the job because your occupation has physical requirements. What should you do?

a. Give the employee a chance to perform the job without any interference.
b. Tell the employee that you noticed he's gained weight and you are concerned he won't be able to keep up with the workflow.
c. Tell the employee that you're glad to have him on your team and to let you know if he finds the work too physically taxing.
d. Tell your supervisor that the job is physical and you hope the coworker can keep up.

40. You are employed as a writer in a small office. You have submitted a completed document for your supervisor's review. The supervisor has heavily edited the document and has deleted several important pieces of information. What should you do?

a. Accept the changes as is because your supervisor is the lead on this project.
b. Ask to speak to your supervisor privately, and explain why the information should be included in the document.
c. Tell you supervisor that you don't appreciate the changes to your document because you are an expert on the topic.
d. Accept the changes, but tell your supervisor that you would prefer not to work on these types of projects in the future.

41. Your supervisor has asked you to mentor a new employee and orient him or her to the department and your job duties. You are unhappy about this request because you are busy with other tasks, and an orientee will slow you down. What should you do?

a. Introduce yourself to the orientee, tell him or her you are glad to have him or her aboard, and ask if he or she has any questions about the position.
b. Tell the orientee that you don't normally do orientation because you are always so busy, but you are happy to do it.
c. Tell the orientee that you hope he or she can keep up with your speedy work pace.
d. Tell the orientee that you don't know why the supervisor asked you to be a mentor because orientees slow you down.

42. You are an hourly employee who is working on an important report that is due at the end of the week. You are running behind on the project and are not likely to finish it on time. What should you do?

a. Stay late and come in early to finish the report on time.
b. Tell your supervisor that you are not going to meet your deadline.
c. Ask coworkers for help on your project so that you can finish it faster.
d. Ask your supervisor if you can have extra time to work on your report.

43. You are asked to manage the social media accounts for a small charitable organization. What should you do?

a. Share important information and community outreach events sponsored by your facility.
b. Like and comment on political topics that align with the charity's ideals.
c. Support local small businesses by retweeting and sharing their posts.
d. Treat the accounts as if they were your own, by liking and commenting on stories you find interesting.

44. You work for a small nonprofit organization overseas where you provide health and wellness products for the community members. You are asked to give a presentation to community members highlighting some of your organization's services. What should you do?

a. Present medical information using technical jargon to impress your supervisor and the attendees.
b. Begin your presentation with health-related information on a variety of topics, and then narrow your focus on the services your facility offers.
c. Focus your presentation on the services provided to the community and how community members can access them.
d. Ask your supervisor if you can offer free samples and screenings after the presentation to help increase attendance.

45. You are the team lead on a large project. After a department meeting, one of your team members asks to speak to you regarding a personal issue that is affecting her work. What should you do?

a. Tell the team member that you can speak with her now, but you will need to answer a few emails while she's talking.
b. Tell the team member to stop by your office next week so you can give her your undivided attention.
c. Tell the team member to schedule a time to speak with you during her lunch break so that she doesn't miss work during your meeting.
d. Speak with the team member now.

46. Your director wants to increase awareness of your facility's values, services, and accomplishments in the surrounding area. He asks you to devise a global initiative to accomplish this task. What should you do?

a. First, form a team of coworkers to canvas the local area with flyers advertising your organization's services.
b. Offer to create a social media presence for the organization, highlighting its services and culture.
c. Give presentations at local schools and community centers.
d. Send email blasts to employees, and ask them to forward them on to their friends and family.

47. You have been recently assigned to a foreign embassy but do not speak the country's native language. You will be working closely with citizens of that country as well as local community members and will need to be able to effectively communicate. What should you do?

a. Begin learning slang conversational phrases to help fit in with the community when you arrive.
b. Take a formal foreign language course at your local community college.
c. Ask the recruiter for guidance as to how to best learn the local language.
d. Wait until you begin work, and then attempt to pick up the language as you go along.
e. Learn a few key phrases to help you get by until you are able to start work

48. Your supervisor asks you to conduct research on environmental changes and write a report about your findings. You have to gather accurate information from reputable sources to complete this task. What should you do?

a. Begin with an internet search, and use all available information, citing your references as required.
b. Use the internet to identify and access government-approved sources for information.
c. Use only evidence-based information from governmental and nonprofit organizations found via the internet.
d. Gather information from encyclopedias at the local library.

49. Your team is asked to devise a plan to recruit new customers for your business. Your location is having financial problems, and new customers are vital to keeping the business afloat. What should you do?

a. Gather a team of coworkers from different backgrounds and positions to brainstorm ideas on how to recruit new business.
b. Ask a senior coworker about how new business was recruited in the past.
c. At the department meeting next month, ask the team if anyone has ideas on how to recruit new customers.
d. Canvass the neighborhood with flyers advertising your company's services.

50. You are an hourly employee in a small office. In your annual review, your supervisor tells you that you need to improve your punctuality as you are punching in a few minutes late several times a week. You are a single parent with a child who needs to be dropped off at school before you go to work. You are often rushing in the morning and getting to school just before the bell rings, making you late to work. What should you do?

a. Organize your work and school supplies the night before so you have less of a morning rush.
b. Investigate other options for school transportation such as buses or carpool.
c. Ask a coworker to punch you in when he or she arrives at work so that you aren't shown as late in the system.
d. Tell your supervisor that the reason you are late is because you have to drop your child off at school on the way to work.

51. You are working in an industrial setting that utilizes large pieces of machinery. A new piece of equipment is introduced that you are not comfortable using. You feel that you were not properly trained on this machine, and you aren't sure exactly how to use it. Your supervisor hands out the daily assignments and then leaves for a meeting. You see that you're assigned to the area that utilizes the machine. What should you do?

a. Wait to do anything until your supervisor returns, then ask him or her if you can have extra training on the machine.
b. Avoid using the machine as much as possible today.
c. Ask a coworker to help you use the machine.
d. Page your supervisor, tell him or her that you aren't comfortable using the machine, and ask if you can be reassigned for the day.

52. You have been working at your company for two years. You enjoy your work and would like to take on more responsibility and work toward a promotion. What should you do?

a. Tell your supervisor that you have worked here for two years and you think it is time to consider a promotion.
b. Volunteer for leadership roles on new projects and teams.
c. Offer ideas on how to streamline processes in the department.
d. Ask your supervisor if he or she can mentor you at work so you can learn more about leadership roles.

53. You work in a large industrial department. During a conversation with a colleague who works at another company, you discover that there are other products on the market that may make your workplace run more efficiently. What should you do?

a. Tell your supervisor that there are new products that might be helpful for your department.
b. Research the product, and then call a meeting with your supervisor to discuss your findings.
c. Ask your friend to call your supervisor and tell him or her about the new product.
d. Tell your supervisor that he or she should purchase the new product because it will help your department become more efficient.

54. You work in a foreign embassy in a community outreach position. As part of your job description, you are required to hold a cardiopulmonary resuscitation (CPR) certification in case of medical emergency while in the field. You look at your CPR card and see that it expired last month. What should you do?

a. Look for a recertification class, and take it as soon as possible.
b. Notify your supervisor, and ask how you should proceed.
c. Continue working without the certification because you remember all the skills you learned in the class.
d. Finish your shift, and then notify your team lead of your certification lapse.

55. You have recently been promoted to team lead in your department. You are nervous about the new position because you have many friends there, and you're not sure how to act around them now that you are in a leadership position. What should you do?

a. Continue your friendship with your coworkers.
b. Avoid social outings with your coworkers as they are now your subordinates.
c. Ask your supervisor for guidance on how to navigate your new position.
d. Call a meeting for your team, and tell your coworkers that because you are now their lead, you will not be socializing with them outside of work.

56. You are employed by a government agency that provides medical supplies and treatment for underprivileged members of a community. You are a new employee who was hired to help create a task force that will distribute supplies and organize medical screenings for the community. You have extensive medical experience as you have worked in health care in the private sector for over fifteen years. What should you do?

a. Take charge of your department, and educate coworkers on how things are done elsewhere.
b. Offer to train coworkers on aseptic techniques and other medical safety tasks.
c. Tell your supervisor that you have extensive medical experience and would like to take a leadership role on this project.
d. Wait for instruction from your supervisor, but speak up if current medical practice standards aren't being upheld
e. Introduce yourself to the community and offer to provide your own medical care at no cost to them.

57. You are employed in an agricultural group similar to the Peace Corps. You help local farmers in Ethiopia combat erosion of soil, increase crop production, and assist with care of the livestock. During your time of service, you learn of political unrest in the village. You disagree with the current governmental regime in the nation and are interested in learning more about the political changes taking place within the community. What should you do?

a. Spend your working hours doing only agricultural work as this is what you were hired to do.
b. Read local newspapers and flyers regarding the political changes in the area to better familiarize yourself with the conflict.
c. Attend political meetings in the community when you are off duty.
d. Speak with the community members you are serving, and attempt to learn more about their struggles.
e. Organize a political action group within your service area, and recruit coworkers and community members to join.

58. You are a new employee of a governmental office. When you were interviewing for the position, the supervisor asked if you were comfortable with using a well-known brand of word processor and spreadsheet tool. You have extensive experience with this tool and expressed your confidence in the interview. Now, a few weeks later, you begin work and discover that these word processor and spreadsheet tools are being phased out and a more specialized series of tools are being implemented. Your coworkers have used these tools before, but you have not. What should you do?

a. Try your best to follow along with your coworkers, and learn as you go.
b. Take classes on the new tools at your local library.
c. Conduct an internet search for online tutorials on the use of the tools.
d. Tell your supervisor that you are not familiar with these tools and will need extra help.
e. Use the old tools as long as possible until you are comfortable with the new tools.

59. You are a new employee at a foreign embassy. When reporting for your first day of orientation, you are shown a handbook on the Department of State Civil Service and Foreign Service culture in your department. The book stays in the department as reference material for the workers, and all new employees are expected to know its contents. You have a full day of training ahead of you, including an orientation lecture. What should you do?

a. Begin reading the handbook during your lunch break.
b. Skim over most of the handbook while you are in your orientation lecture.
c. Ask your supervisor if you may take the handbook home to study.
d. Ask your coworkers if anyone needs the book because you'd like to borrow it for a few days.
e. Note where the handbook is kept, but don't study it. The most important information will likely be relayed during orientation.

60. You are employed as an agent for a Japanese embassy. Your job includes meeting with community members and conducting business transactions. You have a meeting with local businesspeople scheduled for noon. You have several nonurgent tasks to accomplish this morning and may be running late to the meeting. What should you do?

a. Call the meeting leader and ask if it can be rescheduled for 30 minutes later
b. Arrive at the meeting ten minutes late, but apologize profusely and offer a handshake.
c. Cancel one of your morning tasks, and reschedule it for the afternoon.
d. Attempt to arrive at the meeting on time, but don't be concerned if you are a few minutes late.
e. Cancel the meeting and reschedule it for a less busy day.

61. You are assigned to an embassy in India. You are meeting with local businesspeople to discuss ways your organization can help the community with their agricultural efforts. You plan to meet for an early dinner at a local American-style restaurant. You are a newcomer in this country and are not familiar with local customs. What should you do?

a. Arrive on time, and wait for the businesspeople to order first before placing your order.
b. Arrive on time, and order your favorite dish: a hamburger.
c. Arrive five minutes late due to unforeseen circumstances, but be ready to work as soon as you arrive.
d. Ask your coworkers if there are any local customs you should be aware of before you dine with the group.

62. You are employed in a small office. There is a senior colleague in the office who offers you congratulations for passing your recent board examination. This colleague has begun giving you congratulatory hugs and pats on your lower back when you achieve different milestones within the company. Most recently, you passed your board examination, and your colleague gave you a hug and kiss on your cheek. You notice that this behavior is happening more often, and you are beginning to feel uncomfortable with the unwanted touching. What should you do?

a. Report your colleague to human resources for sexual harassment.
b. Tell your colleague that although you appreciate the congratulations, the touching makes you uncomfortable, and you'd like it to stop.
c. Tell your supervisor that your colleague's unwanted touching is making you uncomfortable.
d. Address your colleague in a "chilly" professional manner from now on in the hopes that your colleague gets the message to not be as friendly to you in the future.
e. Tell your colleague to stop touching you immediately.

63. You are employed in a small office within a foreign embassy. Your coworker is a senior member of your department. She serves on the leadership team but is not your immediate supervisor and you do not report to her. Lately, she has been asking you to help her with some of her tasks, even though you have time-sensitive projects to complete. You feel pressured to help her because she is likely to become the next department supervisor, and you want to form a good working relationship with her, but you are annoyed that she keeps asking you to do tasks that are assigned to her. What should you do?

a. Tell her that you will be happy to help her with her tasks if you have time once yours are complete.
b. Set some of your tasks aside, and complete a few of hers first.
c. Tell her that she is not your supervisor and you should not have to take on more work.
d. Tell your supervisor that your colleague is asking you to help her with her work, and ask which projects your supervisor would prefer you work on first.
e. Complain to your supervisor that your colleague is attempting to delegate her work to you.

64. You are the team lead in a small office environment. You notice one of your team members using the copy machine to make flyers for her daughter's school talent show. You tell her that the copy machine is for business use. She tells you that she has volunteered to make the flyers, but she does not have a copy machine in her home. What should you do?

a. Tell her that you appreciate her dedication but that she cannot use the copy machine for her own personal use.
b. Suggest that she take her flyer to a local print shop where there is a copy machine for public use.
c. Suggest that she ask the local library to use their copy machine
d. Tell her that if she continues to use office supplies for her own use, she may be reprimanded.
e. Tell your supervisor that she is using the copy machine for nonwork-related projects.

65. You are the team lead for an office within a foreign embassy. You are in the middle of a phone call when one of your team members asks you if he may leave early to go to the doctor. He looks tired, sweaty, and pale. What should you do?

a. Offer to drive him to the medical facility after you finish your phone call.
b. Tell your team member that he may leave immediately.
c. Ask your team member why he feels he needs to go to the doctor in the middle of his shift.
d. End your phone call, and ask other team members if they can take over your team member's assignment so he can leave.
e. Tell your team member that she may leave as soon as she wraps up her time sensitive work.

66. You are the team lead in a small office. You are leading a group discussion on a project that is currently in progress. You notice that one of your team members is quiet and rarely participates in group discussion. What should you do?

a. During the meeting, ask the team member if she has anything to add.
b. During the meeting, ask the team member why she is being so quiet.
c. After the meeting, tell the team member that you notice she's been quiet lately, but you value her input on the project.
d. After the meeting, tell the team member that you would prefer that she participates more often in the group discussion.

67. You are employed in a department that utilizes on-call scheduling to cover the night shift in the event of absence or high workloads. Your department has suffered from a high level of employee turnover, with several employees quitting at the same time. This has left the night shift sparsely covered, with many vacancies in the schedule. Your director says that there will be additional mandatory on-call days that will be assigned via lottery system, and you are expected to cover that shift regardless of any previous engagements. You have a special trip planned in the coming week. What should you do?

a. Accept the changes, and work your on-call shift even though you have plans.
b. Accept the changes, but try to get a coworker to switch shifts with you so that you can still go on your trip.
c. Tell your supervisor that you have upcoming plans and won't be able to cover any additional shifts.
d. Ask your supervisor if you can attempt to fill the schedule vacancies by asking your coworkers to voluntarily sign up for shifts rather than utilizing a lottery system.

68. You are the team leader in an office environment. Your director calls a meeting and says you must take on additional work because of several time-sensitive projects taking place simultaneously. You realize that your assignment will be 50 percent heavier than it normally is, and you are concerned about how you will complete all your tasks. What should you do?

a. Accept the changes, and work as quickly as you can to finish your tasks on time.
b. Ask your director if you may have extra time to complete your tasks.
c. Delegate some of your tasks to other team members.
d. Tell your director that you can't complete all of these tasks at once, and you will have to skip some.

69. There is a mandatory department meeting scheduled today, where important financial information and new policies will be shared. You are planning to attend, but you are awaiting an important phone call from your daughter's allergist. What should you do?

a. Keep your cell phone on vibrate in your pocket.
b. Keep your cell phone on silent on the table within your view.
c. Explain to your supervisor that you are awaiting an important call, and ask how to proceed.
d. Turn off your phone while in the meeting
e. Keep the phone on the lowest volume possible, and store it in your purse under the conference room table

70. You are the team lead in an office within a foreign embassy, and your team prepares reports for your supervisor to review. You notice that one of your team member's reports often misses important information and sometimes appears disorganized. What should you do?

a. Tell your supervisor that your coworker's reports are missing crucial information.
b. Ask your team member if he or she needs any help with the workload.
c. Tell your team member that you noticed some information is missing from the report.
d. Tell your team member that you think his or her reports could be more comprehensive and offer to help

71. You are a new employee and have a question about a procedure. Your supervisor is in a meeting with several executives in his or her office, and you need instruction on how to proceed. Your coworkers are all out of the department working on tasks. What should you do?

a. Knock on your supervisor's door, and apologize for disrupting the meeting.
b. Page one of your coworkers, and ask him or her for assistance.
c. Call your supervisor's office, and apologize for interrupting.
d. Call the director of the facility, and ask for help.

72. Your facility is organizing a fund-raising event to benefit a local charity. The chosen event is a 5K walk/run during which participants raise funds by asking for donations and sponsors. You want to help with the cause and get your coworkers involved. What should you do?

a. Organize a walk team with volunteers from your department.
b. Tell your coworkers that you will be walking in the event and are accepting donations.
c. Tell your coworkers that if they aren't participating in the walk, then they will need to sponsor you to run.
d. Organize a donation from your department by collecting voluntary contributions.

73. You are employed at a facility at which shift work is required. The coworker who normally relieves you is consistently late to work, causing you to have to wait to give your shift report. This also makes you late to pick up your child at school. You have made subtle hints about this lateness, but the problem has not resolved. What should you do?

a. Tell your supervisor that you have to leave on time even if your coworker is late.
b. Tell your coworker that you have to pick up your child at school and you need him or her to arrive on time so you can leave.
c. Tell your supervisor that your coworker is always late, and it is becoming a problem.
d. Tell your coworker that if he or she doesn't arrive to work on time, you will have to notify your supervisor.

74. You are scheduled to attend a mandatory department meeting by your director. The one-hour meeting is taking place on your day off, and you have no childcare options for that day for your school-age children. What should you do?

a. Ask your director if you may bring your children to the meeting, and offer to bring quiet activities to occupy them.
b. Tell your director that you can't make the meeting due to childcare issues.
c. Bring your children to the meeting, and make them sit outside the conference room.
d. Tell your director that you cannot make the meeting, and in the future, you will need more notice before mandatory events as you have children that require babysitters

75. Your director has scheduled training sessions for your day off. The equipment being covered in the training are pieces that you use daily as well as new ones that will be implemented soon. You do not have plans that day but don't want to spend your day off in the office doing training. What should you do?

a. Skip the training because it is your day off.
b. Attend the training.
c. Ask your supervisor if you can catch up on the information presented on another day.
d. Look for webinars about the new equipment that is being implemented.

76. A coworker has reported you for an ethics violation, and the matter is currently being investigated. You are not aware of any wrongdoing and feel you are wrongfully accused. What should you do?

a. Tell your supervisor that you are not aware of any ethics violations but will cooperate with the investigation.
b. Tell your supervisor that your coworker has been stealing office supplies for the past six months.
c. Tell your coworker that there seems to be a misunderstanding.
d. Read through your company's policies, and see if you've inadvertently violated any.

77. You are leading a group discussion about a new project in your department. The team members cannot agree on one approach and have started to argue with each other. The debate is becoming heated, and you need to come to an agreement. What should you do first?

a. Adjourn the meeting, and reschedule for another date and time.
b. Tell the team members that arguing doesn't solve anything
c. Tell the team members that each member will have a chance to speak.
d. Raise your voice slightly, and ask for everyone's attention in an assertive tone.
e. Cancel the project, and reassign it to another group.

78. You are the team lead in your department. A team member has pulled you aside to tell you that he or she feels that you appear distracted and don't listen to employees when they bring a problem to you. What should you do?

a. Tell the team member that although you appreciate his or her candor, you don't agree with the assessment.
b. Tell the team member that you've been working on several projects that have caused you to become distracted.
c. Tell the team member that when staff members speak to you, you will give him or her your undivided attention.
d. Tell the team member that you will institute and open-door policy for the airing of grievances.

79. You are the leader of a team that is working on an important project within your department. During group discussions, one member of your team consistently volunteers for all of the important tasks and convinces the other team members to support his or her ideas even if they are not in the company's best interest. What should you do?

a. Dismiss the team member from your team.
b. Speak with the team member privately, and tell him or her that others need a chance to take on more responsibility.
c. During the meeting, tell the team member that he or she will take a supportive role in future tasks.
d. During the group discussion, call on team members individually so that all ideas are presented.

80. You are a male supervisor at an embassy located in Israel. Many of your customers are of the Orthodox Jewish faith. You are meeting a female customer for a business meeting and are waiting to greet her. What should you do?

a. Wait politely for her to address you in a way that is comfortable for her.
b. Greet her with a warm hello, and introduce yourself.
c. Introduce yourself, and attempt a handshake.
d. Tell her you are "a hugger," and ask if you can give her a hug.

81. You are employed in an office within an Asian embassy. You are mentoring a new employee who is of Japanese ethnicity and citizenship. You notice that the employee refers to you as "Karen-san" rather than just Karen. You aren't sure why this employee is pronouncing your name this way. What should you do?

a. Tell the staff member that he or she may call you Karen.
b. Ask the staff member to stop calling you Karen-san because you don't like it.
c. Continue your workday without mentioning the issue.
d. Conduct an internet search to determine why the staff member is adding "san" to your name.

82. You are the newly assigned team leader for a group that has been under other management for several months. Upon starting with the group, you notice that one staff member consistently leaves early on Friday evenings. Rather than staying until 6:00 p.m. like the rest of the staff, he leaves at 4:00 p.m. You question the staff member, and he says that he must leave before sundown on Fridays because he has to uphold the laws of the Sabbath. What should you do?

a. Tell the staff member that you can't guarantee that he will be able to leave at exactly 4:00 p.m. every Friday, but you will do your best to ensure that he leaves before sundown.
b. Tell the staff member that you appreciate his explanation and that he should continue with his current practice.
c. Tell the staff member that although you respect his religion, you are now the new leader and will make your own rules.
d. Tell the staff member to enjoy his time off.

83. You were recently hired to the United States Foreign Service. You are excited about this new opportunity but aren't sure what to expect. You want to learn more about the organization. What should you do?

a. Conduct an internet search to find information regarding the organization.
b. Begin with studying information found on the Foreign Service website.
c. Wait until you report for work as your supervisor will be training you.
d. Ask friends if they have any knowledge of the organization.

84. You are currently employed in the information technology (IT) department of a foreign embassy. You accepted the position because you have several years of experience with IT, but you have an interest in pursuing a career in the medical field. Your embassy offers a job shadowing program for employees who are interested in other fields, and you would like to apply for the health-care version of the program. What should you do?

a. Ask your supervisor for a meeting, and explain your goals to him or her.
b. Email your supervisor and ask if you can have a few days off to complete the job shadowing program.
c. Attend the job shadowing program without notifying your manager or coworkers because your personal choices are none of their business.
d. Ask a coworker to cover your shifts so that you can complete the program.

English Expression

1

A nuclear nonproliferation treaty was signed in 1968 to attempt to stop the spread of nuclear technology. The United Nations was instrumental in [1] ensuring that the text of the treaty conveyed what it meant to—that the United States and other so-called nuclear states (France, United Kingdom, the then–Soviet Union, [2] Peoples Republic Of China) could not provide nuclear weapons to nonnuclear states—those states that did not have them. The treaty was signed by over sixty countries, but some refused. [3] Israel, Pakistan, India, and North Korea have admitted having nuclear weapons but won't agree to abide by the treaty.

2

[4] The first pillar ensures safety with all nuclear weaponry presently in possession of countries in the treaty. Those countries that have signed the treaty agree that they will not receive, create, or otherwise get or use another country's help to acquire nuclear weapons. They vow that they won't use those nuclear weapons they may already have [5] excepting to protect [6] their self.

3

The second pillar of the treaty says that those [7] nuclear weapons' countries should work toward disarmament, meaning [8] therefore, that they are to eliminate those weapons that they may already have. This part of the treaty may be difficult to enforce and [9] implying international trust that all countries will eventually work toward that end. Since the treaty asks countries to negotiate this pillar in [10] Good Faith, it may make enforcement procedures difficult as the treaty is presently written. Still, countries signing the treaty have agreed that disarmament is an ultimate goal.

4

The third pillar of the treaty allows for [11] peacetime use of nuclear energy. Compliance [12] about this part of the [13] treaty; means that countries are still able to use the nuclear energy they presently have, but not as part of nuclear weaponry. Nuclear materials [14] that are generally considered to be ingredients for nuclear weapons (e.g., uranium, plutonium) should be carefully overseen.

The United Nations was instrumental in (1) <u>ensuring</u> that the text of the treaty conveyed what it meant to—that the United States and other so-called nuclear states (France, United Kingdom, the then–Soviet Union, Peoples Republic Of China) could not provide nuclear weapons to nonnuclear states—those states that did not have them.

1. Which of the following is the most correct?

a. ensuring
b. assuring
c. insuring
d. reassuring

The United Nations was instrumental in ensuring that the text of the treaty conveyed what it meant to—that the United States and other so-called nuclear states (France, United Kingdom, the then–Soviet Union, (2) Peoples Republic Of China) could not provide nuclear weapons to nonnuclear states—those states that did not have them.

2. Which of the following is the most correct?

a. Peoples Republic Of China
b. People's Republic of China
c. Peoples Republic of China
d. People's Republic Of China

(3) Israel, Pakistan, India, and North Korea have admitted having nuclear weapons but won't agree to abide by the treaty.

3. Which sentence best joins the previous sentence with the one following?

a. Here are the names of the countries.
b. All of these countries cite the same reasons.
c. There are a variety of reasons.
d. They won't sign the treaty.

(4) The first pillar ensures safety with all nuclear weaponry presently in possession of countries in the treaty. Those countries that have signed the treaty agree that they will not receive, create, or otherwise get or use another country's help to acquire nuclear weapons. They vow that they won't use those nuclear weapons they may already have excepting to protect their self.

4. Which sentence best introduces this paragraph?

a. The nuclear nonproliferation treaty comprises three parts, or pillars.
b. The nuclear nonproliferation treaty is made up of pillars.
c. The nuclear nonproliferation treaty is multi-faceted.
d. The nuclear nonproliferation treaty is three-tiered.

They vow that they won't use those nuclear weapons they may already have (5) excepting to protect their self.

5. Which of the following is the most correct?

a. excepting
b. accepting
c. except
d. accept

They vow that they won't use those nuclear weapons they may already have excepting to protect (6) their self.

6. Which of the following is the most correct?

a. their self.
b. their selves.
c. them self.
d. themselves.

The second pillar of the treaty says that those (7) <u>nuclear weapons' countries</u> should work toward disarmament, meaning therefore, that they are to eliminate those weapons that they may already have.

7. Which of the following is the most correct?

a. nuclear weapons' countries
b. nuclear weapons countries
c. countries with nuclear weapons
d. countries with nuclear weapons'

The second pillar of the treaty says that those nuclear weapons' countries should work toward disarmament, meaning (8) <u>therefore, that</u> they are to eliminate those weapons that they may already have.

8. Which of the following is the most correct?

a. therefore, that
b. therefore that
c. that
d. OMIT phrase

This part of the treaty may be difficult to enforce and (9) <u>implying</u> international trust that all countries will eventually work toward that end.

9. Which of the following is the most correct?

a. implying
b. implies
c. applying
d. applies

Since the treaty asks countries to negotiate this pillar in (10) <u>Good Faith</u>, it may make enforcement procedures difficult as the treaty is presently written.

10. Which of the following is the most correct?

a. Good Faith
b. good faith
c. "Good Faith"
d. "good faith"

The third pillar of the treaty allows for (11) <u>peacetime</u> use of nuclear energy.

11. Which of the following is the most correct?

a. peacetime
b. peaceable
c. peacelike
d. peaceful

Compliance (12) <u>about</u> this part of the treaty; means that countries are still able to use the nuclear energy they presently have, but not as part of nuclear weaponry.

12. Which of the following is the most correct?

a. about
b. among
c. with
d. over

Compliance about this part of the (13) <u>treaty; means</u> that countries are still able to use the nuclear energy they presently have, but not as part of nuclear weaponry.

13. Which of the following is the most correct?

a. treaty; means
b. treaty, means
c. treaty. Means
d. treaty means

Nuclear materials (14) <u>that are</u> generally considered to be ingredients for nuclear weapons (e.g., uranium, plutonium) should be carefully overseen.

14. Which of the following is the most correct?

a. that are
b. which are
c. are
d. OMIT the underlined portion

15. Which sentence could best be used as a final sentence of this passage?

a. The three pillars of the treaty combine for a strong program among those who have signed.
b. The treaty is ultimately meaningless, since not all nuclear materials are being overseen in this way.
c. The three pillars contain essentially the same information and should be combined into one.
d. The three pillars of the treaty ensure that there are no nuclear problems in our world.

1

Most journalists would agree that print newspapers today are in survival mode. The past decade has been an unsettled one for national and local papers, as online technology has provided [16] enhanced opportunity's" for readers to get news that is usually [17] free, extensive, and available at any time of the day or night. Add our [18] countries' current poor economic conditions to the equation and publishers of most large national newspapers don't need to read quarterly figures. They know that the [19] circulation figures for print newspapers continue to fall.

2

Since they employ so many people in a variety of capacities, newspaper publishers have a dilemma that is [20] not only going to get more worse with time. They know that their reading audience is moving to online content. Although most of [21] there older readers are still loyal to the print edition of the newspaper, the number of new, younger readers is in decline. These tech-savvy readers get almost all of their news through the electronic [22] media their computers cell phones and handheld devices. News executives, many of them not completely comfortable with technology themselves, must figure out a way to be successful in this easily accessible electronic world.

3

Advertising online may not have the impact a print advertisement can have. Think of [23] a full page advertisement in [24] The New York Times or USA Today. A well-placed print ad is often difficult for readers [25] to ignore it. The opposite tends to be true with online advertising—savvy readers can click past an ad in a second. Advertisers are still gauging the effectiveness of placing their ads on online [26] newscites.

4

Some newspapers have experimented with charging a [27] fee for access to their online news sites. Successful [28] subscription, based online newspapers have content that is [29] both unique or valuable. Since many reputable websites offer their news at no charge and update it constantly, it is difficult for most newspapers to compete online. [30] Subscribers' seem to have no reason to pay for [31] his newspaper's content.

5

News is big business. Publishers and owners of print newspapers must figure out ways to [32] keep their readers loyal, produce revenue, and stay viable in [33] todays' changing world. Most newspaper executives know that the window of time [34] to adopted to the changing market narrows each week.

The past decade has been an unsettled one for national and local papers, as online technology has provided (16) enhanced opportunity's" for readers to get news that is usually free, extensive, and available at any time of the day or night.

16. Which of the following is the most correct?

a. "enhanced opportunity's"
b. enhanced opportunity's
c. "enhanced opportunities"
d. enhanced opportunities

The past decade has been an unsettled one for national and local papers, as online technology has provided enhanced opportunity's" for readers to get news that is usually (17) free, extensive, and available at any time of the day or night.

17. Which of the following is the most correct?

a. free, extensive, and available
b. free extensive and available
c. free, extensive, and available,
d. free extensive, and available

Add our (18) countries' current poor economic conditions to the equation and publishers of most large national newspapers don't need to read quarterly figures.

18. Which of the following is the most correct?

a. countries'
b. country's
c. countries
d. countrys'

They know that the (19) circulation figures for print newspapers continue to fall.

19. Which of the following is the most correct?

a. circulation figures for print newspapers continue
b. circulation figures for print newspapers continues
c. circulation figure for print newspapers continue
d. circulation figure for print newspapers continues

Since they employ so many people in a variety of capacities, newspaper publishers have a dilemma that is (20) not only going to get more worse with time.

20. Which of the following is the most correct?

a. not only going to get more worse
b. not only going to get more worse
c. only going to get more worse
d. only going to get worse

Although most of (21) there older readers are still loyal to the print edition of the newspaper, the number of new, younger readers is in decline.

21. Which of the following is the most correct?

a. there
b. their
c. theyre
d. they're

22. The writer wants to add this sentence to the paragraph:

They must solve their problem before their company is no longer viable.

The best place to put this sentence would be after the sentence ending with:

a. . . . moving to online content.
b. . . . younger readers is in decline.
c. . . . cell phones, and handheld devices.
d. . . . in this easily accessible electronic world.

These tech-savvy readers get almost all of their news through the electronic (23) <u>media their computers cell phones and handheld devices</u>.

23. Which of the following is the most correct?

a. media their computers cell phones and handheld devices
b. media, their computers, cell phones, and handheld devices
c. media: their computers, cell phones, and handheld devices
d. media: their computers, cell, phones and handheld devices

Advertising online may not have the impact a print advertisement can have. Think of a full page advertisement in *The New York Times* or *USA Today*. A well-placed print ad is often difficult for readers to ignore it. The opposite tends to be true with online advertising—savvy readers can click past an ad in a second. Advertisers are still gauging the effectiveness of placing their ads on online newscites.

24. Which of the following sentences would provide the best introduction to paragraph 3?

a. Many newspapers contain advertisements of different sizes.
b. A logical place to gain revenue is advertising.
c. Advertising is big business.
d. Don't count out advertising.

Think of (25) <u>a full page advertisement</u> in *The New York Times* or *USA Today*. A well-placed print ad is often difficult for readers to ignore it.

25. Which of the following is the most correct?

a. a full page advertisement
b. a full, page advertisement
c. a full-page-advertisement
d. a full-page advertisement

Think of a full page advertisement in (26) *The New York Times* or *USA Today*. A well-placed print ad is often difficult for readers to ignore it.

26. Which of the following is the most correct?

a. The New York Times
b. The New York Times:
c. The New York Times,
d. The New York Times—

Think of a full page advertisement in *The New York Times* or *USA Today*. A well-placed print ad is often difficult for readers (27) to ignore it.

27. Which of the following is the most correct?

a. to ignore it
b. to ignore them
c. to be ignored
d. to ignore

Advertisers are still gauging the effectiveness of placing their ads on online (28) newscites.

28. Which of the following is the most correct?

a. newscites
b. news sites
c. news sights
d. newsites

Some newspapers have experimented with charging a (29) fee for access to their online news sites.

29. Which of the following is the most correct?

a. fee for access to their
b. fee for accessing to their
c. fees for assess to their
d. fee assessing to their

Successful (30) subscription, based online newspapers have content that is both unique or valuable.

30. Which of the following is the most correct?

a. subscription, based
b. subscription based
c. subscription-based
d. subscription based,

Successful subscription, based online newspapers have content that is (31) both unique or valuable.

31. Which of the following is the most correct?

a. both unique or valuable
b. both unique, or valuable
c. both unique, and valuable
d. both unique and valuable

(32) Subscribers' seem to have no reason to pay for his newspaper's content.

32. Which of the following is the most correct?

a. Subscribers'
b. Subscriber's
c. Subscribers
d. Subscriber

Subscribers' seem to have no reason to pay for (33) his newspaper's content.

33. Which of the following is the most correct?

a. his
b. her
c. their
d. its

34. What is the best place to put this additional sentence?

That's why the next year will be crucial to this market.

a. Before Sentence 1
b. After Sentence 1
c. After Sentence 2
d. After Sentence 3

Publishers and owners of print newspapers must figure out ways to (35) keep their readers loyal, produce revenue, and stay viable in todays' changing world.

35. Which of the following is the most correct?

a. keep their readers loyal, produce revenue, and
b. keep their readers loyal produce revenue and
c. keep their readers loyal, produce, revenue, and
d. keep their readers, loyal produce, revenue and

Publishers and owners of print newspapers must figure out ways to keep their readers loyal, produce revenue, and stay viable in (36) todays' changing world.

36. Which of the following is the most correct?

a. today's changing world
b. todays changing world
c. today's changing world
d. to-day's changing world

Most newspaper executives know that the window of time (37) to adopted to the changing market narrows each week.

37. Which of the following is the most correct?

a. to adopted
b. to adapted
c. to adapt
d. to adopt

Cronyism (38) was best described as when a person in (39) an authoritarian position gives a job to a loyal friend or social contact simply because of (40) their relationship to each other.

38. Which of the following is the most correct?

a. was
b. were
c. is
d. are

39. Which of the following is the most correct?

a. an authoritative position
b. a position of authority
c. a position
d. the know

40. Which of the following is the most correct?

a. their relationship to each other.
b. each's relationship to the other.
c. ones' relationship with the other.
d. the relationship one has with the other.

Many times the person hired or appointed is not particularly qualified to perform the job and learns the duties once in (41) place—on-the-job-training.

41. Which of the following is the most correct?

a. place—on
b. place. On
c. place; on
d. place on

About fifty years ago, most of the public schools in the United States (42) were segregated, that is, the schools were racially unbalanced.

42. Which of the following is the most correct?

a. were segregated, that is; the schools were racially unbalanced
b. were segregated that is, the schools were racially unbalanced
c. were segregated, that is the schools were racially unbalanced
d. were segregated that is the schools were racially unbalanced

The United States Border Patrol works hard to ensure that our country's borders are safe. The job formerly consisted of mainly halting entry of illegal aliens and contraband across our borders. The job has become much more than that. (43)

43. If the writer wants to add a sentence here to explain how the job has become "more than that," which of the following sentences best accomplishes that goal?

a. Border patrol agents now must protect against terrorists and illegal weapons crossing the border.
b. Border patrol agents work constantly to protect our country's citizens.
c. Border patrol agents must know how to recognize all sorts of ways illegal aliens may be able to sneak into the country.
d. Border patrol agents must recognize that they have a dangerous job.

The North Korean security forces are notorious for interfering with the decisions of the court. Most of the time, the end result of court cases can easily be concluded before the judiciary have even started discussions.

44. Which of the following would be the best opening sentence for this paragraph?

a. The North Korean court system is known for its widespread corruption.
b. Most court systems in the world are conducted differently from the United States.
c. North Korea's citizens must endure inequities throughout the court system.
d. Judges in North Korea are not equitable with their decisions.

Some historians cite President John Kennedy's appointment of his longtime friend Robert McNamara as Secretary of Defense as a classic case of cronyism. McNamara had no experience at all in foreign affairs or defense strategies, yet was given this highly influential and important appointment by his friend. Robert McNamara is often mentioned as the person directly responsible for getting the United States involved in the war in Vietnam— (45)

45. Which ending to this sentence provides the best conclusion to the passage?

a. a war that is said to be a disastrous event in our country's history.
b. a war that was fought for many years.
c. a war that many people today may not understand.
d. a war that has cronyism to thank for its inception.

Written Essay

You will have 30 minutes to write an essay on an assigned topic. Sample topics are provided below. Choose one.

As you create your essay, you should present and support your point of view. Your writing will be evaluated on the quality of the writing and not on your opinion. A good essay will have an organized structure, clear thesis, and logical supporting details. Ensure that you are presenting your topic in a way that appeals to your target audience. Use clear and appropriate word choice throughout. Ensure that grammar, punctuation, and spelling are correct. Your response can be of any length.

1. Sudan's borders were drawn during British colonial times. The Sudanese north comprises Muslim Arabs, while Africans of various faiths are mainly in the south. The people living in Sudan's south have experienced slave raids since Islamic law was imposed there in 1983. Describe how and why the conflict in Sudan has become even more serious since 1989.

2. Conservative and liberal thinkers have vastly differing views about fundamental components of our society, our government, our rights, and life in general. Identify at least three key issues and the differences of viewpoints held by those thinkers coming from the left as contrasted with those coming from the right.

Answer Key and Explanations

Job Knowledge

1. C: "Bcc" means "blind carbon copy." When an email is sent this way, the original recipient does not know who else may be getting it. Sending a cc means that all recipients know who is getting a copy. Forwarding an email is a way to send it to someone else without letting the intended recipient know, but it is not the most efficient way.

2. D: The mode is the value that occurs most often in a listing.

3. D: The U.S. banking system is one of the most regulated banking systems in the world, with regulations within each state and the federal government.

4. A: Although many programs were introduced under Franklin Roosevelt's New Deal, the Medicaid and Medicare programs were started by Johnson.

5. A: The Federal Reserve System raises and lowers the prime rate to regulate the nation's money supply.

6. B: The waterways of the United States are closely tied to its ability to transport the goods that are able to be grown year-round within the country. This greatly affects the economy. The U.S. government has a laissez-faire policy as it applies to the economy. Russia's geography means that there is a short growing season. The country has a very small coastline and waterways that do not connect. Their economy is defined by their geography.

7. A: The EU is committed to the environment, humanitarian values, peace, stability, European solidarity, and a common market. The first two treaties shared a common theme. The Treaty of Paris, 1951, created a common steel and coal market between the original members. The Treaty of Rome, 1957, built the European Economic Community (EEC). These treaties both focused on creating a common market.

8. A: Among the choices listed, a database is best defined as a tool that is used for collecting and organizing information. The other choices are all potential uses for a database, but choice A is the best general definition.

9. A: Good managers will set up an environment where people will be motivated to work.

10. B: Title VII prohibits intentional discrimination and practices with the effect of discriminating against individuals because of their race, color, national origin, religion, or gender.

11. B: Noncitizens are able to receive Medicaid, food stamps, and Social Security benefits. They contribute to the economy by working, paying taxes, and buying products.

12. B: In an attempt to keep the population down, China instituted a one-child policy. Nigeria has the largest population in Africa. The government has provided more access to birth control and encouraged families to limit themselves to four children.

13. C: Lech Walesa was the president during this time. Helmut Kohl was the German chancellor. Ceausescu was a Communist dictator. Havel was elected president of the Czech Republic in 1989.

14. C: The Irish Republican Army (IRA) was a paramilitary organization wanting Northern Ireland's independence from Britain. Al-Qaeda is a Muslim terrorist group.

15. A: Insurgency is a military struggle involving guerilla warfare of small rural bands. Insurgents can hold to different causes or ideologies. While it is commonly thought to be caused by ethnic or religious differences, weakened governments are more likely to see insurgency.

16. C: The Maastricht Treaty was signed in the Netherlands and created both the European Union and the euro as its currency.

17. B: Neoliberalism is an economic model encouraged by the United States which encourages free markets and private ownership of businesses.

18. A: Germany developed rocket technology and the United States put a man on the moon in 1969.

19. C: In absolutism, the ruler is sovereign. Kings often said that they were governed by divine right and were responsible to only God. Patriarchy is a social organization where descent follows the male line. An oligarchy is a small group of people who control a government. Communism is where a communist party holds power alone.

20. C: There are Federal Reserve banks in (1) Boston; (2) New York; (3) Philadelphia; (4) Cleveland; (5) Richmond; (6) Atlanta; (7) Chicago; (8) St. Louis; (9) Minneapolis; (10) Dallas; (11) Kansas City; and (12) San Francisco.

21. D: A stateless nation is one that wants statehood but does not have it (Kurds in the Middle East). An industrialized but not democratic country is how a Second World country is usually described. An impoverished and unstable country is a description of a Third World country.

22. D: In 2002, the United States was involved with nation building in Afghanistan.

23. A: The Patriot Act was specifically formed to combat terrorism.

24. B: The First Amendment covers freedom of the press, petitioning the government, and assembling peacefully. "Cruel and unusual punishment" is covered in the Eighth Amendment.

25. B: The Fourth Amendment outlaws unreasonable search and seizure. The Eighth Amendment protects against excessive bail. The Fourteenth Amendment states the rights of citizenship.

26. D: Free speech means that people can generally say what they want to. Propaganda is misinformation and half-truths about something. "Penny press" is the phrase used to describe the early newspapers published in the United States.

27. D: Senators are elected for a term of 6 years.

28. D: Although an immigrant or a nonresident alien can be a refugee, the term for people who flee for political reasons is "refugee."

29. C: Chairpersons for standing committees of Congress are chosen by leaders of the majority party.

30. A: Although Congress must agree to pay for foreign policy dictated by the president, it does not decide foreign policy.

31. D: The education of the workforce generally does not affect GDP. The size of the workforce implies that there are people who are ready and willing to work. The amount of capital means that there is a sufficient number of factories and assets available to create goods and services. Technology includes the skills and knowledge people have to direct and enable the workforce.

32. C: While many Communist regimes limit international trade, liberals, Marxists, social democrats, and conservatives support the idea of free international trade. Mercantilists do not support free international trade, but mercantilism is not a widely respected ideology.

33. D: Raising the minimum wage ultimately causes a rise in the rate of inflation, since employers' labor costs are raised. Employers pass this increase on as higher prices for their goods and services.

34. A: Price determines what goods will be produced, who will be producing them, and how they will be produced. Banks and demand are both affected by price. Government is not a big part of a market economy and is more a part of a command economy.

35. C: An inelastic demand is not very sensitive to changes in price. "Utility" means satisfaction or usefulness, which is not affected if the athlete buys the same amount of spinach every week.

36. B: Car A would arrive in 2 hours (150 miles/75 mph = 2). Car B would arrive in 2 hours and 30 minutes. In 2 hours at 60 mph, the car would go 120 miles, with 30 miles left to travel.

37. B: To find the correct price, first subtract 15% from the price of the book ($35.00 – 5.25 = $29.75). Then subtract 10% from the discounted price ($29.75 – $2.97 = $26.78). Choice A is incorrect because the 2 percent figures cannot be added together. Choice C is just 15% off the original price. Choice D is just 10% off the original price.

38. B: Subtract 325 from 1500, and then divide by the 5 people left. Choice A is incorrect because the resulting figure after subtracting 325 is divided by 6, and not 5. Choice C is incorrect because it is the total (1500) divided by 6. Choice D is incorrect because it is the total divided by 5.

39. B: Multiply $10,000 by .32 = $3,200. Subtract this amount from the total winnings: $10,000 – $3,200 = $6,800.

40. B: Multiply $25,000 by .06 = $1,500. Add the interest to the principal: $25,000 + $1,500 = $26,500. Subtract the $5,000 payment: $26,500 – $5,000 = $21,500.

41. A: In a 24-hour day, one-fourth = 6 hours. Subtract this from 24 to get 18 hours. One-twelfth of his day = 2 hours. Subtract this from 18 to get 16 hours. One-half of his day = 12 hours. Subtract this from 16 to get 4 hours.

42. D: A subject line is an important part of an email and should contain a strong clue about what the message is about.

43. A: The group will be made up of people with varying education levels, attitudes, prior knowledge, and interests.

44. C: Douglas MacArthur was Roosevelt's general who advised him during this time but was not one of the Big Three. Winston Churchill was the British prime minister, Roosevelt was the ailing U.S. president, and Joseph Stalin was the head of the Soviet Union.

45. C: A firewall protects a computer from other computers and viruses. Encryption is a way to send something so that it can be read by only the recipient. A filter screens incoming messages. A bug is a problem with a computer.

46. A: Regional and ethnic cleavages have been a political struggle for the government of Nigeria. Although English is the official language of Nigeria, the country is made up of a variety of languages and cultures. Religious influences also vary. Most citizens align themselves with Muslim, Christian, and indigenous African beliefs.

47. A: The CPU is the most important part of the computer. RAM is the type of memory a computer uses. A URL is part of a web address. The OS is software used by the computer.

48. A: The denominator is the number on the bottom of a fraction. The denominator must be the same to add fractions, so before adding, the least common denominator must be found.

49. B: Goals should closely align with what the company or organization is trying to do. Although employees are usually rewarded for reaching their goals, they are not typically penalized for not reaching them. They should be set by the employee and should be attainable—but not necessarily difficult.

50. C: The law requires employers to ensure that those they hire are legally permitted to work in the United States.

Situational Judgment

1. Best: C. Worst: B. Telling your supervisor that you have not performed this task before and may have questions about it demonstrates good communication skills and offers the supervisor insight on your comfort level regarding the new task. Telling your supervisor that you will get started right away is not the best answer because the employee in this vignette is currently "busy with other work" that was previously assigned and might need to be completed first. Similarly, option A is not the best answer because telling your supervisor that you're "busy" is never a good approach. However, the worst answer is B. Telling your supervisor that the task is outside of your scope of practice is rude and insubordinate.

2. Best: B. Worst: C. It is never appropriate to alter a coworker's workspace as you are unfamiliar with her current work plans. Closing her screen or logging her out of the computer could result in loss of work or other mistakes. Therefore, waiting until your coworker returns and then discussing the problem with her is the best option. The worst option is C, to immediately discuss the problem with the supervisor as this is a small security infringement and no imminent danger is present. It is best to first discuss the issue with the coworker rather than involving a supervisor.

3. Best: A. Worst: D. It is always good business practice to express appreciation for workers that go above and beyond expectations and offer new ideas and suggestions, no matter how feasible they are. This level of engagement makes a workplace run more smoothly. Although option C is similar to A, the main difference is in the execution. Telling a coworker that changes need to be made before the idea can be implemented leads the worker to believe that the idea will be implemented, when in reality, it will not. The worst answer is D. Team leaders are not dictators and must not behave as such. Team leaders must take a collaborative approach and listen to any and all ideas from their team.

4. Best: B. Worst: A. When conflict happens in the workplace, it is always appropriate to discuss the matter privately. This allows for the free exchange of ideas without outside interjection. The worst option is A. To refuse to participate in the new policy and voice your concerns immediately is a knee-jerk reaction that is rarely helpful. Refusal to follow directions is insubordinate and in many facilities, insubordination may end in termination.

5. Best: B. Worst: C. If you are unfamiliar with the culture of a community, especially one who is experiencing civil unrest, it is most beneficial to participate in company-approved events that provide you with support from coworkers as well as structured, safe interactions with the community. If the area is dangerous, it is best to visit with an existing group who knows the area and its culture. Scheduling meet-and-greet and open-house events may be useful in meeting the community as well; however, these don't provide you with support and safety from coworkers who have familiarity with the culture. Option C is the worst answer as reading the local newspaper may offer you news stories about the civil unrest; it will not reveal as much about the culture as an immersive, firsthand experience.

6. Best: A. Worst: D. A polite redirection of the interview is best in this situation. Asking personal questions such as marital status, how many children an applicant has, and other sensitive information are illegal and potentially discriminatory. This line of questioning must be stopped immediately; therefore, option D is the worst answer.

7. Best: C. Worst: D. Your department is in turmoil. Offering daily 5-minute meetings with staff provides an immediate response to a problem within the department. When morale is low, productivity suffers. Therefore, it is good business practice to take immediate action and begin the communication process. Option A is an appropriate action to take but is not as timely as an immediate meeting with the staff. Option B is also not a wrong answer, but it takes the personal touch out of the interaction. Face-to-face discussion is always better than a memo as tone and emotion are rarely accurately conveyed in writing. The worst answer is D, as this prolongs the unrest in the department.

8. Best: D. Worst: A. This employee has several years of experience at this company and offers solutions and new ideas. This employee would be more successful in management than a new graduate who has minimal experience or a new employee who is not as experienced. The worst answer is A. Seniority is not the only factor that should be taken into consideration when offering a promotion. This employee is frequently tardy, which may indicate a lack of interest in the job or simply poor time management skills, both of which are not conducive to a successful managerial position.

9. Best: B. Worst: C. Delegating some of the projects to responsible team members ensures that all of the projects will be completed in a timely manner. Although prioritizing is helpful, it is more beneficial to prioritize which tasks you need to complete personally and then delegate other less-important projects to your team members. Option C is the worst answer as you have been assigned tasks that must be completed regardless of your busy schedule.

10. Best: A. Worst: D. If your department is having financial difficulties, immediate action is needed. Sending email notices rather than paper newsletters is a quick and easy way to reduce costs as you are eliminating the need for any paper use on that project. Reducing the publication of the newsletter is also helpful but does not have as much of an impact as stopping paper use completely. Options C and E are also helpful but not quite as impactful as stopping paper use completely. Option D is the worst choice as it is not good practice to require employees to incur the expense of bringing their own office supplies when other actions can be taken first.

11. Best: A. Worst: C. In customer service situations, it is good practice to apologize to the customer for your part in the altercation. This helps to "save" a sale, and the business will not lose a customer. The worst option is C. Customer service agents must take ownership of their mistakes and make every effort to rectify them, even if they are not fully to blame for the altercation.

12. Best: B. Worst: A. The audience for your presentation is a group of customers who may be interested in purchasing the new equipment. They are likely laypeople who have no prior knowledge of technical terminology or scientific jargon. Therefore, it is important to use lay terms whenever possible but highlight and explain any important technical jargon that is critical for the understanding of how the product works or its application. Option A is the worst choice as these customers may be confused by the technical jargon, which can lead to confusion and a lack of interest in the product.

13. Best: C. Worst: A. Open communication is critical in the workplace. Speaking to your supervisor about the cost increase and possible solutions shows enthusiasm and initiative. Option A is the worst choice because you are basing your assessment of the situation on hearsay from your coworker. It is best to discuss the problem with your supervisor first and then, if there is an ethical issue, report it to the proper chain of command in your unit or organization.

14. Best: A. Worst: C. Although option B is a kind gesture, your generosity may be abused in the future. Therefore, other options should be considered first. Option A allows for you to attempt to rectify the situation in a fair manner. Many stores and organizations do offer discounts or credit in certain situations, and it is acceptable to ask a supervisor for guidance. The worst option is C. Changing prices without permission is considered theft.

15. Best: C. Worst: A. The director has stated that the diversity training is a facility-wide initiative, which indicates that attendance is required of all employees. The worst answer is A. Skipping a required training without giving prior notice or without giving a valid reason for the absence is unacceptable and could be grounds for termination in some instances.

16. Best: C. Worst: B. It is considered rude to speak in a foreign language in front of other non-fluent members of a workplace. Speaking with a coworker privately about the issue shows maturity and tactfulness. The coworker might not realize that he or she is making other colleagues uncomfortable and should be given the benefit of the doubt. Option B is the worst option as interrupting the conversation is a rude gesture in itself, and it can also be considered confrontational. It is not acceptable workplace behavior to instigate a potential altercation when a more tactful approach can be taken.

17. Best: A. Worst: D. It is unknown if the coworker was actually reading the document, so it is best to simply put the document away. At that point, you can speak to the coworker about the classified nature of the document and inform your supervisor of any possible security breach. Option D is the worst answer because it is unknown whether the coworker read the document, reporting him or her is premature.

18. Best: A. Worst: D. Politely correcting a coworker in a hazardous situation is an appropriate course of action. Offering to help while performing the task correctly is also an appropriate choice, but clear, direct instructions in a dangerous situation are preferred. The worst answer is D. If a situation is potentially unsafe, immediate action is required.

19. Best: B. Worst: D. After any work-related injury, it is important to immediately fill out an incident report. This should take place before any other intervention, including labeling the equipment as "broken." Once a report is filled out, your facility's human resources department or your supervisor will instruct you on further actions to take, including seeking medical care. Unless the situation is life-threatening or critical, medical care should be sought out after receiving instructions from your workplace. The worst option is D. Ignoring the incident and continuing with your workday is dangerous and can result in further injury.

20. Best: B. Worst: D. Occupational Safety and Health Administration (OSHA) requires that all exits remain clear at all times. Boxes and equipment should never block an exit, even for only a few minutes. The worst answer is D. A blocked exit is a safety hazard and could cause injury or death in an emergency situation.

21. Best: C. Worst: A. E cylinders of oxygen are pressurized and highly combustible. If they topple over or are struck, they could explode, causing facility damage and personal injury. All gas cylinders must be secured at all times. Therefore, the worst answer is A.

22. Best: D. Worst: A. Although the employer can ask for concessions, these employees are not required to give them. Practice of religion is protected under federal law, and these employees have a right to continue to take their prayer breaks as they have done previously. The worst answer is A. It is unlawful to require employees to work with no breaks, whether that time is taken for prayer, meals, or other activities.

23. Best: B. Worst: A. Apologizing for any inconvenience is good business etiquette. Your job requires you to check the visitor's identification, log the information, and record the in and out times. Therefore, you must follow these steps with every individual every time unless told otherwise. You may choose to check with your supervisor after the encounter to ensure that you are following proper procedure, but you should first perform your job duties as previously instructed. Although both options A and C are poor choices, A is the worst choice. Waving him through without logging any information can be a potentially serious security breach. C is also a poor choice as it is a confrontational and unprofessional way to conduct your job responsibilities, but you are still logging his information as required. This is better than simply waving him through the security checkpoint, possibly putting employees and the facility at risk.

24. Best: D. Worst: B. Because you have already brought the issue to your supervisor, and she is unwilling or unable to help, it is time to follow the chain of command and make a formal complaint. The worst answer is B. The chemicals are known to be hazardous to your health, and you must not be in contact with them without the proper personal protective equipment in place. If you are unable to obtain a splash mask and gloves from other sources (such as your home or another department), then work must cease until the stocking issue is resolved.

25. Best: E. Worst: C. Whenever a medical emergency takes place and someone loses consciousness, the first thing you should do is assess the person and make sure he or she has a pulse and is breathing. This is important because to call for help, you have to describe the situation. Treating a pulseless person is different from treating a fainting victim. The next best answer is B, activating the emergency response system. This should take place shortly after you assess the severity of the emergency. The worst answer is C. This woman has hit her head and could have a cervical spine injury, so moving her may cause further injury. You should never move an accident victim of any kind unless there is immediate danger to his or her safety.

26. Best: B. Worst: A. You have been asked to assess and move victims to the medical tents. That is enough instruction to begin working. Choice A is the worst choice because waiting for more specific instruction from the medical team wastes valuable time when trying to transport critically injured civilians. Therefore, option A is the worst answer. Moving the most severely injured patients first ensures quicker access to medical care and can help prevent more casualties.

27. Best: B. Worst: C. When managing a crisis, it is important to take instruction from the leader who is managing the situation. Option C is the worst answer because taking it upon yourself to begin working without instruction can result in confusion, mistakes, and chaos. The emergency coordinator will give instructions based on the severity of the situation and will determine what actions need to take place first. They will then assign tasks to individuals.

28. Best: A. Worst: B. When greeting colleagues, it is best to take a warm but professional approach. Saying hello, introducing yourself, and offering a handshake is an appropriate greeting for a professional situation. Hugging a new acquaintance is never appropriate as you don't know the other person's comfort level with that type of personal touch. Option B is the worst answer because hugging is not a socially appropriate greeting in the professional setting. Although C and D are also appropriate greetings, they aren't as comprehensive or welcoming as option A. Option A offers a handshake, an introduction, a greeting, and a personal escort to the department. Options C and D do not include all of these components.

29. Best: A. Worst: B. Attempting to pronounce an unfamiliar name is always good business practice. It shows that you care about addressing the customer in a respectful way, even if you make a mistake. Option B is the worst choice. Your facility requires you to address customers by their last names (i.e., Mrs. Smith), and you should make every attempt to do so. Referring to a customer by his or her first name is not only inappropriate but can also be considered rude and disrespectful to some individuals.

30. Best: C. Worst: A. The best approach is to attempt to quiet the chatter in a polite manner. You are a team leader and are therefore in a position of authority. The coworkers may not realize they are interrupting the speaker, so a gentle reminder is acceptable. Ignoring your coworker and the other talkers is acceptable but may not stop the distracting chatter. Moving your seat can be disruptive and distracting to the speaker but is a valid option if none of the other approaches succeed in stopping the background noise. Option A is the worst choice as loudly "shushing" the coworkers can be as disruptive as the talkers themselves.

31. Best: D. Worst: A. Presenting the supervisor with information on your measurable successes in your position will help him to determine if a salary raise is warranted. Demonstrated success such as increasing revenue, recruiting and retaining new customers, and sales quota reports all offer objective information that the supervisor can consider. The worst answer is A. This approach is referred to as "quid pro quo," in other words, "do something for me, and I'll do something for you." At a minimum, this approach is rude and inappropriate but could also be considered harassment in many instances.

32. Best: D. Worst: A. You are tasked with learning as much as possible about the culture of the customer's business and determining the benefits of a partnership. The best way to do this is to ask open-ended questions, which can reveal extensive details about the customer's business. You should also ask the customer if they have questions for you, and share information about your business as well. Option A is the worst choice as the best way to learn is to be an active listener. If you are doing all the talking and "selling" your company, you are not achieving your goal of discovering new information about the customer's company.

33. Best: A. Worst: C. Despite the customer's lateness, it is good manners to introduce yourself and make pleasant small talk before beginning the discussions. You don't know why the customer was late, and he is likely embarrassed or concerned about his tardiness. Asking him why he's late or making mention of it in general can cause the customer to be uncomfortable. You may also lose the partnership or sale if the customer is offended. Therefore, option C is the worst answer as you are mentioning his lateness and potentially causing unnecessary embarrassment.

34. Best: C. Worst: D. You don't know why John is eager to take on more responsibility at work. John is not doing anything wrong and does not need to be reprimanded by you or anyone else. In this situation, it is best to simply speak to your supervisor and tell them that you'd like to have more responsibility at work. The worst answer is D. Complaining to your supervisor that your coworker is "upstaging" you because he works on all the new projects makes you appear childish and unprofessional.

35. Best: C. Worst: A. You are aware of the upcoming vacation because it is taken every year at the same time in that country. Therefore, you can work ahead or formulate a plan together that will help limit the amount of catch-up work that must be completed when they return. This is the best option for everyone as the work will continue while they are gone, and you are able to stay on schedule. Option A is the worst answer. It is not culturally sensitive to belittle a country's customs even if they are inconvenient for you and your time-sensitive project.

36. Best: A. Worst: B. Your supervisor may not realize help is needed and may assume that the department is running smoothly. Bringing the issue to her attention privately, and asking for help in a specific area, helps her understand where the issue lies and how to rectify it. Option B is the worst answer. Here you are making assumptions that your supervisor doesn't like you or your coworkers, when she may simply not realize that there is a problem. Telling her that you notice she doesn't like your team is accusatory and could be perceived as hostile. This approach puts the supervisor in a defensive position that is not conducive to open, honest communication.

37. Best: C. Worst: B. Your project was cancelled, and your supervisor is asking you to join another team. Your first course of action should be integrating with the other team and helping them complete their project. Being friendly and asking how you can help is always a good approach. Then, once the task is underway, you may ask for additional projects or responsibilities. It is also acceptable to join the other team and wait for them to instruct you because they have been working together on that project for an extended period of time. The worst answer is B. Working together with other colleagues is a common occurrence in the business setting and must be navigated even if you don't enjoy group work. Flexibility is essential in the workplace. In addition, there is no indication that this project was cancelled because you performed subpar work, and therefore, you should not assume that the cancellation was your fault.

38. Best: D. Worst: B. It is best to not comment on a coworker's health or ask questions about it. A coworker's personal issues that require him or her to go on leave is not anyone's business. Asking personal questions or commenting on health is not appropriate in the workplace. If her leave was due to a medical reason, then her privacy is protected by Health Insurance Portability and Accountability Act (HIPPA) laws. Therefore, the worst answer is B.

39. Best: A. Worst: B. You do not yet know how well this employee can perform the job requirements; therefore, you should give him the opportunity to work without interference or questioning. The worst answer is B. Although it is rude to comment to a supervisor about a person's weight or insinuate that he or she can't keep up with the workload, it's even worse to mention these concerns to the colleague directly. This approach is likely to cause hurt feelings as well as conflict between yourself and the colleague.

40. Best: B. Worst: C. Speaking to your supervisor privately about the issue is a professional and courteous approach to resolving this conflict. The worst answer is C. Boasting about your abilities does not resolve the problem of the omitted information. The issue should be brought to your supervisor's attention in a respectful manner.

41. Best: A. Worst: D. Making an orientee fell welcome is the first step in building a successful working relationship. Soon, the orientee will be a seasoned coworker whom you may rely on in the future. It is best to form a cordial working relationship from the start despite your hesitation for being "slowed down." The worst answer is D. Telling a new employee that they "will just slow you down" is an offensive and upsetting remark that is completely unacceptable in the workplace. This approach is likely to upset the orientee and cause him or her to not feel welcome in the office.

42. Best: D. Worst: B. Although staying late or coming in early is helpful in the completion of a time-sensitive project, hourly workers are not always allowed to put in overtime. These hours should be approved ahead of time by your supervisor. Therefore, D is the best option because you are asking for more time to work on your report. This can include moving the deadline or adding extra work hours. The worst answer is B. It is premature to tell your supervisor that you won't meet the deadline. First, you must think of ways to help yourself meet the deadline rather than simply giving up.

43. Best: A. Worst: D. When asked to manage the social media accounts for a small charitable organization, it is best to share only information and events that are sponsored by your facility unless you are instructed otherwise. The worst answer is D. Treating the accounts as if they are your own and liking and commenting on stories you find interesting is not professional. You are assigned to manage the accounts for a business, and that business's best interest must be considered at all times. Your personal feelings and opinions may not align with the charity's ideals and can cause conflict in the future.

44. Best: C. Worst: D. Members of the community will be attending your presentation to find out what services your facility provides and how to access those services. Focusing on those topics will make your presentation streamlined and efficient. The worst option is D. The audience is made up of community members who are laypeople. Using medical jargon will not impress them but may in fact cause them to be disinterested in the presentation and result in the members not utilizing your facility's services in the future.

45. Best: D. Worst: C. If a colleague is having an issue that affects her work, immediate action should take place. Offering to speak to her immediately shows that you care about her and take her problems seriously. The worst answer is C. Delaying the conversation and requiring the colleague to miss her lunch break is unacceptable. Missing a few minutes of work is appropriate when solving an important problem.

46. Best: B. Worst: D. The director has requested a large-scale marketing strategy to highlight the company's services and values. Social media can reach millions of people in a short period of time and, therefore, should be the first step in a global public outreach initiative. The worst option is D. Employees are already aware of the services and accomplishments of their organization. Forwarding emails to a small number of friends and family does not have the same effectiveness as larger-scale campaigns.

47. Best: C. Worst: A. You are unfamiliar with this country's language and will need to find a way to effectively communicate. Some countries have different dialects depending on the part of the country you are visiting, so a formal foreign language course might not be helpful to you. The best action to take is to ask your recruiter or supervisor for guidance on how to learn the local language. You may not need to have extensive knowledge of the language prior to starting work, and you may receive tutoring in the language as part of the assignment. Therefore, it is best not to take action on your own until you know more. The worst answer is A. Learning slang is not always helpful as you will be in a professional position and will need to maintain the dignity of your position. Slang conversation can be used incorrectly or can include rude phrases that should be avoided.

48. Best: C. Worst: A. You are asked to gather information on environmental changes from reputable sources. An internet search is a quick and easy way to access information, but care must be taken to ensure the sources are indeed reputable. Therefore, using only evidence-based information from governmental and nonprofit organizations is appropriate. This type of information has been studied and is proven to be accurate. The worst answer is A. Although the internet can be helpful in identifying and gathering accurate information, it is easy to find inaccurate information as well. It is not good practice to use all information found in an internet search, but instead you should carefully assess the sources of information to determine their accuracy and reputability.

49. Best: A. Worst: D. If your company is in financial distress, immediate action should be taken. Gathering a team of diverse coworkers allows for open brainstorming of ideas and sharing of knowledge. A team made up of people from different backgrounds with different opinions is more helpful than taking action on your own. Each coworker has a unique perspective on the problem, and sharing differing ideas on how to approach the problem can result in a more successful outcome. The worst option is D. Although advertising your services to the local area may be helpful, it is not a multifaceted approach utilizing critical thinking skills to solve the problem.

50. Best: A. Worst: C. Although investigating other transportation options is helpful, it is not an immediate solution to the problem. Organizing your supplies, making lunches the night before, and other similar actions can help save time in the morning and potentially solve your tardiness problem immediately. The worst option is C. Asking a coworker to punch you in when you aren't physically in the building is fraudulent behavior that can also be considered theft. This can be grounds for termination.

51. Best: D. Worst: A. When utilizing heavy machinery, safety is the utmost concern. Serious injury can occur if you are using a machine that you are unfamiliar with. Being honest with your supervisor and telling him or her that you're uncomfortable is the best course of action. You are asking to be reassigned only for the day, after which time you can ask for more training or guidance. The worst option is A. Waiting until your supervisor returns from the meeting to ask for more training is not helpful as you were supposed to be using the machine already. It is not in the company's best interest to delay work while you wait for your supervisor to return and then have an in-service on the machine. It is best to ask to be reassigned so that work can continue uninterrupted until you are able to complete training.

52. Best: B. Worst: A. Taking on a leadership role on new projects and teams demonstrates initiative and a desire to learn more. This is the first step in being considered for a promotion or supervisory role. The worst answer is A. Promotions are not determined by how long someone has worked in a role but instead are based on merit, initiative, and skill. Telling your supervisor that you should have a promotion because you've worked at your office for two years demonstrates an attitude of entitlement, which is not a positive attribute.

53. Best: B. Worst: D. Although a product may work well for one office, it may not be beneficial for another. Therefore, it is best to first research the product on your own and then ask your supervisor to review your findings. This demonstrates initiative and critical-thinking skills that are essential to being successful in the workplace. The worst answer is D. No research has been conducted to make sure that the product is a good fit for your department, so suggesting that your supervisor purchase it is premature.

54. Best: B. Worst: C. The certification is required for your position, and you should notify your supervisor immediately if your certification has lapsed. He or she may choose to remove you from active duty until the recertification is complete or may simply help you find a recertification course while you continue working. Either way, this issue is your supervisor's decision, and he or she should be immediately notified of the problem. The worst option is C. If an emergency takes place during your shift, you could possibly injure someone if your skills are not current. Ignoring a lapse in certification is unacceptable and could lead to dismissal in some cases.

55. Best: C. Worst: D. It is always appropriate to ask for guidance when you're not sure of how to behave in a workplace situation. The worst answer is D. There is no need to upset the interpersonal relationships in the department by telling your team members that you won't socialize with them any longer. This can cause animosity, especially because these coworkers may assume they are no longer your friends. This can result in strained relationships and poor morale.

56. Best: C. Worst: E. You are a new employee, and although you have extensive medical expertise, you should not take a leadership role without being appointed one. It is best to ask your supervisor if you can lead the team rather than taking it upon yourself to advise the group. The worst answer is E. Offering to treat the community on your own is kind but potentially dangerous. You are assuming all risk and liability for your actions, which can negatively impact the organization by which you are employed. Your personal safety may also be at risk because you will be treating patients on your own with no assistance from others.

57. Best: A. Worst: E. You were hired as part of a peaceful agricultural service group to do farming work in the community. This should be your sole focus during your work hours. If you choose to learn about local politics during your time of service, you should do so with caution and only on your off-duty times. The worst answer is E. You are not hired to take any kind of political action on the community's behalf. Your enthusiasm for local politics may have negative effects as you are a newcomer in this land and are not well versed in the topic. Taking political action can cause unrest and potential danger for you, your coworkers, and your local community.

58. Best: D. Worst: A. If you are not familiar with a particular tool used in your office, you should be honest and tell your supervisor. Telling him or her that you need extra help with the new technology shows initiative and eagerness to learn. The worst option is A. If you are unsure of how to use the tools, you should ask for help. Attempting to use them without proper training can result in poor productivity and mistakes.

59. Best: C. Worst: E. This handbook outlines the culture of the organization for which you now work. You are a new employee and need to familiarize yourself with all aspects of the job, including the organization's culture and purpose. Therefore, it is good practice to study the handbook that outlines this information. The book generally stays in the office, so it is polite to ask the supervisor if you may borrow it as he or she is the head of the department. The worst answer is E. You are expected to read and understand the handbook. Skipping this task is insubordinate and detrimental to your knowledge, growth, and advancement in this department.

60. Best: C. Worst: D. Your scheduled meeting is a formal commitment with local businesspeople. You need to be as professional and punctual as possible, especially because tardiness is considered an insult in the Japanese culture. Being late is not acceptable, and therefore you should rearrange your schedule and move one of your morning tasks to later in the day. Canceling the meeting may be acceptable for an emergency but not for extra tasks that are not urgent. The worst answer is D. Tardiness is insulting and unprofessional. If you are late to a meeting, you must apologize and take steps not to repeat this error in the future. Option B is not a good choice because while you are taking steps to rectify your tardiness, Japanese culture dictates that people bow to each other, not shake hands. Bowing is a sign of respect.

61. Best: A. Worst: B. Although tardiness is not insulting in the Indian culture, it is best to arrive on time if at all possible. Local customs may dictate what is appropriate to order in a business setting, so it is good practice to follow the lead of your companions when ordering. Option D is the second-best choice because your coworkers may not be as knowledgeable about local customs as they think, so you could be relying on information that may not be accurate. The worst answer is B. Although punctuality is the goal, the food you've ordered is unacceptable in Hinduism. Beef is likely on the menu because this is an American-style restaurant; however, although not everyone in India is Hindu, it would be wise to avoid any potential offense.

62. Best: B. Worst: A. A cordial but firm statement is required in this situation as the colleague may not realize that this behavior is unacceptable to you. Your colleague may see these actions as friendly and not inappropriate. The worst option is A. Reporting your colleague to human resources for sexual harassment is premature at this point in time. First, you should address the problem with the individual, and if you are not successful in stopping the behavior, then further corrective action can take place.

63. Best: A. Worst: C. You should complete your assigned tasks first, especially because they are time sensitive. Once those tasks are complete, then you can help your colleague with her projects if time allows. The worst choice is C. Telling your colleague that she is "not your boss" is rude and childish behavior and not appropriate for the office.

64. Best: A. Worst: E. You are the team leader and are therefore in a position of authority. It is appropriate to make a firm but kind statement on the use of office supplies. If, after that warning, she does not stop, then you may choose to speak with your supervisor. Therefore, option E is the worst answer because that action is premature at this time.

65. Best: B. Worst: C. Although it is kind to offer to drive the team member to the doctor, he may not want you to know where he is going as the type of doctor he visits may reveal his medical problem. Therefore, it is best to allow him to leave immediately, especially because he doesn't look well. The worst answer is C. It is not your business as to why this team member needs to visit a doctor. He looks unwell, so his motivation is not in question. His medical privacy is protected by Health Insurance Portability and Accountability Act (HIPPA) laws.

66. Best: C. Worst: B. Asking the team member during the meeting about her opinions may make her uncomfortable. She may simply be shy and not comfortable with public speaking or group discussions. Therefore, it is best to wait until after the meeting and speak with her privately about her participation. The worst answer is B. Asking the team member why she's so quiet is rude and potentially embarrassing to the worker. The question can be posed in a more polite way, preferably in private.

67. Best: D. Worst: C. Attempting to fill the vacancies by asking colleagues to volunteer for shifts shows innovation and drive, which are desirable qualities in employees. The worst answer is C. This on-call schedule is mandatory and refusing to work your assigned shift can result in corrective action and/or termination.

68. Best: C. Worst: D. Delegating some tasks to other team members is good business strategy when dealing with several time-sensitive tasks at once. The worst answer is D. Skipping tasks is not an option, and you must find a way to complete them in a timely manner.

69. Best: C. Worst: E. It is not necessary to share medical information with your supervisor, but you should tell him or her that you are expecting an important call from a physician and you would like to know how he or she prefers the situation to be handled. The supervisor will then choose an approach that is the least disruptive to the meeting. The worst answer is E. Keeping your phone on the lowest volume can be disruptive to the meeting attendees if your phone does ring. Keeping the phone on silent, vibrate, or turning it off completely are all better choices.

70. Best: D. Worst: A. You are the team lead and are therefore in a position of authority. Politely bringing a mistake to a team member's attention is appropriate, especially if you are offering to help rectify the situation. The worst answer is A. There is no need to involve a supervisor at this time as you have not addressed the problem personally with your team member yet. If you make an effort to help your team member and he or she is still unsuccessful, then your supervisor may need to be involved.

71. Best: B. Worst: D. Your supervisor is in an important meeting with executives and should not be disturbed unless absolutely necessary. As a new employee, you should ask your coworkers for help. If they are unable to assist you, then you may need to ask your supervisor for assistance. Asking the director of the facility for help is unwise because he or she may not be unfamiliar with the daily workings of your department. Therefore, option D is the worst answer.

72. Best: A. Worst: C. This is a facility-approved charity, and therefore, it is acceptable to organize a walk team for your department. The walk team must be composed of volunteers, and involvement should not be mandatory. The worst answer is C. Participation, especially financial contributions, should be voluntary. It is rude and presumptuous to insist on donations from your coworkers. They may not have the interest or means to donate.

73. Best: B. Worst: A. Giving your coworker subtle hints has not been successful, so it is time to be direct. Politely explaining the problem is an appropriate and professional way to resolve an interpersonal issue. The coworker may not realize he or she is causing you distress and inconvenience by being tardy. You should talk about the problem directly. If that doesn't solve the problem, then you may bring the issue to your supervisor. The worst answer is A. You have not told your supervisor about the tardiness issue, and therefore he or she is unaware that there is a problem. You are also not offering any solutions to the issue or talking with your coworker directly to help solve the problem.

74. Best: A. Worst: D. In some facilities, children are welcome in meetings as long as they are not disruptive to the proceedings. These children are school-age and are likely to have an attention span conducive to quiet play for an hour. If the director will not allow this, then you will have to try a different option. The worst answer is D. You should at least try other options before saying that you can't make the meeting. Also, it is not your place to tell your director how to do his or her job. The meeting's timing may not have been under his or her control, and there is no reason to be rude and insubordinate.

75. Best: B. Worst: A. Although there is no mention of the training being mandatory, it still benefits you to learn about the new equipment that is being implemented, especially because you will be responsible for it. Attending the training without complaint is the best course of action. The worst option is A. Skipping the training, especially without notifying your supervisor ahead of time, could be seen as disinterest and a lack of motivation.

76. Best: A. Worst: B. Cooperating fully with the investigation is the best action to take. Discussing the matter with coworkers isn't necessary and could possibly hinder the investigation. Option B is the worst choice as this is considered retaliation and is punishable by termination in most organizations.

77. Best: D. Worst: E. Although raising your voice is not generally recommended, it is important to stop the arguing immediately so that the conflict does not continue to escalate. Once you have everyone's undivided attention, you may give further instruction or choose to end the meeting entirely. However, this is a time-sensitive project that needs to be completed in a timely fashion. Therefore, option E is the worst answer because it is essentially giving up on the task and your group. Instead, you should employ team-building techniques to help foster communication and free exchange of ideas within the group.

78. Best: C. Worst: A. Listening to the staff member and then taking immediate action is the best choice in this situation. This staff member was assertive and direct while remaining respectful by speaking with you in private about the issue. You should give him or her the same courtesy by employing active listening skills and then taking action. The worst answer is A. This dismissive attitude is unacceptable for a leader of a group.

79. Best: D. Worst: A. When conducting group discussions, it is essential for all ideas to be presented and considered. As the team leader, it is your responsibility to allow each team member to present his or her opinions and ideas without interference from other staff members. The best way to accomplish this is to take an active role during each group discussion. The worst answer is A. Although this team member may be more assertive and persuasive than other team members, there is no reason to dismiss him or her.

80. Best: B. Worst: C. You are greeting a potential customer, so you should greet her warmly and introduce yourself. Many Orthodox Jewish women are not allowed to touch men who they are not married to. Even the seemingly harmless handshake can be a grave offense in that community. Therefore, a non-touching greeting is appropriate. The worst option is C because you are attempting to shake her hand, which is taboo touching in her culture.

81. Best: C. Worst: B. In the Japanese culture, adding "san" after someone's name shows respect in a professional environment or with elders. This team member is attempting to convey respect for you and your title, and you should not correct him or her. The worst answer is B. Telling the staff member that you don't like this will likely cause offense and hurt feelings.

82. Best: B. Worst: C. Thanking the employee for his explanation of his cultural and religious beliefs is good manners. His religious rights are protected by law, and you must make every effort to uphold his work restrictions. Therefore, the worst answer is C.

83. Best: B. Worst: C. If you want to gather information about the organization you are joining, you should first look at the organization's website. This will offer the most timely and accurate information. Option C is the worst answer because you should have a basic knowledge of the organization you are joining before you actually arrive for your first day of work. This shows initiative and eagerness to learn.

84. Best: A. Worst: C. Being open, honest, and direct is always a good approach is business. Your supervisor should be the first person to know of your plans for the future as you may be leaving a void in the schedule if you pursue a position elsewhere after completing your program. You may also complete the program and realize that health care is not what you expected, and you may not want to pursue that field. Therefore, you should be open with your supervisor about your actions. The program is offered by the embassy, and you will need to miss work to attend, so you should include your supervisor and coworkers in the conversation because it is unprofessional to assume that you will be able to attend the program and miss work without making arrangements to do so. Therefore, option C is the worst choice.

English Expression

1. A: The word "ensuring" means "making certain," and it is used correctly in this sentence.

2. B: "Of" is not capitalized in this country's official name (nor would it be in a title), and "People" is in its possessive form.

3. B: The sentence that follows implies that each of these non-signing countries provides the same reason for not signing.

4. A: The sentence provides a meaning for the word "pillar," which is introduced at the beginning of the next sentence and used within the rest of the passage.

5. C: "Except" means "but" or "only in this instance.

6. D: This sentence is talking about the countries involved with the treaty, so "themselves" is used.

7. C: "Nuclear weapons' countries" is awkward phrasing and should not be used here. There is no possessive form when the phrase is converted to "countries with nuclear weapons."

8. D: This phrase can be omitted without changing the meaning of the sentence.

9. B: The sentence is written in the present tense. "Applies" means "pertains to" or "relates to." This is not the meaning conveyed in this sentence.

10. B: "Good faith" is a phrase meaning "with fairness and trust." It is not presented in quotes or capitalized, since it is an accepted English-language phrase.

11. D: The sentence infers that nuclear energy should be used only for good.

12. C: Countries comply "with" an agreement or treaty—meaning that they will uphold what they have signed.

13. D: This part of the sentence does not need a semicolon, comma, or period, since it is not a clause or phrase.

14. D: The phrase can be omitted and the sentence does not lose its meaning.

15. A: The pillars are only as effective as those who have signed them.

16. D: There is no indication that the phrase is a quote, so quotation marks should not be used here. The plural of "opportunity" is "opportunities."

17. A: The words "free" and "extensive" should be separated by a comma, and so should "extensive" and "and." There should not be a comma after "available," since it is not part of the list.

18. B: The passage is referring to one country (the United States), and the noun "country" is in the possessive form here—apostrophe s.

19. A: Since "figures" is the subject of the sentence (it must be "figures" and not "figure," since it refers to more than one newspaper), "continue" must align with that word. "The figures continue" is correct but not "The figures continues."

20. D: "More worse" is considered to be bad grammar. Using "not only" implies that there will be a "but" to complete the thought, which is not the case here.

21. B: The word refers to the newspaper's older readers—the possessive form. "There" means "in that place." "Theyre" is not a word. "They're" is the contracted form of "they are."

22. D: The sentence ties up the paragraph and is best used to conclude it.

23. C: The colon after "media" indicates that the words that follow will further explain it. These items are listed, so there should be a comma after each one.

24. B: The sentence provides an overview of the solution to the problem. Sentence A provides a fact about print advertising, which is not really what the paragraph is about. Sentence C provides a statement that does not address the main idea of the paragraph—that advertising may not work as well online as it does in a print paper. Sentence D infers that advertising may work well online, which contradicts what the paragraph seems to state.

25. D: The words "full-page" are hyphenated to form an adjective phrase describing "advertisement."

26. A: There are only two newspapers listed and they are separated by "or." They do not have to be additionally separated by a comma or any other punctuation mark.

27. D: The word "it" is not needed here, since it is clear from the sentence that "ignore" is referring to "ads." Adding "it" or "them" is incorrect grammatically. "To be ignored" implies that the readers will be ignored, changing the meaning of the sentence.

28. B: "News sites" is short for "news websites." This is the only acceptable spelling.

29. A: The fee is charged for readers to gain access to the site. "Assess" means to evaluate or review something. The -ing form of either word is not grammatically correct here.

30. C: The words "subscription based" describe "online newspapers." The words must be joined with a hyphen to form an adjective phrase that is read together. The commas are not necessary.

31. D: The word "both" means that the words following will go together. The conjunction "or" can't be used here, as it means "either." There is no need for a comma, since there are only two adjectives listed to describe the content.

32. C: The plural form of "subscriber" is used with "seem." There is no apostrophe, since the word is not in the possessive form.

33. C: The subject of the sentence is plural: subscribers. The pronoun "their" is plural.

34. D: The sentence provides a summary and conclusion to the passage, so should appear at the end of the piece.

35. A: The phrases "keep their readers loyal" and "produce revenue" are part of a list of ways newspaper owners will try to save their business. The listed phrases must each be separated by a comma.

36. C: The noun "today's" is in the singular possessive form, with "changing world" further describing "today."

37. C: "Adapt" refers to what the news executives have to do. "Adopt" is not used correctly here. The present tense is used in the sentence, so the verb "adapt" should correctly be used in the present tense.

38. C: The sentence is written in the present tense, and the noun "cronyism" is written in the singular form.

39. B: An authoritarian position is a strict position. The person appointing another to a job must be in a position of authority—one that will allow him or her to make such appointments or hires.

40. A: This response provides the most succinct way to make this point.

41. A: The dash is used here to add words, almost as an afterthought. A semicolon is used to join two simple sentences. The words appearing after "place" cannot stand alone, so cannot be considered a simple sentence.

42. A: The phrase "that is" continues with the same thought as what precedes it, so it belongs in the same sentence, but it begins a new independent clause, which requires a semicolon rather than a comma.

43. A: This sentence provides details to explain the statement made in the sentence above it.

44. A: The sentence provides a general introduction to what comes next in the short paragraph.

45. A: The end of this sentence provides a reason why McNamara's decision to enter the war may not have been one an experienced official may have made. It provides a conclusion to the article by giving an example of how cronyism can backfire.

How to Overcome Test Anxiety

Just the thought of taking a test is enough to make most people a little nervous. A test is an important event that can have a long-term impact on your future, so it's important to take it seriously and it's natural to feel anxious about performing well. But just because anxiety is normal, that doesn't mean that it's helpful in test taking, or that you should simply accept it as part of your life. Anxiety can have a variety of effects. These effects can be mild, like making you feel slightly nervous, or severe, like blocking your ability to focus or remember even a simple detail.

If you experience test anxiety—whether severe or mild—it's important to know how to beat it. To discover this, first you need to understand what causes test anxiety.

Causes of Test Anxiety

While we often think of anxiety as an uncontrollable emotional state, it can actually be caused by simple, practical things. One of the most common causes of test anxiety is that a person does not feel adequately prepared for their test. This feeling can be the result of many different issues such as poor study habits or lack of organization, but the most common culprit is time management. Starting to study too late, failing to organize your study time to cover all of the material, or being distracted while you study will mean that you're not well prepared for the test. This may lead to cramming the night before, which will cause you to be physically and mentally exhausted for the test. Poor time management also contributes to feelings of stress, fear, and hopelessness as you realize you are not well prepared but don't know what to do about it.

Other times, test anxiety is not related to your preparation for the test but comes from unresolved fear. This may be a past failure on a test, or poor performance on tests in general. It may come from comparing yourself to others who seem to be performing better or from the stress of living up to expectations. Anxiety may be driven by fears of the future—how failure on this test would affect your educational and career goals. These fears are often completely irrational, but they can still negatively impact your test performance.

Review Video: 3 Reasons You Have Test Anxiety
Visit mometrix.com/academy and enter code: 428468

Elements of Test Anxiety

As mentioned earlier, test anxiety is considered to be an emotional state, but it has physical and mental components as well. Sometimes you may not even realize that you are suffering from test anxiety until you notice the physical symptoms. These can include trembling hands, rapid heartbeat, sweating, nausea, and tense muscles. Extreme anxiety may lead to fainting or vomiting. Obviously, any of these symptoms can have a negative impact on testing. It is important to recognize them as soon as they begin to occur so that you can address the problem before it damages your performance.

Review Video: 3 Ways to Tell You Have Test Anxiety
Visit mometrix.com/academy and enter code: 927847

The mental components of test anxiety include trouble focusing and inability to remember learned information. During a test, your mind is on high alert, which can help you recall information and stay focused for an extended period of time. However, anxiety interferes with your mind's natural processes, causing you to blank out, even on the questions you know well. The strain of testing during anxiety makes it difficult to stay focused, especially on a test that may take several hours. Extreme anxiety can take a huge mental toll, making it difficult not only to recall test information but even to understand the test questions or pull your thoughts together.

Review Video: How Test Anxiety Affects Memory
Visit mometrix.com/academy and enter code: 609003

Effects of Test Anxiety

Test anxiety is like a disease—if left untreated, it will get progressively worse. Anxiety leads to poor performance, and this reinforces the feelings of fear and failure, which in turn lead to poor performances on subsequent tests. It can grow from a mild nervousness to a crippling condition. If allowed to progress, test anxiety can have a big impact on your schooling, and consequently on your future.

Test anxiety can spread to other parts of your life. Anxiety on tests can become anxiety in any stressful situation, and blanking on a test can turn into panicking in a job situation. But fortunately, you don't have to let anxiety rule your testing and determine your grades. There are a number of relatively simple steps you can take to move past anxiety and function normally on a test and in the rest of life.

Review Video: How Test Anxiety Impacts Your Grades
Visit mometrix.com/academy and enter code: 939819

Physical Steps for Beating Test Anxiety

While test anxiety is a serious problem, the good news is that it can be overcome. It doesn't have to control your ability to think and remember information. While it may take time, you can begin taking steps today to beat anxiety.

Just as your first hint that you may be struggling with anxiety comes from the physical symptoms, the first step to treating it is also physical. Rest is crucial for having a clear, strong mind. If you are tired, it is much easier to give in to anxiety. But if you establish good sleep habits, your body and mind will be ready to perform optimally, without the strain of exhaustion. Additionally, sleeping well helps you to retain information better, so you're more likely to recall the answers when you see the test questions.

Getting good sleep means more than going to bed on time. It's important to allow your brain time to relax. Take study breaks from time to time so it doesn't get overworked, and don't study right before bed. Take time to rest your mind before trying to rest your body, or you may find it difficult to fall asleep.

Review Video: The Importance of Sleep for Your Brain
Visit mometrix.com/academy and enter code: 319338

Along with sleep, other aspects of physical health are important in preparing for a test. Good nutrition is vital for good brain function. Sugary foods and drinks may give a burst of energy but this burst is followed by a crash, both physically and emotionally. Instead, fuel your body with protein and vitamin-rich foods.

Also, drink plenty of water. Dehydration can lead to headaches and exhaustion, especially if your brain is already under stress from the rigors of the test. Particularly if your test is a long one, drink water during the breaks. And if possible, take an energy-boosting snack to eat between sections.

Review Video: How Diet Can Affect your Mood
Visit mometrix.com/academy and enter code: 624317

Along with sleep and diet, a third important part of physical health is exercise. Maintaining a steady workout schedule is helpful, but even taking 5-minute study breaks to walk can help get your blood pumping faster and clear your head. Exercise also releases endorphins, which contribute to a positive feeling and can help combat test anxiety.

When you nurture your physical health, you are also contributing to your mental health. If your body is healthy, your mind is much more likely to be healthy as well. So take time to rest, nourish your body with healthy food and water, and get moving as much as possible. Taking these physical steps will make you stronger and more able to take the mental steps necessary to overcome test anxiety.

Review Video: How to Stay Healthy and Prevent Test Anxiety
Visit mometrix.com/academy and enter code: 877894

Mental Steps for Beating Test Anxiety

Working on the mental side of test anxiety can be more challenging, but as with the physical side, there are clear steps you can take to overcome it. As mentioned earlier, test anxiety often stems from lack of preparation, so the obvious solution is to prepare for the test. Effective studying may be the most important weapon you have for beating test anxiety, but you can and should employ several other mental tools to combat fear.

First, boost your confidence by reminding yourself of past success—tests or projects that you aced. If you're putting as much effort into preparing for this test as you did for those, there's no reason you should expect to fail here. Work hard to prepare; then trust your preparation.

Second, surround yourself with encouraging people. It can be helpful to find a study group, but be sure that the people you're around will encourage a positive attitude. If you spend time with others who are anxious or cynical, this will only contribute to your own anxiety. Look for others who are motivated to study hard from a desire to succeed, not from a fear of failure.

Third, reward yourself. A test is physically and mentally tiring, even without anxiety, and it can be helpful to have something to look forward to. Plan an activity following the test, regardless of the outcome, such as going to a movie or getting ice cream.

When you are taking the test, if you find yourself beginning to feel anxious, remind yourself that you know the material. Visualize successfully completing the test. Then take a few deep, relaxing breaths and return to it. Work through the questions carefully but with confidence, knowing that you are capable of succeeding.

Developing a healthy mental approach to test taking will also aid in other areas of life. Test anxiety affects more than just the actual test—it can be damaging to your mental health and even contribute to depression. It's important to beat test anxiety before it becomes a problem for more than testing.

Review Video: Test Anxiety and Depression
Visit mometrix.com/academy and enter code: 904704

Study Strategy

Being prepared for the test is necessary to combat anxiety, but what does being prepared look like? You may study for hours on end and still not feel prepared. What you need is a strategy for test prep. The next few pages outline our recommended steps to help you plan out and conquer the challenge of preparation.

Step 1: Scope Out the Test

Learn everything you can about the format (multiple choice, essay, etc.) and what will be on the test. Gather any study materials, course outlines, or sample exams that may be available. Not only will this help you to prepare, but knowing what to expect can help to alleviate test anxiety.

Step 2: Map Out the Material

Look through the textbook or study guide and make note of how many chapters or sections it has. Then divide these over the time you have. For example, if a book has 15 chapters and you have five days to study, you need to cover three chapters each day. Even better, if you have the time, leave an extra day at the end for overall review after you have gone through the material in depth.

If time is limited, you may need to prioritize the material. Look through it and make note of which sections you think you already have a good grasp on, and which need review. While you are studying, skim quickly through the familiar sections and take more time on the challenging parts. Write out your plan so you don't get lost as you go. Having a written plan also helps you feel more in control of the study, so anxiety is less likely to arise from feeling overwhelmed at the amount to cover.

Step 3: Gather Your Tools

Decide what study method works best for you. Do you prefer to highlight in the book as you study and then go back over the highlighted portions? Or do you type out notes of the important information? Or is it helpful to make flashcards that you can carry with you? Assemble the pens, index cards, highlighters, post-it notes, and any other materials you may need so you won't be distracted by getting up to find things while you study.

If you're having a hard time retaining the information or organizing your notes, experiment with different methods. For example, try color-coding by subject with colored pens, highlighters, or post-it notes. If you learn better by hearing, try recording yourself reading your notes so you can listen while in the car, working out, or simply sitting at your desk. Ask a friend to quiz you from your flashcards, or try teaching someone the material to solidify it in your mind.

Step 4: Create Your Environment

It's important to avoid distractions while you study. This includes both the obvious distractions like visitors and the subtle distractions like an uncomfortable chair (or a too-comfortable couch that makes you want to fall asleep). Set up the best study environment possible: good lighting and a comfortable work area. If background music helps you focus, you may want to turn it on, but otherwise keep the room quiet. If you are using a computer to take notes, be sure you don't have any other windows open, especially applications like social media, games, or anything else that could distract you. Silence your phone and turn off notifications. Be sure to keep water close by so you stay hydrated while you study (but avoid unhealthy drinks and snacks).

Also, take into account the best time of day to study. Are you freshest first thing in the morning? Try to set aside some time then to work through the material. Is your mind clearer in the afternoon or evening? Schedule your study session then. Another method is to study at the same time of day that you will take the test, so that your brain gets used to working on the material at that time and will be ready to focus at test time.

Step 5: Study!

Once you have done all the study preparation, it's time to settle into the actual studying. Sit down, take a few moments to settle your mind so you can focus, and begin to follow your study plan. Don't give in to distractions or let yourself procrastinate. This is your time to prepare so you'll be ready to fearlessly approach the test. Make the most of the time and stay focused.

Of course, you don't want to burn out. If you study too long you may find that you're not retaining the information very well. Take regular study breaks. For example, taking five minutes out of every hour to walk briskly, breathing deeply and swinging your arms, can help your mind stay fresh.

As you get to the end of each chapter or section, it's a good idea to do a quick review. Remind yourself of what you learned and work on any difficult parts. When you feel that you've mastered the material, move on to the next part. At the end of your study session, briefly skim through your notes again.

But while review is helpful, cramming last minute is NOT. If at all possible, work ahead so that you won't need to fit all your study into the last day. Cramming overloads your brain with more information than it can process and retain, and your tired mind may struggle to recall even previously learned information when it is overwhelmed with last-minute study. Also, the urgent nature of cramming and the stress placed on your brain contribute to anxiety. You'll be more likely to go to the test feeling unprepared and having trouble thinking clearly.

So don't cram, and don't stay up late before the test, even just to review your notes at a leisurely pace. Your brain needs rest more than it needs to go over the information again. In fact, plan to finish your studies by noon or early afternoon the day before the test. Give your brain the rest of the day to relax or focus on other things, and get a good night's sleep. Then you will be fresh for the test and better able to recall what you've studied.

Step 6: Take a practice test

Many courses offer sample tests, either online or in the study materials. This is an excellent resource to check whether you have mastered the material, as well as to prepare for the test format and environment.

Check the test format ahead of time: the number of questions, the type (multiple choice, free response, etc.), and the time limit. Then create a plan for working through them. For example, if you have 30 minutes to take a 60-question test, your limit is 30 seconds per question. Spend less time on the questions you know well so that you can take more time on the difficult ones.

If you have time to take several practice tests, take the first one open book, with no time limit. Work through the questions at your own pace and make sure you fully understand them. Gradually work up to taking a test under test conditions: sit at a desk with all study materials put away and set a timer. Pace yourself to make sure you finish the test with time to spare and go back to check your answers if you have time.

After each test, check your answers. On the questions you missed, be sure you understand why you missed them. Did you misread the question (tests can use tricky wording)? Did you forget the information? Or was it something you hadn't learned? Go back and study any shaky areas that the practice tests reveal.

Taking these tests not only helps with your grade, but also aids in combating test anxiety. If you're already used to the test conditions, you're less likely to worry about it, and working through tests until you're scoring well gives you a confidence boost. Go through the practice tests until you feel comfortable, and then you can go into the test knowing that you're ready for it.

Test Tips

On test day, you should be confident, knowing that you've prepared well and are ready to answer the questions. But aside from preparation, there are several test day strategies you can employ to maximize your performance.

First, as stated before, get a good night's sleep the night before the test (and for several nights before that, if possible). Go into the test with a fresh, alert mind rather than staying up late to study.

Try not to change too much about your normal routine on the day of the test. It's important to eat a nutritious breakfast, but if you normally don't eat breakfast at all, consider eating just a protein bar. If you're a coffee drinker, go ahead and have your normal coffee. Just make sure you time it so that the caffeine doesn't wear off right in the middle of your test. Avoid sugary beverages, and drink enough water to stay hydrated but not so much that you need a restroom break 10 minutes into the test. If your test isn't first thing in the morning, consider going for a walk or doing a light workout before the test to get your blood flowing.

Allow yourself enough time to get ready, and leave for the test with plenty of time to spare so you won't have the anxiety of scrambling to arrive in time. Another reason to be early is to select a good seat. It's helpful to sit away from doors and windows, which can be distracting. Find a good seat, get out your supplies, and settle your mind before the test begins.

When the test begins, start by going over the instructions carefully, even if you already know what to expect. Make sure you avoid any careless mistakes by following the directions.

Then begin working through the questions, pacing yourself as you've practiced. If you're not sure on an answer, don't spend too much time on it, and don't let it shake your confidence. Either skip it and come back later, or eliminate as many wrong answers as possible and guess among the remaining ones. Don't dwell on these questions as you continue—put them out of your mind and focus on what lies ahead.

Be sure to read all of the answer choices, even if you're sure the first one is the right answer. Sometimes you'll find a better one if you keep reading. But don't second-guess yourself if you do immediately know the answer. Your gut instinct is usually right. Don't let test anxiety rob you of the information you know.

If you have time at the end of the test (and if the test format allows), go back and review your answers. Be cautious about changing any, since your first instinct tends to be correct, but make sure you didn't misread any of the questions or accidentally mark the wrong answer choice. Look over any you skipped and make an educated guess.

At the end, leave the test feeling confident. You've done your best, so don't waste time worrying about your performance or wishing you could change anything. Instead, celebrate the successful completion of this test. And finally, use this test to learn how to deal with anxiety even better next time.

Review Video: 5 Tips to Beat Test Anxiety
Visit mometrix.com/academy and enter code: 570656

Important Qualification

Not all anxiety is created equal. If your test anxiety is causing major issues in your life beyond the classroom or testing center, or if you are experiencing troubling physical symptoms related to your anxiety, it may be a sign of a serious physiological or psychological condition. If this sounds like your situation, we strongly encourage you to seek professional help.

How to Overcome Your Fear of Math

The word *math* is enough to strike fear into most hearts. How many of us have memories of sitting through confusing lectures, wrestling over mind-numbing homework, or taking tests that still seem incomprehensible even after hours of study? Years after graduation, many still shudder at these memories.

The fact is, math is not just a classroom subject. It has real-world implications that you face every day, whether you realize it or not. This may be balancing your monthly budget, deciding how many supplies to buy for a project, or simply splitting a meal check with friends. The idea of daily confrontations with math can be so paralyzing that some develop a condition known as *math anxiety*.

But you do NOT need to be paralyzed by this anxiety! In fact, while you may have thought all your life that you're not good at math, or that your brain isn't wired to understand it, the truth is that you may have been conditioned to think this way. From your earliest school days, the way you were taught affected the way you viewed different subjects. And the way math has been taught has changed.

Several decades ago, there was a shift in American math classrooms. The focus changed from traditional problem-solving to a conceptual view of topics, de-emphasizing the importance of learning the basics and building on them. The solid foundation necessary for math progression and confidence was undermined. Math became more of a vague concept than a concrete idea. Today, it is common to think of math, not as a straightforward system, but as a mysterious, complicated method that can't be fully understood unless you're a genius.

This is why you may still have nightmares about being called on to answer a difficult problem in front of the class. Math anxiety is a very real, though unnecessary, fear.

Math anxiety may begin with a single class period. Let's say you missed a day in 6th grade math and never quite understood the concept that was taught while you were gone. Since math is cumulative, with each new concept building on past ones, this could very well affect the rest of your math career. Without that one day's knowledge, it will be difficult to understand any other concepts that link to it. Rather than realizing that you're just missing one key piece, you may begin to believe that you're simply not capable of understanding math.

This belief can change the way you approach other classes, career options, and everyday life experiences, if you become anxious at the thought that math might be required. A student who loves science may choose a different path of study upon realizing that multiple math classes will be required for a degree. An aspiring medical student may hesitate at the thought of going through the necessary math classes. For some this anxiety escalates into a more extreme state known as *math phobia*.

Math anxiety is challenging to address because it is rooted deeply and may come from a variety of causes: an embarrassing moment in class, a teacher who did not explain concepts well and contributed to a shaky foundation, or a failed test that contributed to the belief of math failure.

These causes add up over time, encouraged by society's popular view that math is hard and unpleasant. Eventually a person comes to firmly believe that he or she is simply bad at math. This belief makes it difficult to grasp new concepts or even remember old ones. Homework and test grades begin to slip, which only confirms the belief. The poor performance is not due to lack of ability but is caused by math anxiety.

Math anxiety is an emotional issue, not a lack of intelligence. But when it becomes deeply rooted, it can become more than just an emotional problem. Physical symptoms appear. Blood pressure may rise and heartbeat may quicken at the sight of a math problem – or even the thought of math! This fear leads to a mental block. When someone with math anxiety is asked to perform a calculation, even a basic problem can seem overwhelming and impossible. The emotional and physical response to the thought of math prevents the brain from working through it logically.

The more this happens, the more a person's confidence drops, and the more math anxiety is generated. This vicious cycle must be broken!

The first step in breaking the cycle is to go back to very beginning and make sure you really understand the basics of how math works and why it works. It is not enough to memorize rules for multiplication and division. If you don't know WHY these rules work, your foundation will be shaky and you will be at risk of developing a phobia. Understanding mathematical concepts not only promotes confidence and security, but allows you to build on this understanding for new concepts. Additionally, you can solve unfamiliar problems using familiar concepts and processes.

Why is it that students in other countries regularly outperform American students in math? The answer likely boils down to a couple of things: the foundation of mathematical conceptual understanding and societal perception. While students in the US are not expected to *like* or *get* math, in many other nations, students are expected not only to understand math but also to excel at it.

Changing the American view of math that leads to math anxiety is a monumental task. It requires changing the training of teachers nationwide, from kindergarten through high school, so that they learn to teach the *why* behind math and to combat the wrong math views that students may develop. It also involves changing the stigma associated with math, so that it is no longer viewed as unpleasant and incomprehensible. While these are necessary changes, they are challenging and will take time. But in the meantime, math anxiety is not irreversible—it can be faced and defeated, one person at a time.

False Beliefs

One reason math anxiety has taken such hold is that several false beliefs have been created and shared until they became widely accepted. Some of these unhelpful beliefs include the following:

There is only one way to solve a math problem. In the same way that you can choose from different driving routes and still arrive at the same house, you can solve a math problem using different methods and still find the correct answer. A person who understands the reasoning behind math calculations may be able to look at an unfamiliar concept and find the right answer, just by applying logic to the knowledge they already have. This approach may be different than what is taught in the classroom, but it is still valid. Unfortunately, even many teachers view math as a subject where the best course of action is to memorize the rule or process for each problem rather than as a place for students to exercise logic and creativity in finding a solution.

Many people don't have a mind for math. A person who has struggled due to poor teaching or math anxiety may falsely believe that he or she doesn't have the mental capacity to grasp mathematical concepts. Most of the time, this is false. Many people find that when they are relieved of their math anxiety, they have more than enough brainpower to understand math.

Men are naturally better at math than women. Even though research has shown this to be false, many young women still avoid math careers and classes because of their belief that their math abilities are inferior. Many girls have come to believe that math is a male skill and have given up trying to understand or enjoy it.

Counting aids are bad. Something like counting on your fingers or drawing out a problem to visualize it may be frowned on as childish or a crutch, but these devices can help you get a tangible understanding of a problem or a concept.

Sadly, many students buy into these ideologies at an early age. A young girl who enjoys math class may be conditioned to think that she doesn't actually have the brain for it because math is for boys, and may turn her energies to other pursuits, permanently closing the door on a wide range of opportunities. A child who finds the right answer but doesn't follow the teacher's method may believe that he is doing it wrong and isn't good at math. A student who never had a problem with math before may have a poor teacher and become confused, yet believe that the problem is because she doesn't have a mathematical mind.

Students who have bought into these erroneous beliefs quickly begin to add their own anxieties, adapting them to their own personal situations:

I'll never use this in real life. A huge number of people wrongly believe that math is irrelevant outside the classroom. By adopting this mindset, they are handicapping themselves for a life in a mathematical world, as well as limiting their career choices. When they are inevitably faced with real-world math, they are conditioning themselves to respond with anxiety.

I'm not quick enough. While timed tests and quizzes, or even simply comparing yourself with other students in the class, can lead to this belief, speed is not an indicator of skill level. A person can work very slowly yet understand at a deep level.

If I can understand it, it's too easy. People with a low view of their own abilities tend to think that if they are able to grasp a concept, it must be simple. They cannot accept the idea that they are capable of understanding math. This belief will make it harder to learn, no matter how intelligent they are.

I just can't learn this. An overwhelming number of people think this, from young children to adults, and much of the time it is simply not true. But this mindset can turn into a self-fulfilling prophecy that keeps you from exercising and growing your math ability.

The good news is, each of these myths can be debunked. For most people, they are based on emotion and psychology, NOT on actual ability! It will take time, effort, and the desire to change, but change is possible. Even if you have spent years thinking that you don't have the capability to understand math, it is not too late to uncover your true ability and find relief from the anxiety that surrounds math.

Math Strategies

It is important to have a plan of attack to combat math anxiety. There are many useful strategies for pinpointing the fears or myths and eradicating them:

Go back to the basics. For most people, math anxiety stems from a poor foundation. You may think that you have a complete understanding of addition and subtraction, or even decimals and percentages, but make absolutely sure. Learning math is different from learning other subjects. For example, when you learn history, you study various time periods and places and events. It may be important to memorize dates or find out about the lives of famous people. When you move from US history to world history, there will be some overlap, but a large amount of the information will be new. Mathematical concepts, on the other hand, are very closely linked and highly dependent on each other. It's like climbing a ladder – if a rung is missing from your understanding, it may be difficult or impossible for you to climb any higher, no matter how hard you try. So go back and make sure your math foundation is strong. This may mean taking a remedial math course, going to a tutor to work through the shaky concepts, or just going through your old homework to make sure you really understand it.

Speak the language. Math has a large vocabulary of terms and phrases unique to working problems. Sometimes these are completely new terms, and sometimes they are common words, but are used differently in a math setting. If you can't speak the language, it will be very difficult to get a thorough understanding of the concepts. It's common for students to think that they don't understand math when they simply don't understand the vocabulary. The good news is that this is fairly easy to fix. Brushing up on any terms you aren't quite sure of can help bring the rest of the concepts into focus.

Check your anxiety level. When you think about math, do you feel nervous or uncomfortable? Do you struggle with feelings of inadequacy, even on concepts that you know you've already learned? It's important to understand your specific math anxieties, and what triggers them. When you catch yourself falling back on a false belief, mentally replace it with the truth. Don't let yourself believe that you can't learn, or that struggling with a concept means you'll never understand it. Instead, remind yourself of how much you've already learned and dwell on that past success. Visualize grasping the new concept, linking it to your old knowledge, and moving on to the next challenge. Also, learn how to manage anxiety when it arises. There are many techniques for coping with the irrational fears that rise to the surface when you enter the math classroom. This may include controlled breathing, replacing negative thoughts with positive ones, or visualizing success. Anxiety interferes with your ability to concentrate and absorb information, which in turn contributes to greater anxiety. If you can learn how to regain control of your thinking, you will be better able to pay attention, make progress, and succeed!

Don't go it alone. Like any deeply ingrained belief, math anxiety is not easy to eradicate. And there is no need for you to wrestle through it on your own. It will take time, and many people find that speaking with a counselor or psychiatrist helps. They can help you develop strategies for responding to anxiety and overcoming old ideas. Additionally, it can be very helpful to take a short course or seek out a math tutor to help you find and fix the missing rungs on your ladder and make sure that you're ready to progress to the next level. You can also find a number of math aids online: courses that will teach you mental devices for figuring out problems, how to get the most out of your math classes, etc.

Check your math attitude. No matter how much you want to learn and overcome your anxiety, you'll have trouble if you still have a negative attitude toward math. If you think it's too hard, or just have general feelings of dread about math, it will be hard to learn and to break through the anxiety. Work on cultivating a positive math attitude. Remind yourself that math is not just a hurdle to be cleared, but a valuable asset. When you view math with a positive attitude, you'll be much more likely to understand and even enjoy it. This is something you must do for yourself. You may find it helpful to visit with a counselor. Your tutor, friends, and family may cheer you on in your endeavors. But your greatest asset is yourself. You are inside your own mind – tell yourself what you need to hear. Relive past victories. Remind yourself that you are capable of understanding math. Root out any false beliefs that linger and replace them with positive truths. Even if it doesn't feel true at first, it will begin to affect your thinking and pave the way for a positive, anxiety-free mindset.

Aside from these general strategies, there are a number of specific practical things you can do to begin your journey toward overcoming math anxiety. Something as simple as learning a new note-taking strategy can change the way you approach math and give you more confidence and understanding. New study techniques can also make a huge difference.

Math anxiety leads to bad habits. If it causes you to be afraid of answering a question in class, you may gravitate toward the back row. You may be embarrassed to ask for help. And you may procrastinate on assignments, which leads to rushing through them at the last moment when it's too late to get a better understanding. It's important to identify your negative behaviors and replace them with positive ones:

Prepare ahead of time. Read the lesson before you go to class. Being exposed to the topics that will be covered in class ahead of time, even if you don't understand them perfectly, is extremely helpful in increasing what you retain from the lecture. Do your homework and, if you're still shaky, go over some extra problems. The key to a solid understanding of math is practice.

Sit front and center. When you can easily see and hear, you'll understand more, and you'll avoid the distractions of other students if no one is in front of you. Plus, you're more likely to be sitting with students who are positive and engaged, rather than others with math anxiety. Let their positive math attitude rub off on you.

Ask questions in class and out. If you don't understand something, just ask. If you need a more in-depth explanation, the teacher may need to work with you outside of class, but often it's a simple concept you don't quite understand, and a single question may clear it up. If you wait, you may not be able to follow the rest of the day's lesson. For extra help, most professors have office hours outside of class when you can go over concepts one-on-one to clear up any uncertainties. Additionally, there may be a *math lab* or study session you can attend for homework help. Take advantage of this.

Review. Even if you feel that you've fully mastered a concept, review it periodically to reinforce it. Going over an old lesson has several benefits: solidifying your understanding, giving you a confidence boost, and even giving some new insights into material that you're currently learning! Don't let yourself get rusty. That can lead to problems with learning later concepts.

Teaching Tips

While the math student's mindset is the most crucial to overcoming math anxiety, it is also important for others to adjust their math attitudes. Teachers and parents have an enormous influence on how students relate to math. They can either contribute to math confidence or math anxiety.

As a parent or teacher, it is very important to convey a positive math attitude. Retelling horror stories of your own bad experience with math will contribute to a new generation of math anxiety. Even if you don't share your experiences, others will be able to sense your fears and may begin to believe them.

Even a careless comment can have a big impact, so watch for phrases like *He's not good at math* or *I never liked math*. You are a crucial role model, and your children or students will unconsciously adopt your mindset. Give them a positive example to follow. Rather than teaching them to fear the math world before they even know it, teach them about all its potential and excitement.

Work to present math as an integral, beautiful, and understandable part of life. Encourage creativity in solving problems. Watch for false beliefs and dispel them. Cross the lines between subjects: integrate history, English, and music with math. Show students how math is used every day, and how the entire world is based on mathematical principles, from the pull of gravity to the shape of seashells. Instead of letting students see math as a necessary evil, direct them to view it as an imaginative, beautiful art form – an art form that they are capable of mastering and using.

Don't give too narrow a view of math. It is more than just numbers. Yes, working problems and learning formulas is a large part of classroom math. But don't let the teaching stop there. Teach students about the everyday implications of math. Show them how nature works according to the laws of mathematics, and take them outside to make discoveries of their own. Expose them to math-related careers by inviting visiting speakers, asking students to do research and presentations, and learning students' interests and aptitudes on a personal level.

Demonstrate the importance of math. Many people see math as nothing more than a required stepping stone to their degree, a nuisance with no real usefulness. Teach students that algebra is used every day in managing their bank accounts, in following recipes, and in scheduling the day's events. Show them how learning to do geometric proofs helps them to develop logical thinking, an invaluable life skill. Let them see that math surrounds them and is integrally linked to their daily lives: that weather predictions are based on math, that math was used to design cars and other machines, etc. Most of all, give them the tools to use math to enrich their lives.

Make math as tangible as possible. Use visual aids and objects that can be touched. It is much easier to grasp a concept when you can hold it in your hands and manipulate it, rather than just listening to the lecture. Encourage math outside of the classroom. The real world is full of measuring, counting, and calculating, so let students participate in this. Keep your eyes open for numbers and patterns to discuss. Talk about how scores are calculated in sports games and how far apart plants are placed in a garden row for maximum growth. Build the mindset that math is a normal and interesting part of daily life.

Finally, find math resources that help to build a positive math attitude. There are a number of books that show math as fascinating and exciting while teaching important concepts, for example: *The Math Curse; A Wrinkle in Time; The Phantom Tollbooth;* and *Fractals, Googols and Other Mathematical Tales*. You can also find a number of online resources: math puzzles and games, videos that show math in nature, and communities of math enthusiasts. On a local level, students can compete in a variety of math competitions with other schools or join a math club.

The student who experiences math as exciting and interesting is unlikely to suffer from math anxiety. Going through life without this handicap is an immense advantage and opens many doors that others have closed through their fear.

Self-Check

Whether you suffer from math anxiety or not, chances are that you have been exposed to some of the false beliefs mentioned above. Now is the time to check yourself for any errors you may have accepted. Do you think you're not wired for math? Or that you don't need to understand it since you're not planning on a math career? Do you think math is just too difficult for the average person?

Find the errors you've taken to heart and replace them with positive thinking. Are you capable of learning math? Yes! Can you control your anxiety? Yes! These errors will resurface from time to time, so be watchful. Don't let others with math anxiety influence you or sway your confidence. If you're having trouble with a concept, find help. Don't let it discourage you!

Create a plan of attack for defeating math anxiety and sharpening your skills. Do some research and decide if it would help you to take a class, get a tutor, or find some online resources to fine-tune your knowledge. Make the effort to get good nutrition, hydration, and sleep so that you are operating at full capacity. Remind yourself daily that you are skilled and that anxiety does not control you. Your mind is capable of so much more than you know. Give it the tools it needs to grow and thrive.

Thank You

We at Mometrix would like to extend our heartfelt thanks to you, our friend and patron, for allowing us to play a part in your journey. It is a privilege to serve people from all walks of life who are unified in their commitment to building the best future they can for themselves.

The preparation you devote to these important testing milestones may be the most valuable educational opportunity you have for making a real difference in your life. We encourage you to put your heart into it—that feeling of succeeding, overcoming, and yes, conquering will be well worth the hours you've invested.

We want to hear your story, your struggles and your successes, and if you see any opportunities for us to improve our materials so we can help others even more effectively in the future, please share that with us as well. **The team at Mometrix would be absolutely thrilled to hear from you!** So please, send us an email (support@mometrix.com) and let's stay in touch.

If you'd like some additional help, check out these other resources we offer for your exam:
http://mometrixflashcards.com/FSOT

Additional Bonus Material

Due to our efforts to try to keep this book to a manageable length, we've created a link that will give you access to all of your additional bonus material.

Please visit https://www.mometrix.com/bonus948/fsot to access the information.

Made in the USA
Coppell, TX
31 January 2021